THE VICTORIES™
TRANSHUMAN

STORY AND ART
Michael Avon Oeming

COLORS Nick Filardi
LETTERS Aaron Walker

DARK HORSE BOOKS

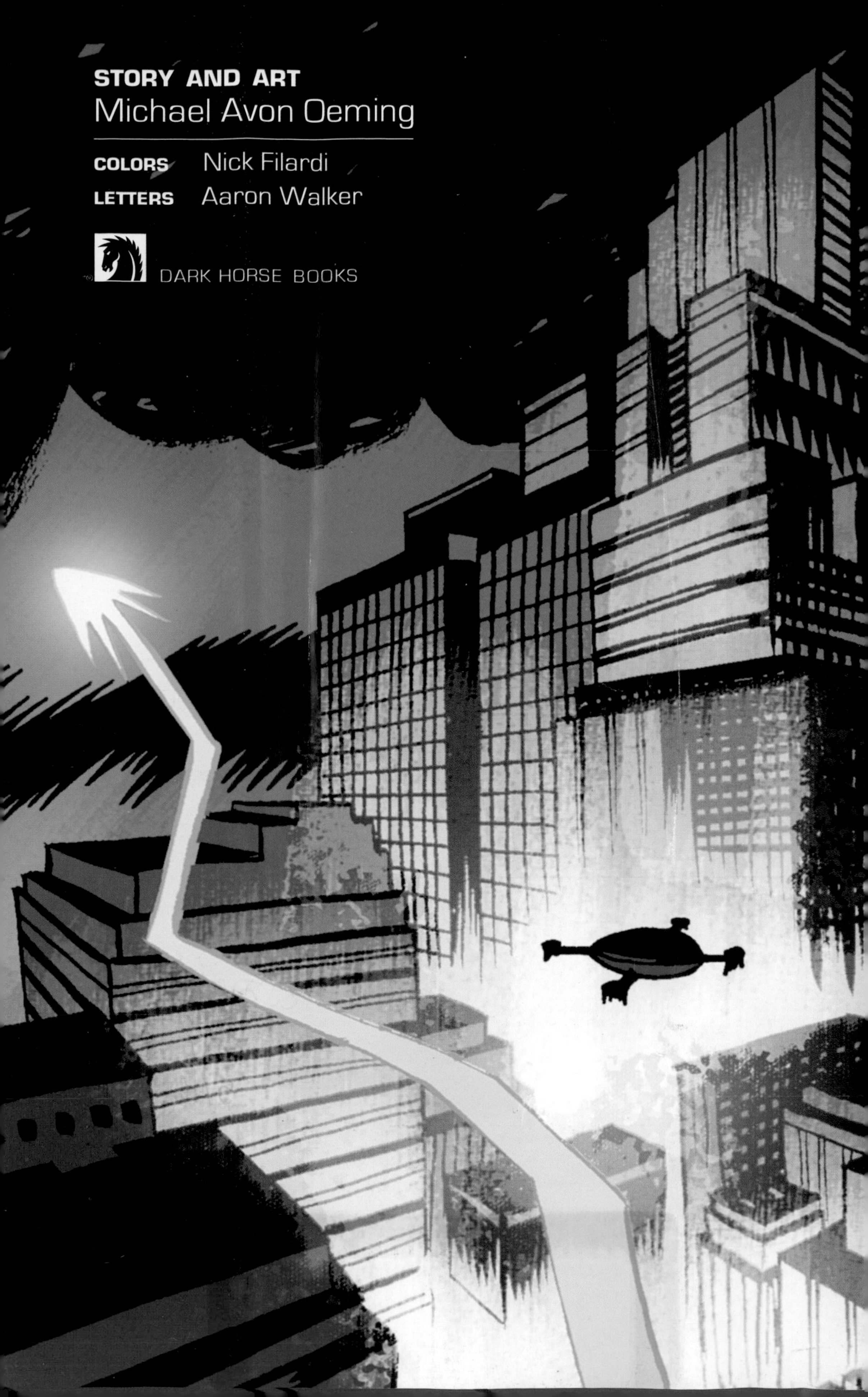

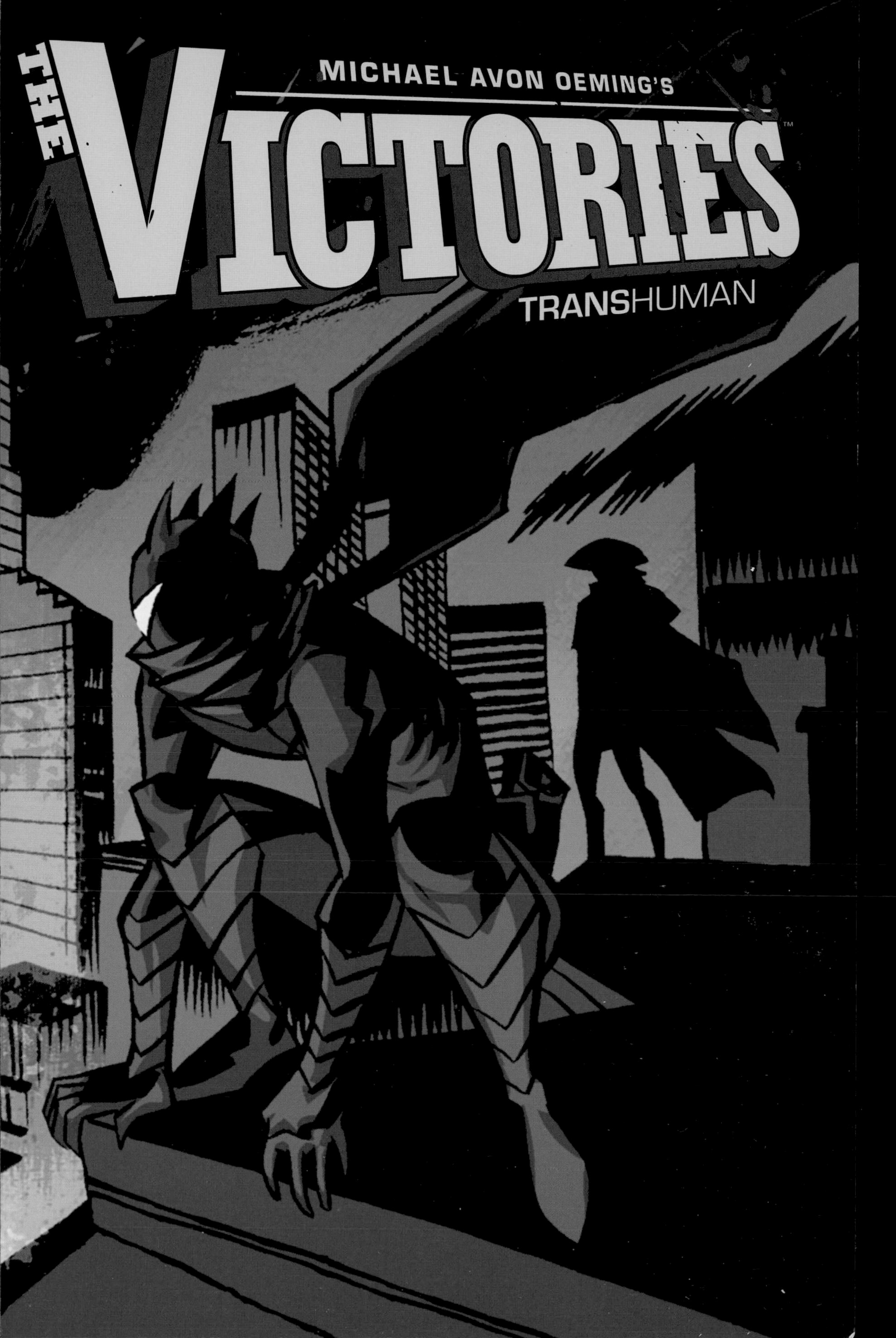
MICHAEL AVON OEMING'S
THE VICTORIES™
TRANSHUMAN

DESIGNER Adam Grano
ASSISTANT EDITOR Shantel LaRocque
EDITOR Scott Allie
PUBLISHER Mike Richardson

Special thanks to Daniel Chabon and Spencer Newlin-Cushing.

Mike Richardson, President and Publisher | Neil Hankerson, Executive Vice President | Tom Weddle, Chief Financial Officer | Randy Stradley, Vice President of Publishing | Michael Martens, Vice President of Book Trade Sales | Anita Nelson, Vice President of Business Affairs | Scott Allie, Editor in Chief | Matt Parkinson, Vice President of Marketing | David Scroggy, Vice President of Product Development | Dale LaFountain, Vice President of Information Technology | Darlene Vogel, Senior Director of Print, Design, and Production | Ken Lizzi, General Counsel | Davey Estrada, Editorial Director | Chris Warner, Senior Books Editor | Diana Schutz, Executive Editor | Cary Grazzini, Director of Print and Development | Lia Ribacchi, Art Director | Cara Niece, Director of Scheduling | Tim Wiesch, Director of International Licensing | Mark Bernardi, Director of Digital Publishing

Published by Dark Horse Books
A division of Dark Horse Comics, Inc.
10956 SE Main Street
Milwaukie, OR 97222

First edition: December 2013
ISBN 978-1-61655-214-5

10 9 8 7 6 5 4 3 2 1
Printed in China

International Licensing: (503) 905-2377
Comic Shop Locator Service: (888) 266-4226

This volume collects issues #1 through #5 of *The Victories* and *The Victories: Babalon* from *Dark Horse Presents* #20 through #22.

CHAPTER ONE

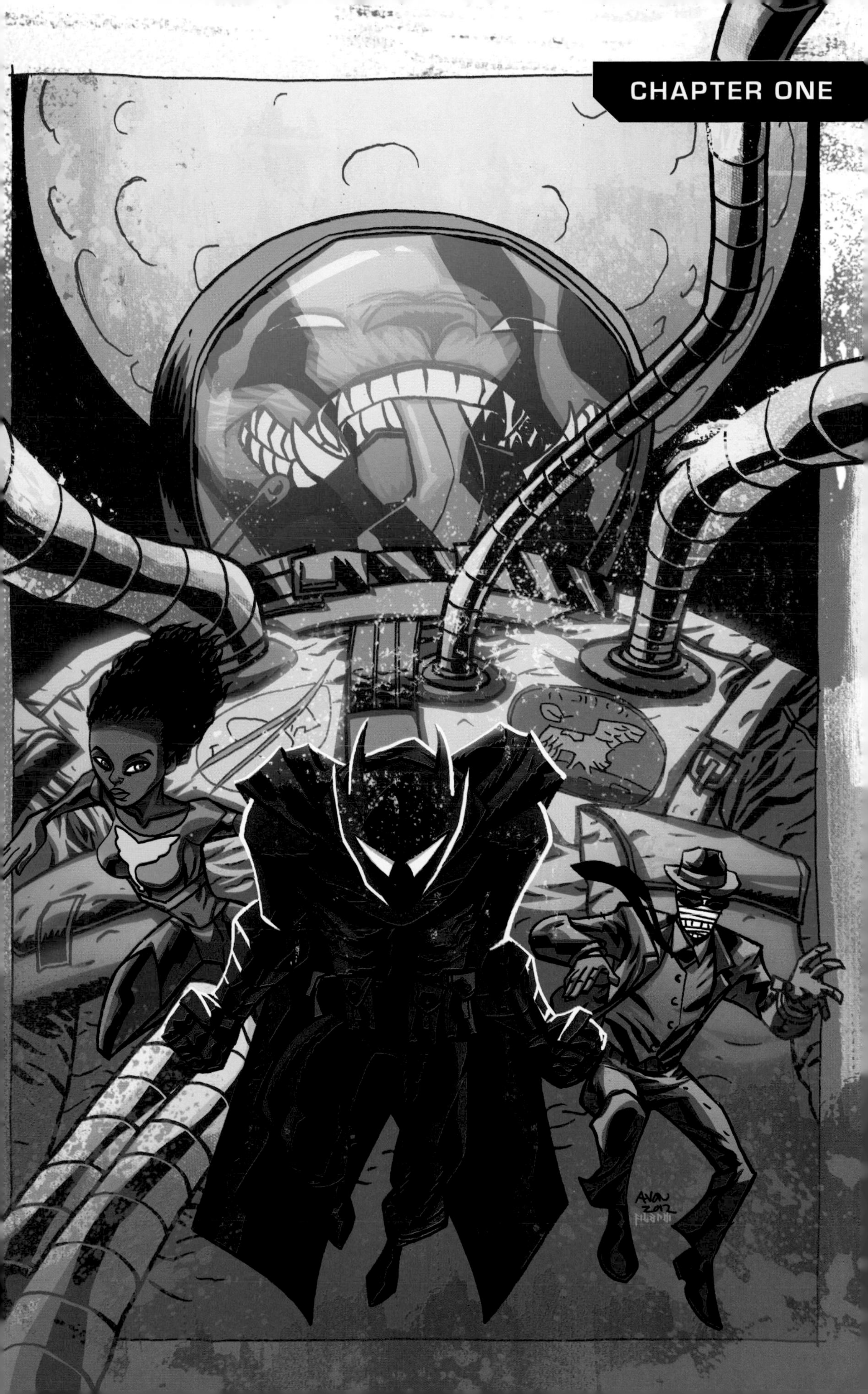

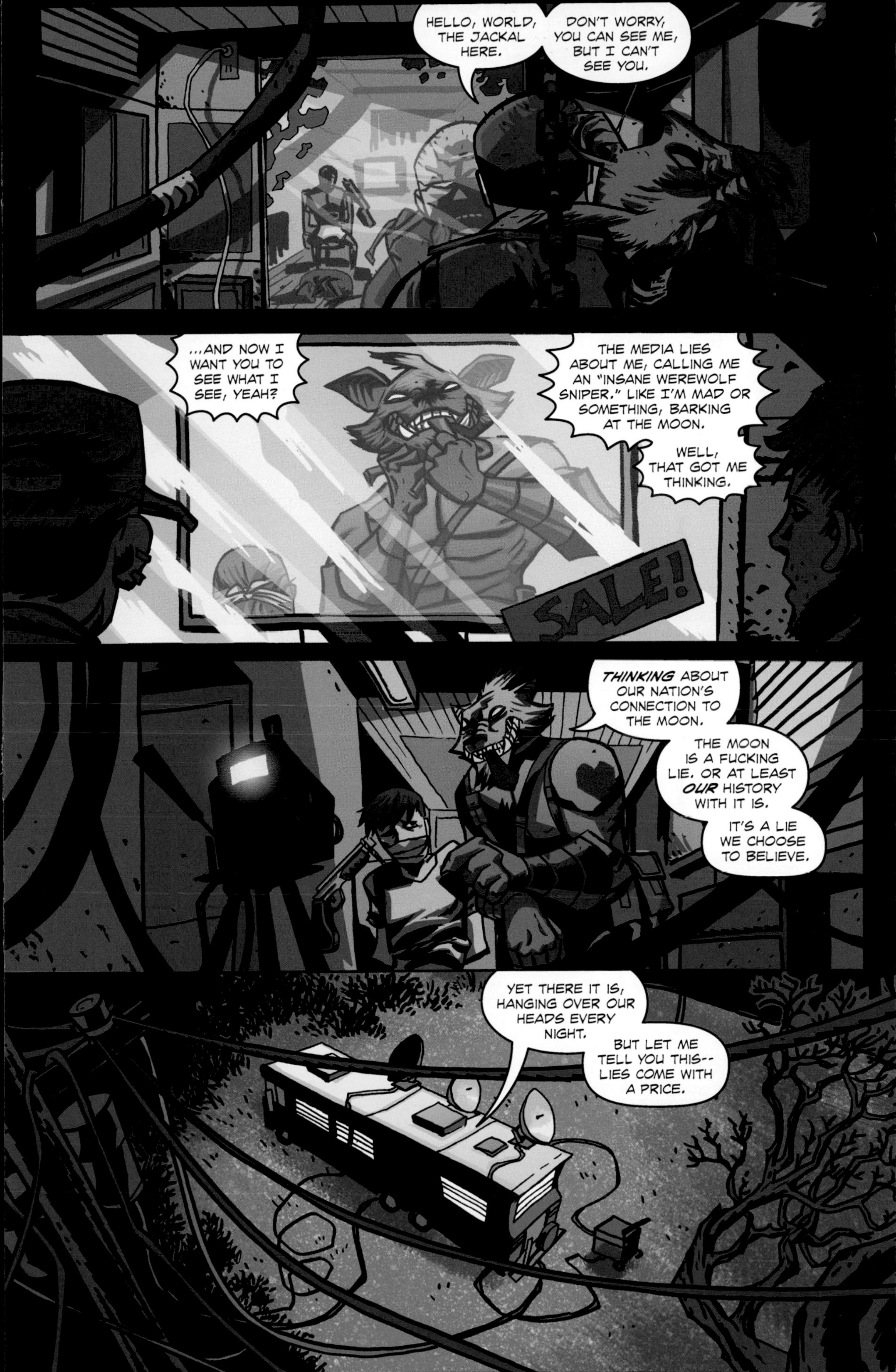
HELLO, WORLD, THE JACKAL HERE.
DON'T WORRY, YOU CAN SEE ME, BUT I CAN'T SEE YOU.
...AND NOW I WANT YOU TO SEE WHAT I SEE, YEAH?
THE MEDIA LIES ABOUT ME, CALLING ME AN "INSANE WEREWOLF SNIPER." LIKE I'M MAD OR SOMETHING, BARKING AT THE MOON.
WELL, THAT GOT ME THINKING.
SALE!
THINKING ABOUT OUR NATION'S CONNECTION TO THE MOON.
THE MOON IS A FUCKING LIE. OR AT LEAST OUR HISTORY WITH IT IS.
IT'S A LIE WE CHOOSE TO BELIEVE.
YET THERE IT IS, HANGING OVER OUR HEADS EVERY NIGHT.
BUT LET ME TELL YOU THIS-- LIES COME WITH A PRICE.

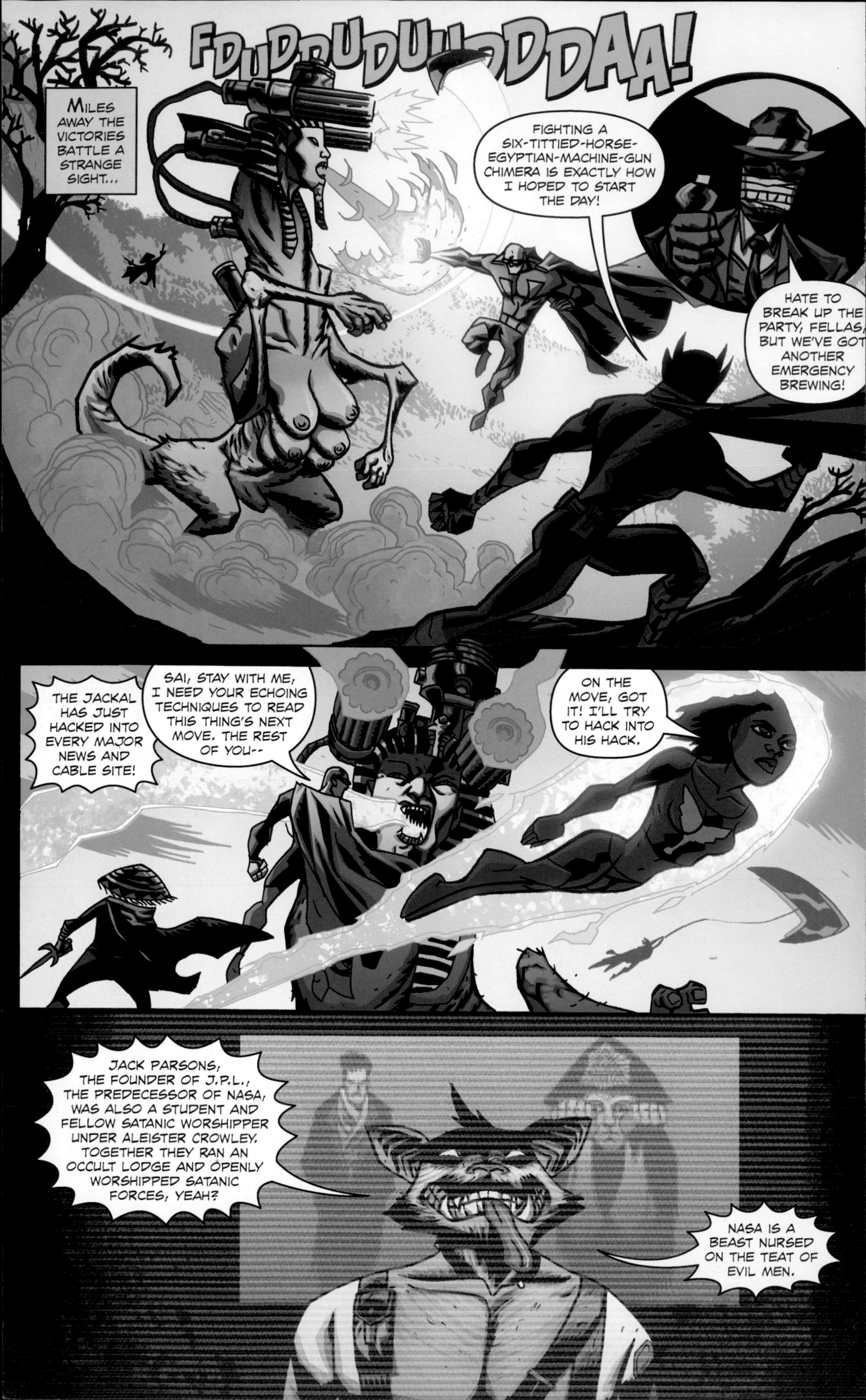

MILES AWAY THE VICTORIES BATTLE A STRANGE SIGHT...
FIGHTING A SIX-TITTIED-HORSE-EGYPTIAN-MACHINE-GUN CHIMERA IS EXACTLY HOW I HOPED TO START THE DAY!
HATE TO BREAK UP THE PARTY, FELLAS, BUT WE'VE GOT ANOTHER EMERGENCY BREWING!
THE JACKAL HAS JUST HACKED INTO EVERY MAJOR NEWS AND CABLE SITE!
SAI, STAY WITH ME, I NEED YOUR ECHOING TECHNIQUES TO READ THIS THING'S NEXT MOVE. THE REST OF YOU--
ON THE MOVE, GOT IT! I'LL TRY TO HACK INTO HIS HACK.
JACK PARSONS, THE FOUNDER OF J.P.L., THE PREDECESSOR OF NASA, WAS ALSO A STUDENT AND FELLOW SATANIC WORSHIPPER UNDER ALEISTER CROWLEY. TOGETHER THEY RAN AN OCCULT LODGE AND OPENLY WORSHIPPED SATANIC FORCES, YEAH?
NASA IS A BEAST NURSED ON THE TEAT OF EVIL MEN.

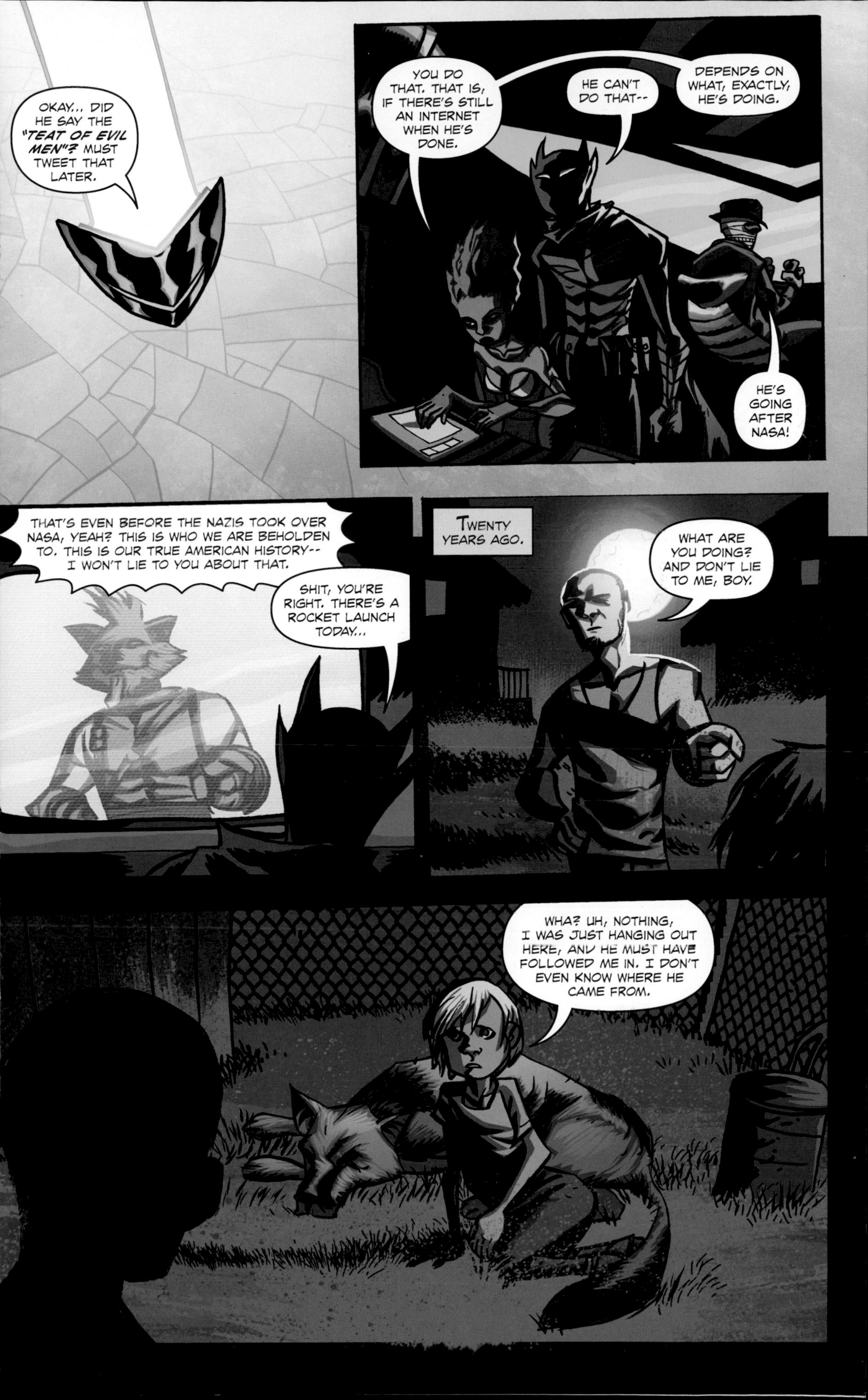
OKAY... DID HE SAY THE "TEAT OF EVIL MEN"? MUST TWEET THAT LATER.
YOU DO THAT. THAT IS, IF THERE'S STILL AN INTERNET WHEN HE'S DONE.
HE CAN'T DO THAT--
DEPENDS ON WHAT, EXACTLY, HE'S DOING.
HE'S GOING AFTER NASA!
THAT'S EVEN BEFORE THE NAZIS TOOK OVER NASA, YEAH? THIS IS WHO WE ARE BEHOLDEN TO. THIS IS OUR TRUE AMERICAN HISTORY-- I WON'T LIE TO YOU ABOUT THAT.
SHIT, YOU'RE RIGHT. THERE'S A ROCKET LAUNCH TODAY...
TWENTY YEARS AGO.
WHAT ARE YOU DOING? AND DON'T LIE TO ME, BOY.
WHA? UH, NOTHING, I WAS JUST HANGING OUT HERE, AND HE MUST HAVE FOLLOWED ME IN. I DON'T EVEN KNOW WHERE HE CAME FROM.

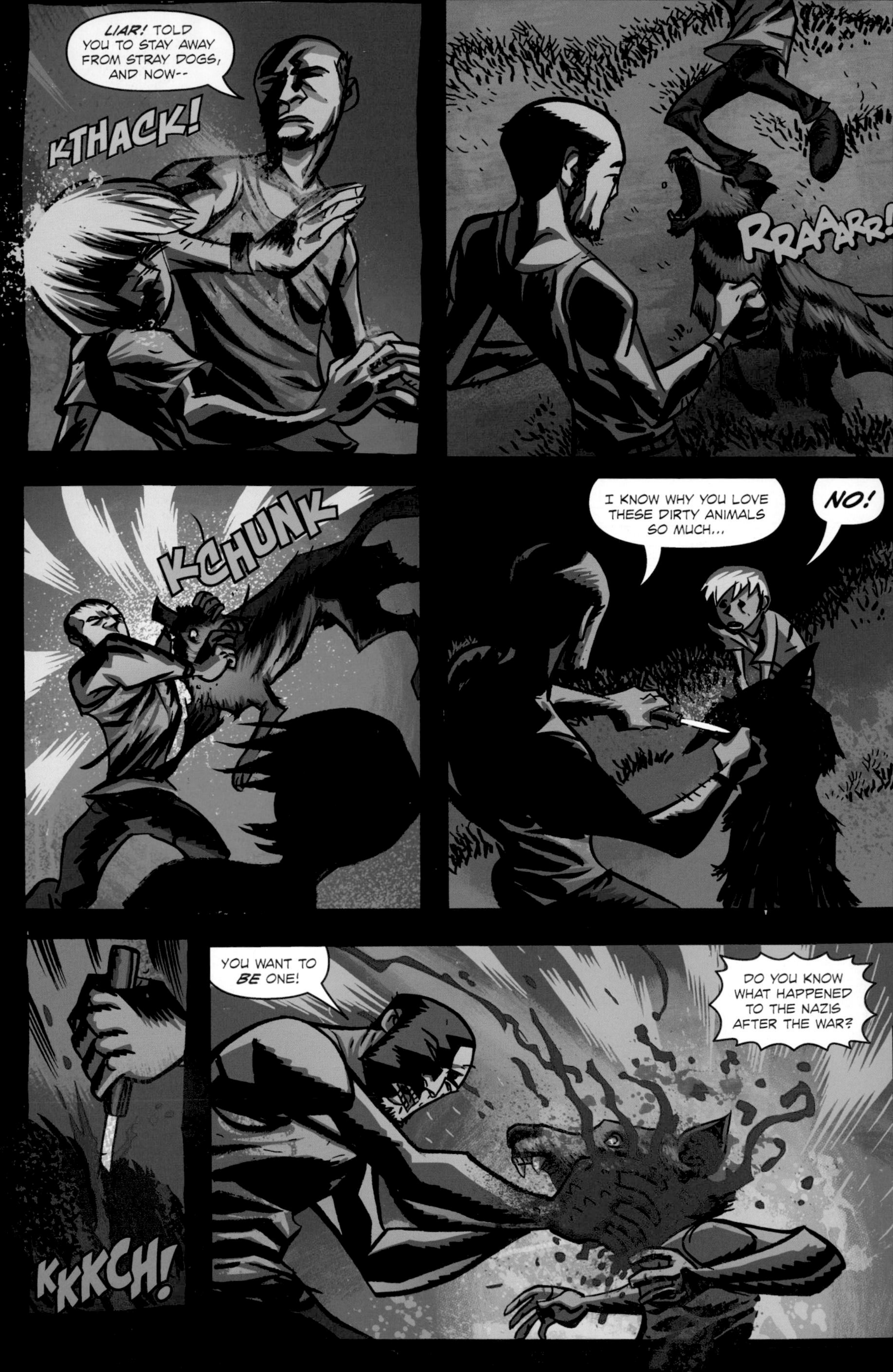
LIAR! TOLD YOU TO STAY AWAY FROM STRAY DOGS, AND NOW--
KTHACK!
RRAAARR!
KCHUNK
I KNOW WHY YOU LOVE THESE DIRTY ANIMALS SO MUCH...
NO!
YOU WANT TO BE ONE!
DO YOU KNOW WHAT HAPPENED TO THE NAZIS AFTER THE WAR?
KKKCH!

WE HIRED THEM. AFTER THE WAR WE GAVE THE NAZIS NEW HISTORIES AND SET THEM LOOSE AT NASA SO WE COULD LEARN THEIR DARK SECRETS AND USE THEM OURSELVES.

HARD LESSONS ARE THE BEST KIND OF LESSONS...

STAY HERE UNTIL YOU CAN FACE THE TRUTH ABOUT YOURSELF.

THE TRUTH IS--TAKE A HARD LOOK AT NASA AND YOU'LL FIND SATAN WORSHIPERS AND A CLUTCH OF NAZIS, YEAH? WERNHER VON BRAUN AND HUNDREDS OF OTHER NAZI SCIENTISTS ARE BEHIND THE MASK OF NASA. THESE WEREN'T JUST "GERMAN SCIENTISTS" THE O.S.A. TRIED TO SELL US.

THEIR "SCIENCE" BENEFITED FROM *PEENEMÜNDE*, A SLAVE-LABOR CAMP WHERE VON BRAUN AND OTHER NASA SCIENTISTS BUILT THE V-2. MORE PRISONERS DIED BUILDING THE ROCKET FACILITIES THAN THE BOMBS KILLED. MORE THAN TWENTY THOUSAND WERE WORKED TO DEATH, STARVED TO DEATH, OR EXPERIMENTED ON FOR SCIENTIFIC GAIN.

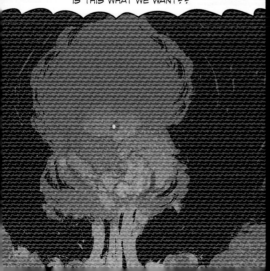

BEFORE THE NAZIS, JACK PARSONS TRIED TO RAISE THE ANTICHRIST DURING TESTS OF THE A-BOMB, USING SEXUAL MAGIC. THE FIRST ATOMIC EXPLOSION WAS A PSYCHOSEXUAL ACT OF EVIL! THESE ARE THE SORTS OF MINDS AT THE FOUNDATION OF NASA, YEAH? IS THIS WHAT WE WANT??

OF ALL THE THINGS TO OBSESS OVER...

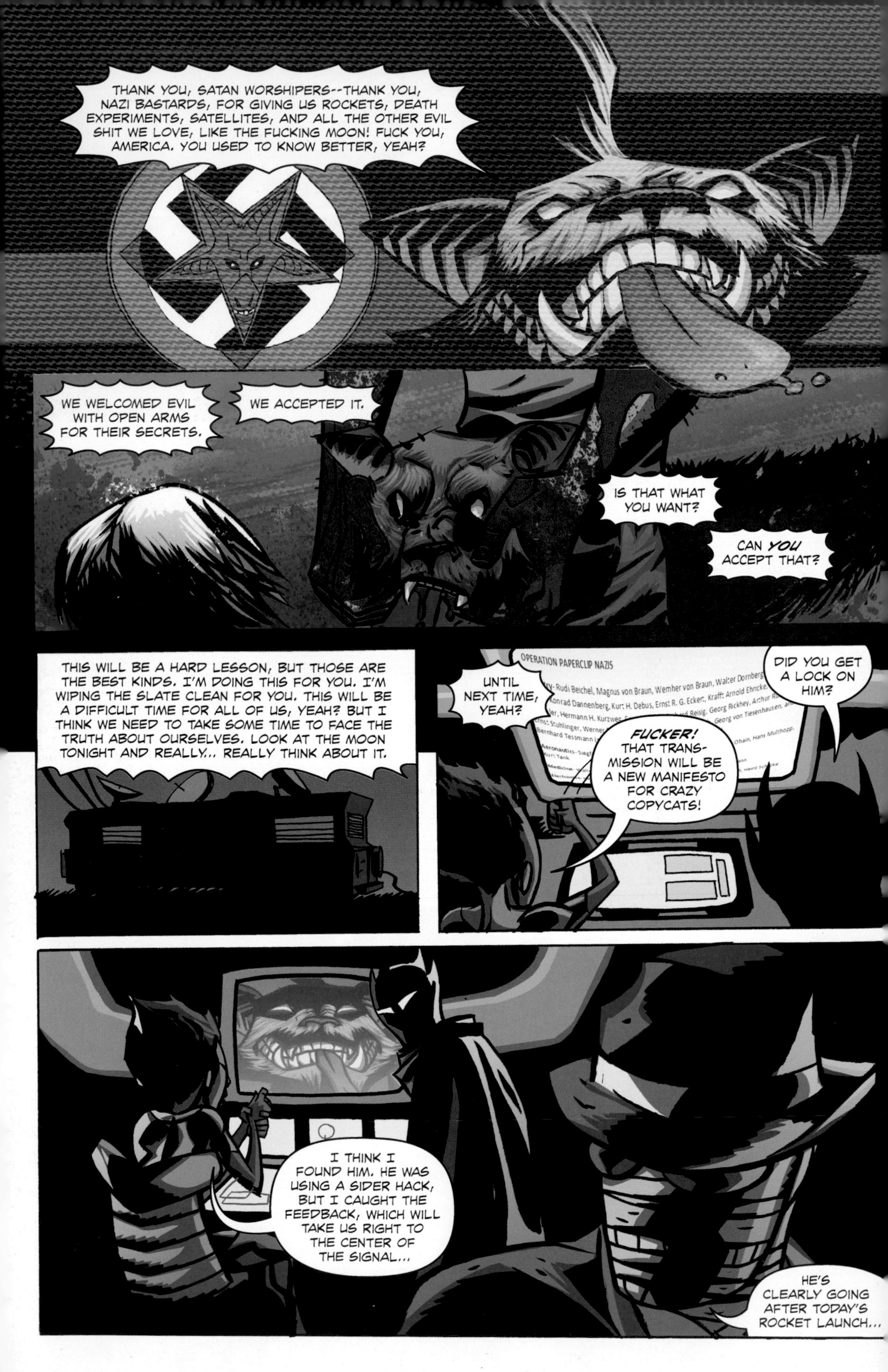
THANK YOU, SATAN WORSHIPERS--THANK YOU, NAZI BASTARDS, FOR GIVING US ROCKETS, DEATH EXPERIMENTS, SATELLITES, AND ALL THE OTHER EVIL SHIT WE LOVE, LIKE THE FUCKING MOON! FUCK YOU, AMERICA. YOU USED TO KNOW BETTER, YEAH?
WE WELCOMED EVIL WITH OPEN ARMS FOR THEIR SECRETS.
WE ACCEPTED IT.
IS THAT WHAT YOU WANT?
CAN *YOU* ACCEPT THAT?
THIS WILL BE A HARD LESSON, BUT THOSE ARE THE BEST KINDS. I'M DOING THIS FOR YOU. I'M WIPING THE SLATE CLEAN FOR YOU. THIS WILL BE A DIFFICULT TIME FOR ALL OF US, YEAH? BUT I THINK WE NEED TO TAKE SOME TIME TO FACE THE TRUTH ABOUT OURSELVES. LOOK AT THE MOON TONIGHT AND REALLY... REALLY THINK ABOUT IT.
OPERATION PAPERCLIP NAZIS
UNTIL NEXT TIME, YEAH?
DID YOU GET A LOCK ON HIM?
FUCKER! THAT TRANS-MISSION WILL BE A NEW MANIFESTO FOR CRAZY COPYCATS!
I THINK I FOUND HIM. HE WAS USING A SIDER HACK, BUT I CAUGHT THE FEEDBACK, WHICH WILL TAKE US RIGHT TO THE CENTER OF THE SIGNAL...
HE'S CLEARLY GOING AFTER TODAY'S ROCKET LAUNCH...

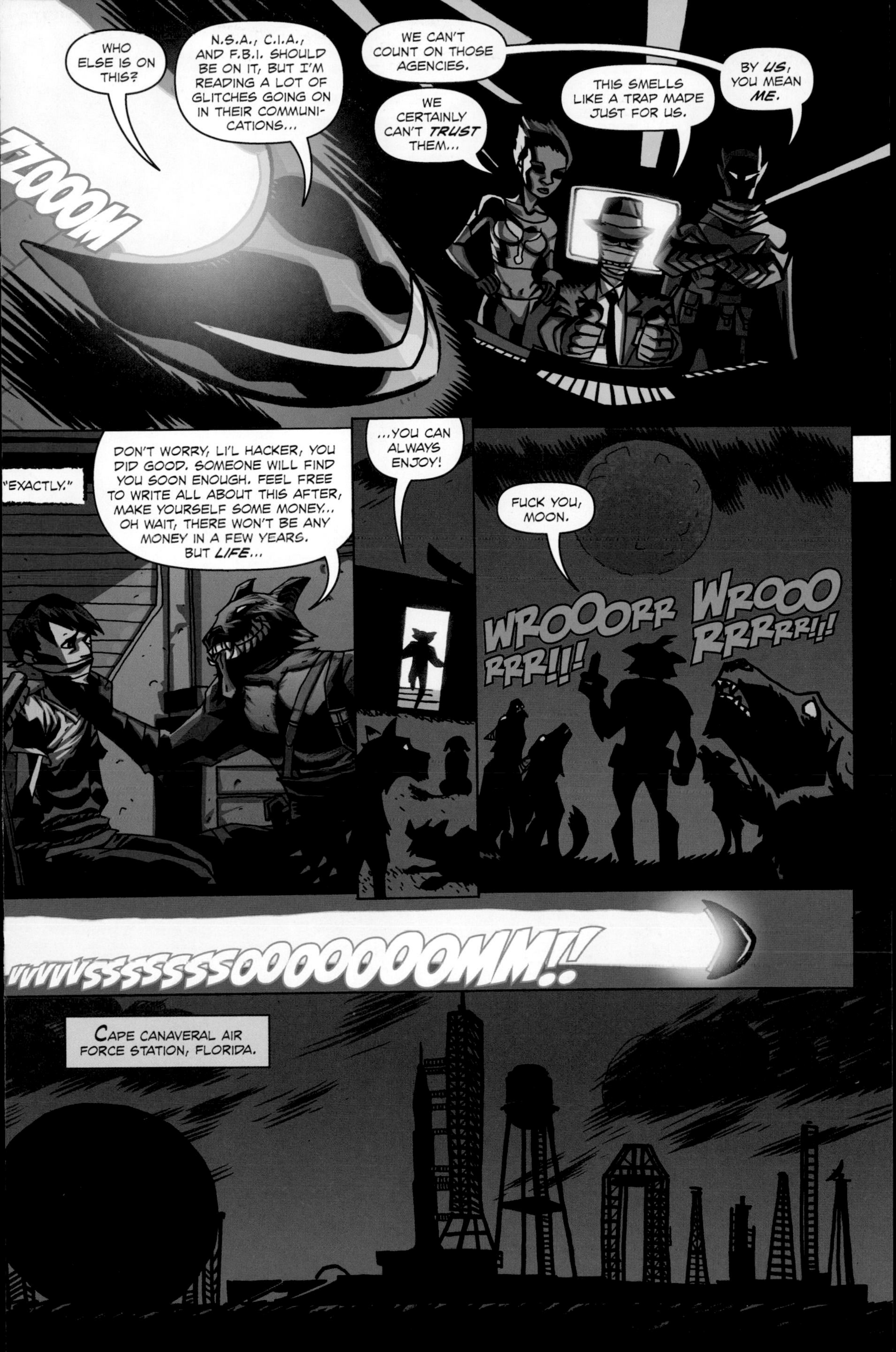
WHO ELSE IS ON THIS?
N.S.A., C.I.A., AND F.B.I. SHOULD BE ON IT, BUT I'M READING A LOT OF GLITCHES GOING ON IN THEIR COMMUNICATIONS...
ZZOOOOM
WE CAN'T COUNT ON THOSE AGENCIES.
WE CERTAINLY CAN'T *TRUST* THEM...
THIS SMELLS LIKE A TRAP MADE JUST FOR US.
BY *US*, YOU MEAN *ME*.
"EXACTLY."
DON'T WORRY, LI'L HACKER, YOU DID GOOD. SOMEONE WILL FIND YOU SOON ENOUGH. FEEL FREE TO WRITE ALL ABOUT THIS AFTER, MAKE YOURSELF SOME MONEY... OH WAIT, THERE WON'T BE ANY MONEY IN A FEW YEARS. BUT *LIFE*...
...YOU CAN ALWAYS ENJOY!
FUCK YOU, MOON.
WROOOORR RRR!!!
WROOO RRRRR!!!
VVVVVSSSSSSOOOOOOOOMM!!
CAPE CANAVERAL AIR FORCE STATION, FLORIDA.

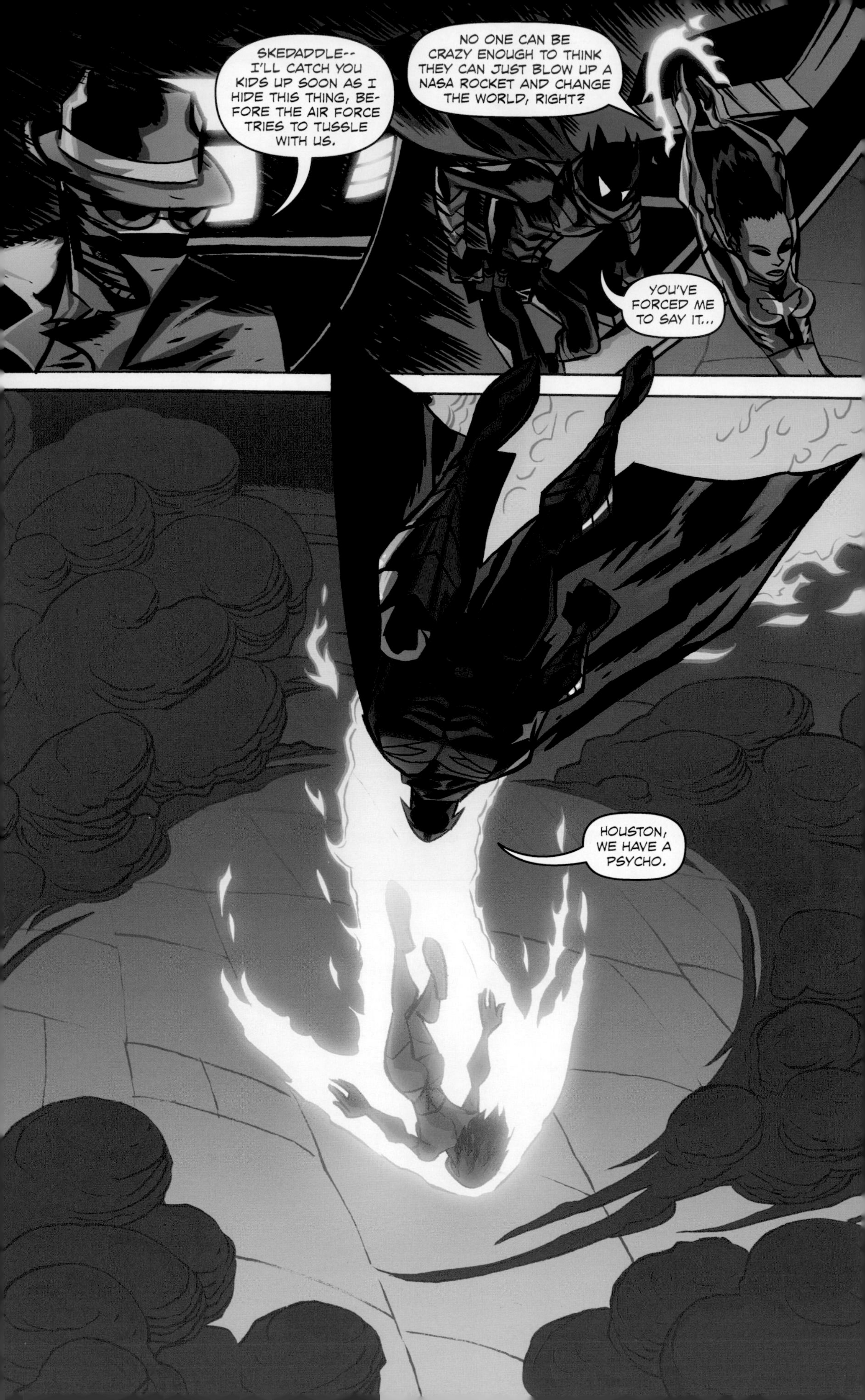
SKEDADDLE-- I'LL CATCH YOU KIDS UP SOON AS I HIDE THIS THING, BEFORE THE AIR FORCE TRIES TO TUSSLE WITH US.
NO ONE CAN BE CRAZY ENOUGH TO THINK THEY CAN JUST BLOW UP A NASA ROCKET AND CHANGE THE WORLD, RIGHT?
YOU'VE FORCED ME TO SAY IT...
HOUSTON, WE HAVE A PSYCHO.

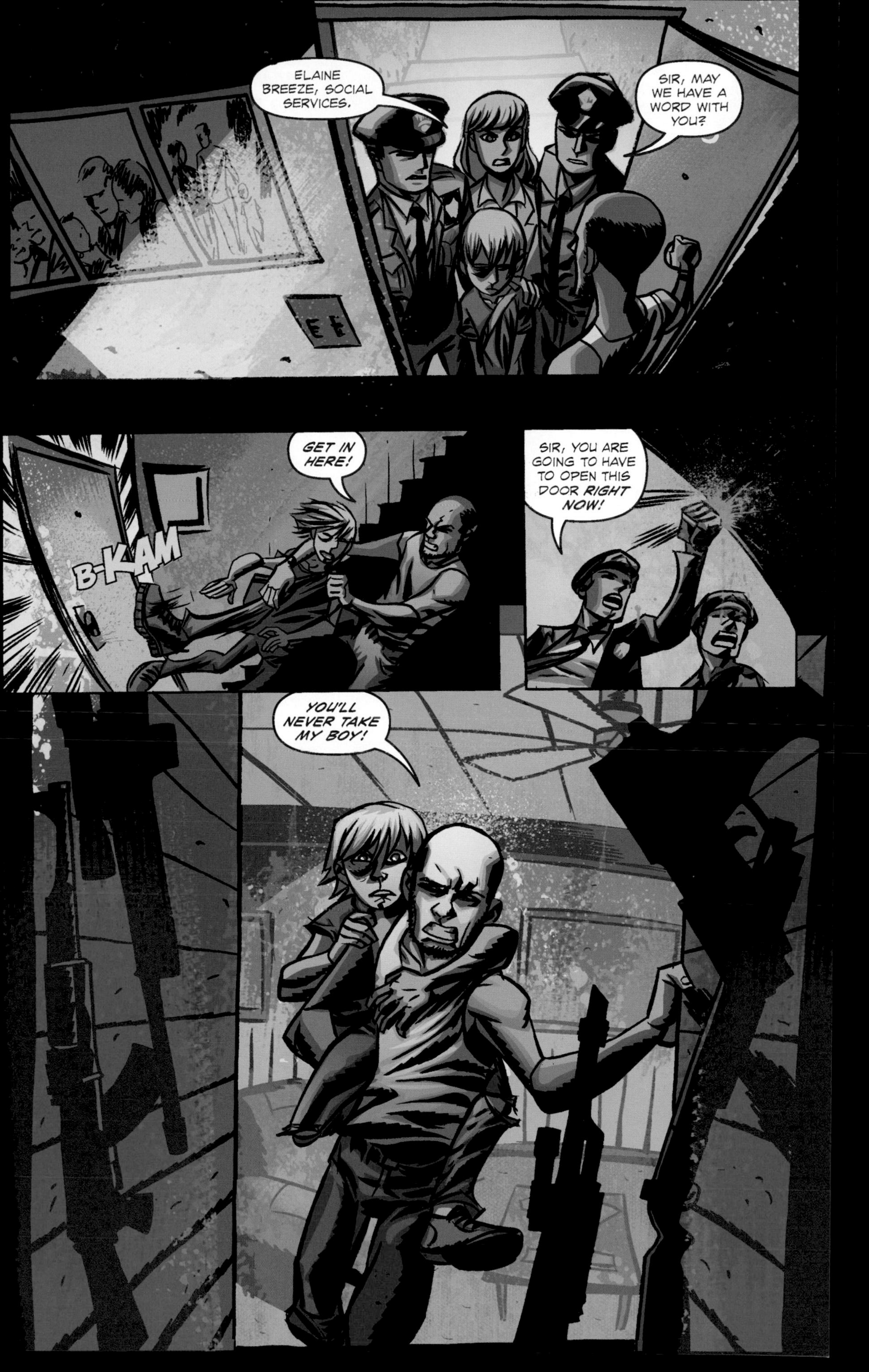
ELAINE BREEZE, SOCIAL SERVICES.
SIR, MAY WE HAVE A WORD WITH YOU?
GET IN HERE!
B-KAM
SIR, YOU ARE GOING TO HAVE TO OPEN THIS DOOR RIGHT NOW!
YOU'LL NEVER TAKE MY BOY!

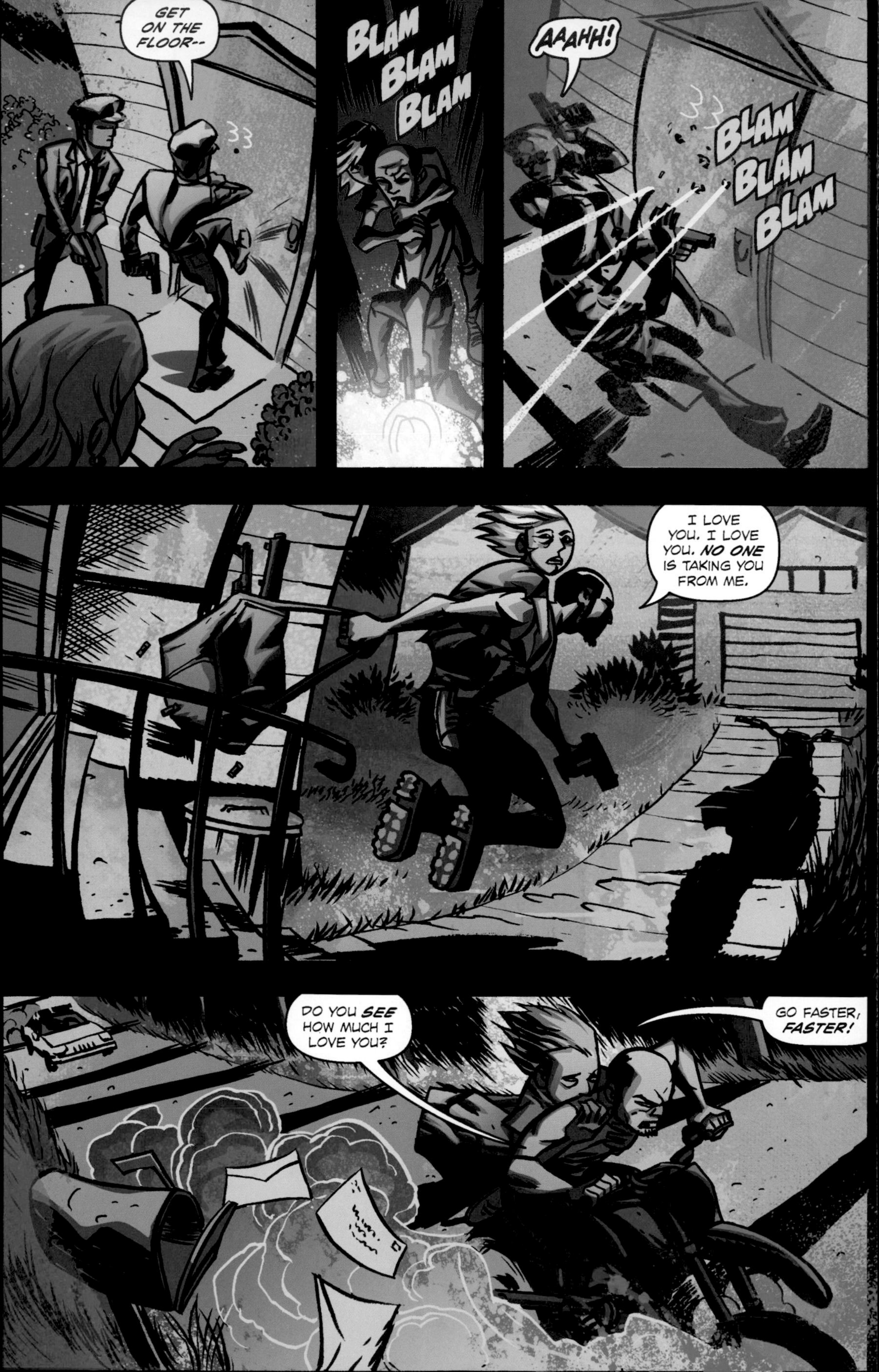
GET ON THE FLOOR--
BLAM BLAM BLAM
AAAHH!
BLAM BLAM BLAM
I LOVE YOU. I LOVE YOU. NO ONE IS TAKING YOU FROM ME.
DO YOU SEE HOW MUCH I LOVE YOU?
GO FASTER, FASTER!

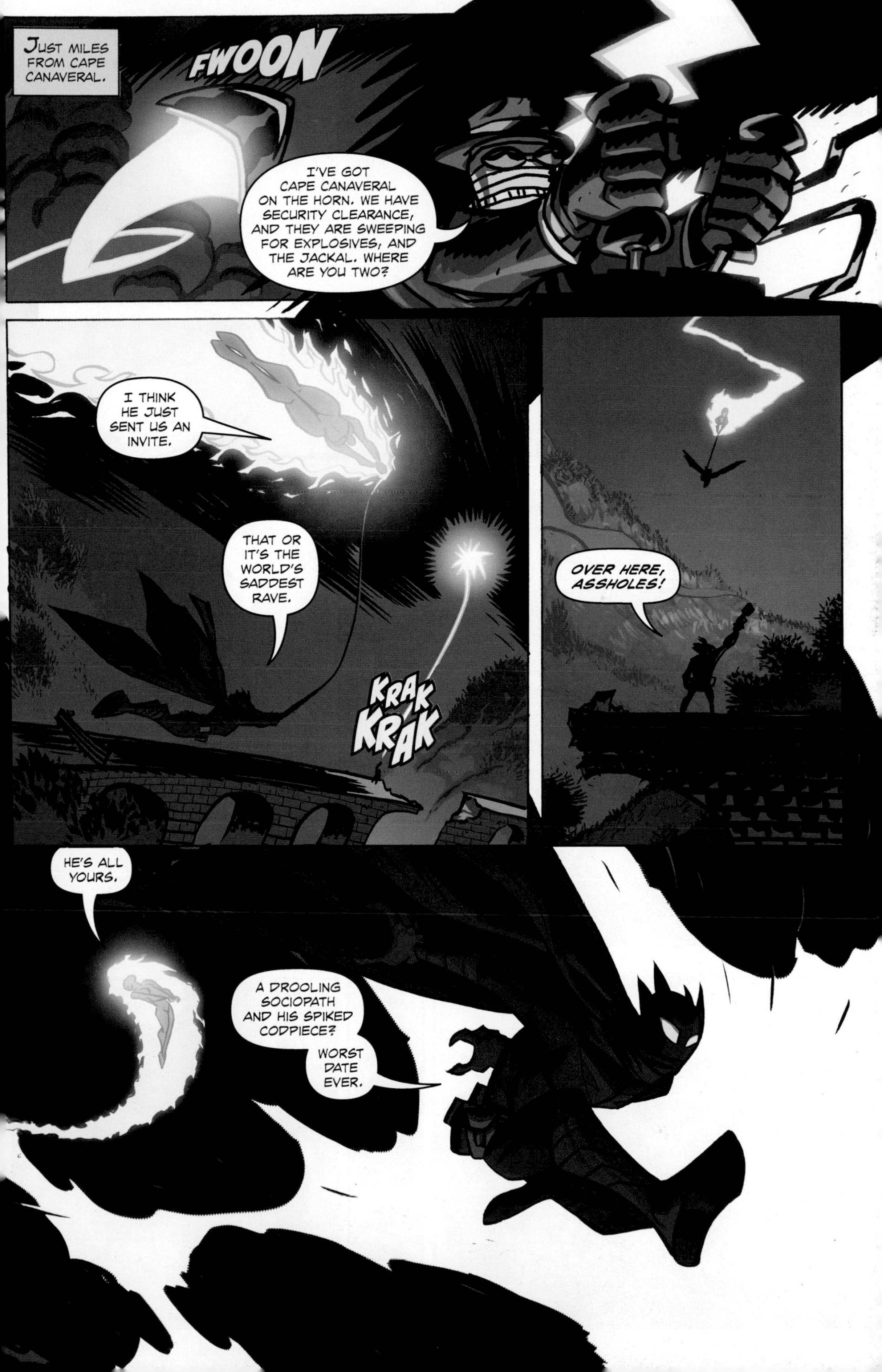
JUST MILES FROM CAPE CANAVERAL.
FWOON
I'VE GOT CAPE CANAVERAL ON THE HORN. WE HAVE SECURITY CLEARANCE, AND THEY ARE SWEEPING FOR EXPLOSIVES, AND THE JACKAL. WHERE ARE YOU TWO?
I THINK HE JUST SENT US AN INVITE.
THAT OR IT'S THE WORLD'S SADDEST RAVE.
KRAK KRAK
OVER HERE, ASSHOLES!
HE'S ALL YOURS.
A DROOLING SOCIOPATH AND HIS SPIKED CODPIECE?
WORST DATE EVER.

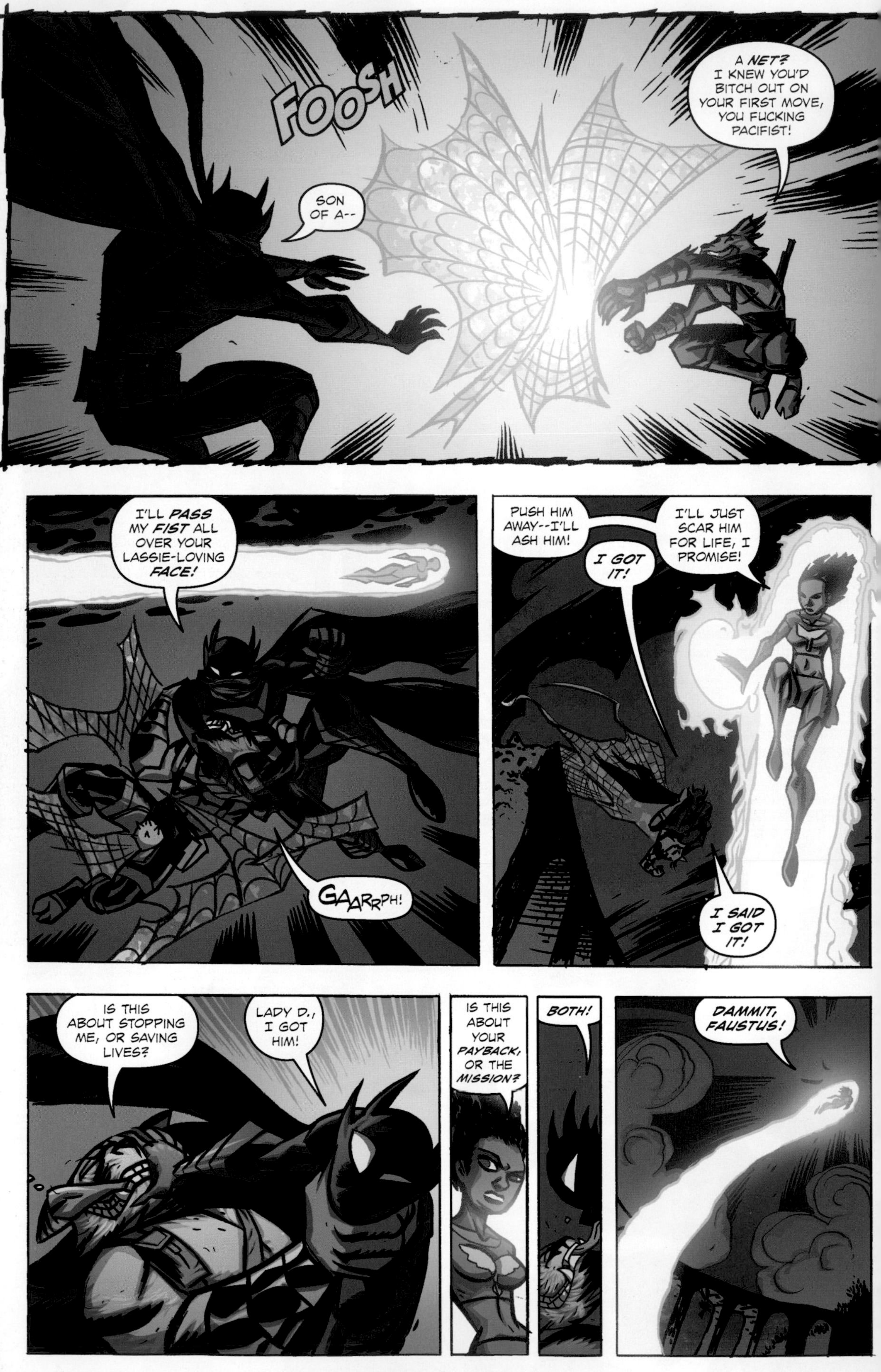
FOOSH
A NET? I KNEW YOU'D BITCH OUT ON YOUR FIRST MOVE, YOU FUCKING PACIFIST!
SON OF A--
I'LL PASS MY FIST ALL OVER YOUR LASSIE-LOVING FACE!
GAARRPH!
PUSH HIM AWAY--I'LL ASH HIM!
I'LL JUST SCAR HIM FOR LIFE, I PROMISE!
I GOT IT!
I SAID I GOT IT!
IS THIS ABOUT STOPPING ME, OR SAVING LIVES?
LADY D., I GOT HIM!
IS THIS ABOUT YOUR PAYBACK, OR THE MISSION?
BOTH!
DAMMIT, FAUSTUS!

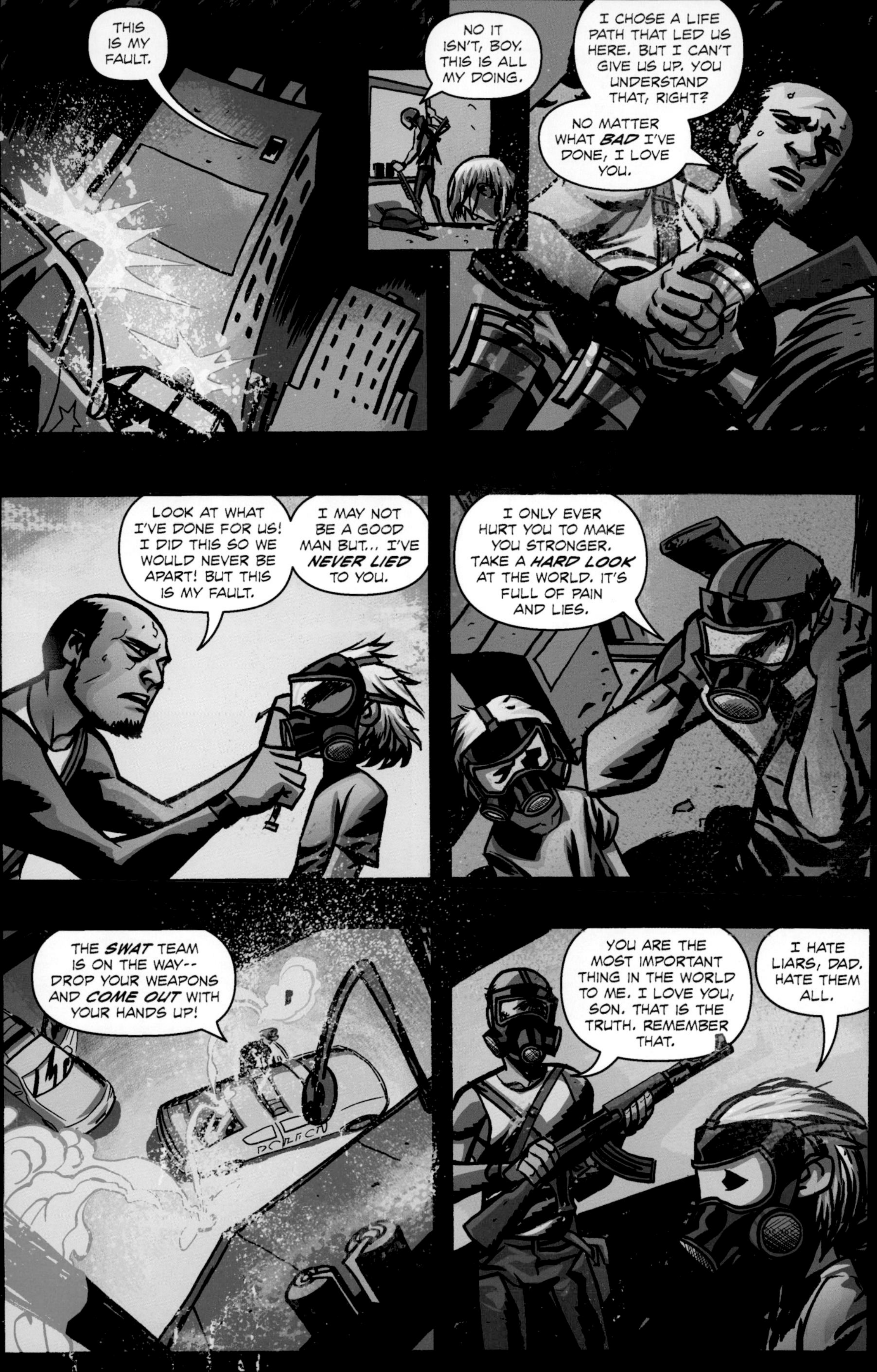
THIS IS MY FAULT.
NO IT ISN'T, BOY. THIS IS ALL MY DOING.
I CHOSE A LIFE PATH THAT LED US HERE. BUT I CAN'T GIVE US UP. YOU UNDERSTAND THAT, RIGHT?
NO MATTER WHAT BAD I'VE DONE, I LOVE YOU.
LOOK AT WHAT I'VE DONE FOR US! I DID THIS SO WE WOULD NEVER BE APART! BUT THIS IS MY FAULT.
I MAY NOT BE A GOOD MAN BUT... I'VE NEVER LIED TO YOU.
I ONLY EVER HURT YOU TO MAKE YOU STRONGER. TAKE A HARD LOOK AT THE WORLD. IT'S FULL OF PAIN AND LIES.
THE SWAT TEAM IS ON THE WAY-- DROP YOUR WEAPONS AND COME OUT WITH YOUR HANDS UP!
POLICE
YOU ARE THE MOST IMPORTANT THING IN THE WORLD TO ME. I LOVE YOU, SON. THAT IS THE TRUTH. REMEMBER THAT.
I HATE LIARS, DAD. HATE THEM ALL.

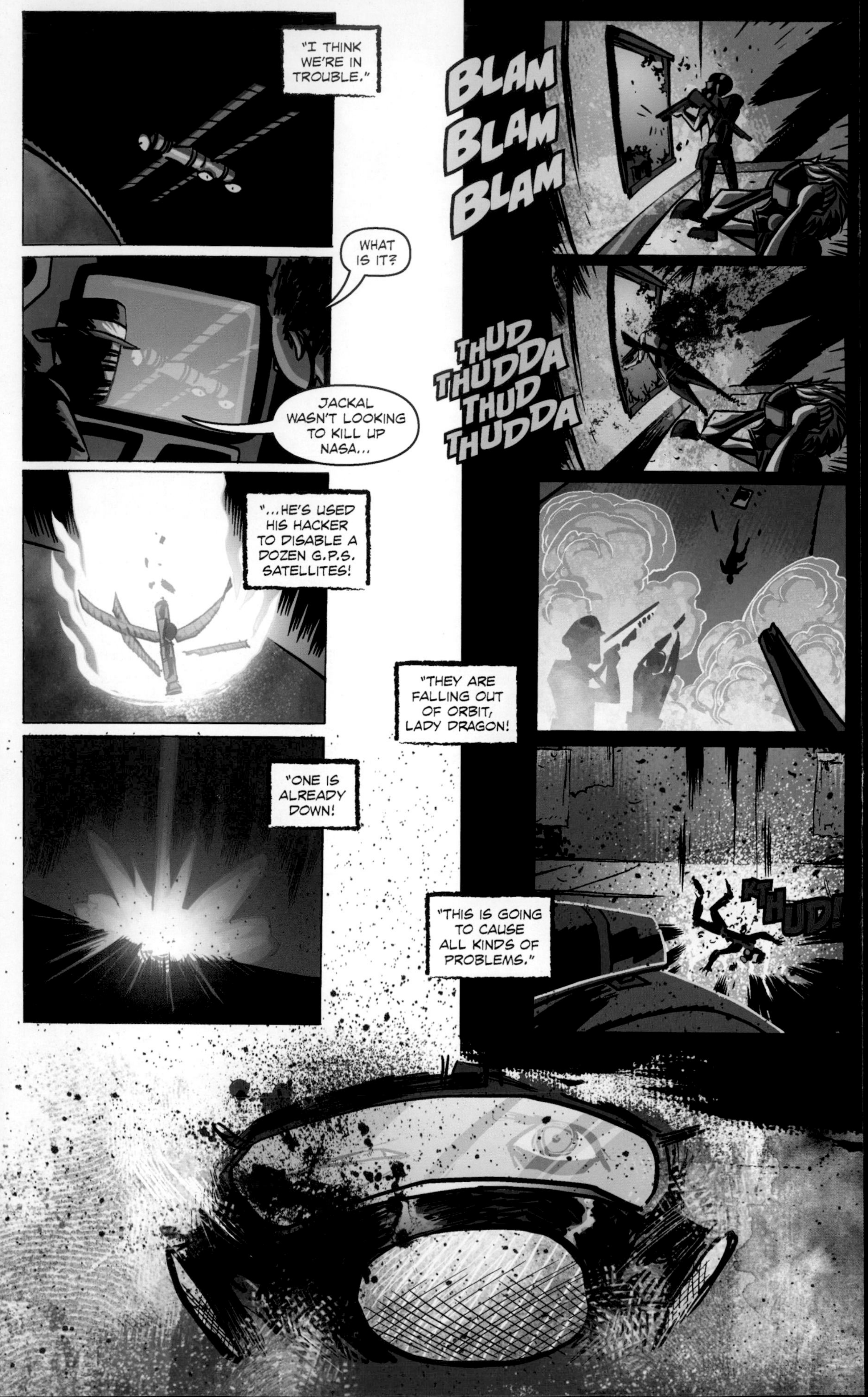
"I THINK WE'RE IN TROUBLE."
BLAM BLAM BLAM
WHAT IS IT?
THUD THUDDA THUD THUDDA
JACKAL WASN'T LOOKING TO KILL UP NASA...
"...HE'S USED HIS HACKER TO DISABLE A DOZEN G.P.S. SATELLITES!
"THEY ARE FALLING OUT OF ORBIT, LADY DRAGON!
"ONE IS ALREADY DOWN!
KTHUD!
"THIS IS GOING TO CAUSE ALL KINDS OF PROBLEMS."

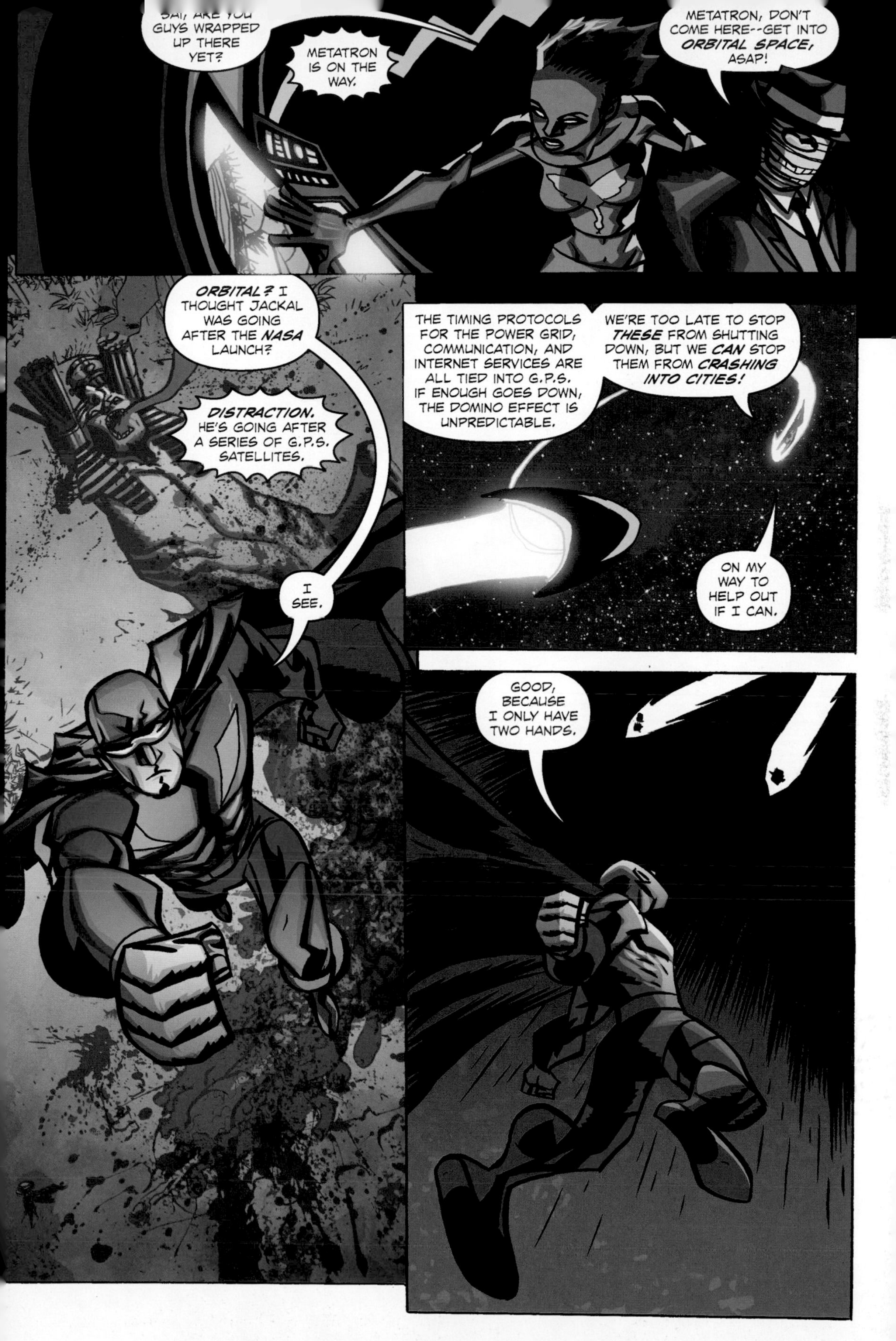
SAY, ARE YOU GUYS WRAPPED UP THERE YET?
METATRON IS ON THE WAY.
METATRON, DON'T COME HERE--GET INTO ORBITAL SPACE, ASAP!
ORBITAL? I THOUGHT JACKAL WAS GOING AFTER THE NASA LAUNCH?
DISTRACTION. HE'S GOING AFTER A SERIES OF G.P.S. SATELLITES.
I SEE.
THE TIMING PROTOCOLS FOR THE POWER GRID, COMMUNICATION, AND INTERNET SERVICES ARE ALL TIED INTO G.P.S. IF ENOUGH GOES DOWN, THE DOMINO EFFECT IS UNPREDICTABLE.
WE'RE TOO LATE TO STOP THESE FROM SHUTTING DOWN, BUT WE CAN STOP THEM FROM CRASHING INTO CITIES!
ON MY WAY TO HELP OUT IF I CAN.
GOOD, BECAUSE I ONLY HAVE TWO HANDS.

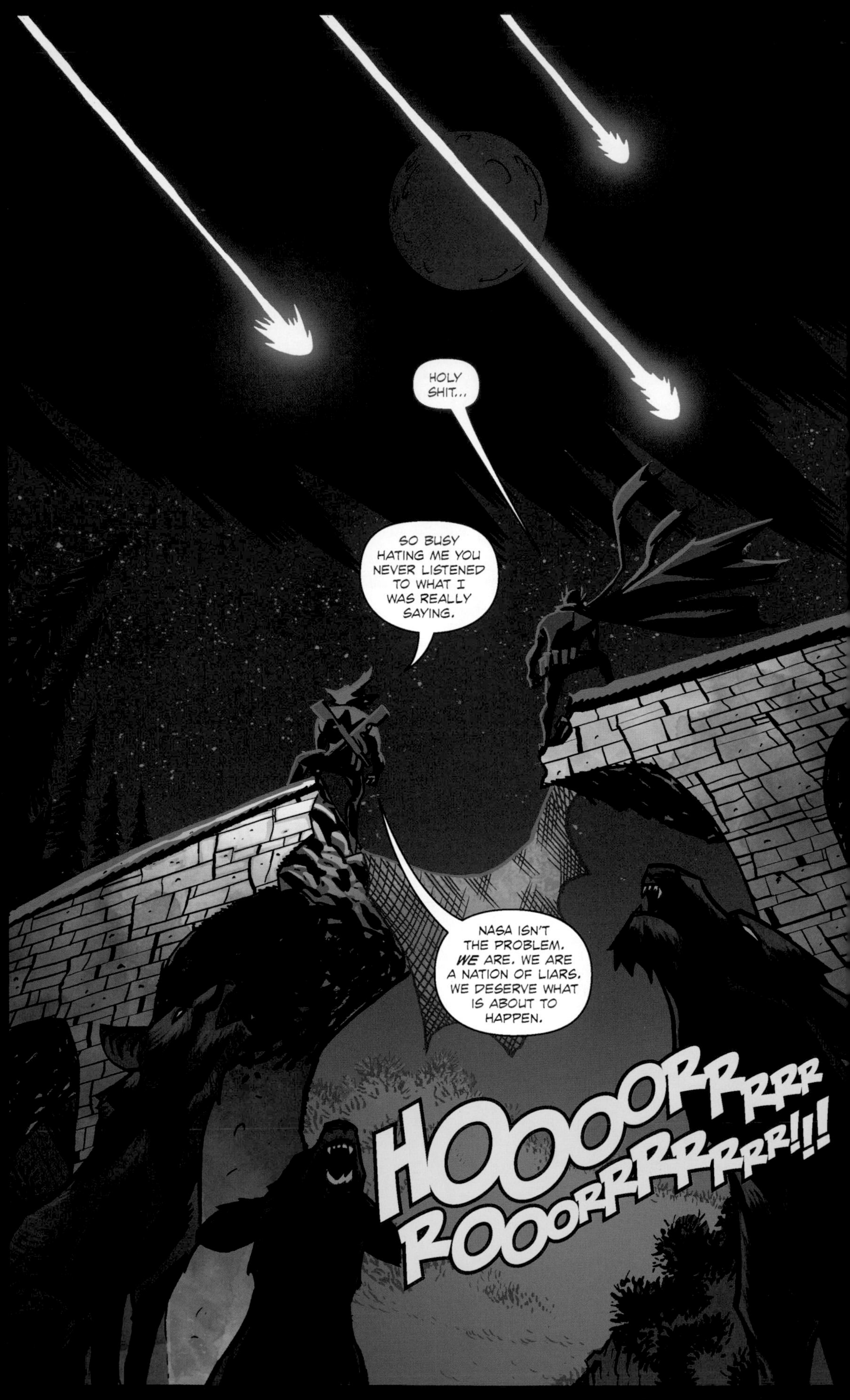
HOLY SHIT...
SO BUSY HATING ME YOU NEVER LISTENED TO WHAT I WAS REALLY SAYING.
NASA ISN'T THE PROBLEM. *WE* ARE. WE ARE A NATION OF LIARS. WE DESERVE WHAT IS ABOUT TO HAPPEN.
HOOOORRRRR ROOORRRRRRR!!!

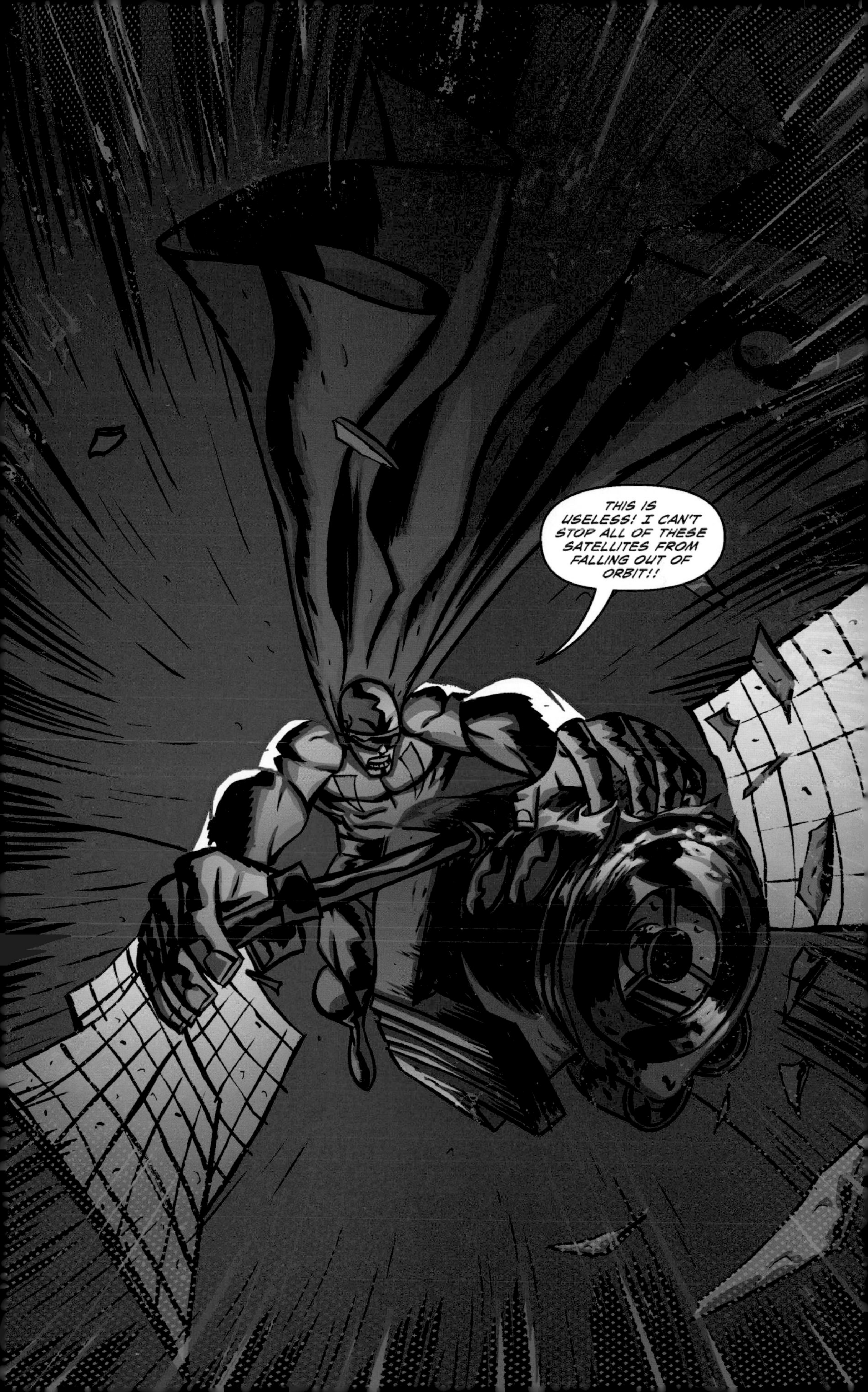
THIS IS USELESS! I CAN'T STOP ALL OF THESE SATELLITES FROM FALLING OUT OF ORBIT!!

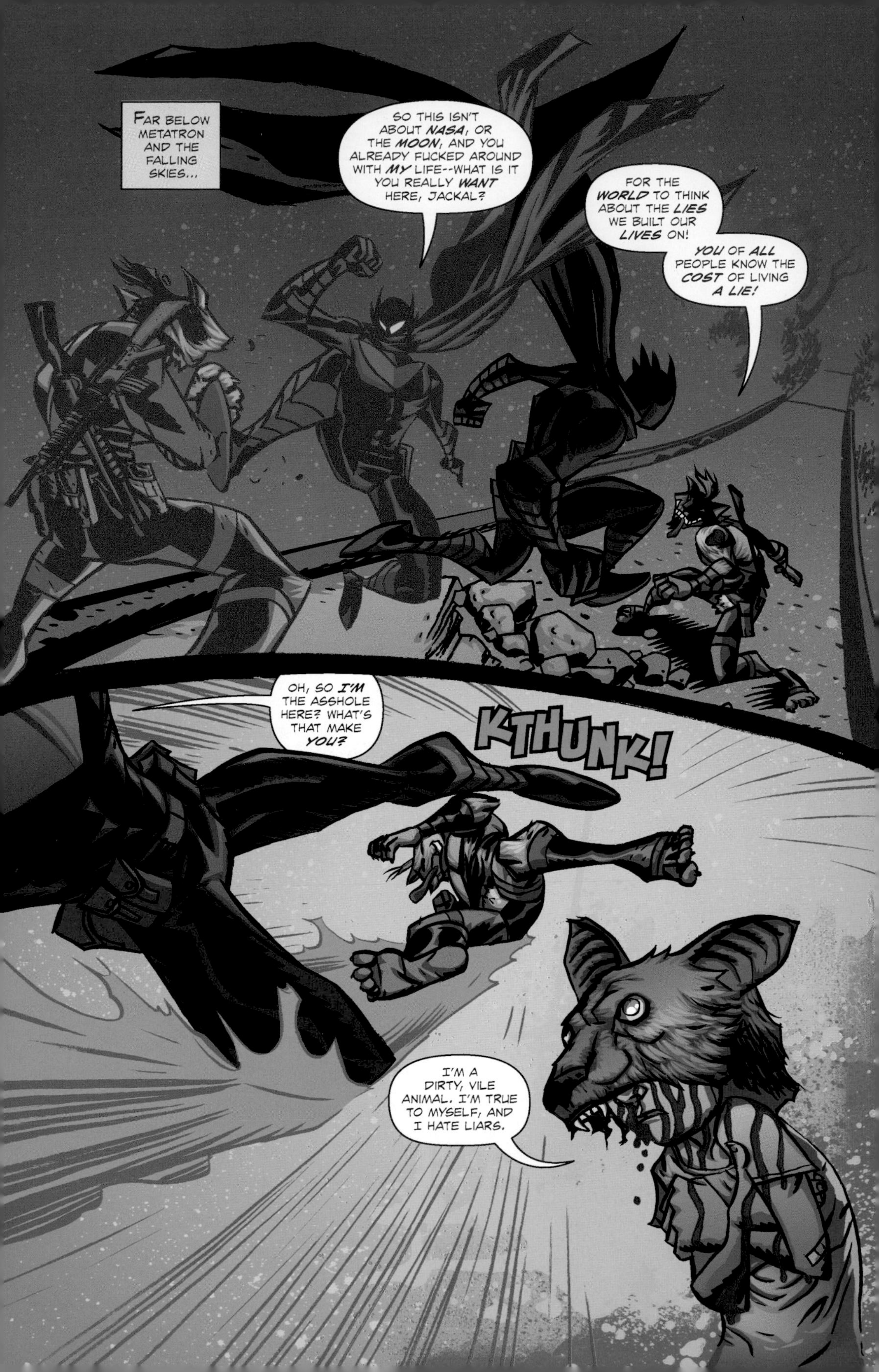
FAR BELOW METATRON AND THE FALLING SKIES...
SO THIS ISN'T ABOUT NASA, OR THE MOON, AND YOU ALREADY FUCKED AROUND WITH MY LIFE--WHAT IS IT YOU REALLY WANT HERE, JACKAL?
FOR THE WORLD TO THINK ABOUT THE LIES WE BUILT OUR LIVES ON!
YOU OF ALL PEOPLE KNOW THE COST OF LIVING A LIE!
OH, SO I'M THE ASSHOLE HERE? WHAT'S THAT MAKE YOU?
KTHUNK!
I'M A DIRTY, VILE ANIMAL. I'M TRUE TO MYSELF, AND I HATE LIARS.

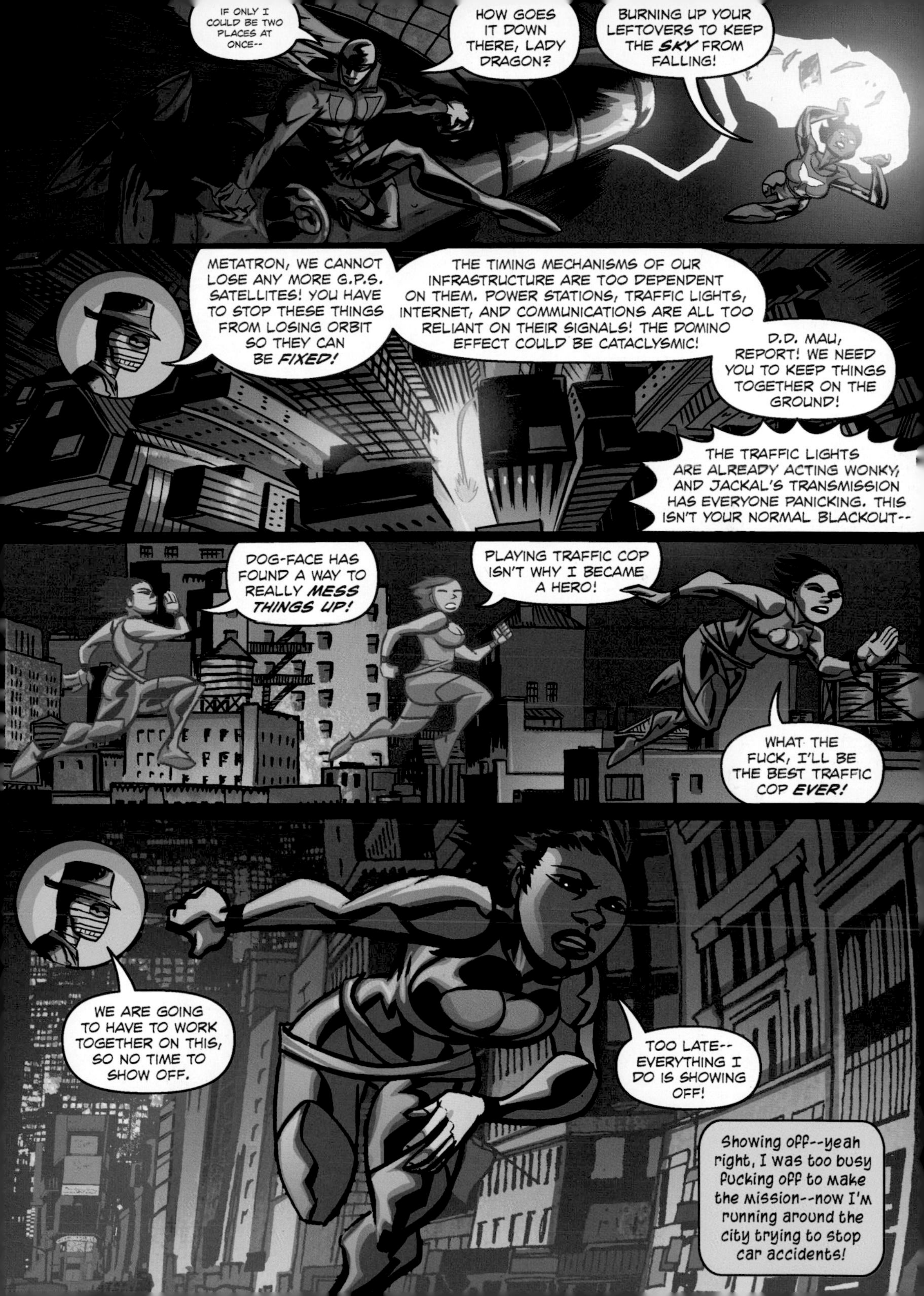
IF ONLY I COULD BE TWO PLACES AT ONCE--
HOW GOES IT DOWN THERE, LADY DRAGON?
BURNING UP YOUR LEFTOVERS TO KEEP THE SKY FROM FALLING!
METATRON, WE CANNOT LOSE ANY MORE G.P.S. SATELLITES! YOU HAVE TO STOP THESE THINGS FROM LOSING ORBIT SO THEY CAN BE FIXED!
THE TIMING MECHANISMS OF OUR INFRASTRUCTURE ARE TOO DEPENDENT ON THEM. POWER STATIONS, TRAFFIC LIGHTS, INTERNET, AND COMMUNICATIONS ARE ALL TOO RELIANT ON THEIR SIGNALS! THE DOMINO EFFECT COULD BE CATACLYSMIC!
D.D. MAU, REPORT! WE NEED YOU TO KEEP THINGS TOGETHER ON THE GROUND!
THE TRAFFIC LIGHTS ARE ALREADY ACTING WONKY, AND JACKAL'S TRANSMISSION HAS EVERYONE PANICKING. THIS ISN'T YOUR NORMAL BLACKOUT--
DOG-FACE HAS FOUND A WAY TO REALLY MESS THINGS UP!
PLAYING TRAFFIC COP ISN'T WHY I BECAME A HERO!
WHAT THE FUCK, I'LL BE THE BEST TRAFFIC COP EVER!
WE ARE GOING TO HAVE TO WORK TOGETHER ON THIS, SO NO TIME TO SHOW OFF.
TOO LATE-- EVERYTHING I DO IS SHOWING OFF!
Showing off--yeah right, I was too busy fucking off to make the mission--now I'm running around the city trying to stop car accidents!

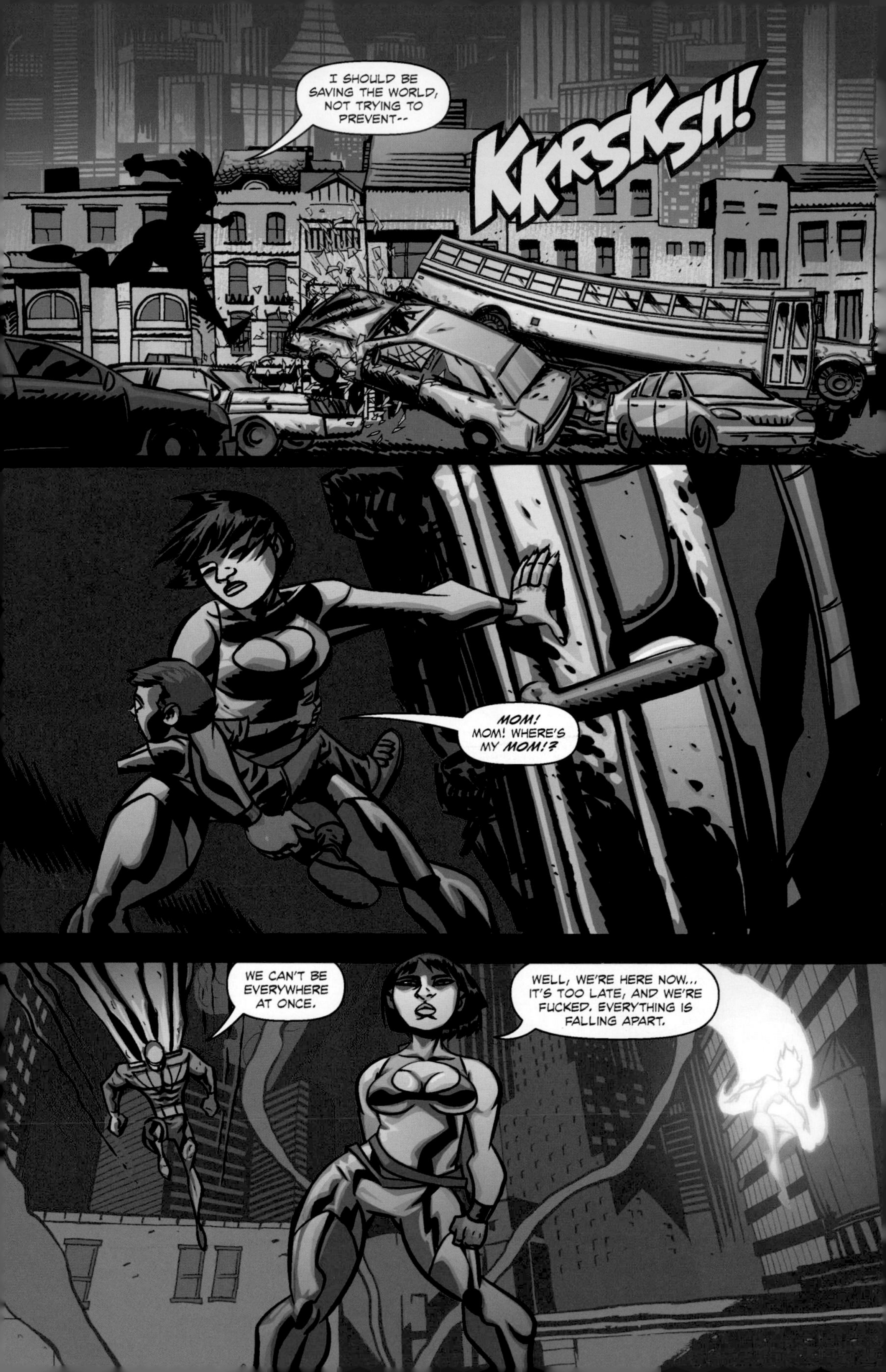

I SHOULD BE SAVING THE WORLD, NOT TRYING TO PREVENT--
KKRSKSH!
MOM! MOM! WHERE'S MY MOM!?
WE CAN'T BE EVERYWHERE AT ONCE.
WELL, WE'RE HERE NOW... IT'S TOO LATE, AND WE'RE FUCKED. EVERYTHING IS FALLING APART.

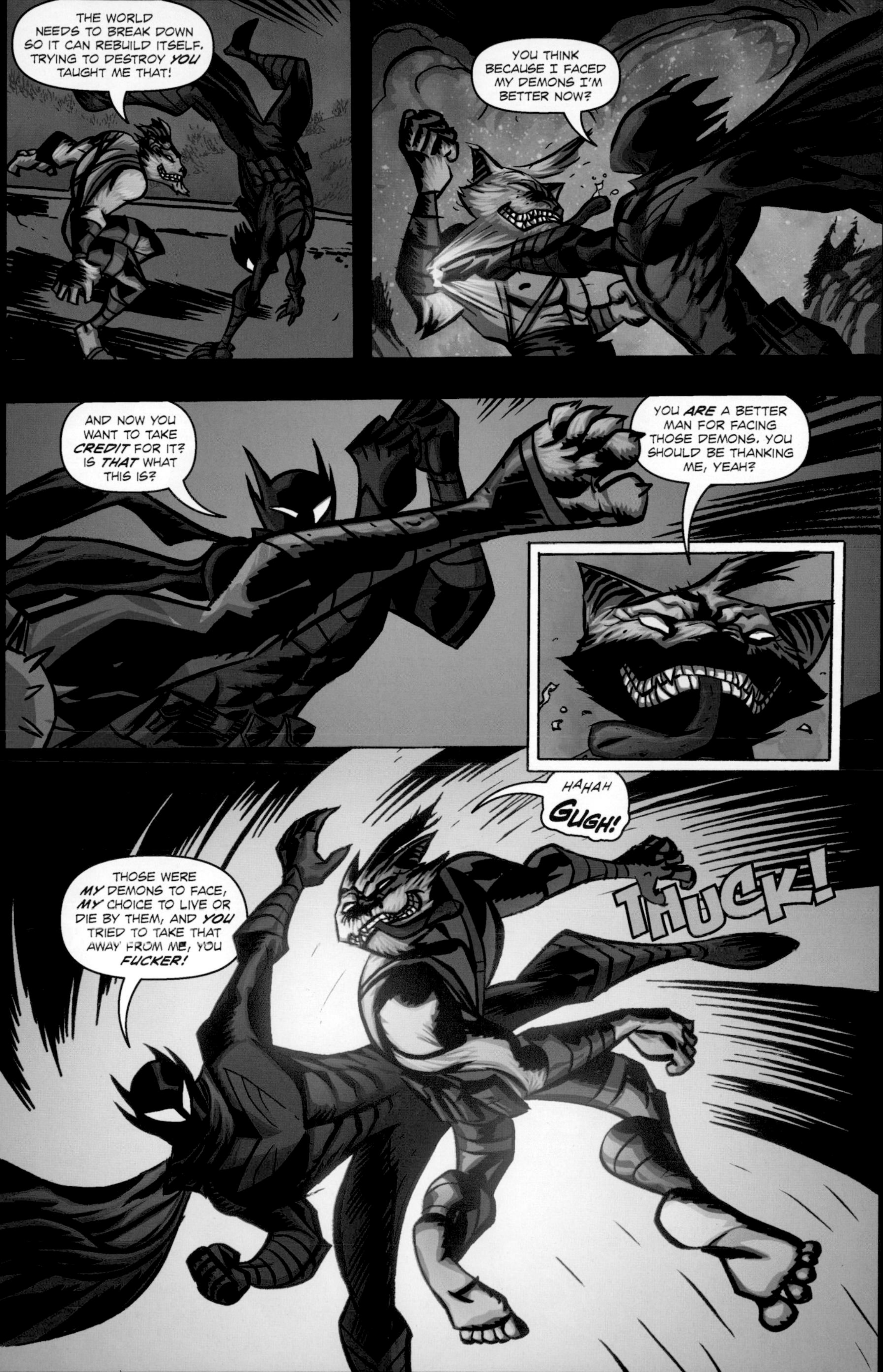
THE WORLD NEEDS TO BREAK DOWN SO IT CAN REBUILD ITSELF. TRYING TO DESTROY YOU TAUGHT ME THAT!
YOU THINK BECAUSE I FACED MY DEMONS I'M BETTER NOW?
AND NOW YOU WANT TO TAKE CREDIT FOR IT? IS THAT WHAT THIS IS?
YOU ARE A BETTER MAN FOR FACING THOSE DEMONS. YOU SHOULD BE THANKING ME, YEAH?
HAHAH
GUGH!
THUCK!
THOSE WERE MY DEMONS TO FACE, MY CHOICE TO LIVE OR DIE BY THEM, AND YOU TRIED TO TAKE THAT AWAY FROM ME, YOU FUCKER!

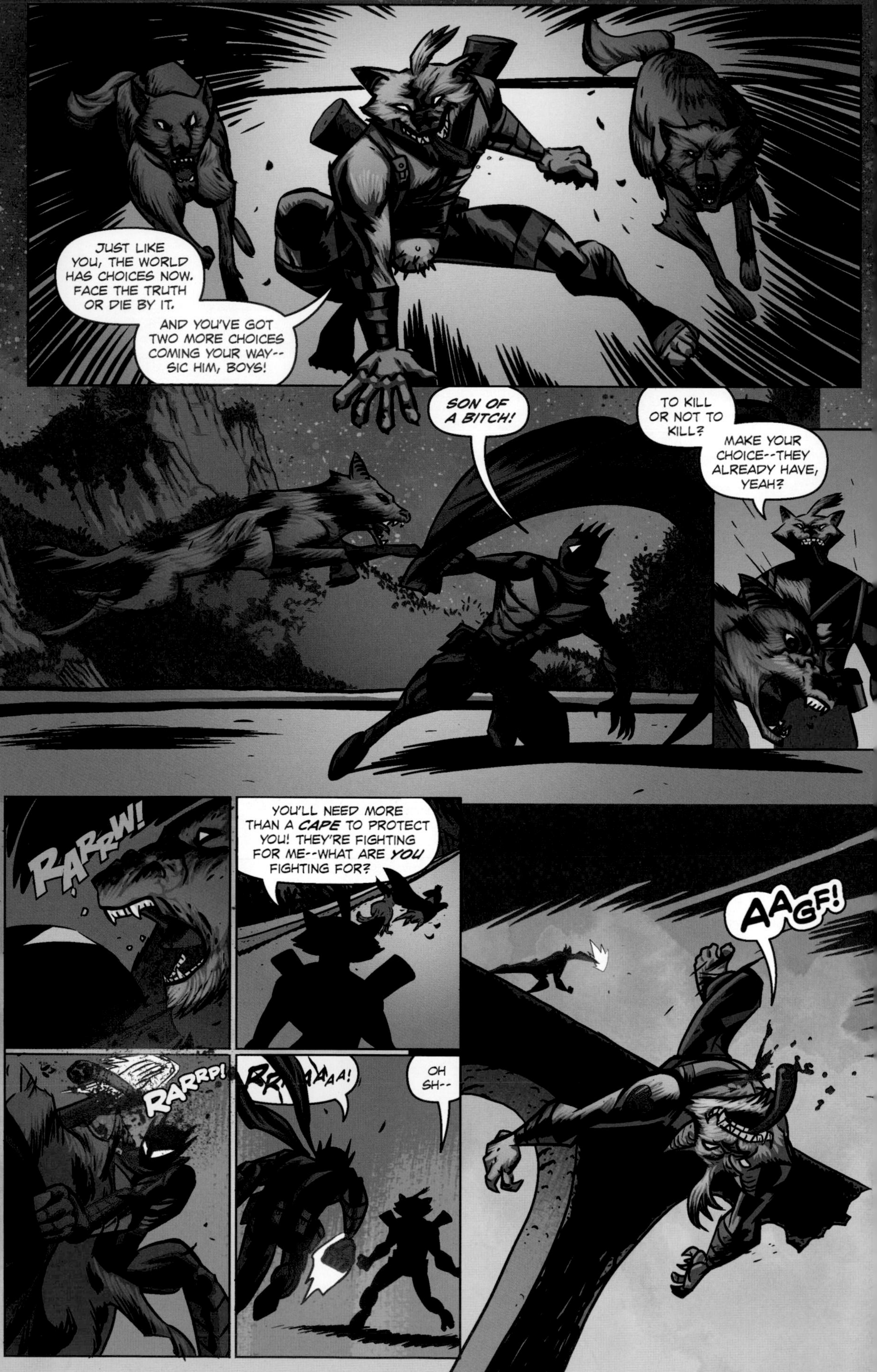
JUST LIKE YOU, THE WORLD HAS CHOICES NOW. FACE THE TRUTH OR DIE BY IT.
AND YOU'VE GOT TWO MORE CHOICES COMING YOUR WAY-- SIC HIM, BOYS!
SON OF A BITCH!
TO KILL OR NOT TO KILL?
MAKE YOUR CHOICE--THEY ALREADY HAVE, YEAH?
RARRW!
YOU'LL NEED MORE THAN A CAPE TO PROTECT YOU! THEY'RE FIGHTING FOR ME--WHAT ARE YOU FIGHTING FOR?
AAGF!
RARRP!
RRAAAAA!
OH SH--

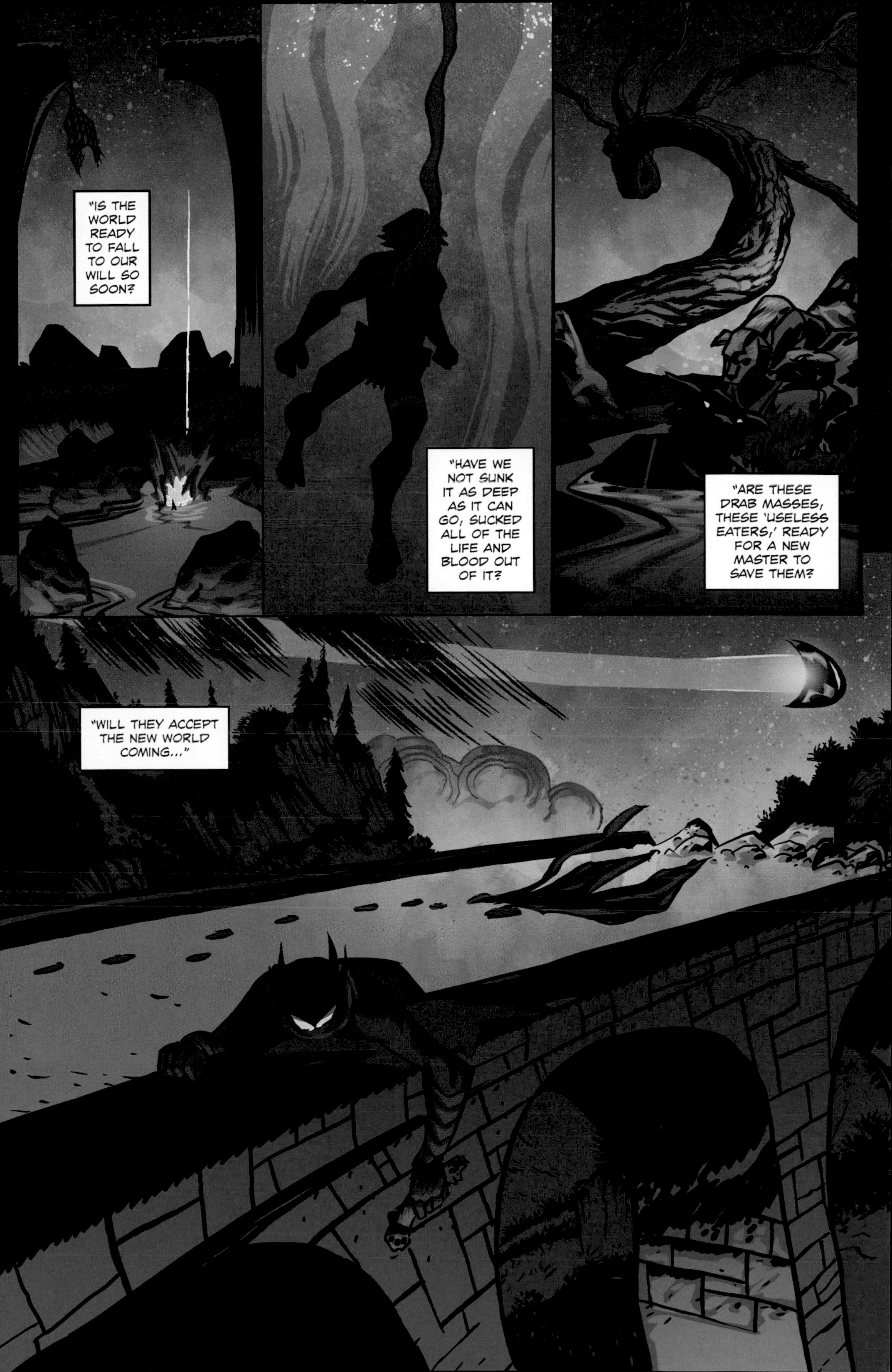
"IS THE WORLD READY TO FALL TO OUR WILL SO SOON?
"HAVE WE NOT SUNK IT AS DEEP AS IT CAN GO, SUCKED ALL OF THE LIFE AND BLOOD OUT OF IT?
"ARE THESE DRAB MASSES, THESE 'USELESS EATERS,' READY FOR A NEW MASTER TO SAVE THEM?
"WILL THEY ACCEPT THE NEW WORLD COMING..."

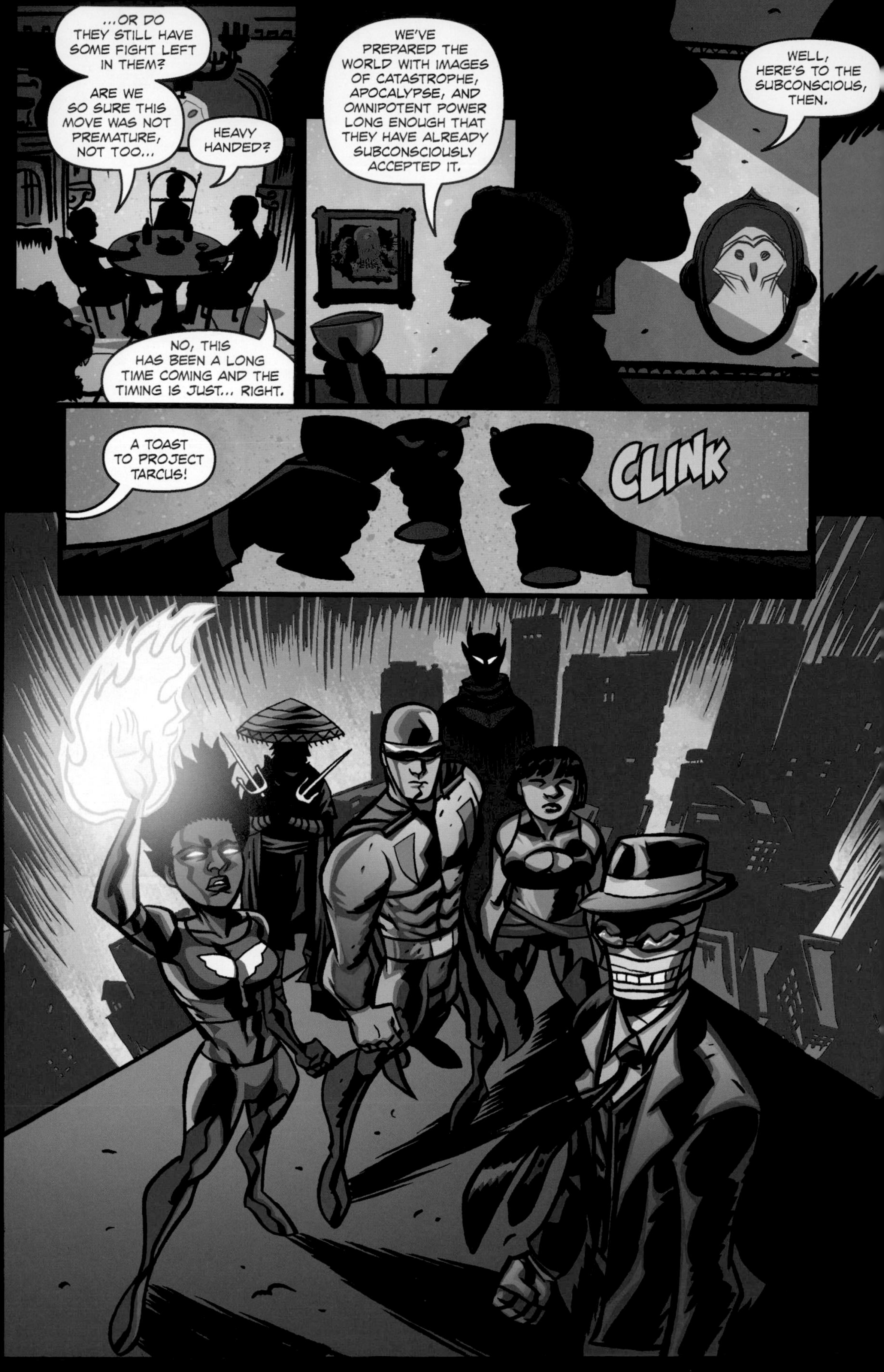
...OR DO THEY STILL HAVE SOME FIGHT LEFT IN THEM?
ARE WE SO SURE THIS MOVE WAS NOT PREMATURE, NOT TOO...
HEAVY HANDED?
NO, THIS HAS BEEN A LONG TIME COMING AND THE TIMING IS JUST... RIGHT.
WE'VE PREPARED THE WORLD WITH IMAGES OF CATASTROPHE, APOCALYPSE, AND OMNIPOTENT POWER LONG ENOUGH THAT THEY HAVE ALREADY SUBCONSCIOUSLY ACCEPTED IT.
WELL, HERE'S TO THE SUBCONSCIOUS, THEN.
A TOAST TO PROJECT TARCUS!
CLINK

CHAPTER TWO

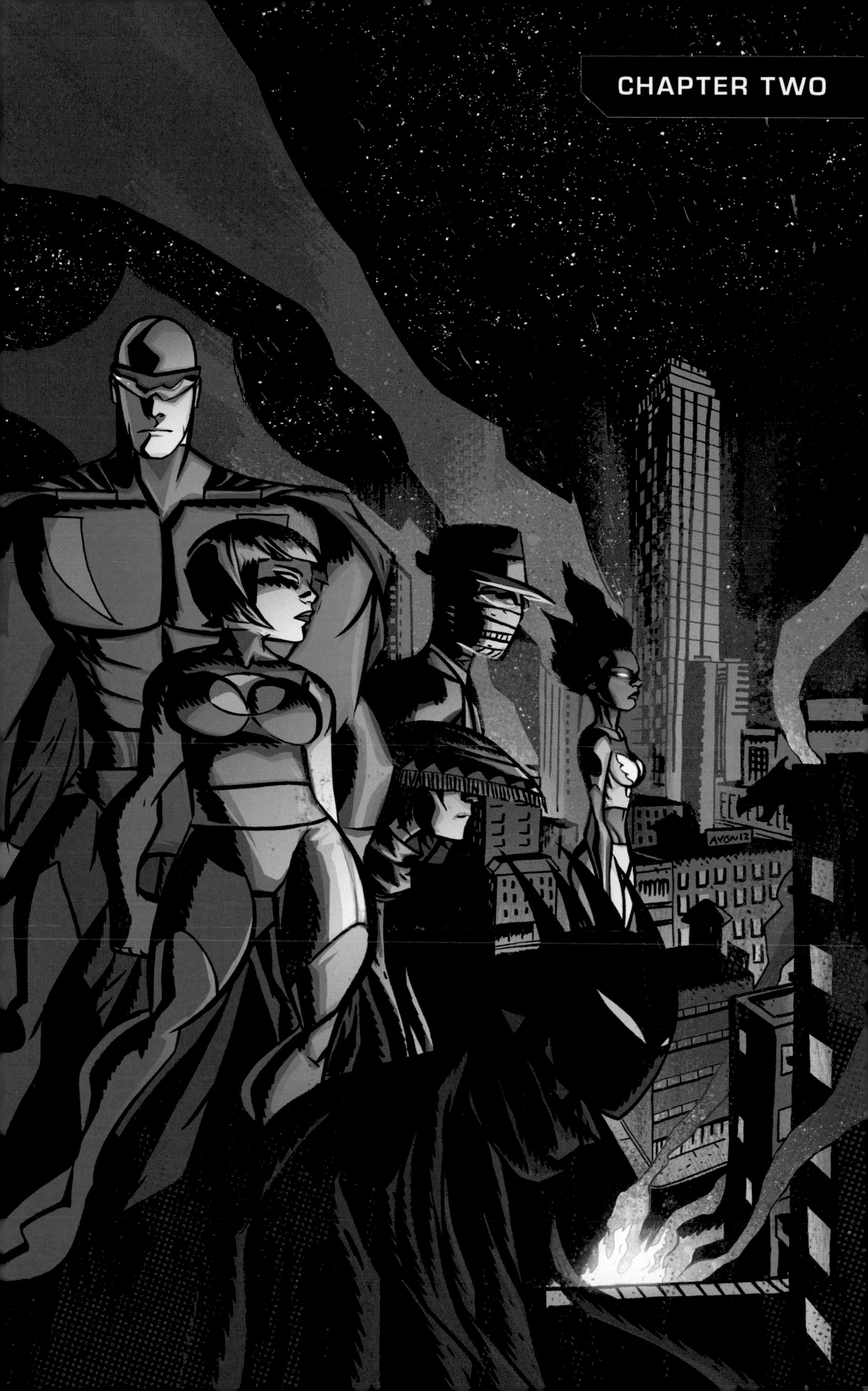

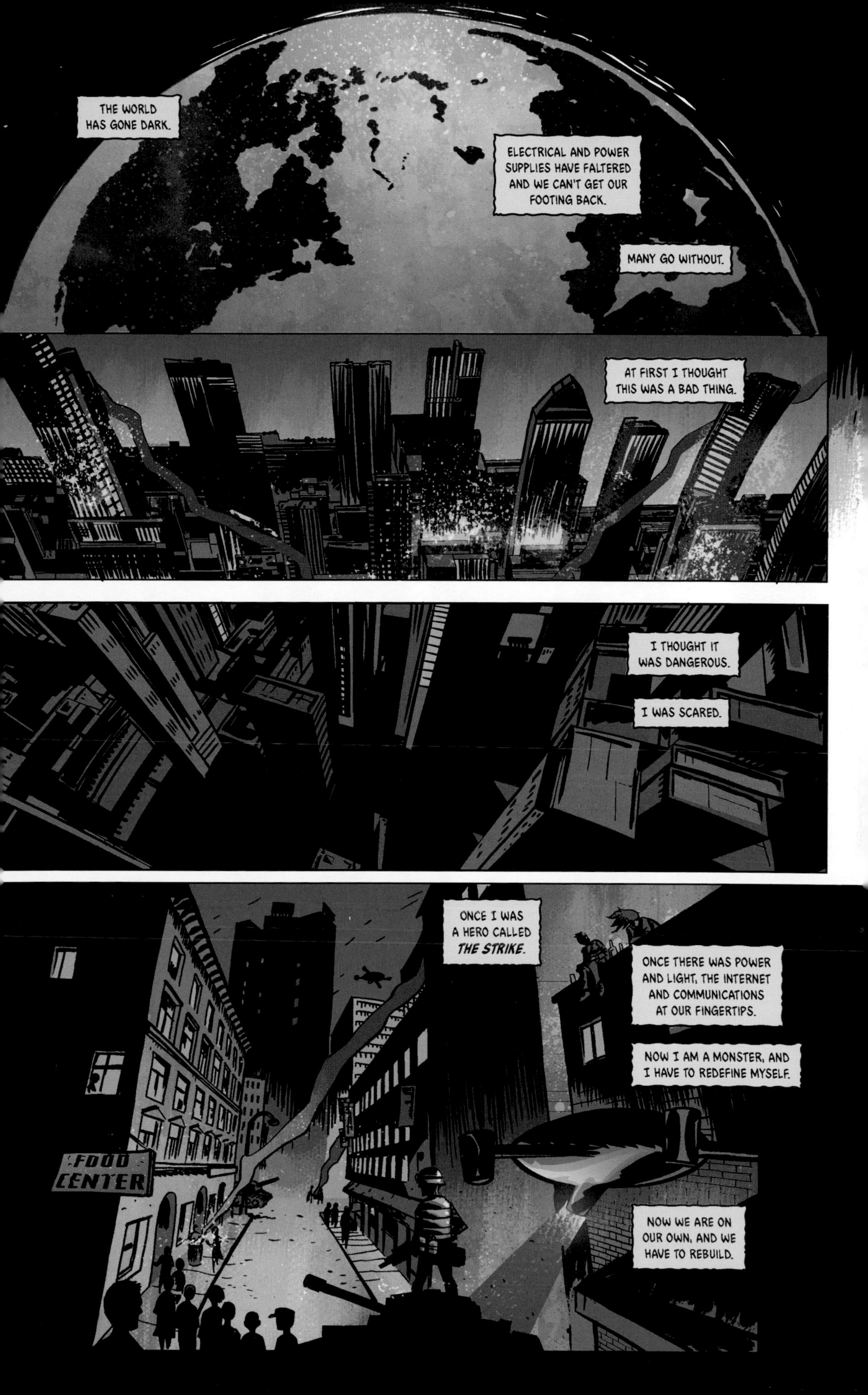
THE WORLD HAS GONE DARK.
ELECTRICAL AND POWER SUPPLIES HAVE FALTERED AND WE CAN'T GET OUR FOOTING BACK.
MANY GO WITHOUT.
AT FIRST I THOUGHT THIS WAS A BAD THING.
I THOUGHT IT WAS DANGEROUS.
I WAS SCARED.
ONCE I WAS A HERO CALLED *THE STRIKE*.
ONCE THERE WAS POWER AND LIGHT, THE INTERNET AND COMMUNICATIONS AT OUR FINGERTIPS.
NOW I AM A MONSTER, AND I HAVE TO REDEFINE MYSELF.
FOOD CENTER
NOW WE ARE ON OUR OWN, AND WE HAVE TO REBUILD.

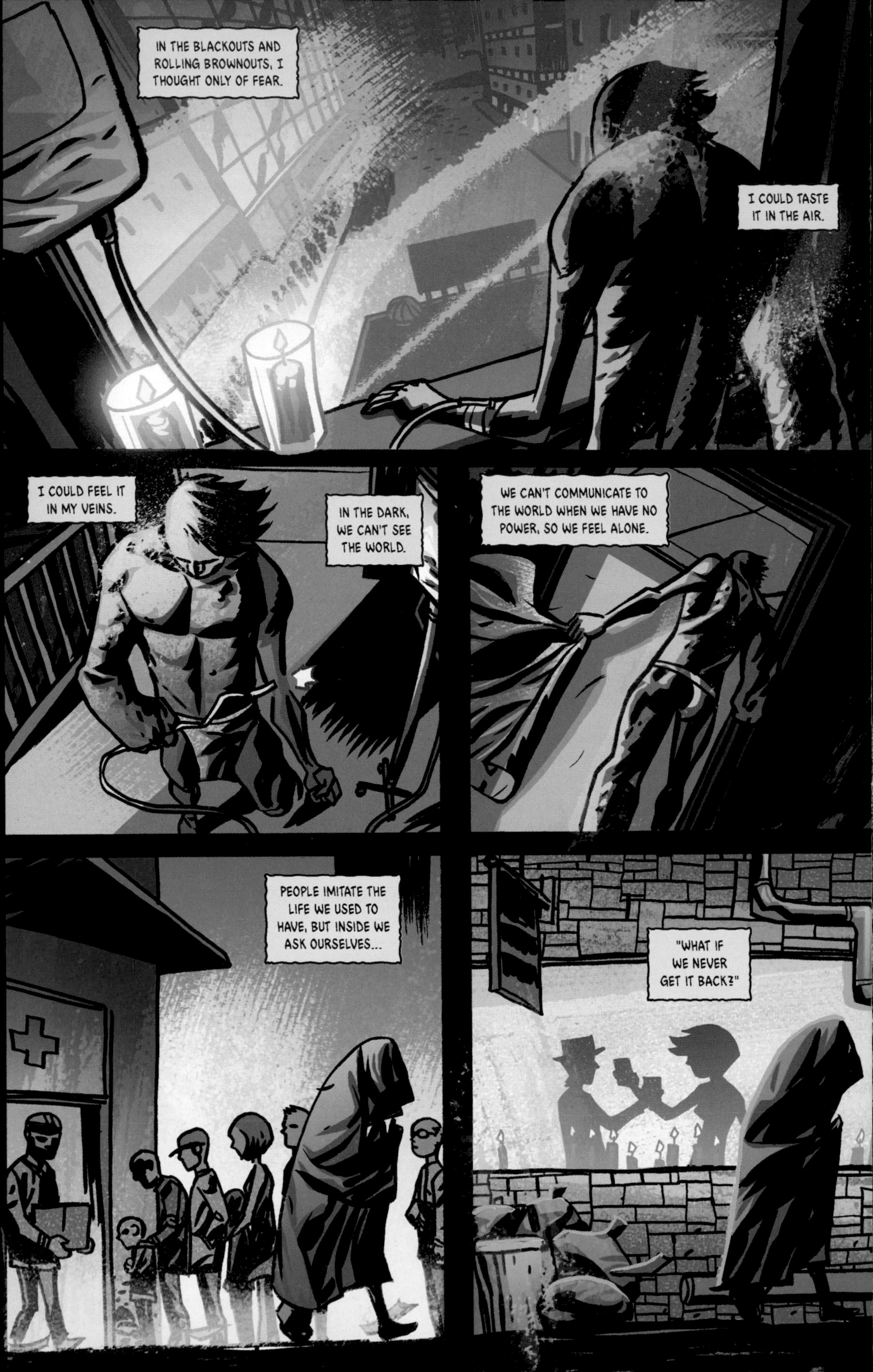
IN THE BLACKOUTS AND ROLLING BROWNOUTS, I THOUGHT ONLY OF FEAR.
I COULD TASTE IT IN THE AIR.
I COULD FEEL IT IN MY VEINS.
IN THE DARK, WE CAN'T SEE THE WORLD.
WE CAN'T COMMUNICATE TO THE WORLD WHEN WE HAVE NO POWER, SO WE FEEL ALONE.
PEOPLE IMITATE THE LIFE WE USED TO HAVE, BUT INSIDE WE ASK OURSELVES...
"WHAT IF WE NEVER GET IT BACK?"

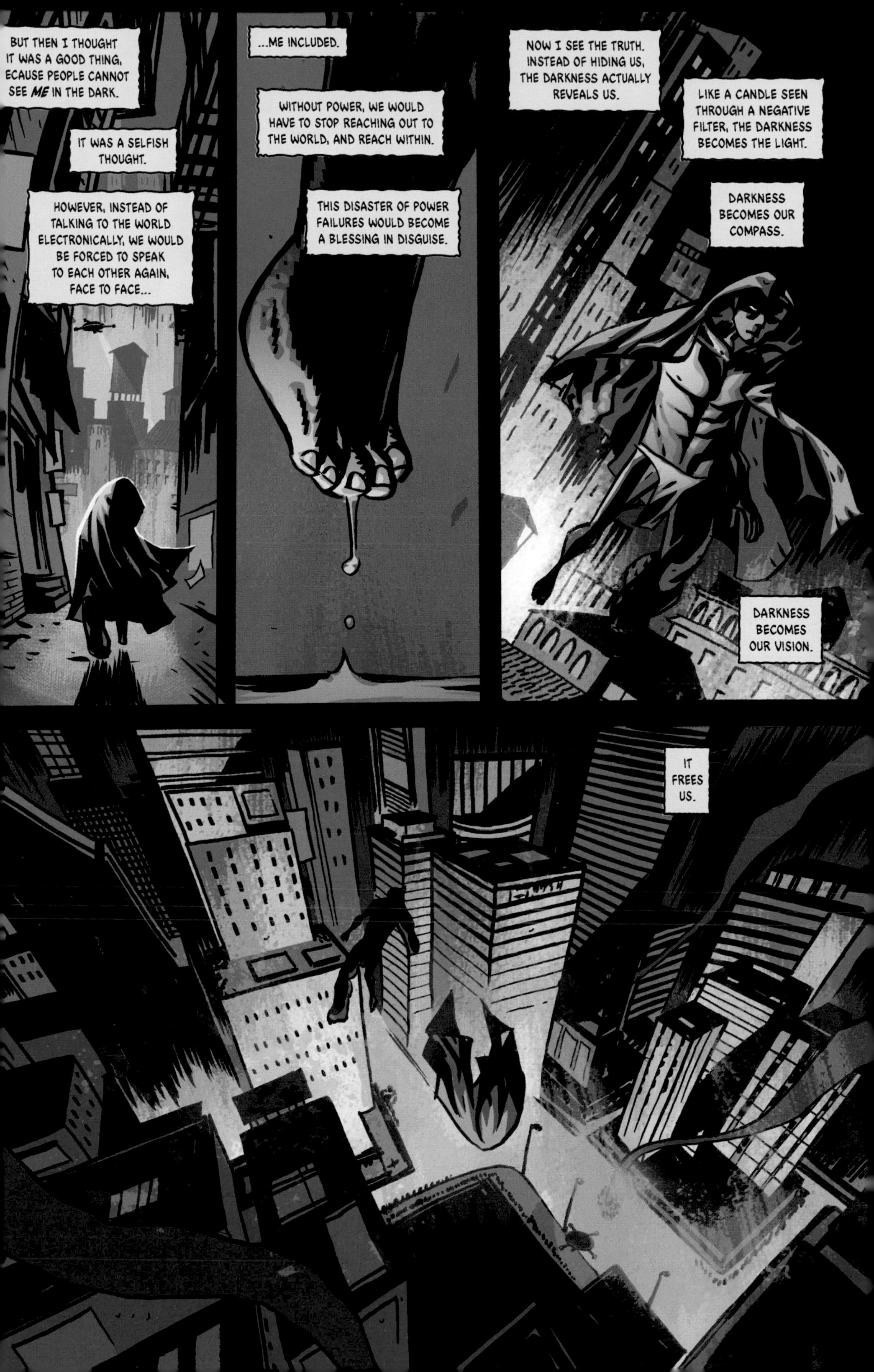
BUT THEN I THOUGHT IT WAS A GOOD THING, ECAUSE PEOPLE CANNOT SEE *ME* IN THE DARK.
IT WAS A SELFISH THOUGHT.
HOWEVER, INSTEAD OF TALKING TO THE WORLD ELECTRONICALLY, WE WOULD BE FORCED TO SPEAK TO EACH OTHER AGAIN, FACE TO FACE...
...ME INCLUDED.
WITHOUT POWER, WE WOULD HAVE TO STOP REACHING OUT TO THE WORLD, AND REACH WITHIN.
THIS DISASTER OF POWER FAILURES WOULD BECOME A BLESSING IN DISGUISE.
NOW I SEE THE TRUTH. INSTEAD OF HIDING US, THE DARKNESS ACTUALLY REVEALS US.
LIKE A CANDLE SEEN THROUGH A NEGATIVE FILTER, THE DARKNESS BECOMES THE LIGHT.
DARKNESS BECOMES OUR COMPASS.
DARKNESS BECOMES OUR VISION.
IT FREES US.

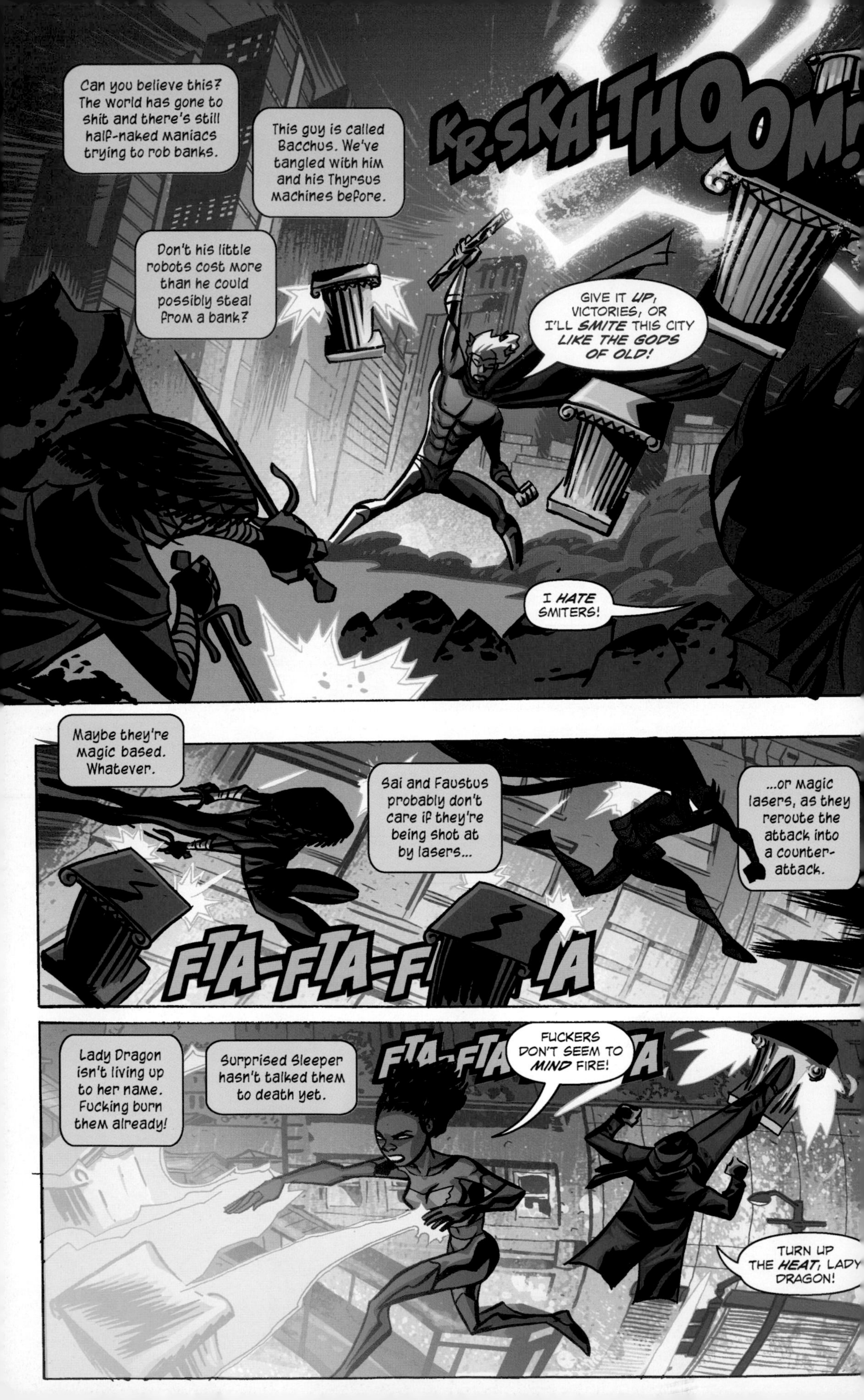

Can you believe this? The world has gone to shit and there's still half-naked maniacs trying to rob banks.
This guy is called Bacchus. We've tangled with him and his Thyrsus machines before.
KR-SKA-THOOOM!
Don't his little robots cost more than he could possibly steal from a bank?
GIVE IT UP, VICTORIES, OR I'LL SMITE THIS CITY LIKE THE GODS OF OLD!
I HATE SMITERS!
Maybe they're magic based. Whatever.
Sai and Faustus probably don't care if they're being shot at by lasers...
...or magic lasers, as they reroute the attack into a counter-attack.
FTA-FTA-F A
Lady Dragon isn't living up to her name. Fucking burn them already!
Surprised Sleeper hasn't talked them to death yet.
FUCKERS DON'T SEEM TO MIND FIRE!
TURN UP THE HEAT, LADY DRAGON!

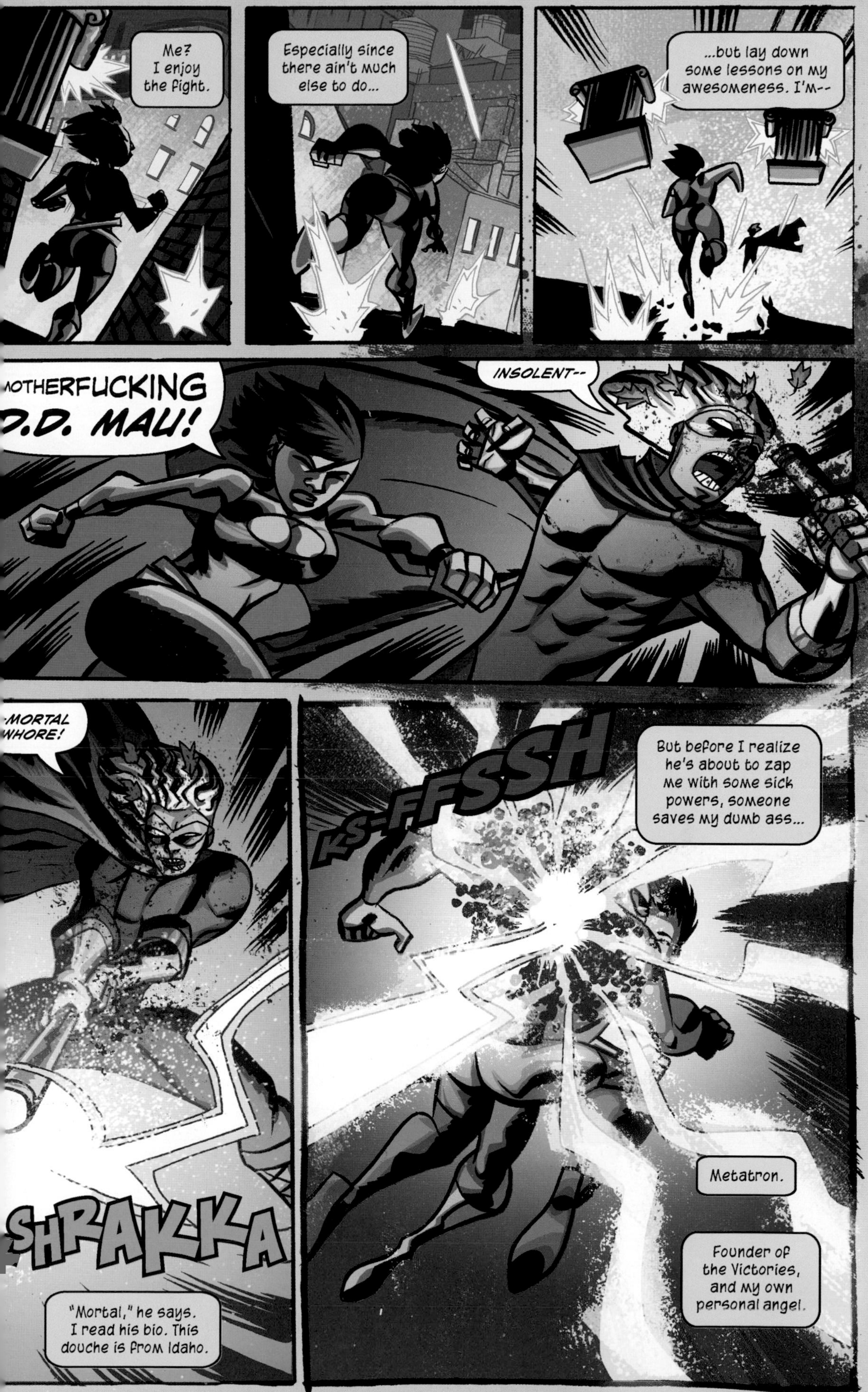
Me? I enjoy the fight.
Especially since there ain't much else to do...
...but lay down some lessons on my awesomeness. I'm--
MOTHERFUCKING D.D. MAU!
INSOLENT--
-MORTAL WHORE!
SHRAKKA
"Mortal," he says. I read his bio. This douche is from Idaho.
KS-FFSSH
But before I realize he's about to zap me with some sick powers, someone saves my dumb ass...
Metatron.
Founder of the Victories, and my own personal angel.

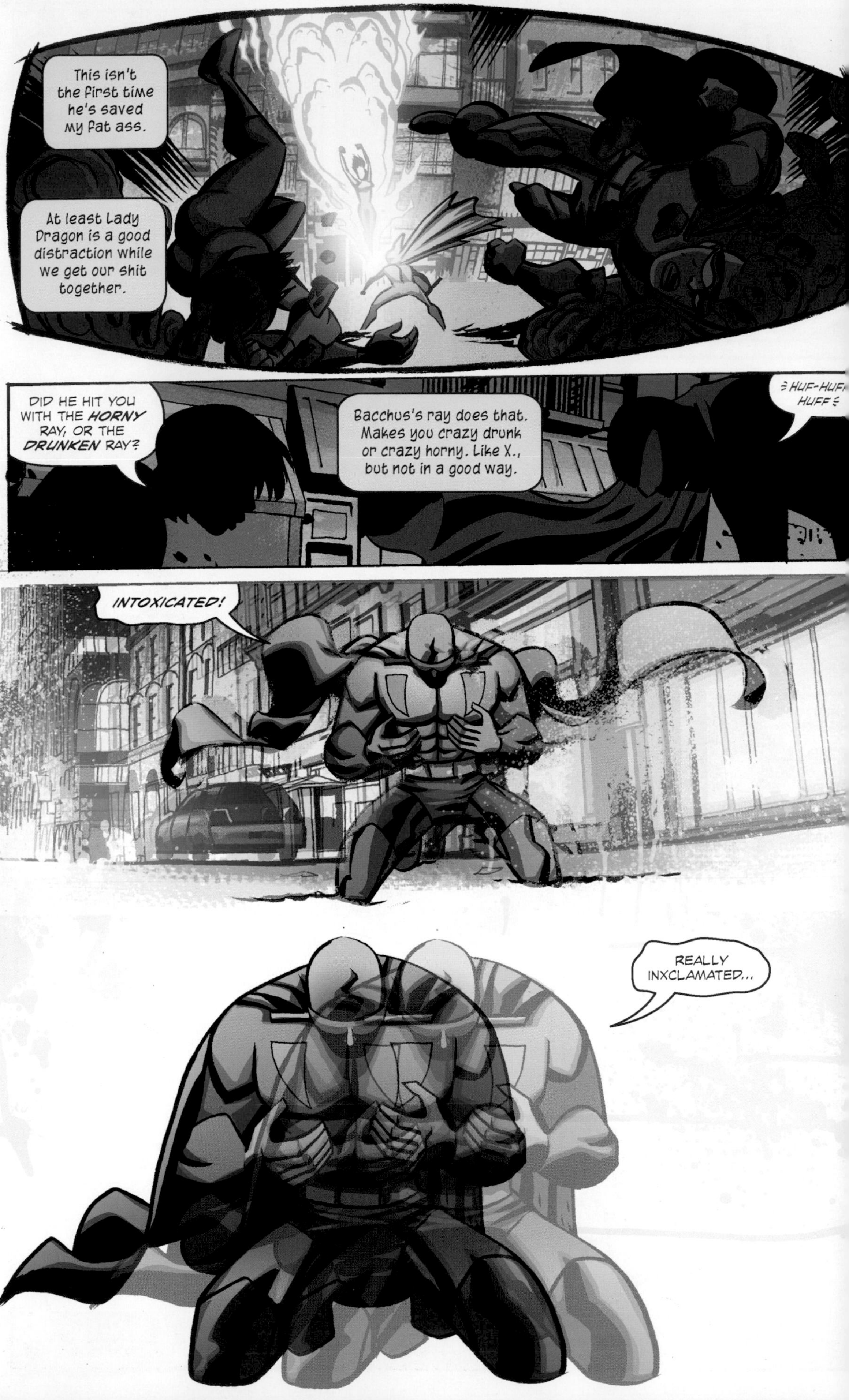
This isn't the first time he's saved my fat ass.
At least Lady Dragon is a good distraction while we get our shit together.
DID HE HIT YOU WITH THE *HORNY* RAY, OR THE *DRUNKEN* RAY?
Bacchus's ray does that. Makes you crazy drunk or crazy horny. Like X., but not in a good way.
HUF-HUF HUFF
INTOXICATED!
REALLY INXCLAMATED...

METATRON?

GOOD, BECAUSE GIVING YOU A *HANDY* SO YOU COULD FIGHT WOULD BE WEIRD.

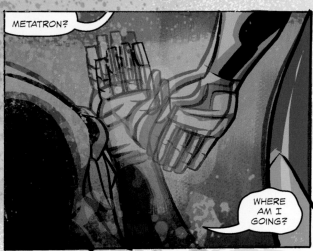

WHERE AM I GOING?

EARTH TO METATRON!

NO, WAIT, I'M NOT HERE--WHERE AM I GOING? *STOP!*

DUDE!

OKAY, BIG GUY, JUST LET ME GET YOU SAFE.

I'M STEPPING AWAY FROM MYSELF...

DAMMIT! I'M GOING TO SHOVE THAT MAGIC DILDO UP BACCHUS'S ASS FOR THIS!

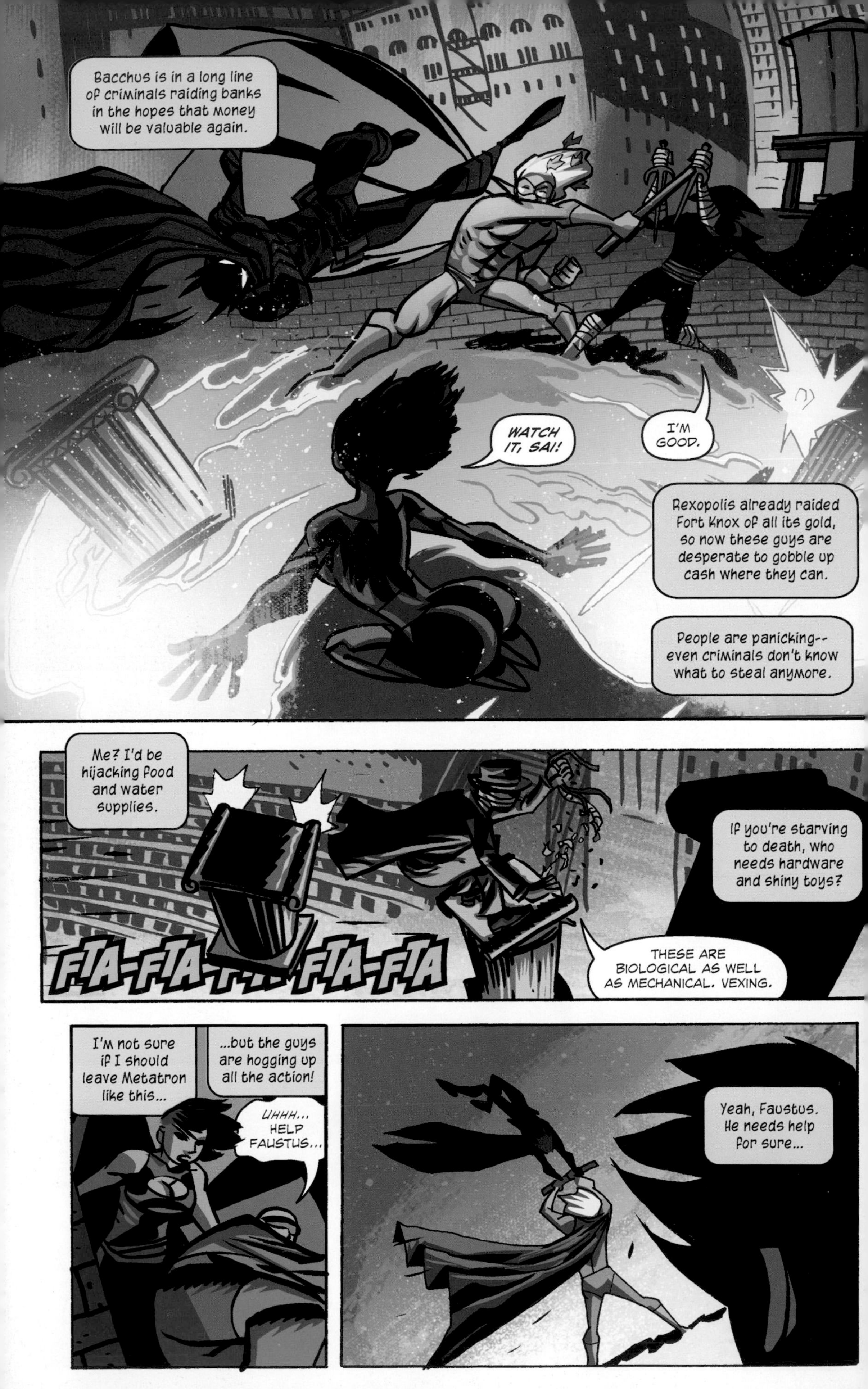
Bacchus is in a long line of criminals raiding banks in the hopes that money will be valuable again.
WATCH IT, SAI!
I'M GOOD.
Rexopolis already raided Fort Knox of all its gold, so now these guys are desperate to gobble up cash where they can.
People are panicking--even criminals don't know what to steal anymore.
Me? I'd be hijacking food and water supplies.
If you're starving to death, who needs hardware and shiny toys?
FTA-FTA-FTA-FTA
THESE ARE BIOLOGICAL AS WELL AS MECHANICAL. VEXING.
I'm not sure if I should leave Metatron like this...
...but the guys are hogging up all the action!
UHHH... HELP FAUSTUS...
Yeah, Faustus. He needs help for sure...

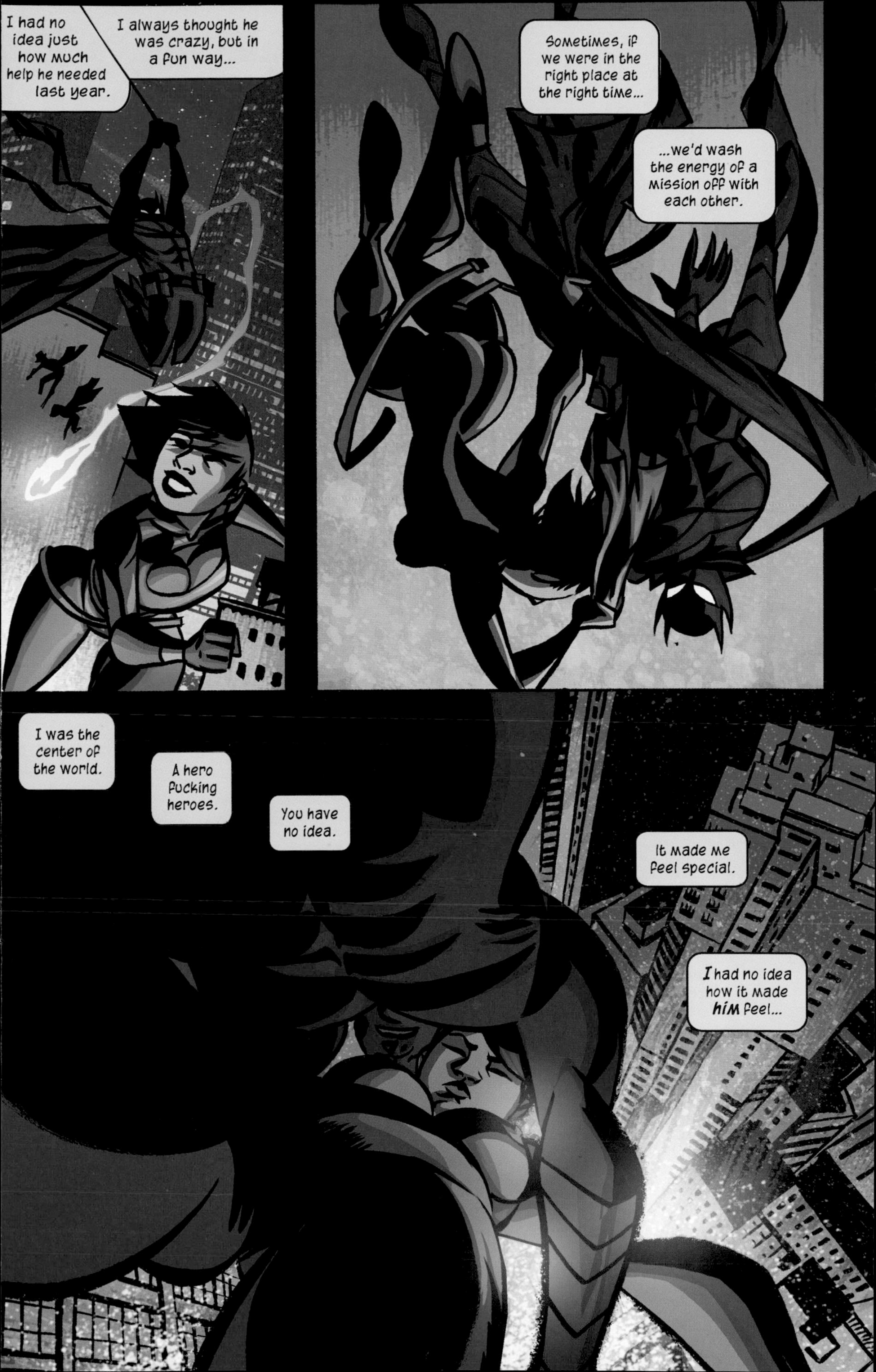
I had no idea just how much help he needed last year.
I always thought he was crazy, but in a fun way...
Sometimes, if we were in the right place at the right time...
...we'd wash the energy of a mission off with each other.
I was the center of the world.
A hero fucking heroes.
You have no idea.
It made me feel special.
I had no idea how it made him feel...

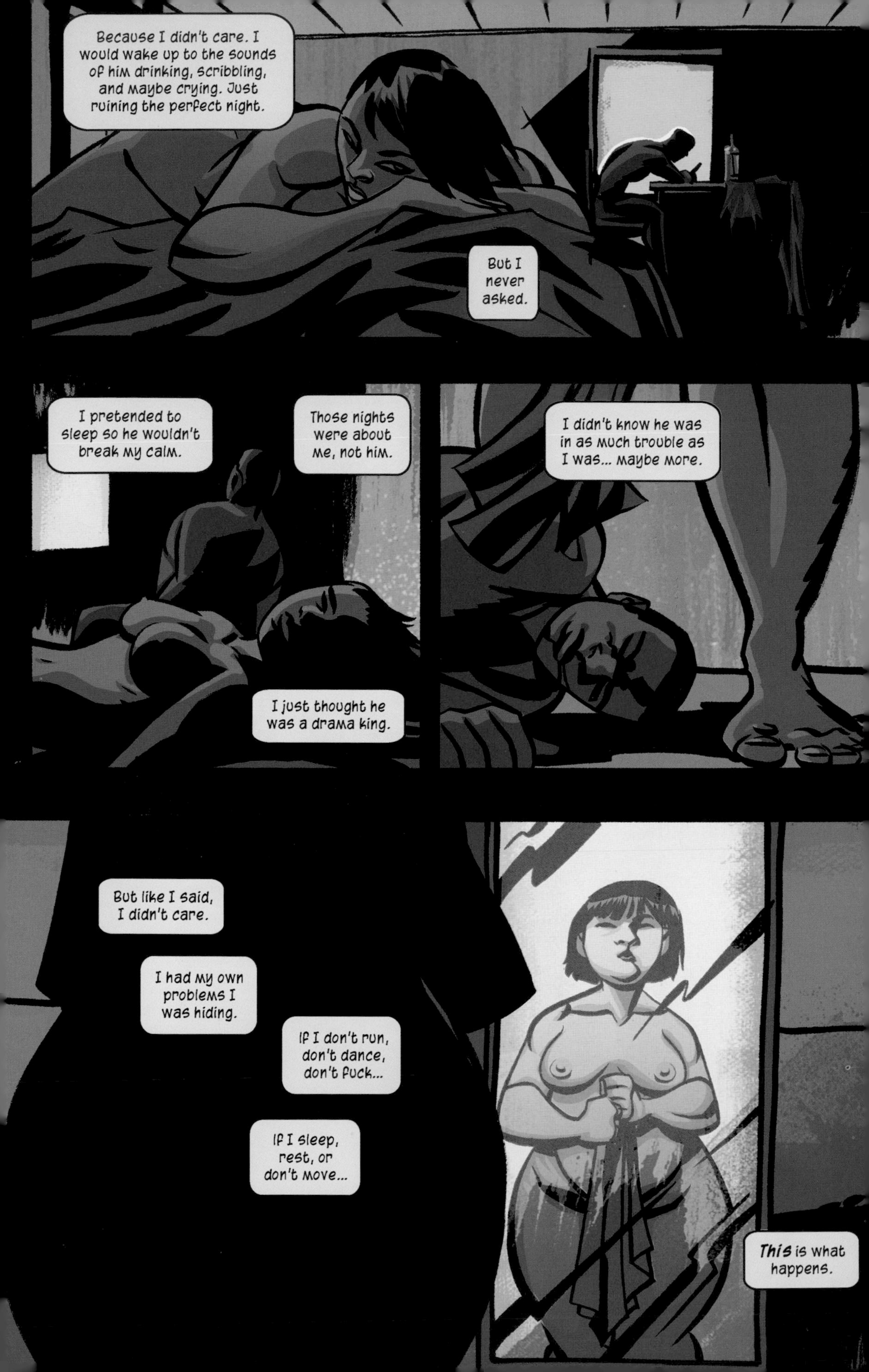
Because I didn't care. I would wake up to the sounds of him drinking, scribbling, and maybe crying. Just ruining the perfect night.
But I never asked.
I pretended to sleep so he wouldn't break my calm.
Those nights were about me, not him.
I just thought he was a drama king.
I didn't know he was in as much trouble as I was... maybe more.
But like I said, I didn't care.
I had my own problems I was hiding.
If I don't run, don't dance, don't fuck...
If I sleep, rest, or don't move...
This is what happens.

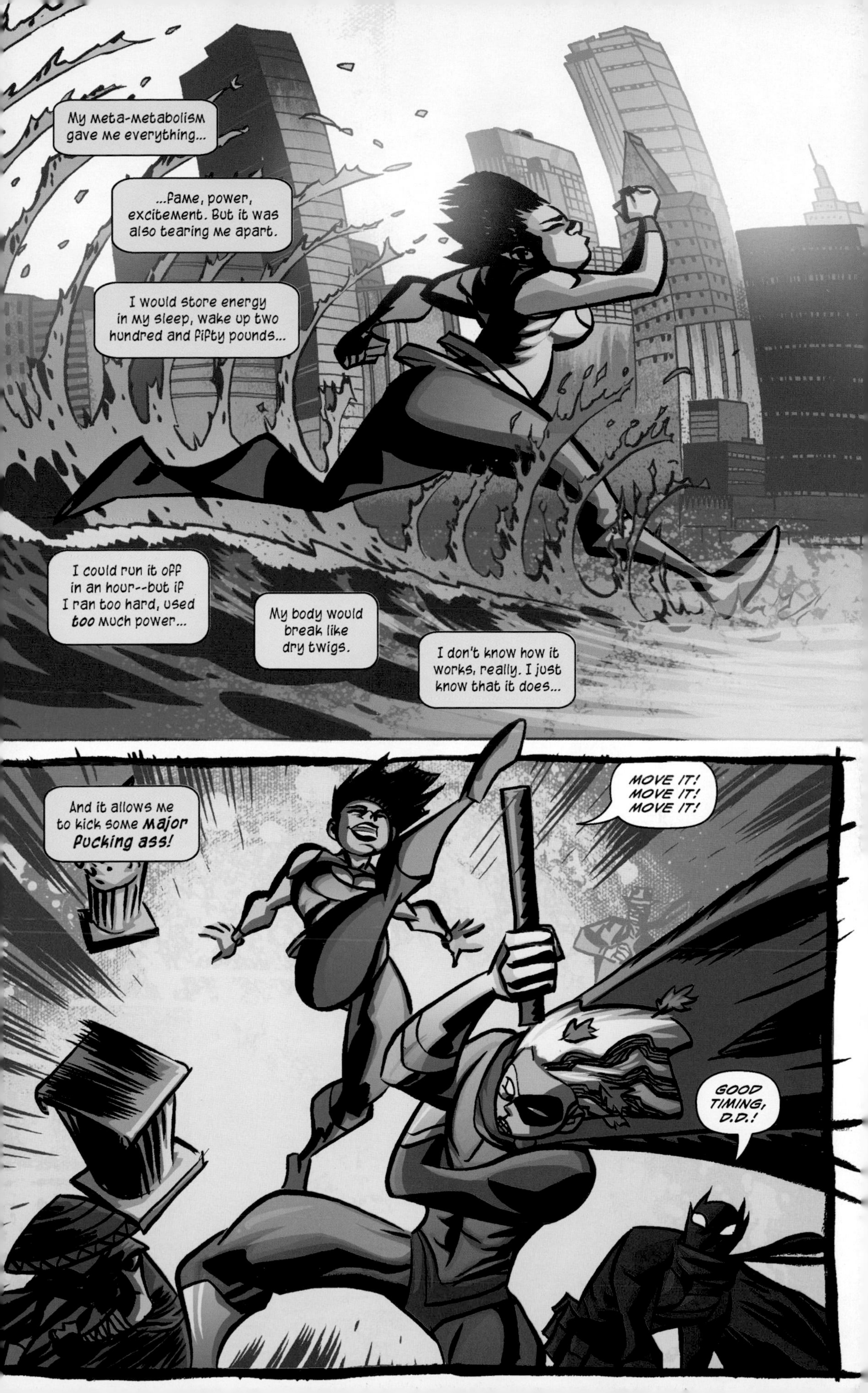
My meta-metabolism gave me everything...
...fame, power, excitement. But it was also tearing me apart.
I would store energy in my sleep, wake up two hundred and fifty pounds...
I could run it off in an hour--but if I ran too hard, used too much power...
My body would break like dry twigs.
I don't know how it works, really. I just know that it does...
And it allows me to kick some major fucking ass!
MOVE IT! MOVE IT! MOVE IT!
GOOD TIMING, D.D.!

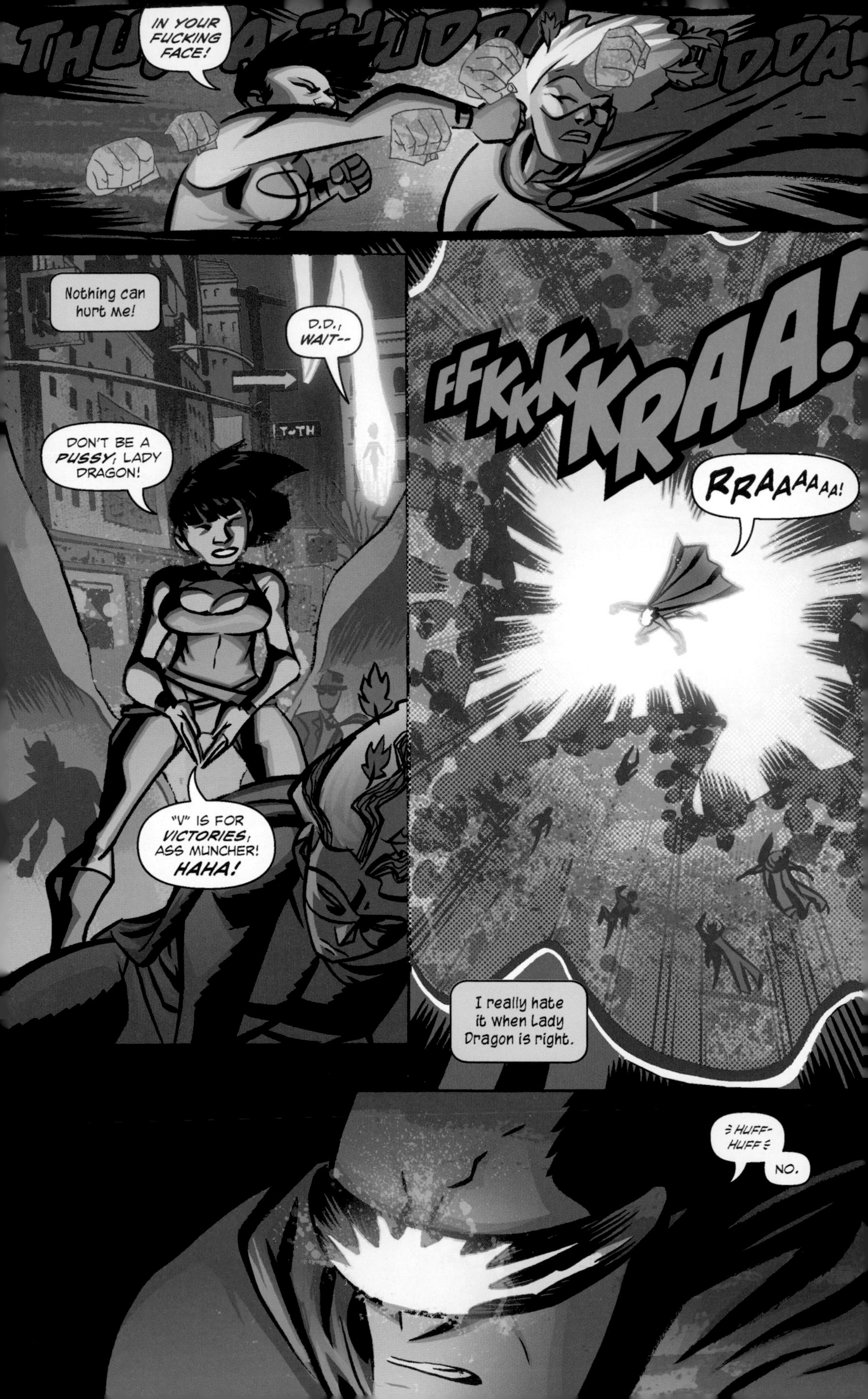

IN YOUR FUCKING FACE!
Nothing can hurt me!
D.D., WAIT--
DON'T BE A PUSSY, LADY DRAGON!
"V" IS FOR VICTORIES, ASS MUNCHER! HAHA!
FFKKKKRAA!
RRAAAAAA!
I really hate it when Lady Dragon is right.
HUFF-HUFF
NO.

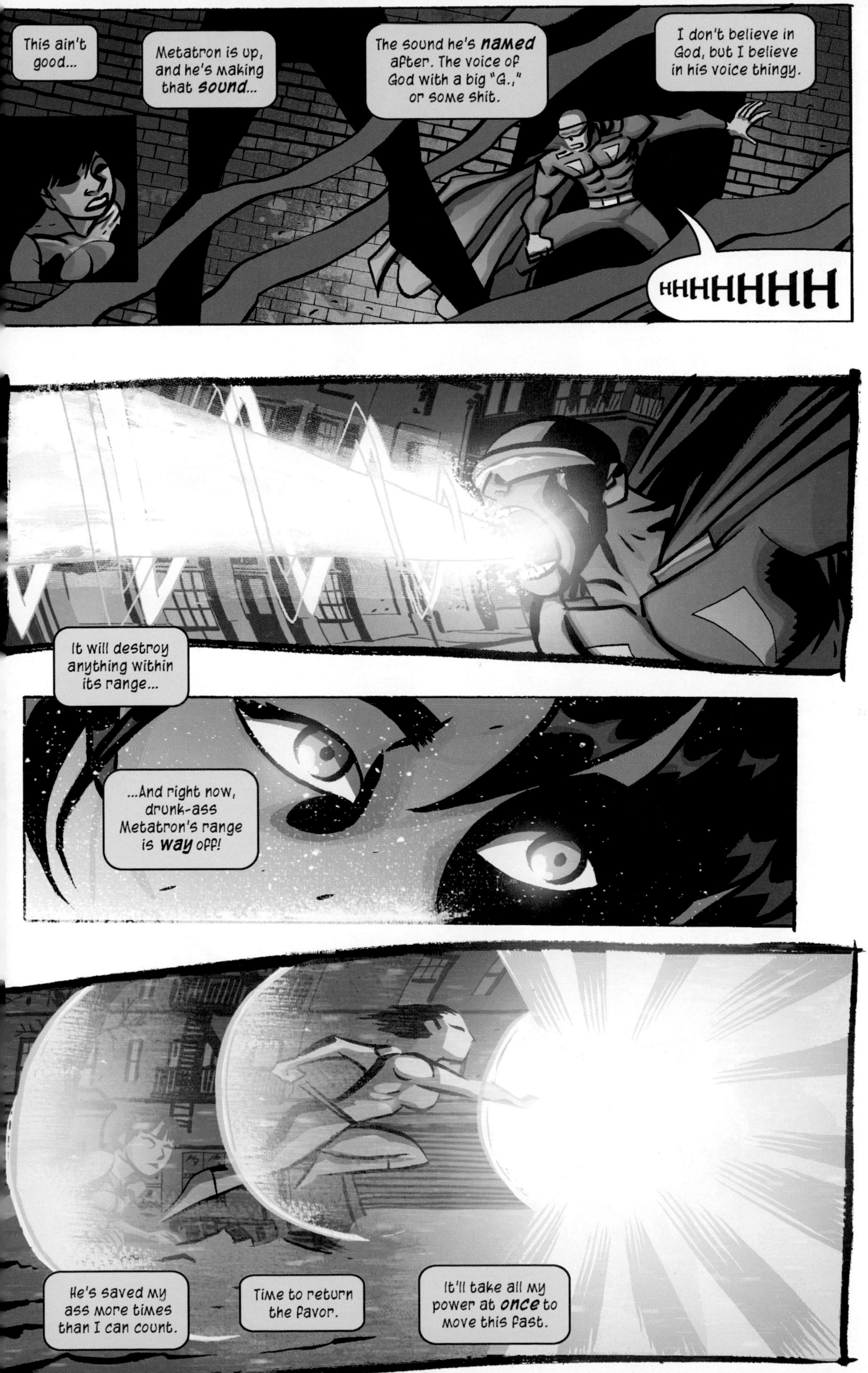
This ain't good...
Metatron is up, and he's making that *sound*...
The sound he's *named* after. The voice of God with a big "G.," or some shit.
I don't believe in God, but I believe in his voice thingy.
HHHHHHH
It will destroy anything within its range...
...And right now, drunk-ass Metatron's range is *way* off!
He's saved my ass more times than I can count.
Time to return the favor.
It'll take all my power at *once* to move this fast.

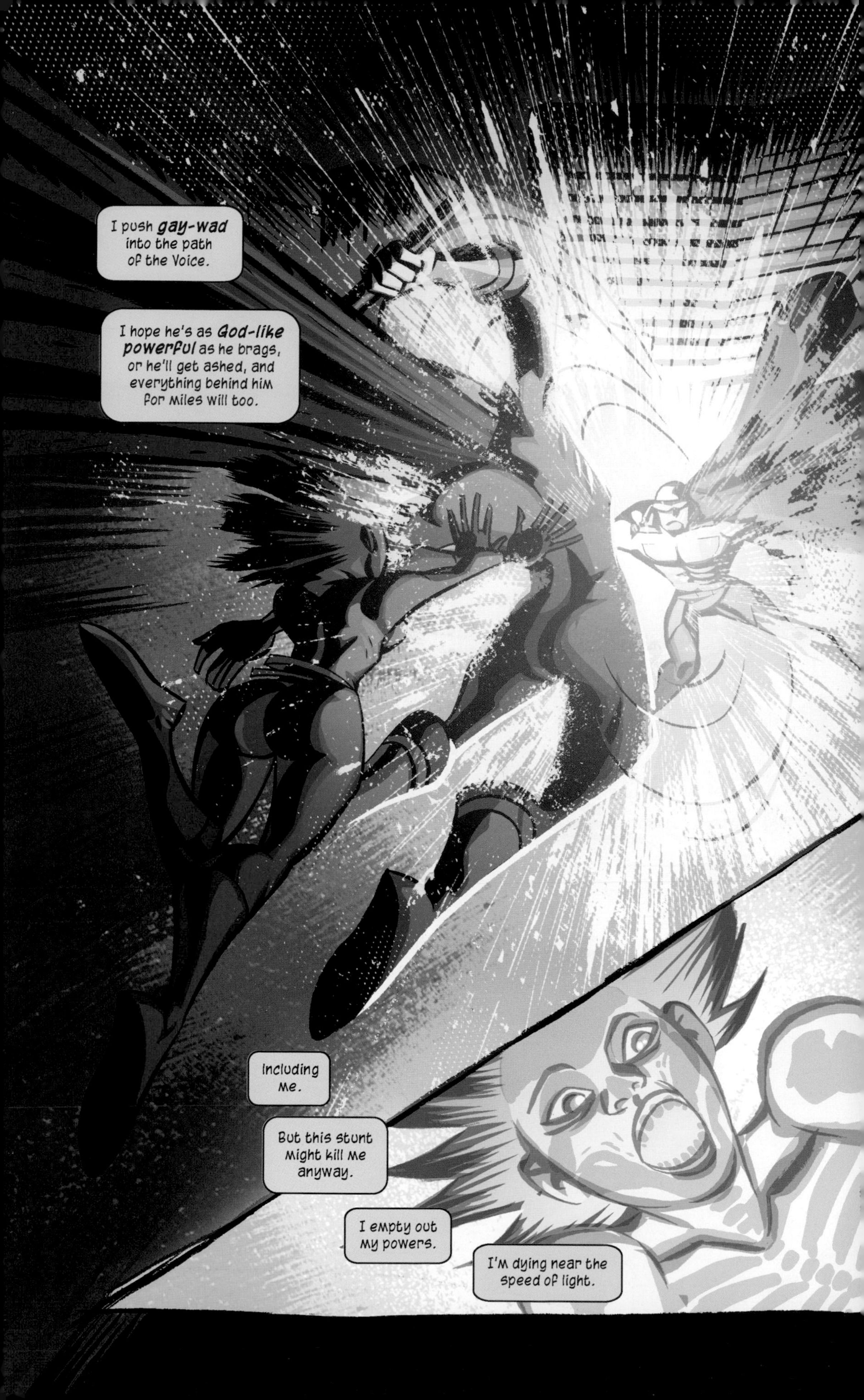
I push **gay-wad** into the path of the Voice.
I hope he's as **God-like powerful** as he brags, or he'll get ashed, and everything behind him for miles will too.
Including me.
But this stunt might kill me anyway.
I empty out my powers.
I'm dying near the speed of light.

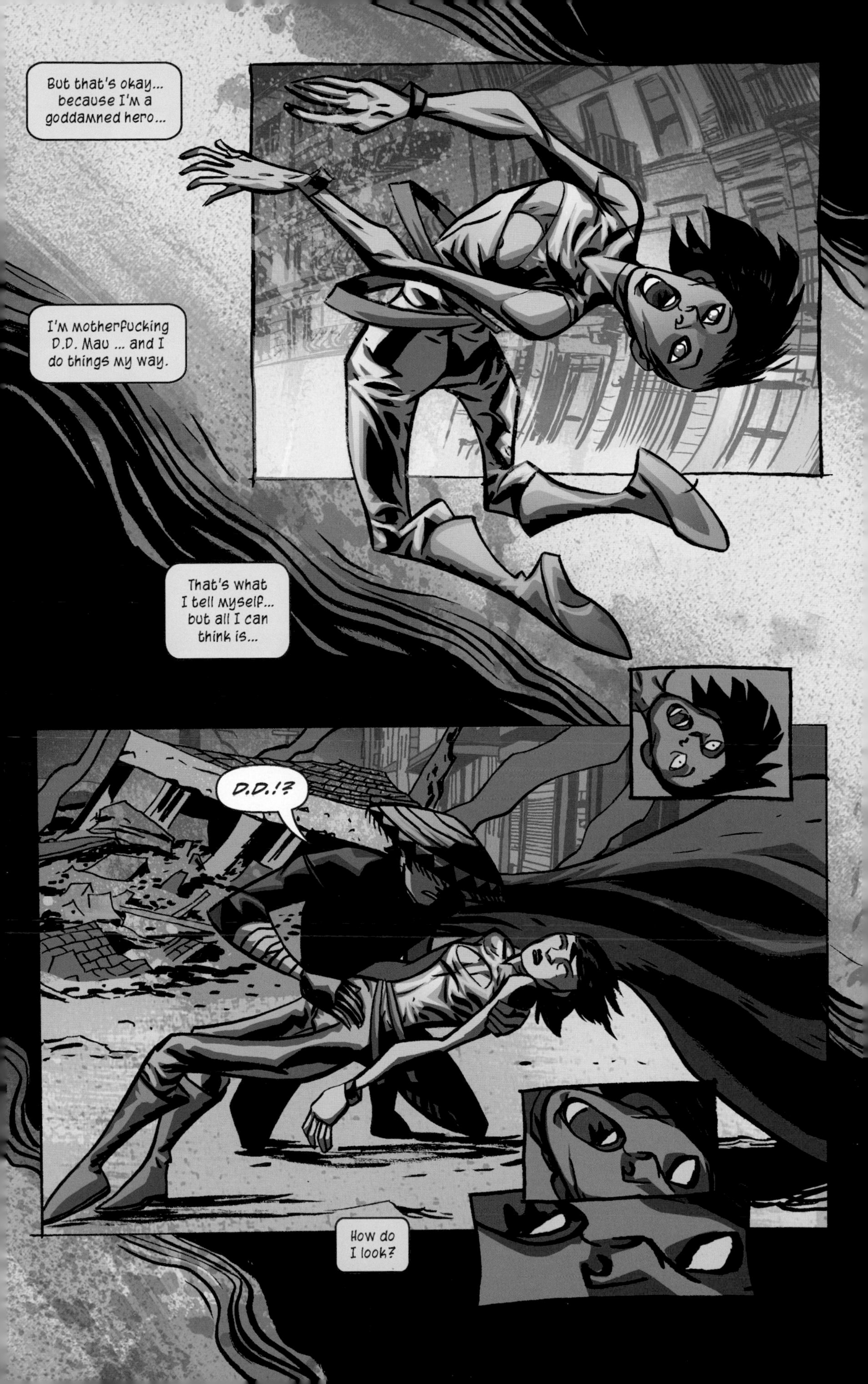
But that's okay... because I'm a goddamned hero...
I'm motherfucking D.D. Mau ... and I do things my way.
That's what I tell myself... but all I can think is...
D.D.!?
How do I look?

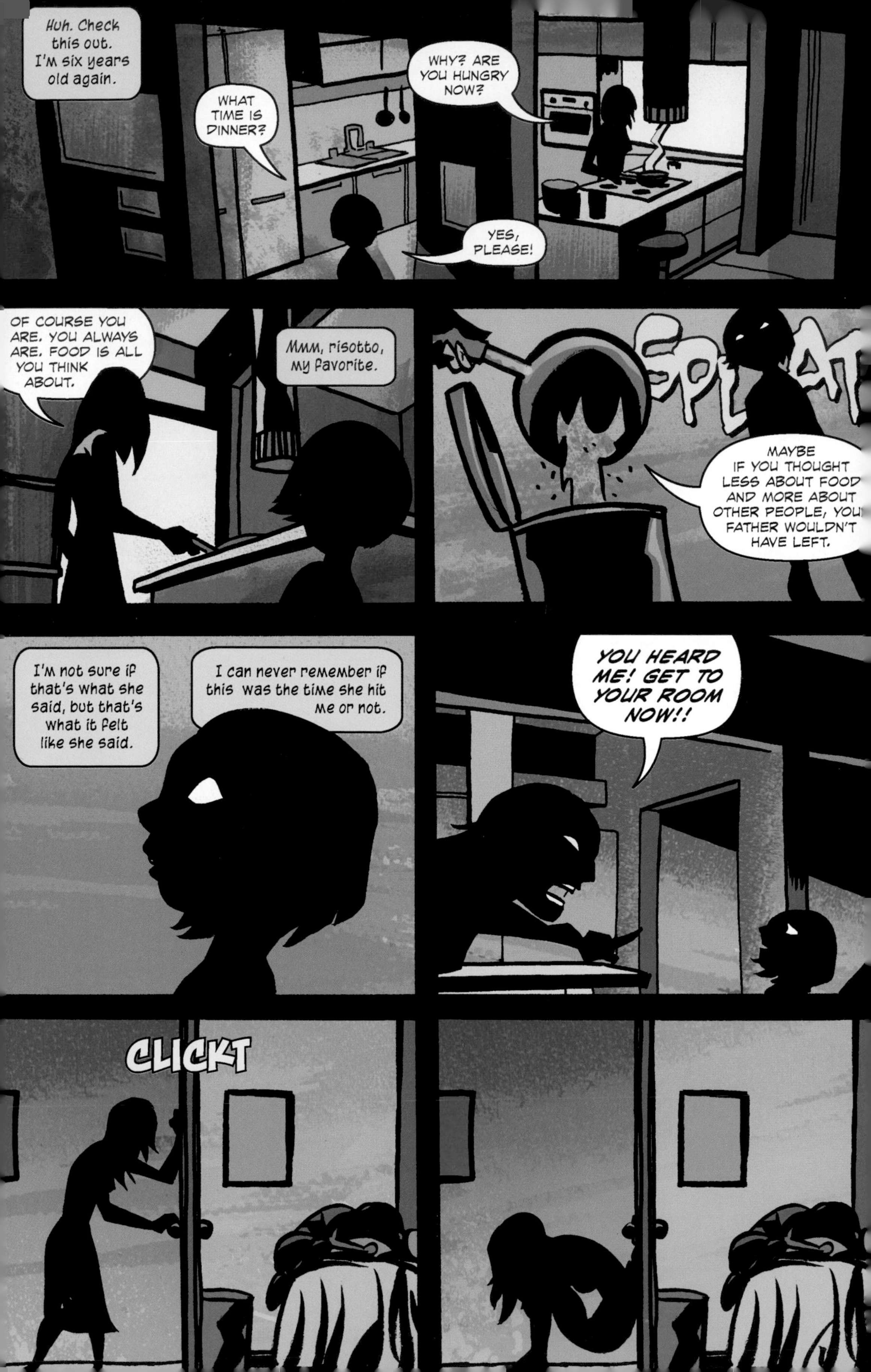
Huh. Check this out. I'm six years old again.
WHAT TIME IS DINNER?
WHY? ARE YOU HUNGRY NOW?
YES, PLEASE!
OF COURSE YOU ARE. YOU ALWAYS ARE. FOOD IS ALL YOU THINK ABOUT.
Mmm, risotto, my favorite.
SPLAT
MAYBE IF YOU THOUGHT LESS ABOUT FOOD AND MORE ABOUT OTHER PEOPLE, YOUR FATHER WOULDN'T HAVE LEFT.
I'm not sure if that's what she said, but that's what it felt like she said.
I can never remember if this was the time she hit me or not.
YOU HEARD ME! GET TO YOUR ROOM NOW!!
CLICKT

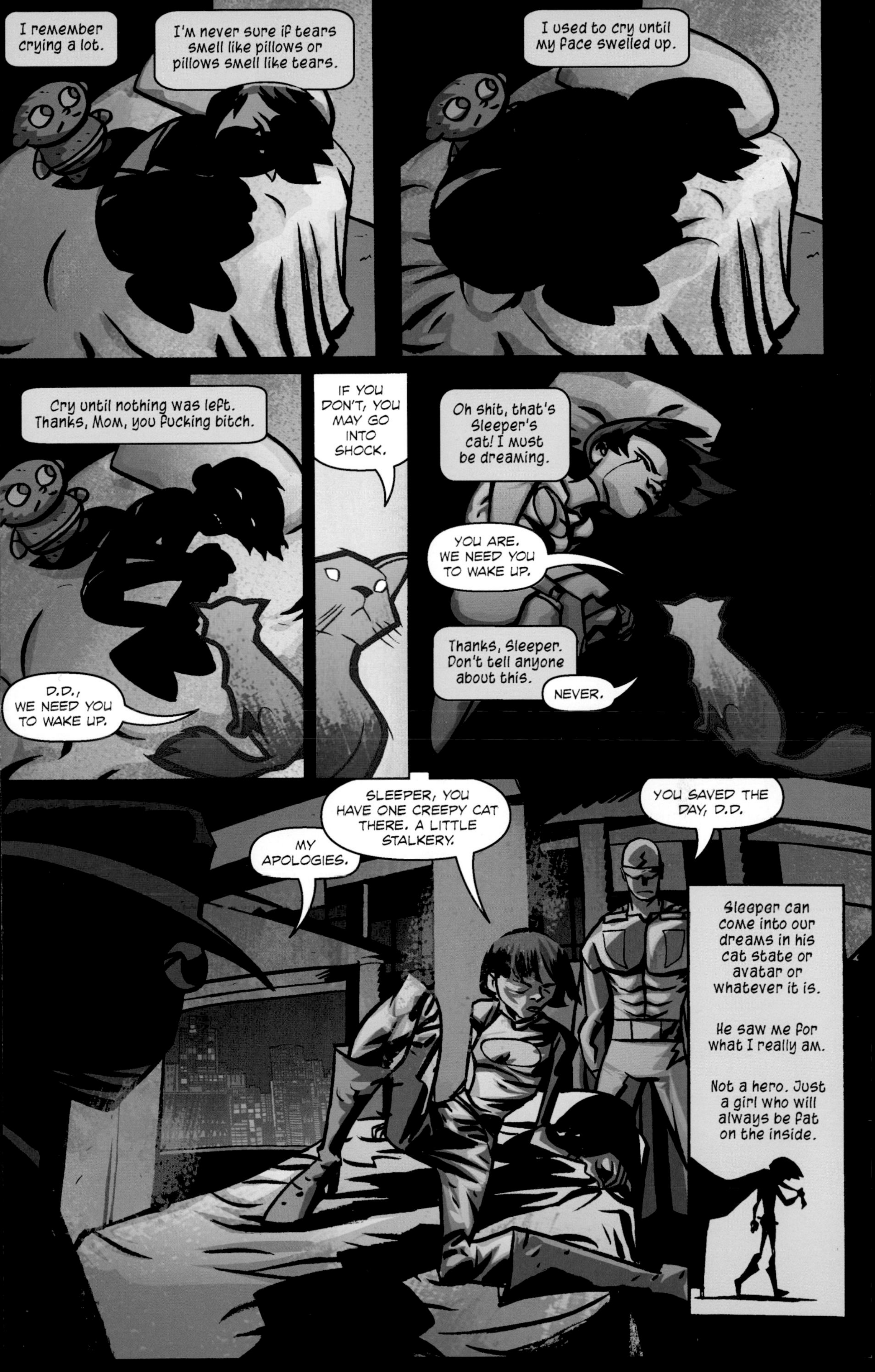
I remember crying a lot.
I'm never sure if tears smell like pillows or pillows smell like tears.
I used to cry until my face swelled up.
Cry until nothing was left. Thanks, Mom, you fucking bitch.
D.D., WE NEED YOU TO WAKE UP.
IF YOU DON'T, YOU MAY GO INTO SHOCK.
Oh shit, that's Sleeper's cat! I must be dreaming.
YOU ARE. WE NEED YOU TO WAKE UP.
Thanks, Sleeper. Don't tell anyone about this.
NEVER.
MY APOLOGIES.
SLEEPER, YOU HAVE ONE CREEPY CAT THERE. A LITTLE STALKERY.
YOU SAVED THE DAY, D.D.
Sleeper can come into our dreams in his cat state or avatar or whatever it is.
He saw me for what I really am.
Not a hero. Just a girl who will always be fat on the inside.

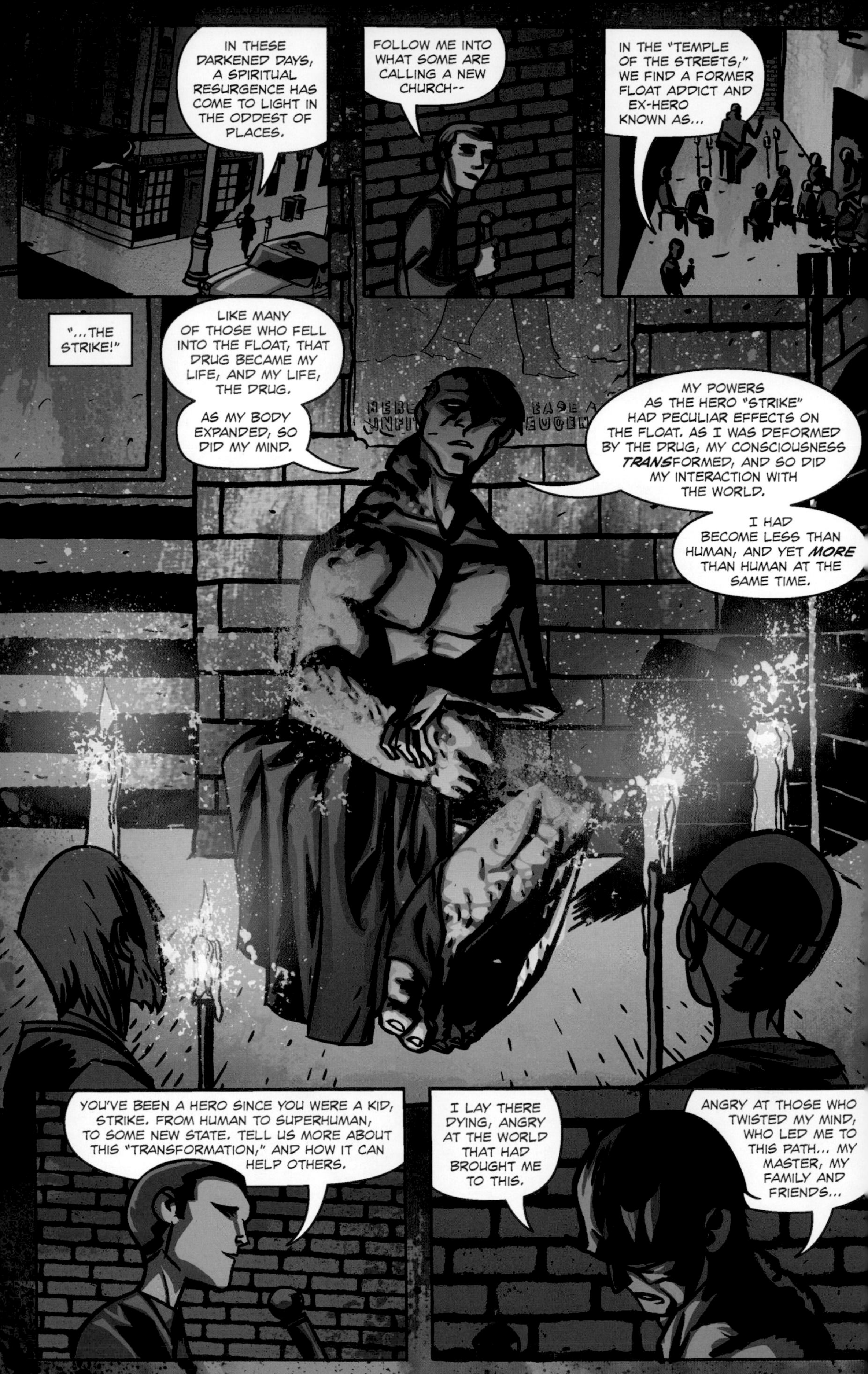
IN THESE DARKENED DAYS, A SPIRITUAL RESURGENCE HAS COME TO LIGHT IN THE ODDEST OF PLACES.
FOLLOW ME INTO WHAT SOME ARE CALLING A NEW CHURCH--
IN THE "TEMPLE OF THE STREETS," WE FIND A FORMER FLOAT ADDICT AND EX-HERO KNOWN AS...
"...THE STRIKE!"
LIKE MANY OF THOSE WHO FELL INTO THE FLOAT, THAT DRUG BECAME MY LIFE, AND MY LIFE, THE DRUG.
AS MY BODY EXPANDED, SO DID MY MIND.
MY POWERS AS THE HERO "STRIKE" HAD PECULIAR EFFECTS ON THE FLOAT. AS I WAS DEFORMED BY THE DRUG, MY CONSCIOUSNESS *TRANS*FORMED, AND SO DID MY INTERACTION WITH THE WORLD.
I HAD BECOME LESS THAN HUMAN, AND YET *MORE* THAN HUMAN AT THE SAME TIME.
YOU'VE BEEN A HERO SINCE YOU WERE A KID, STRIKE. FROM HUMAN TO SUPERHUMAN, TO SOME NEW STATE. TELL US MORE ABOUT THIS "TRANSFORMATION," AND HOW IT CAN HELP OTHERS.
I LAY THERE DYING, ANGRY AT THE WORLD THAT HAD BROUGHT ME TO THIS.
ANGRY AT THOSE WHO TWISTED MY MIND, WHO LED ME TO THIS PATH... MY MASTER, MY FAMILY AND FRIENDS...

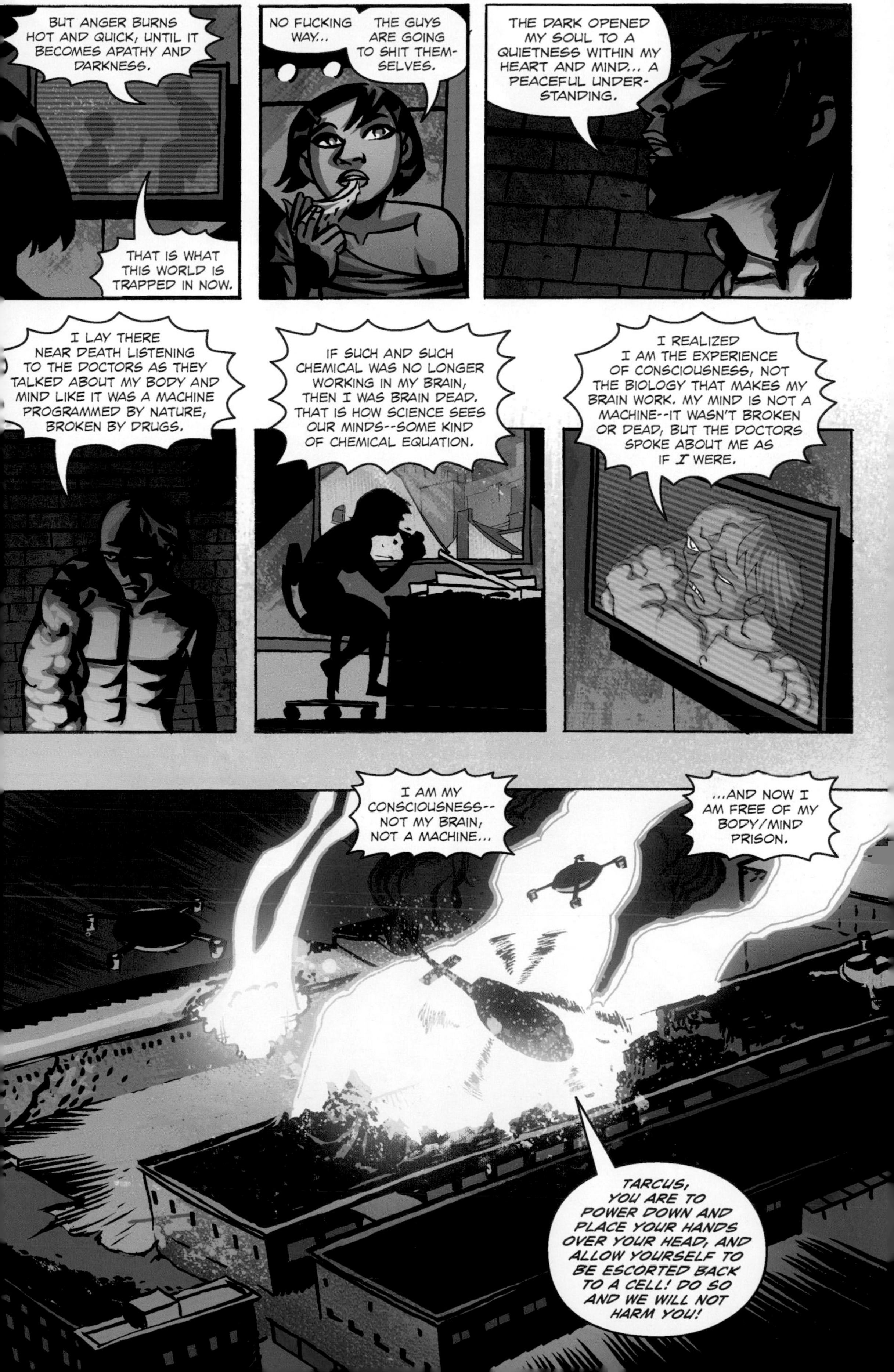
BUT ANGER BURNS HOT AND QUICK, UNTIL IT BECOMES APATHY AND DARKNESS.
THAT IS WHAT THIS WORLD IS TRAPPED IN NOW.
NO FUCKING WAY...
THE GUYS ARE GOING TO SHIT THEMSELVES.
THE DARK OPENED MY SOUL TO A QUIETNESS WITHIN MY HEART AND MIND... A PEACEFUL UNDERSTANDING.
I LAY THERE NEAR DEATH LISTENING TO THE DOCTORS AS THEY TALKED ABOUT MY BODY AND MIND LIKE IT WAS A MACHINE PROGRAMMED BY NATURE, BROKEN BY DRUGS.
IF SUCH AND SUCH CHEMICAL WAS NO LONGER WORKING IN MY BRAIN, THEN I WAS BRAIN DEAD. THAT IS HOW SCIENCE SEES OUR MINDS--SOME KIND OF CHEMICAL EQUATION.
I REALIZED I AM THE EXPERIENCE OF CONSCIOUSNESS, NOT THE BIOLOGY THAT MAKES MY BRAIN WORK. MY MIND IS NOT A MACHINE--IT WASN'T BROKEN OR DEAD, BUT THE DOCTORS SPOKE ABOUT ME AS IF *I* WERE.
I AM MY CONSCIOUSNESS--NOT MY BRAIN, NOT A MACHINE...
...AND NOW I AM FREE OF MY BODY/MIND PRISON.
TARCUS, YOU ARE TO POWER DOWN AND PLACE YOUR HANDS OVER YOUR HEAD, AND ALLOW YOURSELF TO BE ESCORTED BACK TO A CELL! DO SO AND WE WILL NOT HARM YOU!

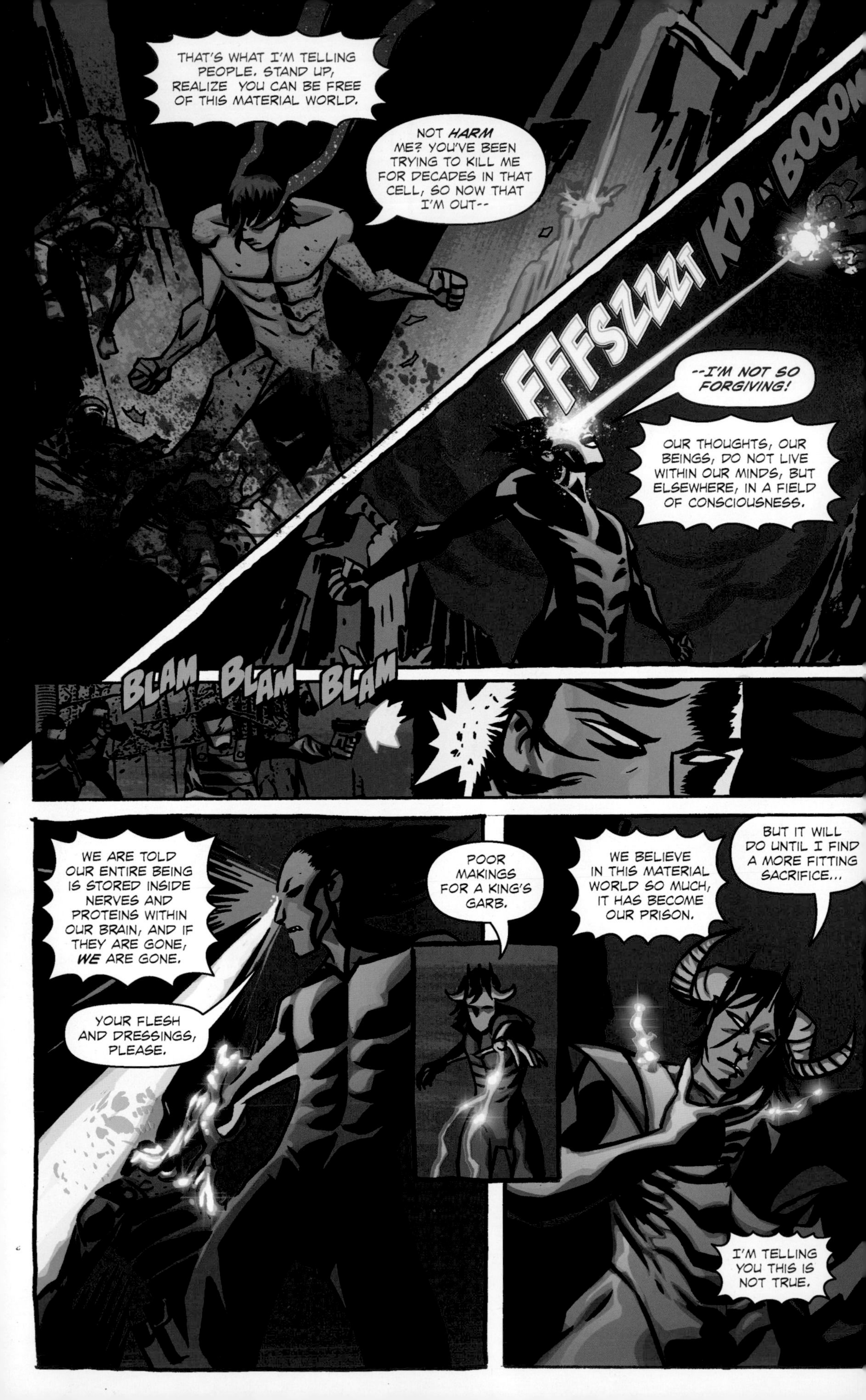
THAT'S WHAT I'M TELLING PEOPLE. STAND UP, REALIZE YOU CAN BE FREE OF THIS MATERIAL WORLD.
NOT *HARM* ME? YOU'VE BEEN TRYING TO KILL ME FOR DECADES IN THAT CELL, SO NOW THAT I'M OUT--
FFFSZZZZT KD-BOOOM
--*I'M NOT SO FORGIVING!*
OUR THOUGHTS, OUR BEINGS, DO NOT LIVE WITHIN OUR MINDS, BUT ELSEWHERE, IN A FIELD OF CONSCIOUSNESS.
BLAM BLAM BLAM
WE ARE TOLD OUR ENTIRE BEING IS STORED INSIDE NERVES AND PROTEINS WITHIN OUR BRAIN, AND IF THEY ARE GONE, ***WE*** ARE GONE.
YOUR FLESH AND DRESSINGS, PLEASE.
POOR MAKINGS FOR A KING'S GARB.
WE BELIEVE IN THIS MATERIAL WORLD SO MUCH, IT HAS BECOME OUR PRISON.
BUT IT WILL DO UNTIL I FIND A MORE FITTING SACRIFICE...
I'M TELLING YOU THIS IS NOT TRUE.

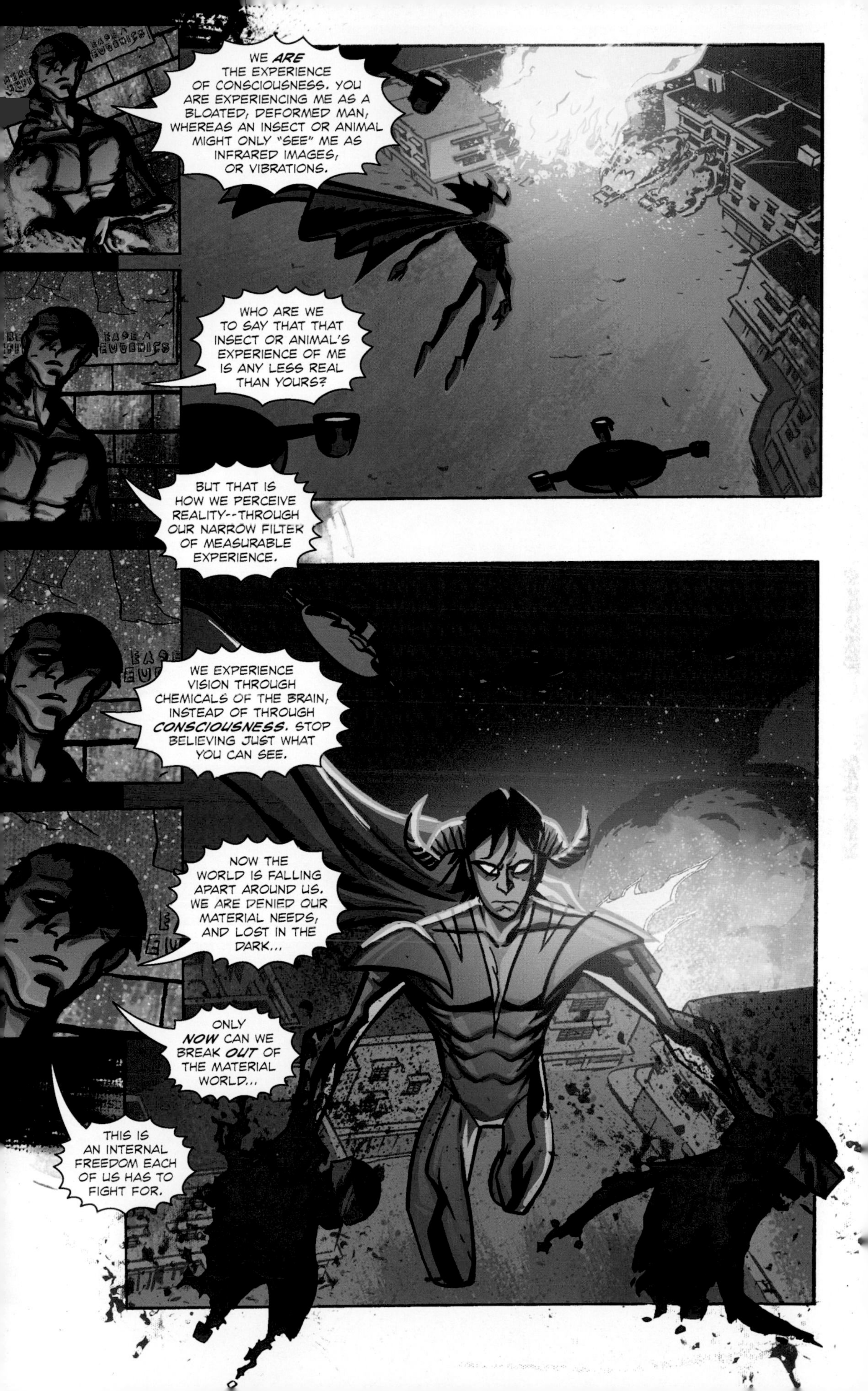
WE ARE THE EXPERIENCE OF CONSCIOUSNESS. YOU ARE EXPERIENCING ME AS A BLOATED, DEFORMED MAN, WHEREAS AN INSECT OR ANIMAL MIGHT ONLY "SEE" ME AS INFRARED IMAGES, OR VIBRATIONS.
WHO ARE WE TO SAY THAT THAT INSECT OR ANIMAL'S EXPERIENCE OF ME IS ANY LESS REAL THAN YOURS?
BUT THAT IS HOW WE PERCEIVE REALITY--THROUGH OUR NARROW FILTER OF MEASURABLE EXPERIENCE.
WE EXPERIENCE VISION THROUGH CHEMICALS OF THE BRAIN, INSTEAD OF THROUGH CONSCIOUSNESS. STOP BELIEVING JUST WHAT YOU CAN SEE.
NOW THE WORLD IS FALLING APART AROUND US. WE ARE DENIED OUR MATERIAL NEEDS, AND LOST IN THE DARK...
ONLY NOW CAN WE BREAK OUT OF THE MATERIAL WORLD...
THIS IS AN INTERNAL FREEDOM EACH OF US HAS TO FIGHT FOR.

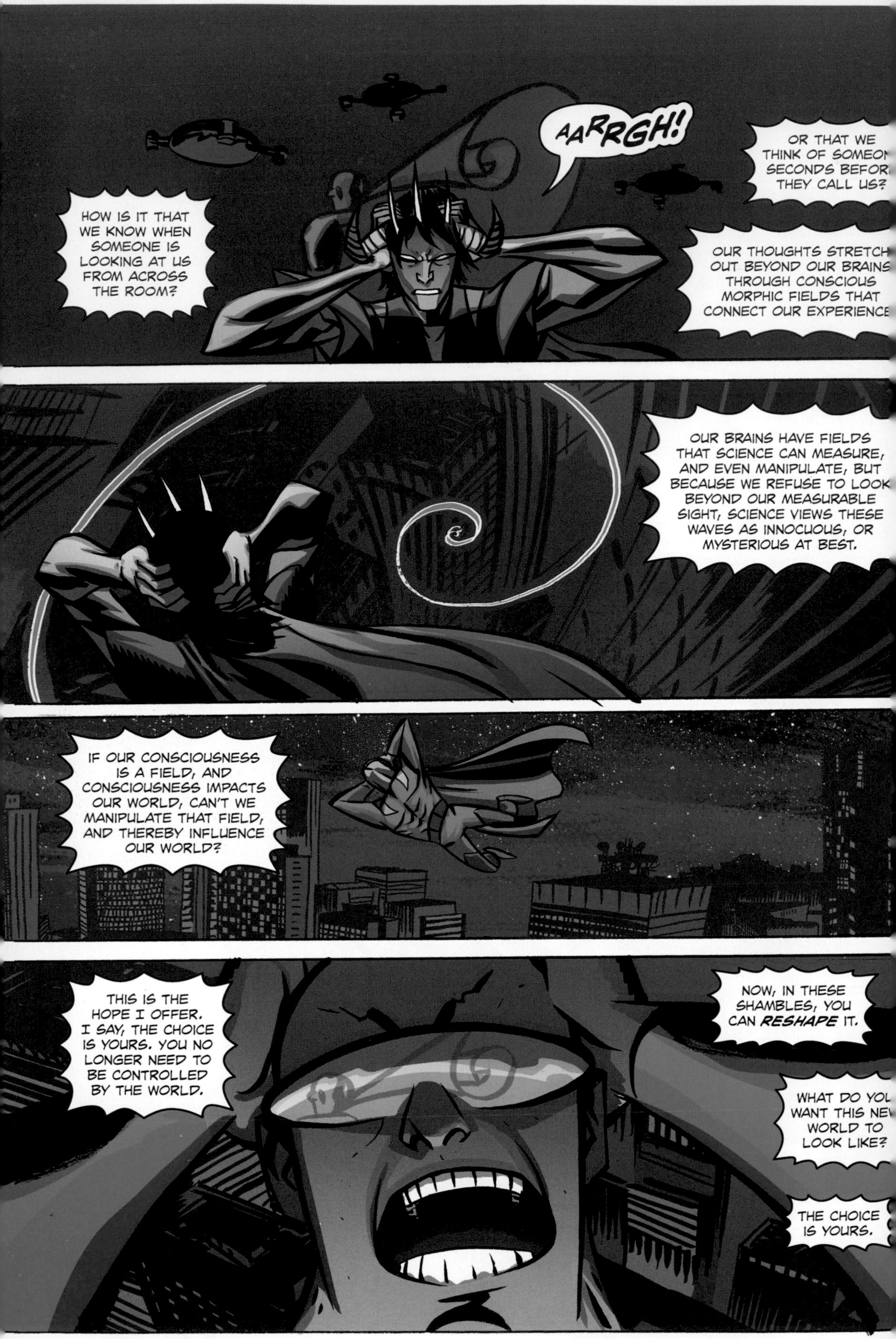

HOW IS IT THAT WE KNOW WHEN SOMEONE IS LOOKING AT US FROM ACROSS THE ROOM?
AARRGH!
OR THAT WE THINK OF SOMEON SECONDS BEFOR THEY CALL US?
OUR THOUGHTS STRETCH OUT BEYOND OUR BRAINS THROUGH CONSCIOUS MORPHIC FIELDS THAT CONNECT OUR EXPERIENCE
OUR BRAINS HAVE FIELDS THAT SCIENCE CAN MEASURE, AND EVEN MANIPULATE, BUT BECAUSE WE REFUSE TO LOOK BEYOND OUR MEASURABLE SIGHT, SCIENCE VIEWS THESE WAVES AS INNOCUOUS, OR MYSTERIOUS AT BEST.
IF OUR CONSCIOUSNESS IS A FIELD, AND CONSCIOUSNESS IMPACTS OUR WORLD, CAN'T WE MANIPULATE THAT FIELD, AND THEREBY INFLUENCE OUR WORLD?
THIS IS THE HOPE I OFFER. I SAY, THE CHOICE IS YOURS. YOU NO LONGER NEED TO BE CONTROLLED BY THE WORLD.
NOW, IN THESE SHAMBLES, YOU CAN *RESHAPE* IT.
WHAT DO YOU WANT THIS NEW WORLD TO LOOK LIKE?
THE CHOICE IS YOURS.

CHAPTER THREE

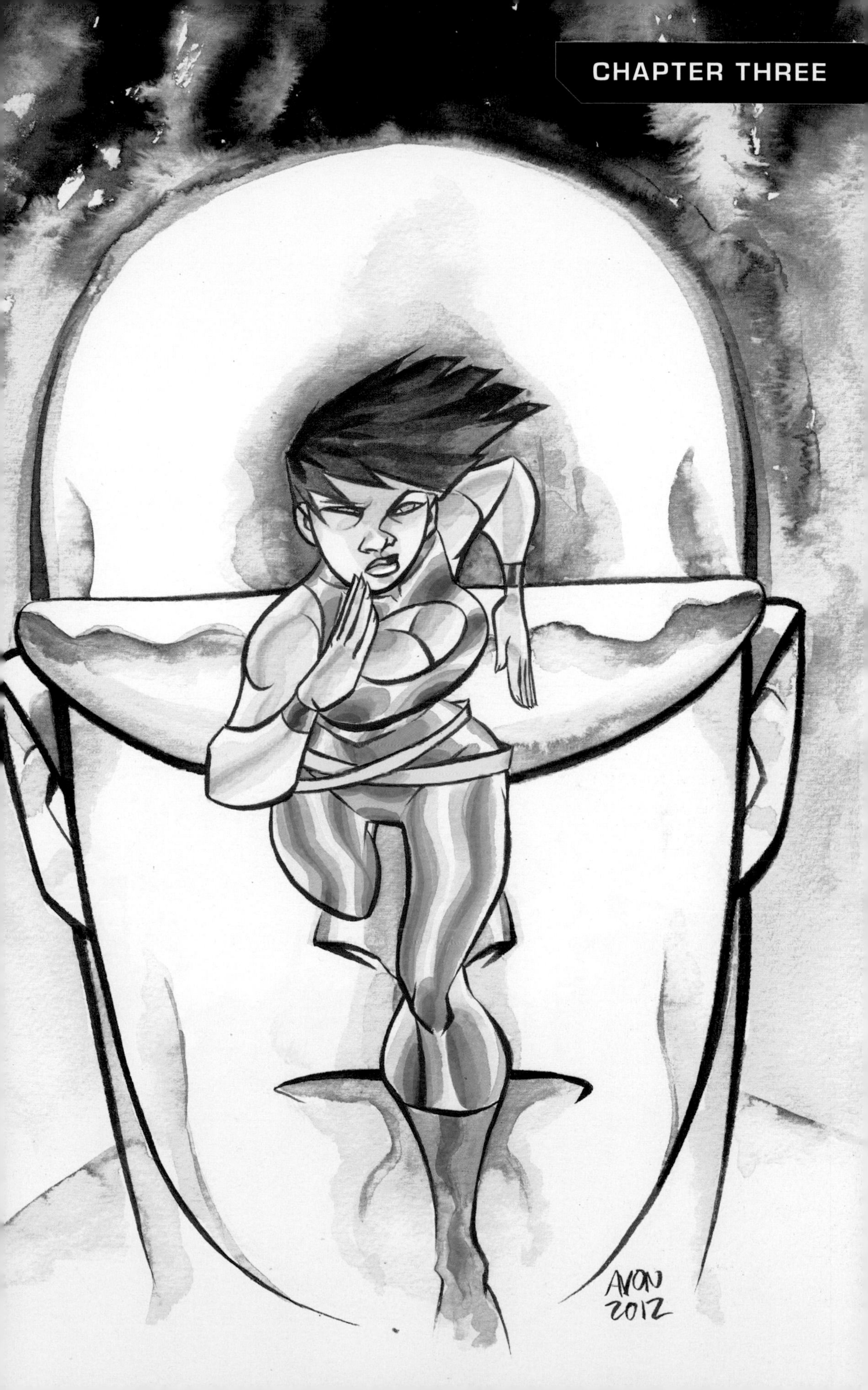
AVON
2012

IN THE WAKE OF THE JACKAL'S ATTACK ON THE GLOBAL INFRASTRUCTURE, FOOD RATION LINES HAVE BECOME A DAILY PART OF LIFE FOR MANY OF US.

IN THOSE LINES TODAY, MANY TOOK A MOMENT TO MOURN THE PASSING OF THE BELOVED HERO KNOWN AS ATLANTIS.

HER BODY WAS FOUND AMID THE DESTRUCTION OF THE OCTAVIA WATER PLANT-- A HIGHLY CONTESTED SITE IN BOLIVIA WHERE THE SO-CALLED WATER WARS HAVE EXPLODED IN VIOLENCE OVER THE PAST MONTHS.

THE EXACT CAUSE OF HER DEATH IS UNKNOWN, BUT MANY SPECULATE IT WAS THE DOING OF THE ERSTE CORP ASSASSINS-- AN ACCUSATION THE ERSTE CORP FIERCELY DENIES.

LITTLE IS KNOWN OF ATLANTIS'S ORIGINS, BUT SOME SPECULATE SHE IS FROM THE ACTUAL FORGOTTEN--

--WAIT--

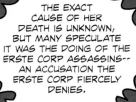

JUST COMING IN, WE MAY HAVE FOOTAGE--

YES, WE ARE CUTTING TO FOOTAGE OF THE ESCAPED CRIMINAL *TARCUS*--

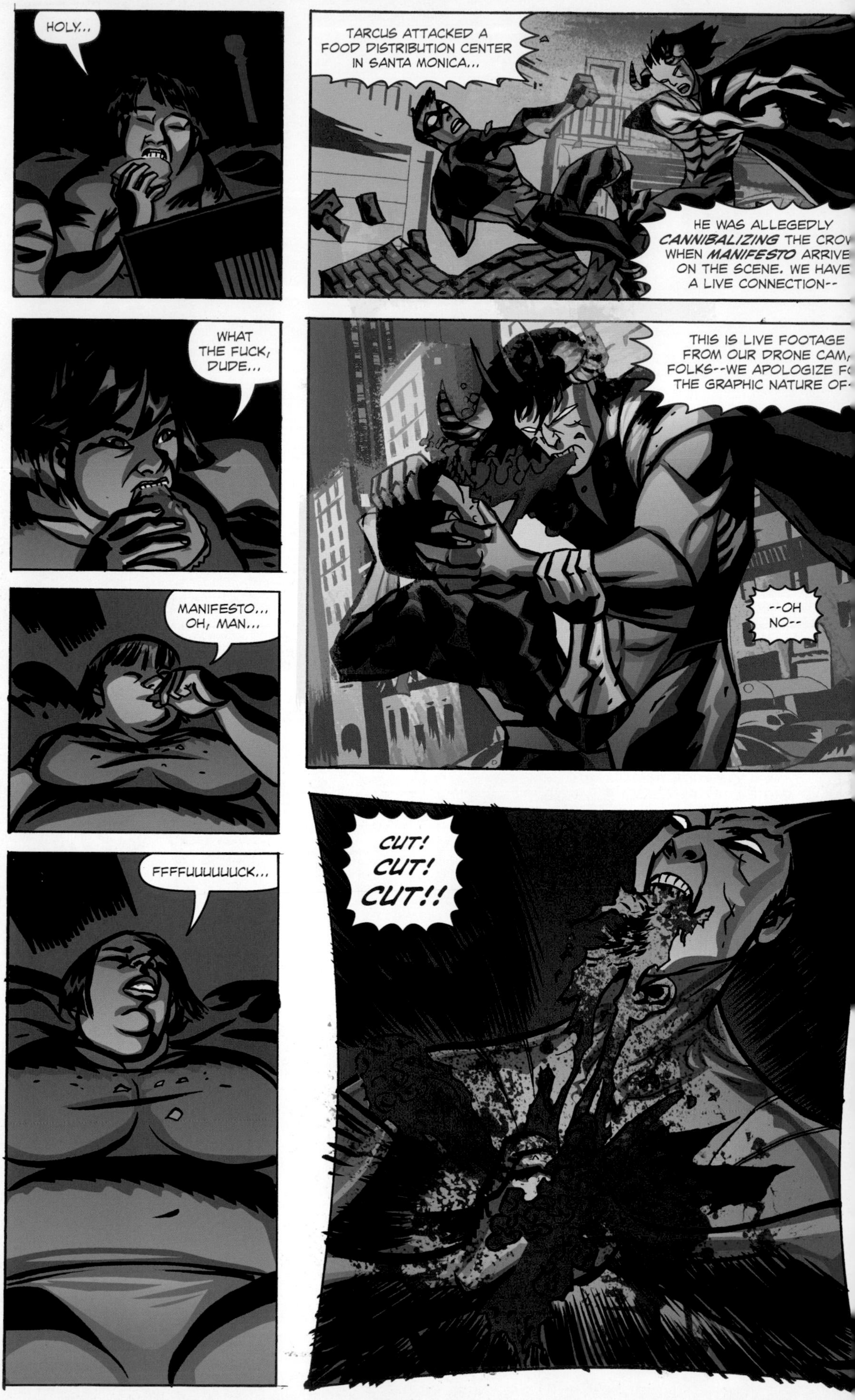

HOLY...
TARCUS ATTACKED A FOOD DISTRIBUTION CENTER IN SANTA MONICA...
HE WAS ALLEGEDLY **CANNIBALIZING** THE CROW
WHEN **MANIFESTO** ARRIVE
ON THE SCENE. WE HAVE A LIVE CONNECTION--
WHAT THE FUCK, DUDE...
THIS IS LIVE FOOTAGE FROM OUR DRONE CAM,
FOLKS--WE APOLOGIZE FO
THE GRAPHIC NATURE OF-
MANIFESTO... OH, MAN...
--OH NO--
FFFFUUUUUUCK...
CUT! CUT! CUT!!

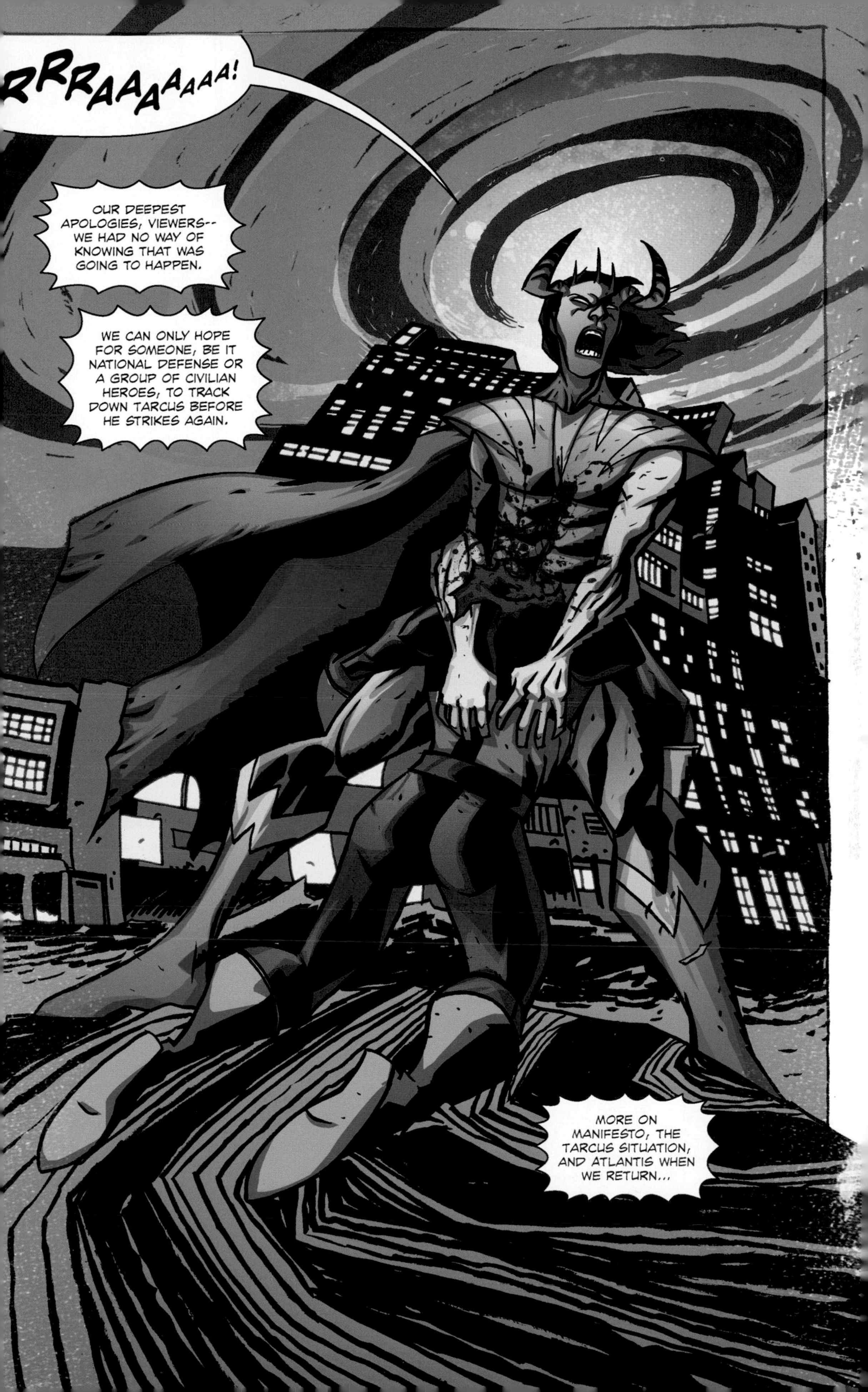
RRRAAAAAAA!
OUR DEEPEST APOLOGIES, VIEWERS-- WE HAD NO WAY OF KNOWING THAT WAS GOING TO HAPPEN.
WE CAN ONLY HOPE FOR SOMEONE, BE IT NATIONAL DEFENSE OR A GROUP OF CIVILIAN HEROES, TO TRACK DOWN TARCUS BEFORE HE STRIKES AGAIN.
MORE ON MANIFESTO, THE TARCUS SITUATION, AND ATLANTIS WHEN WE RETURN...

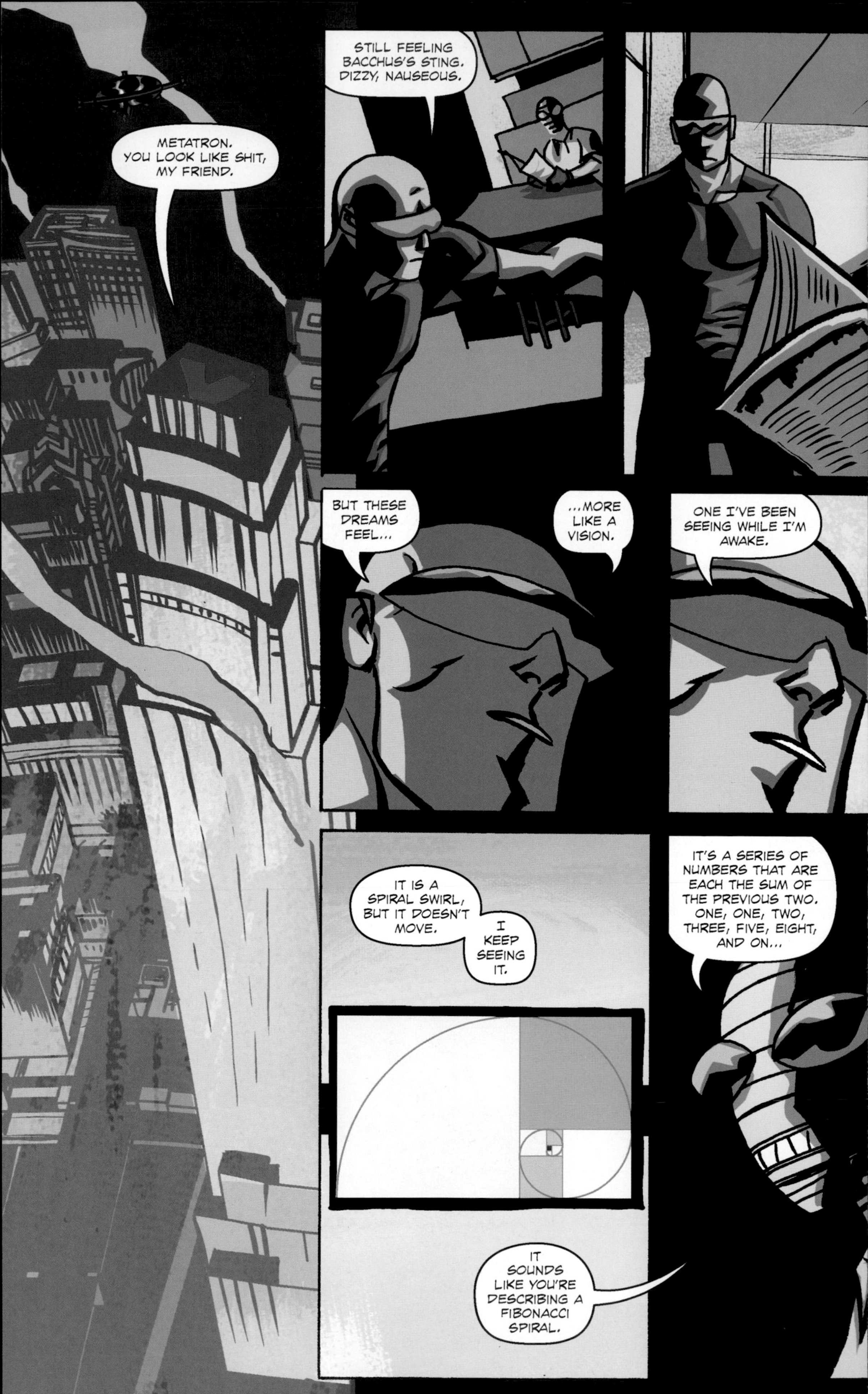
METATRON. YOU LOOK LIKE SHIT, MY FRIEND.
STILL FEELING BACCHUS'S STING. DIZZY, NAUSEOUS.
BUT THESE DREAMS FEEL...
...MORE LIKE A VISION.
ONE I'VE BEEN SEEING WHILE I'M AWAKE.
IT IS A SPIRAL SWIRL, BUT IT DOESN'T MOVE.
I KEEP SEEING IT.
IT'S A SERIES OF NUMBERS THAT ARE EACH THE SUM OF THE PREVIOUS TWO. ONE, ONE, TWO, THREE, FIVE, EIGHT, AND ON...
IT SOUNDS LIKE YOU'RE DESCRIBING A FIBONACCI SPIRAL.

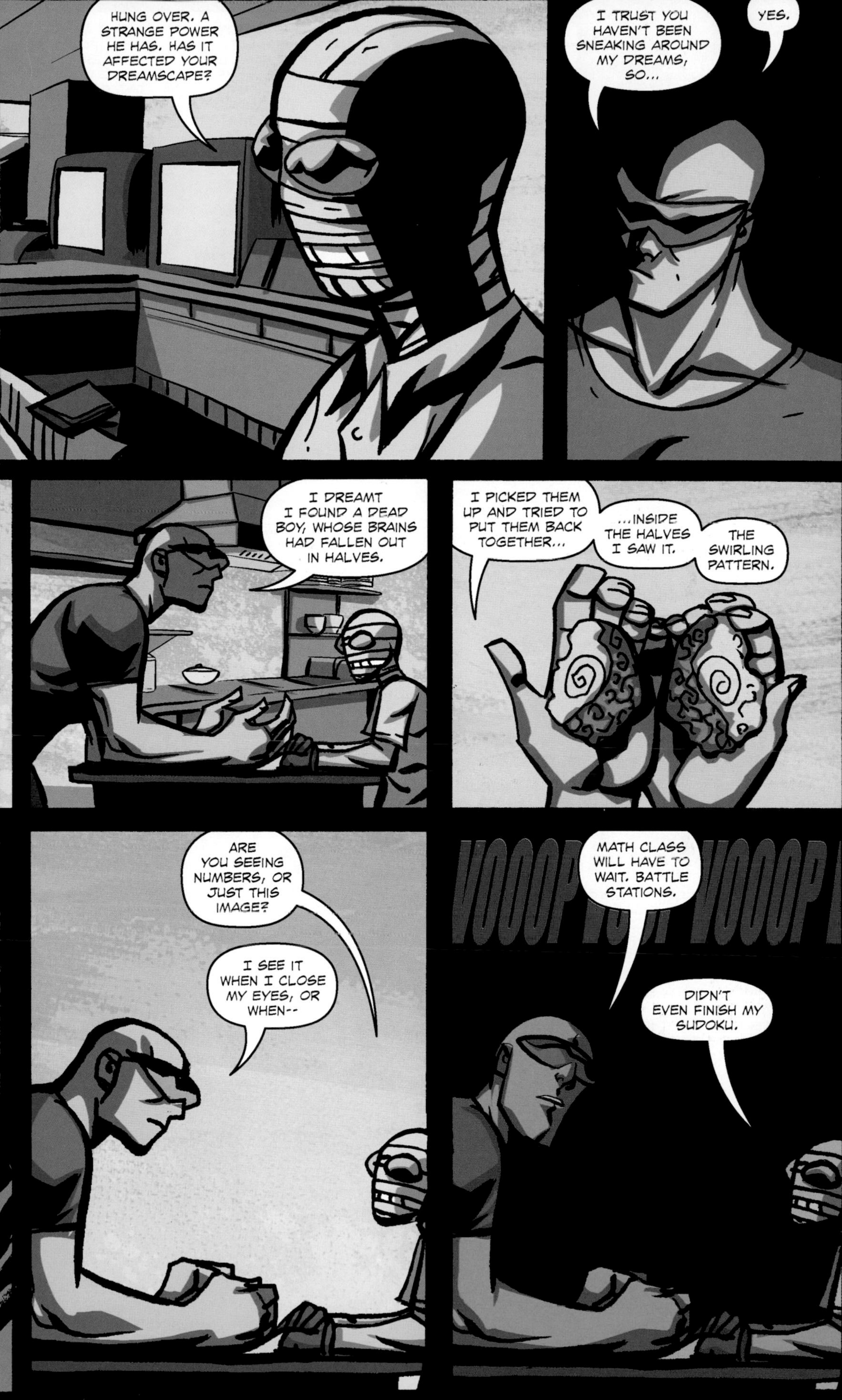
HUNG OVER. A STRANGE POWER HE HAS. HAS IT AFFECTED YOUR DREAMSCAPE?
I TRUST YOU HAVEN'T BEEN SNEAKING AROUND MY DREAMS, SO...
YES.
I DREAMT I FOUND A DEAD BOY, WHOSE BRAINS HAD FALLEN OUT IN HALVES.
I PICKED THEM UP AND TRIED TO PUT THEM BACK TOGETHER...
...INSIDE THE HALVES I SAW IT.
THE SWIRLING PATTERN.
ARE YOU SEEING NUMBERS, OR JUST THIS IMAGE?
I SEE IT WHEN I CLOSE MY EYES, OR WHEN--
VOOOP VOOP VOOOP
MATH CLASS WILL HAVE TO WAIT. BATTLE STATIONS.
DIDN'T EVEN FINISH MY SUDOKU.

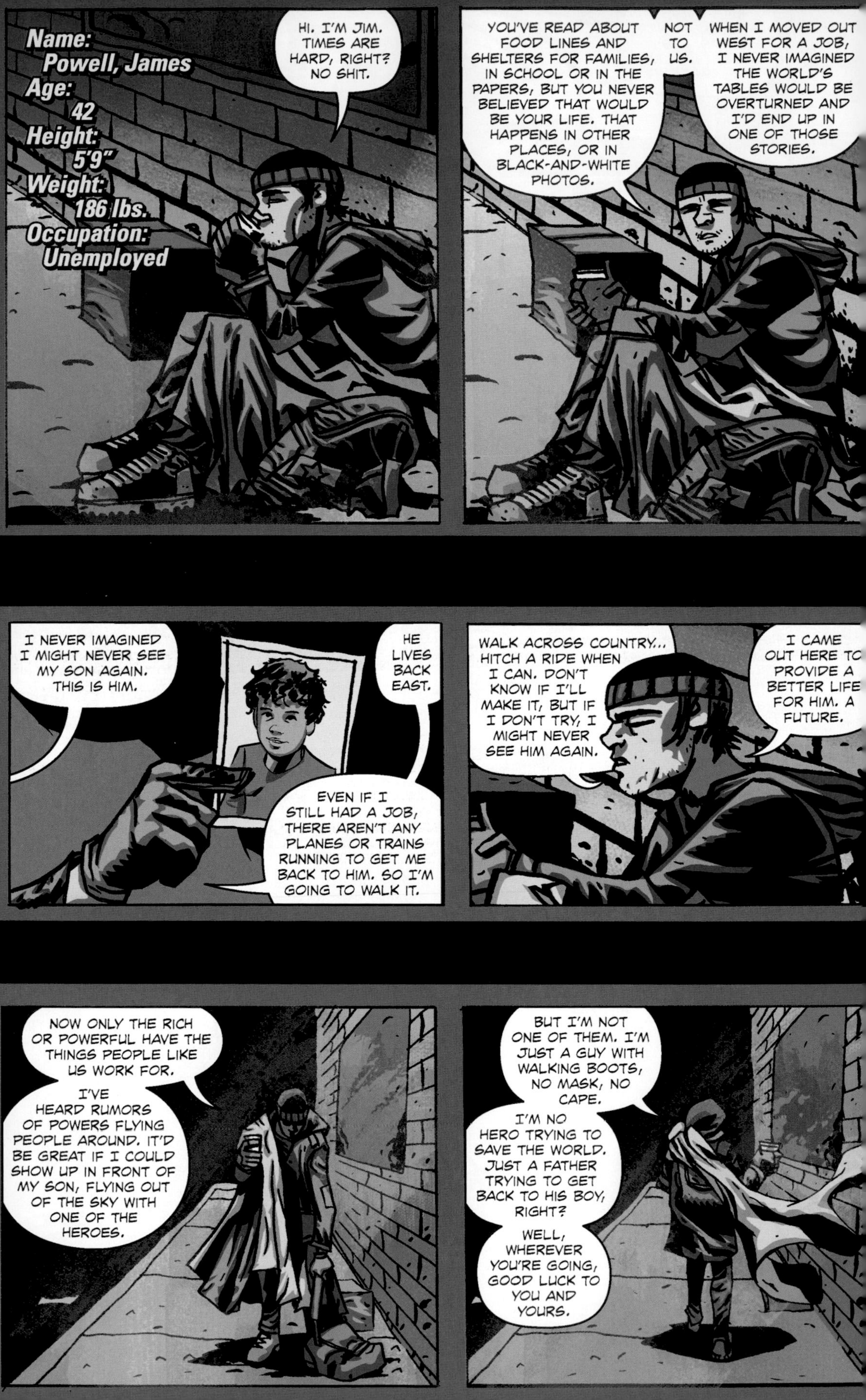

Name: Powell, James
Age: 42
Height: 5'9"
Weight: 186 lbs.
Occupation: Unemployed
HI. I'M JIM. TIMES ARE HARD, RIGHT? NO SHIT.
YOU'VE READ ABOUT FOOD LINES AND SHELTERS FOR FAMILIES, IN SCHOOL OR IN THE PAPERS, BUT YOU NEVER BELIEVED THAT WOULD BE YOUR LIFE. THAT HAPPENS IN OTHER PLACES, OR IN BLACK-AND-WHITE PHOTOS.
NOT TO US.
WHEN I MOVED OUT WEST FOR A JOB, I NEVER IMAGINED THE WORLD'S TABLES WOULD BE OVERTURNED AND I'D END UP IN ONE OF THOSE STORIES.
I NEVER IMAGINED I MIGHT NEVER SEE MY SON AGAIN. THIS IS HIM.
HE LIVES BACK EAST.
EVEN IF I STILL HAD A JOB, THERE AREN'T ANY PLANES OR TRAINS RUNNING TO GET ME BACK TO HIM. SO I'M GOING TO WALK IT.
WALK ACROSS COUNTRY... HITCH A RIDE WHEN I CAN. DON'T KNOW IF I'LL MAKE IT, BUT IF I DON'T TRY, I MIGHT NEVER SEE HIM AGAIN.
I CAME OUT HERE TO PROVIDE A BETTER LIFE FOR HIM. A FUTURE.
NOW ONLY THE RICH OR POWERFUL HAVE THE THINGS PEOPLE LIKE US WORK FOR.
I'VE HEARD RUMORS OF POWERS FLYING PEOPLE AROUND. IT'D BE GREAT IF I COULD SHOW UP IN FRONT OF MY SON, FLYING OUT OF THE SKY WITH ONE OF THE HEROES.
BUT I'M NOT ONE OF THEM. I'M JUST A GUY WITH WALKING BOOTS, NO MASK, NO CAPE.
I'M NO HERO TRYING TO SAVE THE WORLD. JUST A FATHER TRYING TO GET BACK TO HIS BOY, RIGHT?
WELL, WHEREVER YOU'RE GOING, GOOD LUCK TO YOU AND YOURS.

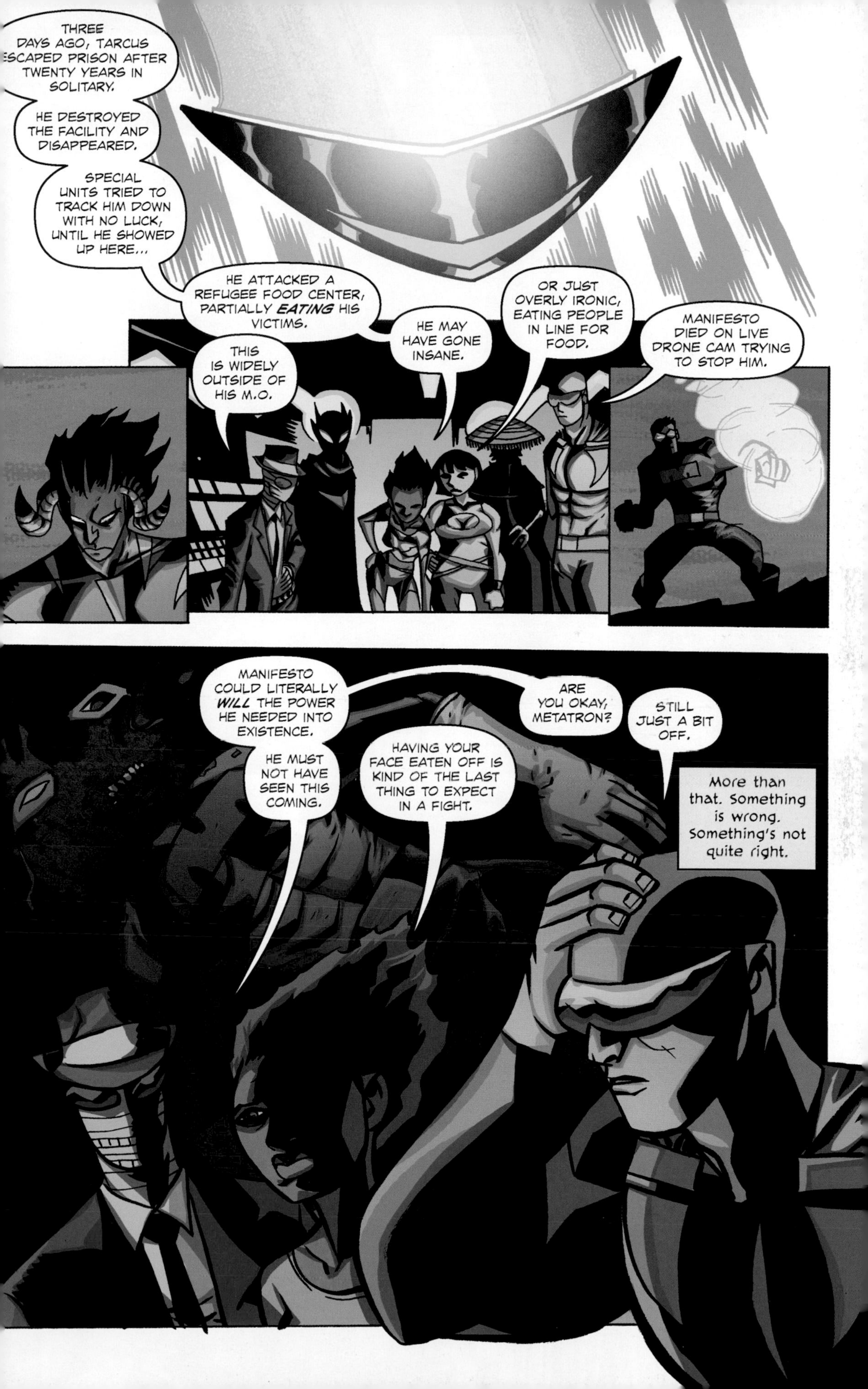
THREE DAYS AGO, TARCUS ESCAPED PRISON AFTER TWENTY YEARS IN SOLITARY.
HE DESTROYED THE FACILITY AND DISAPPEARED.
SPECIAL UNITS TRIED TO TRACK HIM DOWN WITH NO LUCK, UNTIL HE SHOWED UP HERE...
HE ATTACKED A REFUGEE FOOD CENTER, PARTIALLY *EATING* HIS VICTIMS.
THIS IS WIDELY OUTSIDE OF HIS M.O.
HE MAY HAVE GONE INSANE.
OR JUST OVERLY IRONIC, EATING PEOPLE IN LINE FOR FOOD.
MANIFESTO DIED ON LIVE DRONE CAM TRYING TO STOP HIM.
MANIFESTO COULD LITERALLY *WILL* THE POWER HE NEEDED INTO EXISTENCE.
HE MUST NOT HAVE SEEN THIS COMING.
HAVING YOUR FACE EATEN OFF IS KIND OF THE LAST THING TO EXPECT IN A FIGHT.
ARE YOU OKAY, METATRON?
STILL JUST A BIT OFF.
More than that. Something is wrong. Something's not quite right.

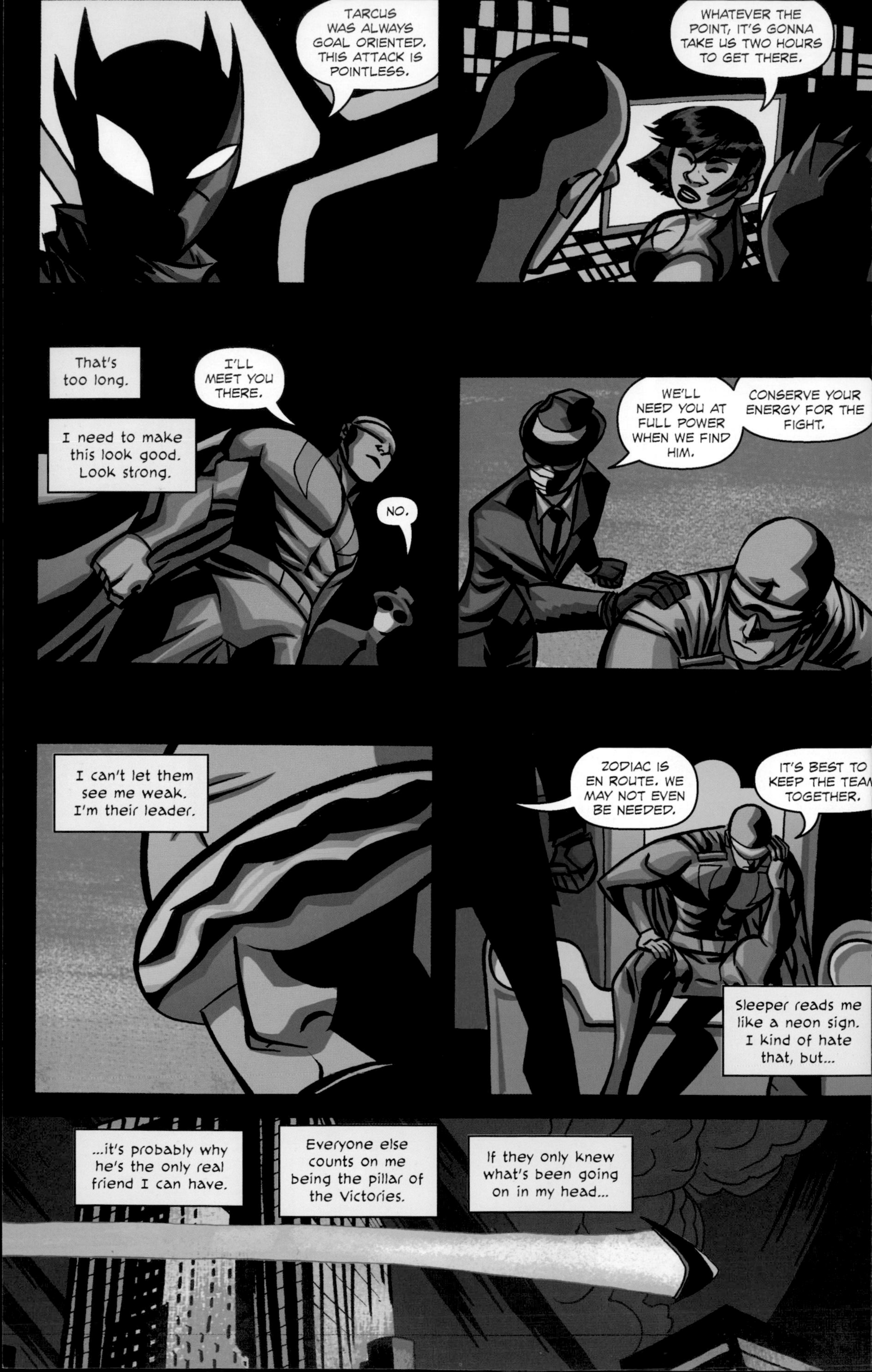
TARCUS WAS ALWAYS GOAL ORIENTED. THIS ATTACK IS POINTLESS.
WHATEVER THE POINT, IT'S GONNA TAKE US TWO HOURS TO GET THERE.
That's too long.
I'LL MEET YOU THERE.
I need to make this look good. Look strong.
NO.
WE'LL NEED YOU AT FULL POWER WHEN WE FIND HIM.
CONSERVE YOUR ENERGY FOR THE FIGHT.
I can't let them see me weak. I'm their leader.
ZODIAC IS EN ROUTE. WE MAY NOT EVEN BE NEEDED.
IT'S BEST TO KEEP THE TEAM TOGETHER.
Sleeper reads me like a neon sign. I kind of hate that, but...
...it's probably why he's the only real friend I can have.
Everyone else counts on me being the pillar of the Victories.
If they only knew what's been going on in my head...

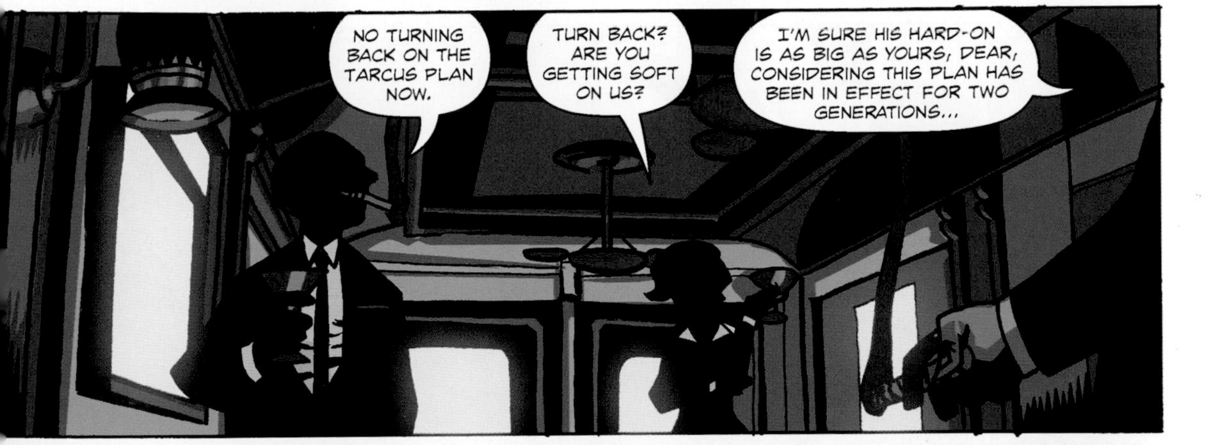
NO TURNING BACK ON THE TARCUS PLAN NOW.
TURN BACK? ARE YOU GETTING SOFT ON US?
I'M SURE HIS HARD-ON IS AS BIG AS YOURS, DEAR, CONSIDERING THIS PLAN HAS BEEN IN EFFECT FOR TWO GENERATIONS...

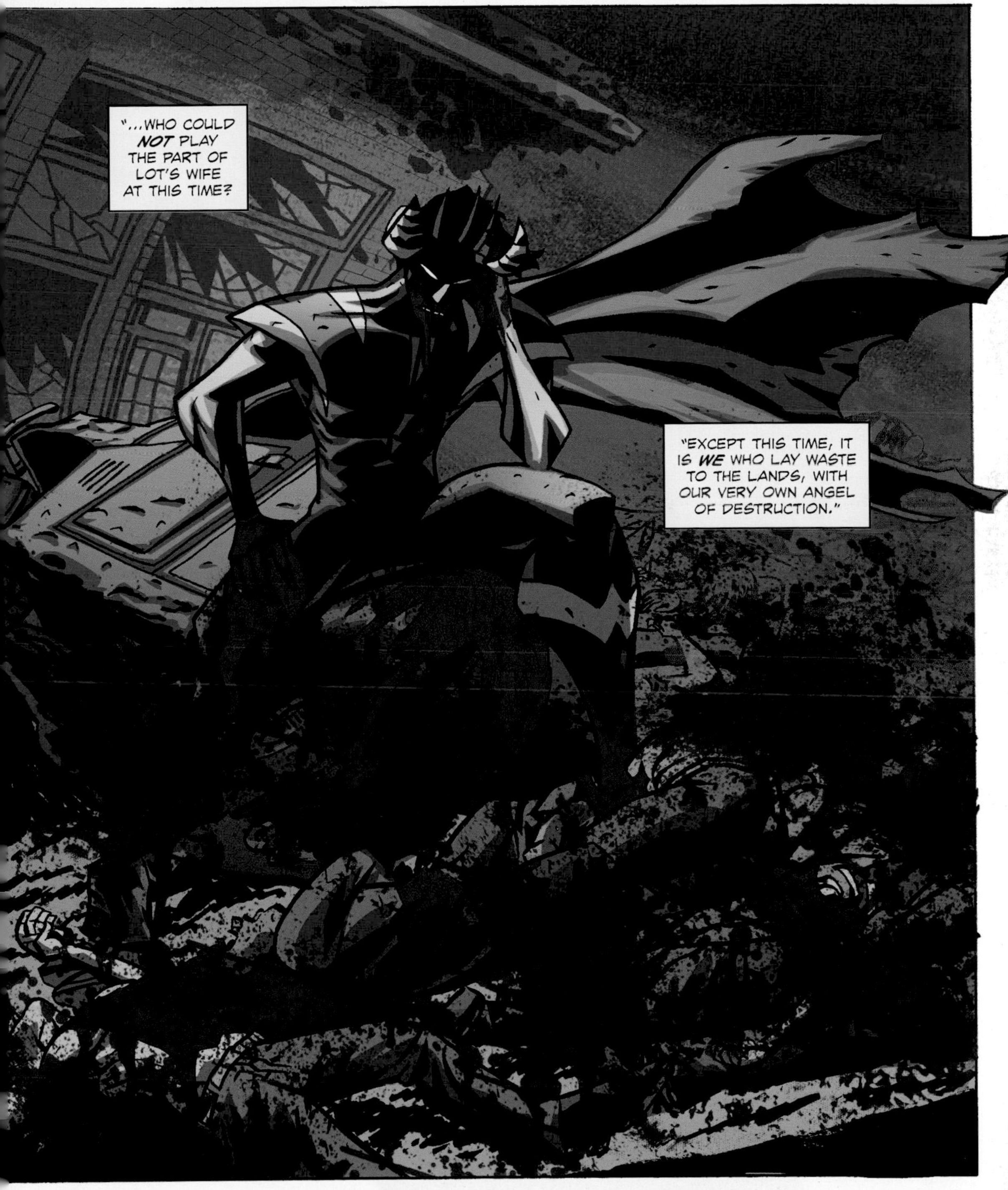
"...WHO COULD NOT PLAY THE PART OF LOT'S WIFE AT THIS TIME?
"EXCEPT THIS TIME, IT IS WE WHO LAY WASTE TO THE LANDS, WITH OUR VERY OWN ANGEL OF DESTRUCTION."

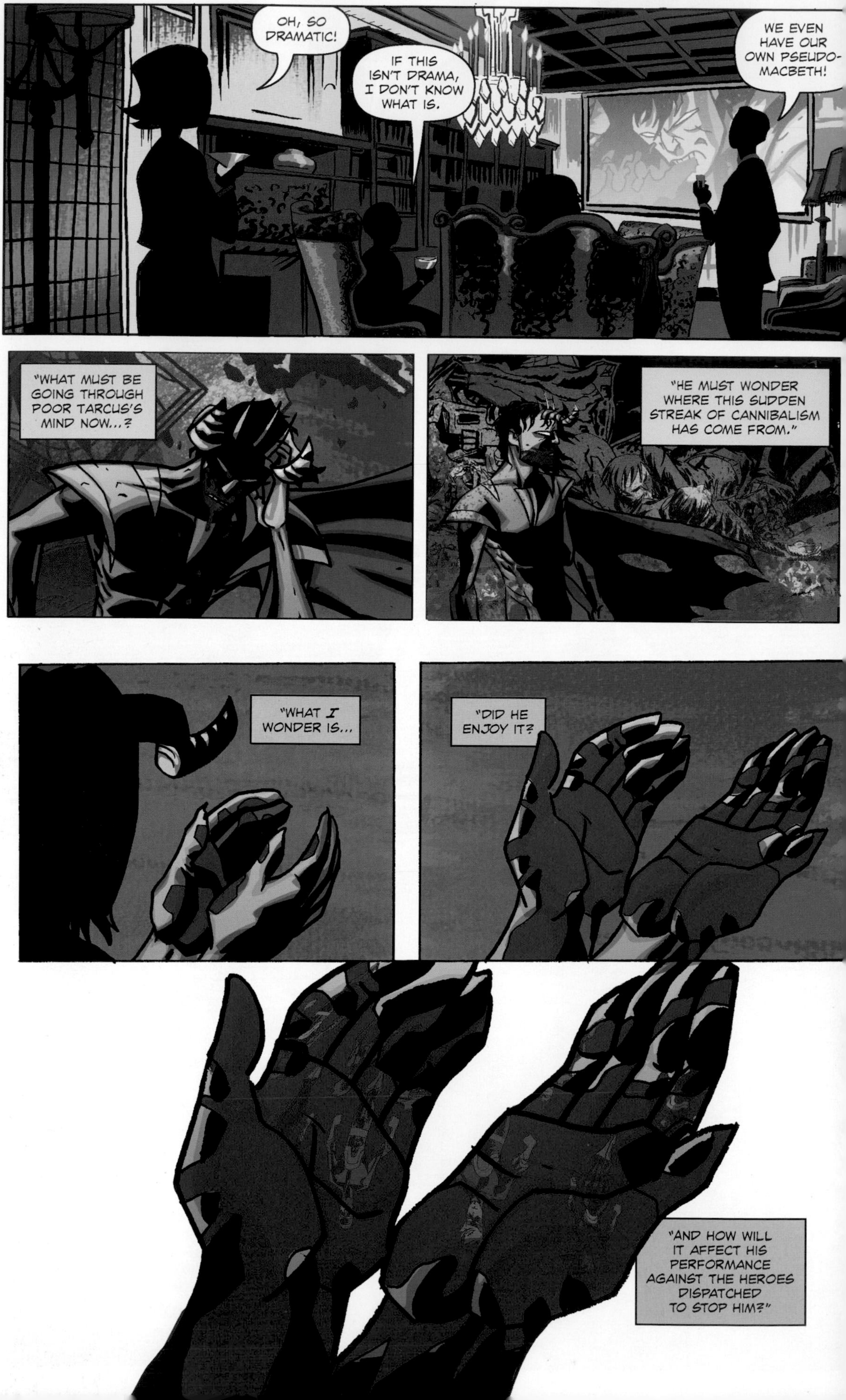
OH, SO DRAMATIC!
IF THIS ISN'T DRAMA, I DON'T KNOW WHAT IS.
WE EVEN HAVE OUR OWN PSEUDO-MACBETH!
"WHAT MUST BE GOING THROUGH POOR TARCUS'S MIND NOW...?
"HE MUST WONDER WHERE THIS SUDDEN STREAK OF CANNIBALISM HAS COME FROM."
"WHAT I WONDER IS...
"DID HE ENJOY IT?
"AND HOW WILL IT AFFECT HIS PERFORMANCE AGAINST THE HEROES DISPATCHED TO STOP HIM?"

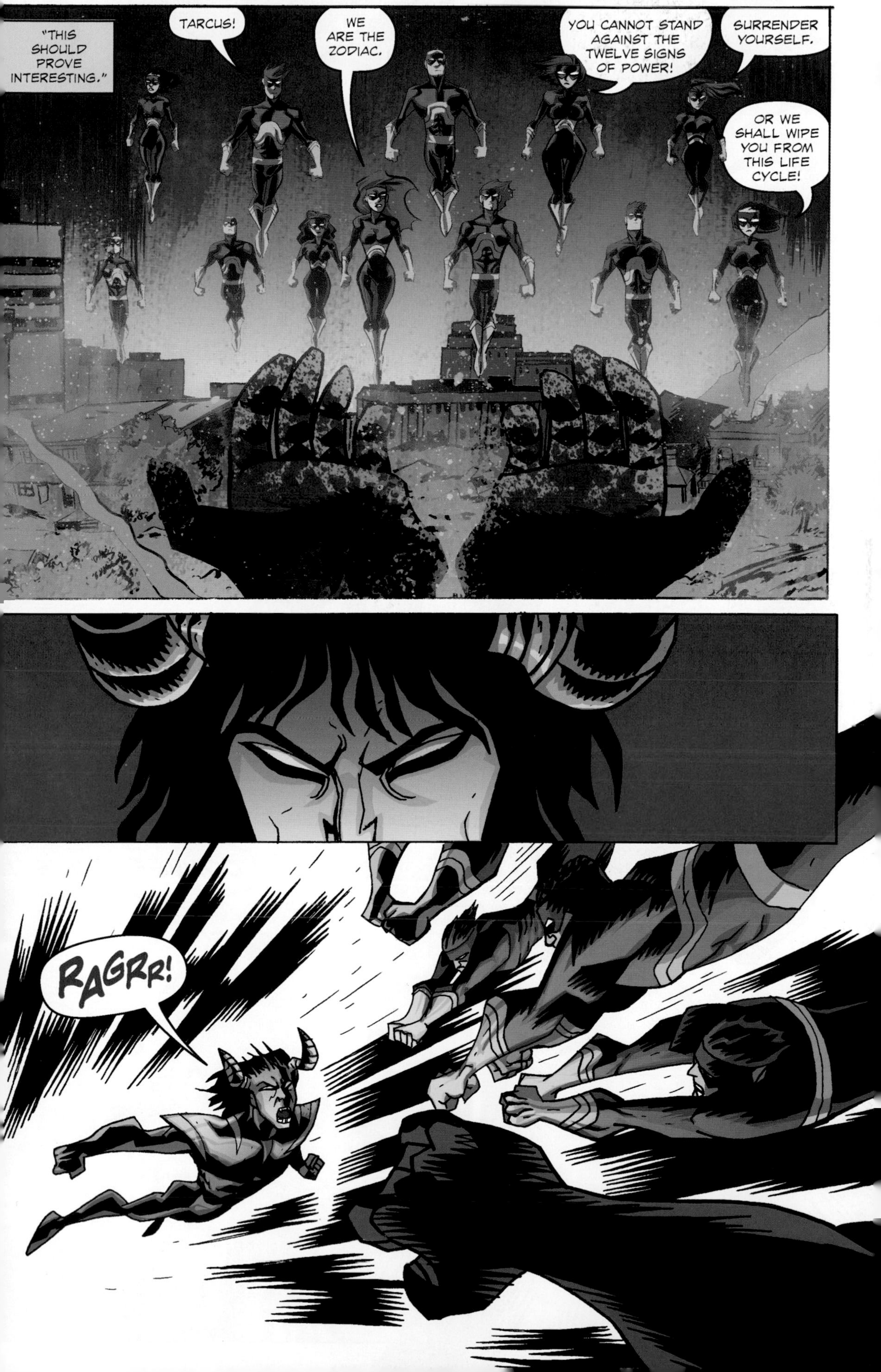
"THIS SHOULD PROVE INTERESTING."
TARCUS!
WE ARE THE ZODIAC.
YOU CANNOT STAND AGAINST THE TWELVE SIGNS OF POWER!
SURRENDER YOURSELF.
OR WE SHALL WIPE YOU FROM THIS LIFE CYCLE!
RAGRR!

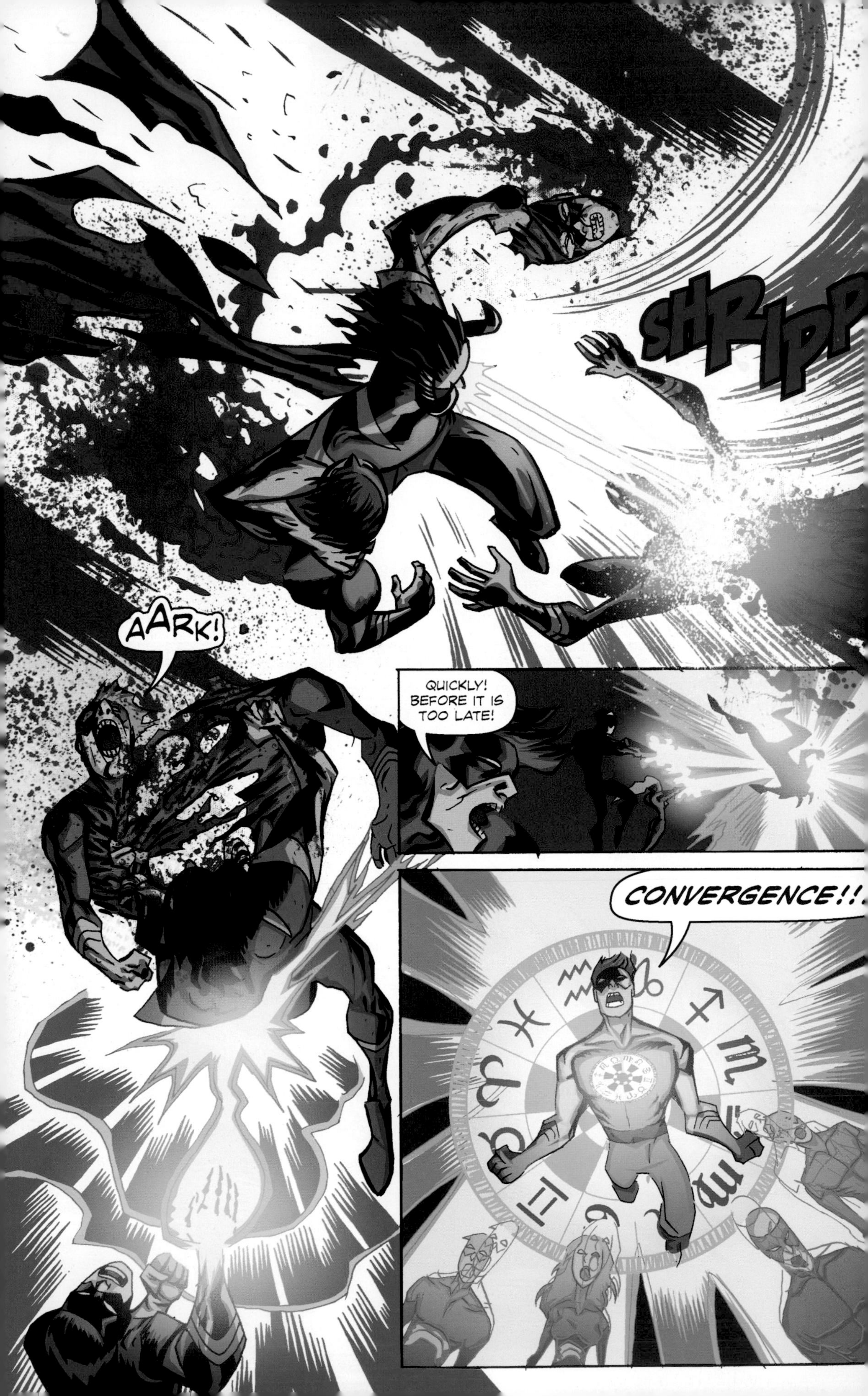
SHRIPP
AARK!
QUICKLY! BEFORE IT IS TOO LATE!
CONVERGENCE!!!

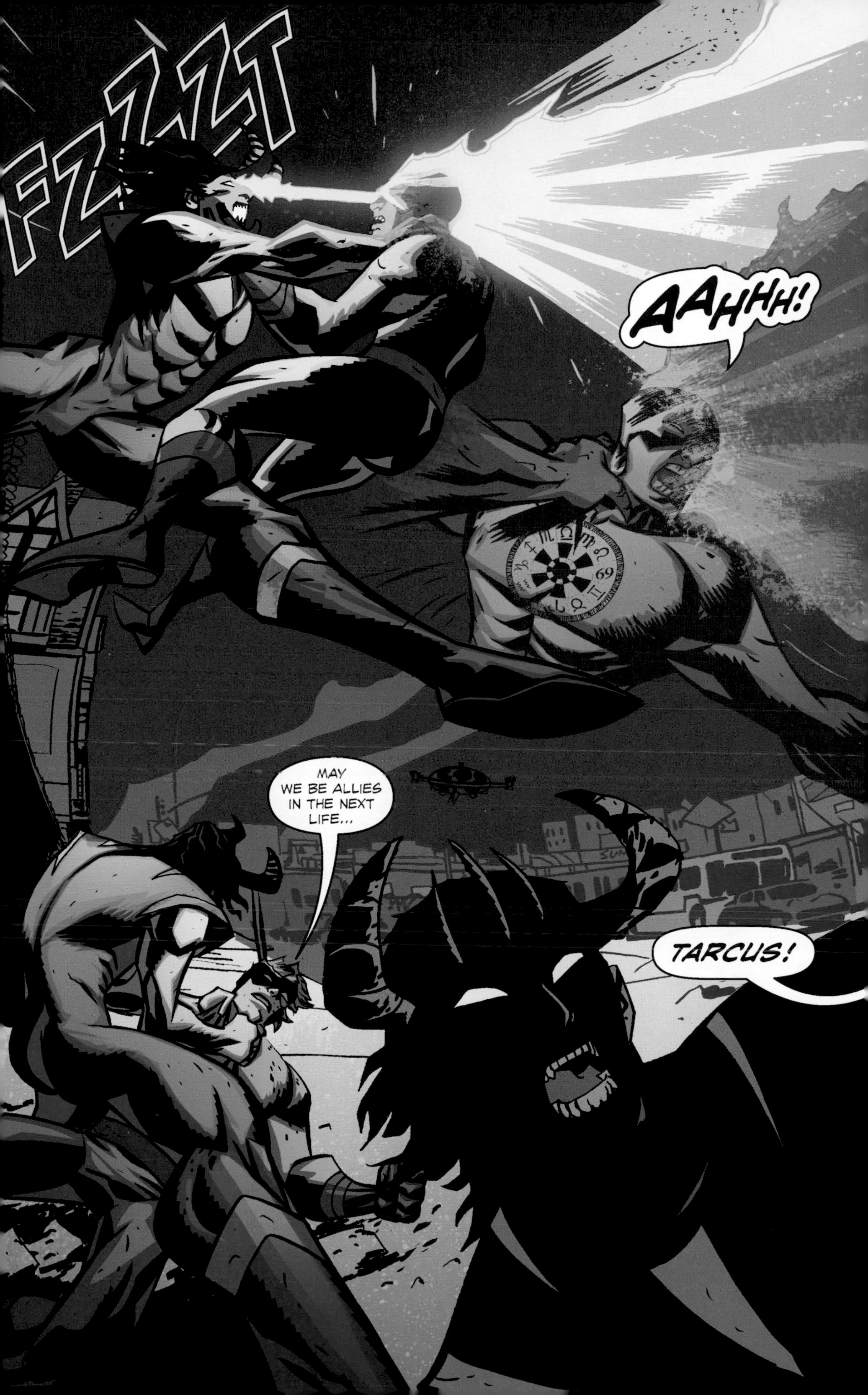
FZZZZT
AAHHH!
MAY WE BE ALLIES IN THE NEXT LIFE...
TARCUS!

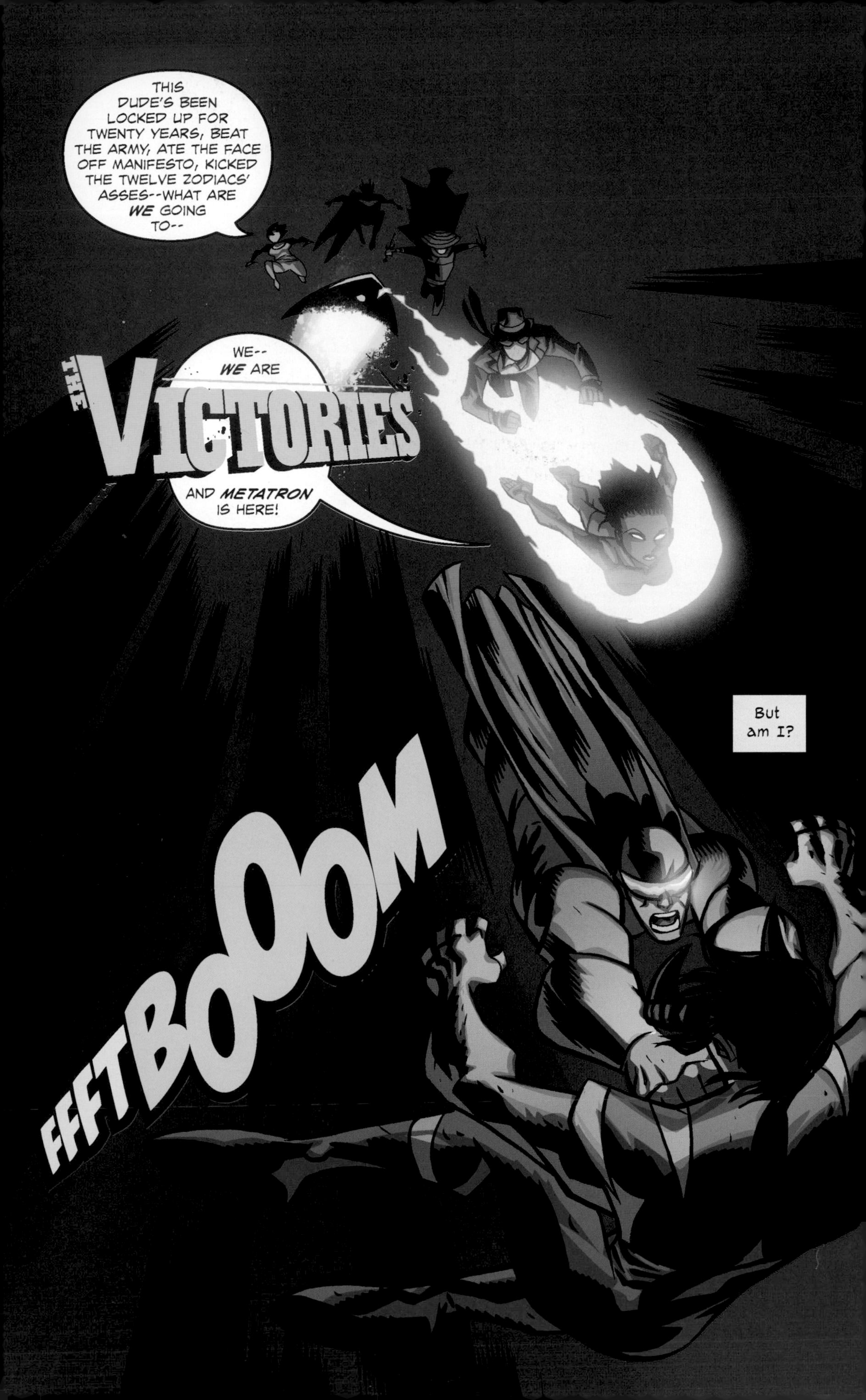
THIS DUDE'S BEEN LOCKED UP FOR TWENTY YEARS, BEAT THE ARMY, ATE THE FACE OFF MANIFESTO, KICKED THE TWELVE ZODIACS' ASSES--WHAT ARE WE GOING TO--
WE-- WE ARE
THE VICTORIES
AND METATRON IS HERE!
But am I?
FFFTBOOOM

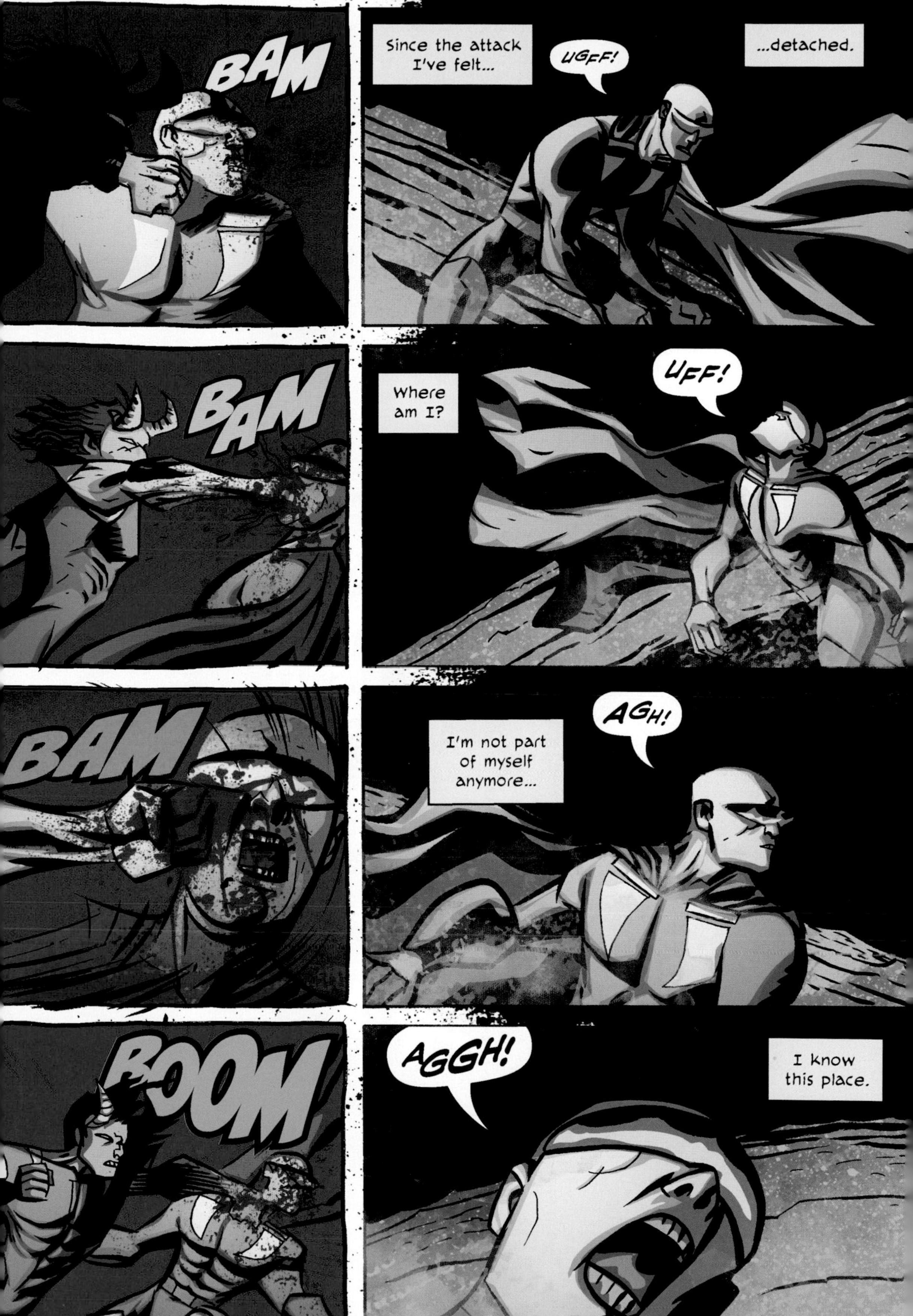
BAM
Since the attack I've felt...
UGFF!
...detached.
BAM
Where am I?
UFF!
BAM
I'm not part of myself anymore...
AGH!
BOOM
AGGH!
I know this place.

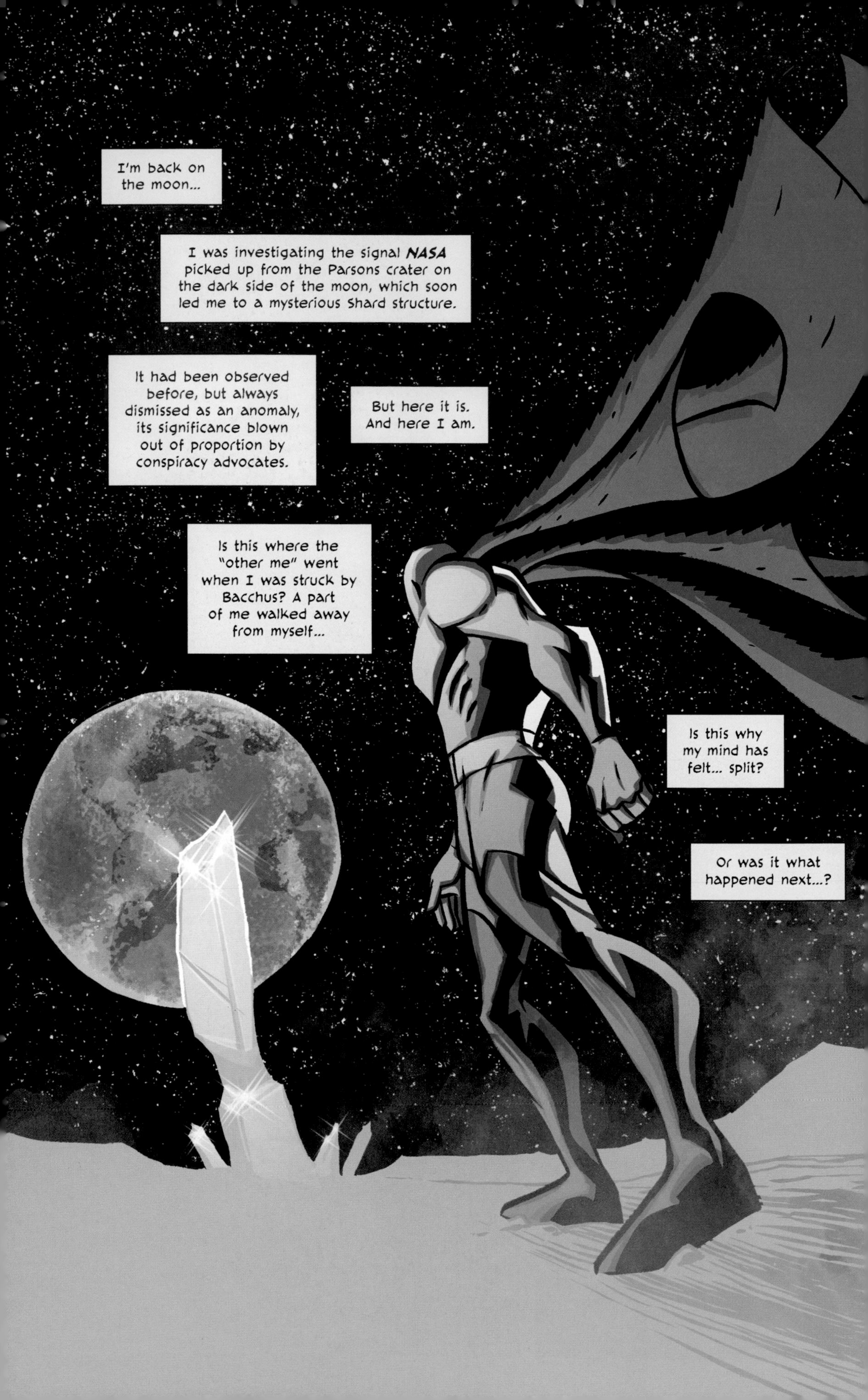
I'm back on the moon...
I was investigating the signal NASA picked up from the Parsons crater on the dark side of the moon, which soon led me to a mysterious Shard structure.
It had been observed before, but always dismissed as an anomaly, its significance blown out of proportion by conspiracy advocates.
But here it is. And here I am.
Is this where the "other me" went when I was struck by Bacchus? A part of me walked away from myself...
Is this why my mind has felt... split?
Or was it what happened next...?

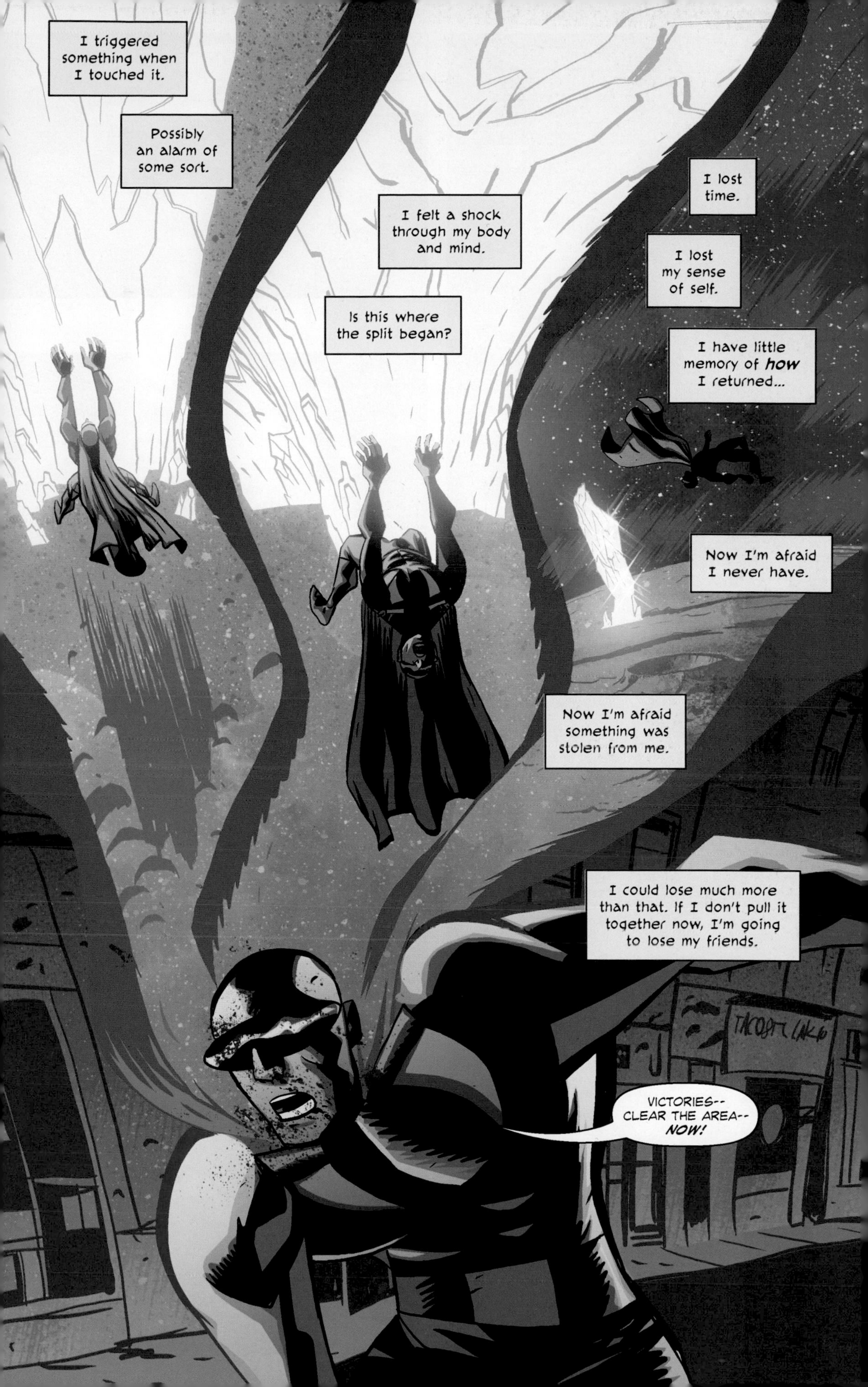
I triggered something when I touched it.
Possibly an alarm of some sort.
I felt a shock through my body and mind.
Is this where the split began?
I lost time.
I lost my sense of self.
I have little memory of *how* I returned...
Now I'm afraid I never have.
Now I'm afraid something was stolen from me.
I could lose much more than that. If I don't pull it together now, I'm going to lose my friends.
VICTORIES-- CLEAR THE AREA-- *NOW!*

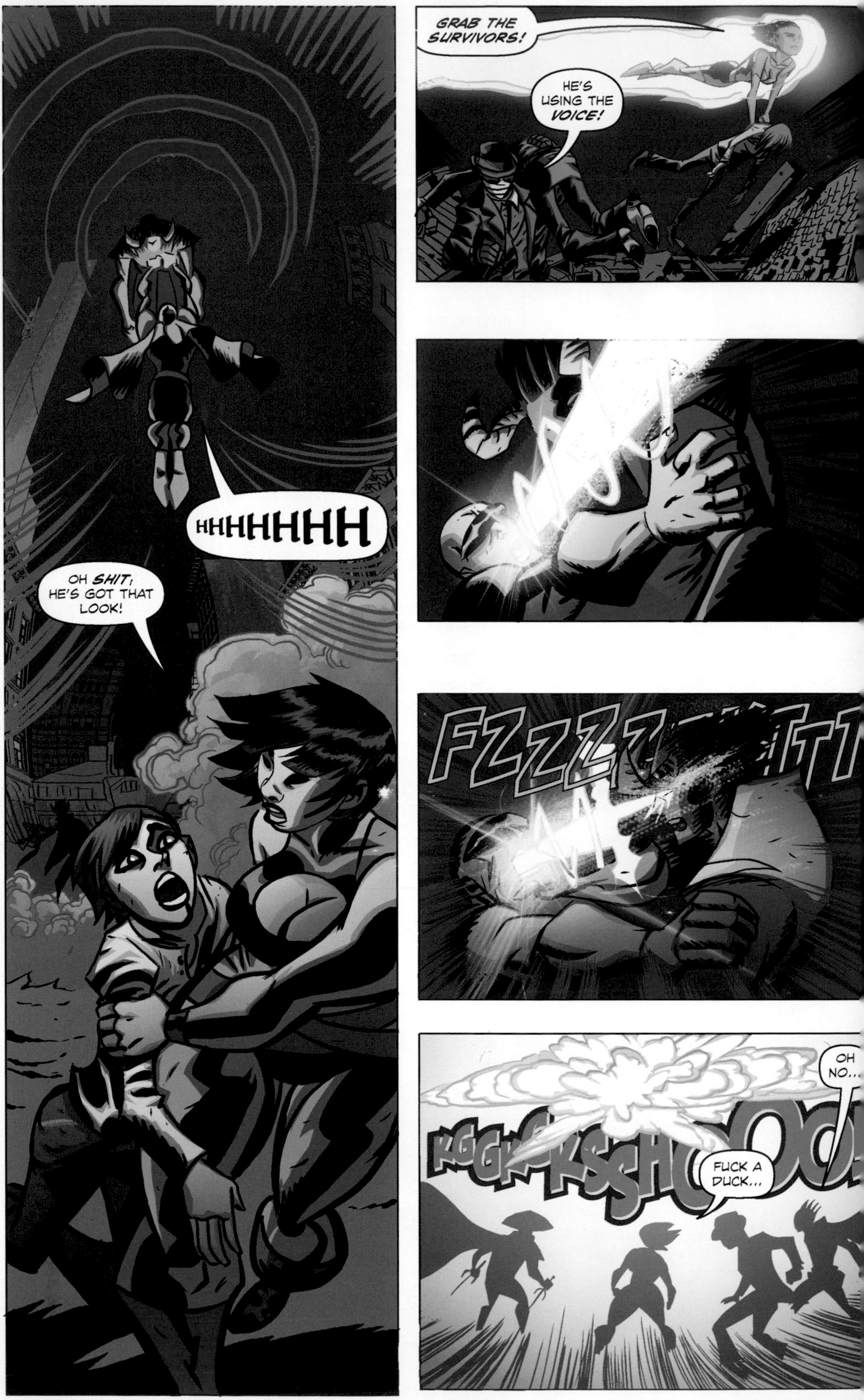
HHHHHHH
OH SHIT, HE'S GOT THAT LOOK!
GRAB THE SURVIVORS!
HE'S USING THE VOICE!
FZZZ
OH NO...
FUCK A DUCK...

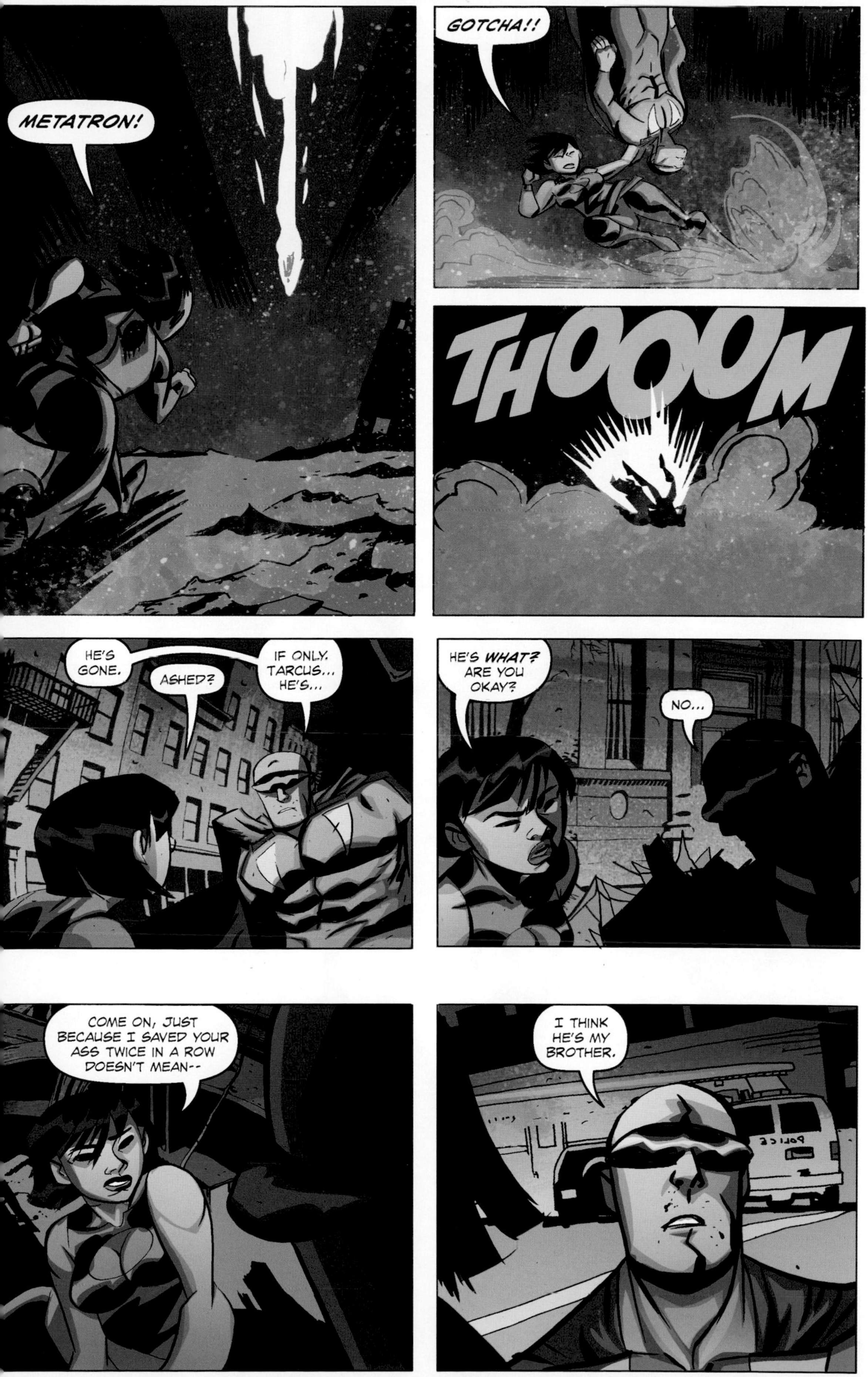
METATRON!
GOTCHA!!
THOOOM
HE'S GONE.
ASHED?
IF ONLY. TARCUS... HE'S...
HE'S WHAT? ARE YOU OKAY?
NO...
COME ON, JUST BECAUSE I SAVED YOUR ASS TWICE IN A ROW DOESN'T MEAN--
I THINK HE'S MY BROTHER.
POLICE

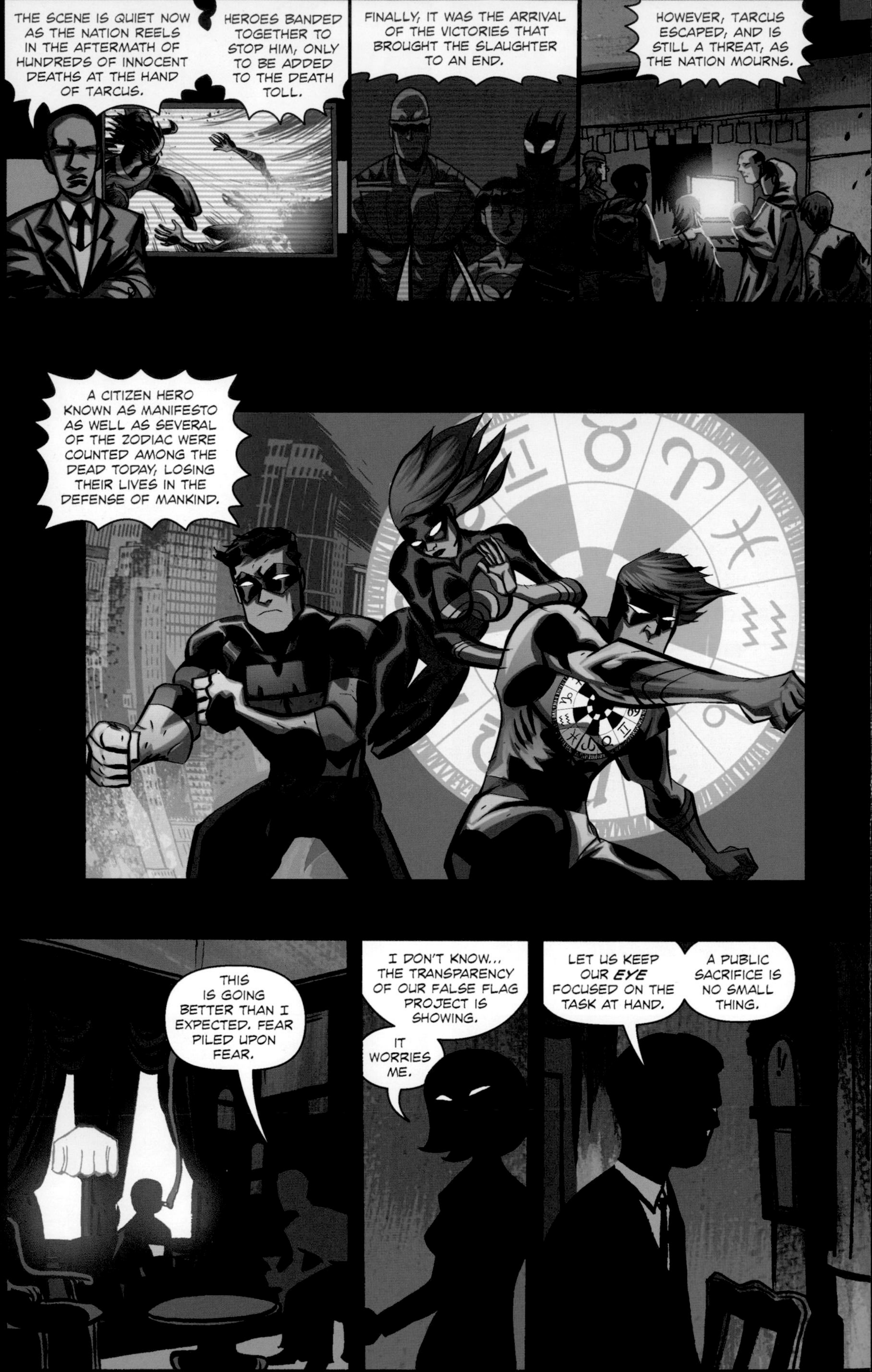

THE SCENE IS QUIET NOW AS THE NATION REELS IN THE AFTERMATH OF HUNDREDS OF INNOCENT DEATHS AT THE HAND OF TARCUS.
HEROES BANDED TOGETHER TO STOP HIM, ONLY TO BE ADDED TO THE DEATH TOLL.
FINALLY, IT WAS THE ARRIVAL OF THE VICTORIES THAT BROUGHT THE SLAUGHTER TO AN END.
HOWEVER, TARCUS ESCAPED, AND IS STILL A THREAT, AS THE NATION MOURNS.
A CITIZEN HERO KNOWN AS MANIFESTO AS WELL AS SEVERAL OF THE ZODIAC WERE COUNTED AMONG THE DEAD TODAY, LOSING THEIR LIVES IN THE DEFENSE OF MANKIND.
THIS IS GOING BETTER THAN I EXPECTED. FEAR PILED UPON FEAR.
I DON'T KNOW... THE TRANSPARENCY OF OUR FALSE FLAG PROJECT IS SHOWING.
IT WORRIES ME.
LET US KEEP OUR *EYE* FOCUSED ON THE TASK AT HAND.
A PUBLIC SACRIFICE IS NO SMALL THING.

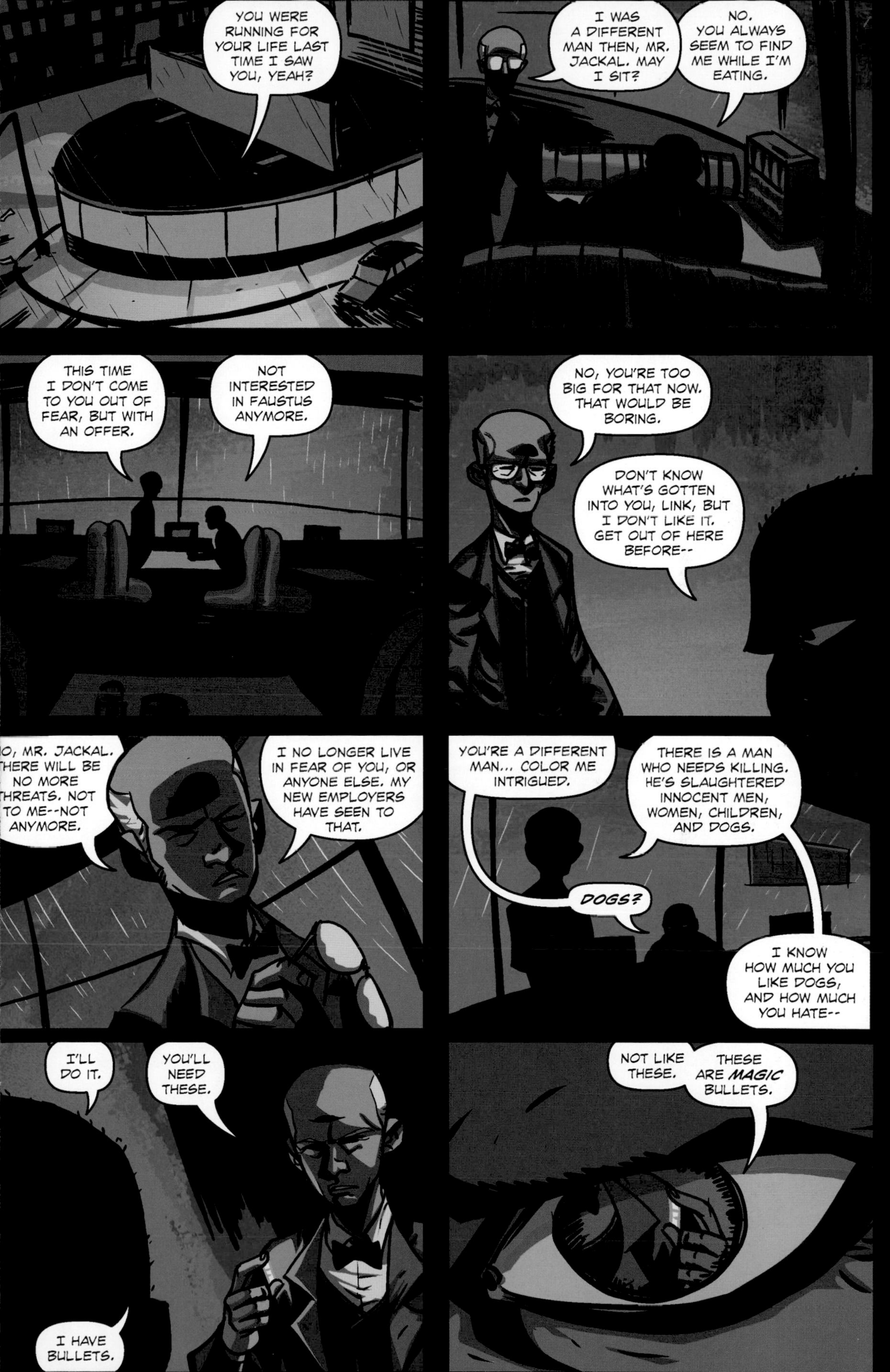
YOU WERE RUNNING FOR YOUR LIFE LAST TIME I SAW YOU, YEAH?
I WAS A DIFFERENT MAN THEN, MR. JACKAL. MAY I SIT?
NO. YOU ALWAYS SEEM TO FIND ME WHILE I'M EATING.
THIS TIME I DON'T COME TO YOU OUT OF FEAR, BUT WITH AN OFFER.
NOT INTERESTED IN FAUSTUS ANYMORE.
NO, YOU'RE TOO BIG FOR THAT NOW. THAT WOULD BE BORING.
DON'T KNOW WHAT'S GOTTEN INTO YOU, LINK, BUT I DON'T LIKE IT. GET OUT OF HERE BEFORE--
O, MR. JACKAL. HERE WILL BE NO MORE HREATS. NOT TO ME--NOT ANYMORE.
I NO LONGER LIVE IN FEAR OF YOU, OR ANYONE ELSE. MY NEW EMPLOYERS HAVE SEEN TO THAT.
YOU'RE A DIFFERENT MAN... COLOR ME INTRIGUED.
THERE IS A MAN WHO NEEDS KILLING. HE'S SLAUGHTERED INNOCENT MEN, WOMEN, CHILDREN, AND DOGS.
DOGS?
I KNOW HOW MUCH YOU LIKE DOGS, AND HOW MUCH YOU HATE--
I'LL DO IT.
YOU'LL NEED THESE.
I HAVE BULLETS.
NOT LIKE THESE.
THESE ARE MAGIC BULLETS.

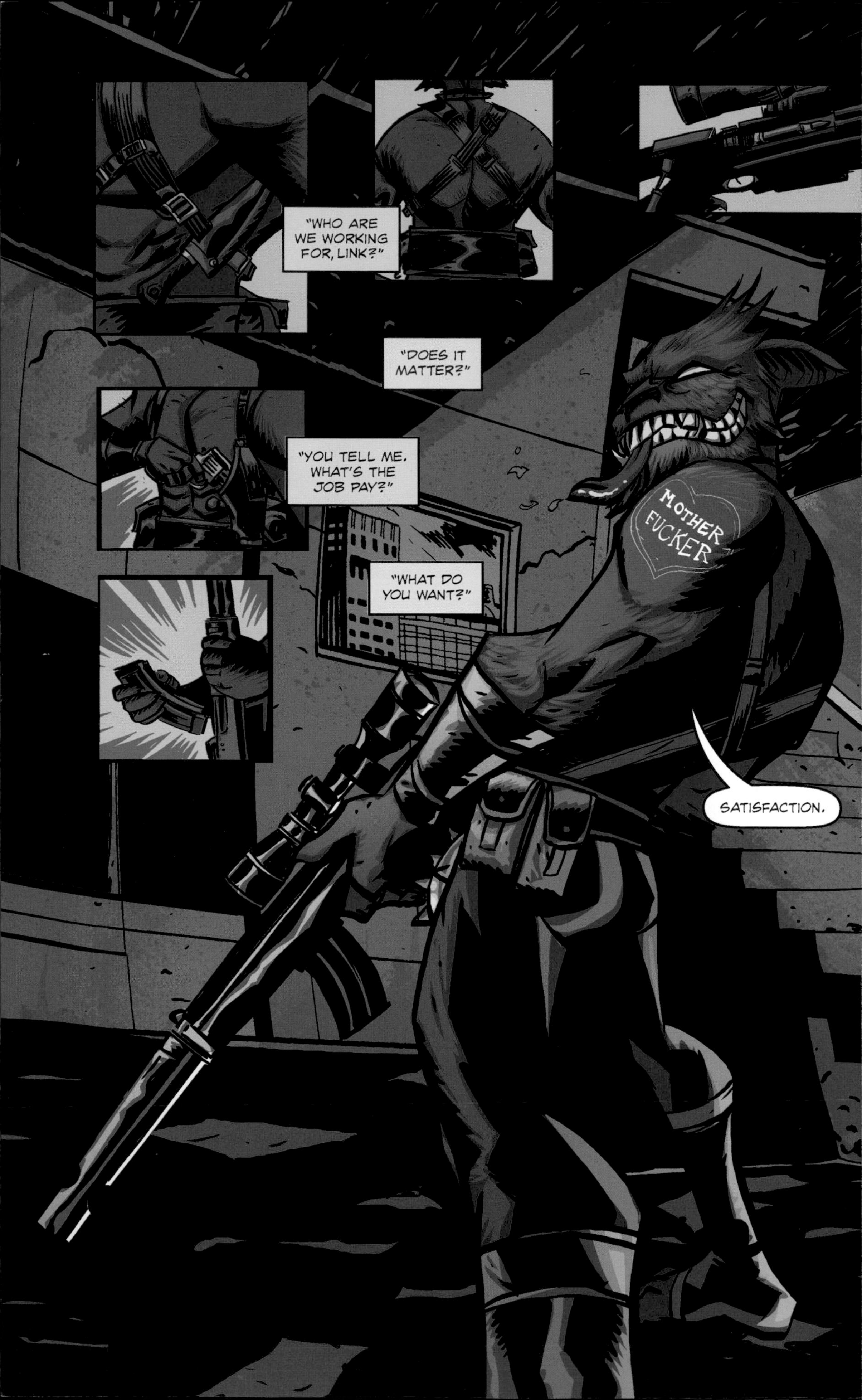
"WHO ARE WE WORKING FOR, LINK?"
"DOES IT MATTER?"
"YOU TELL ME. WHAT'S THE JOB PAY?"
"WHAT DO YOU WANT?"
MOTHER FUCKER
SATISFACTION.

CHAPTER FOUR

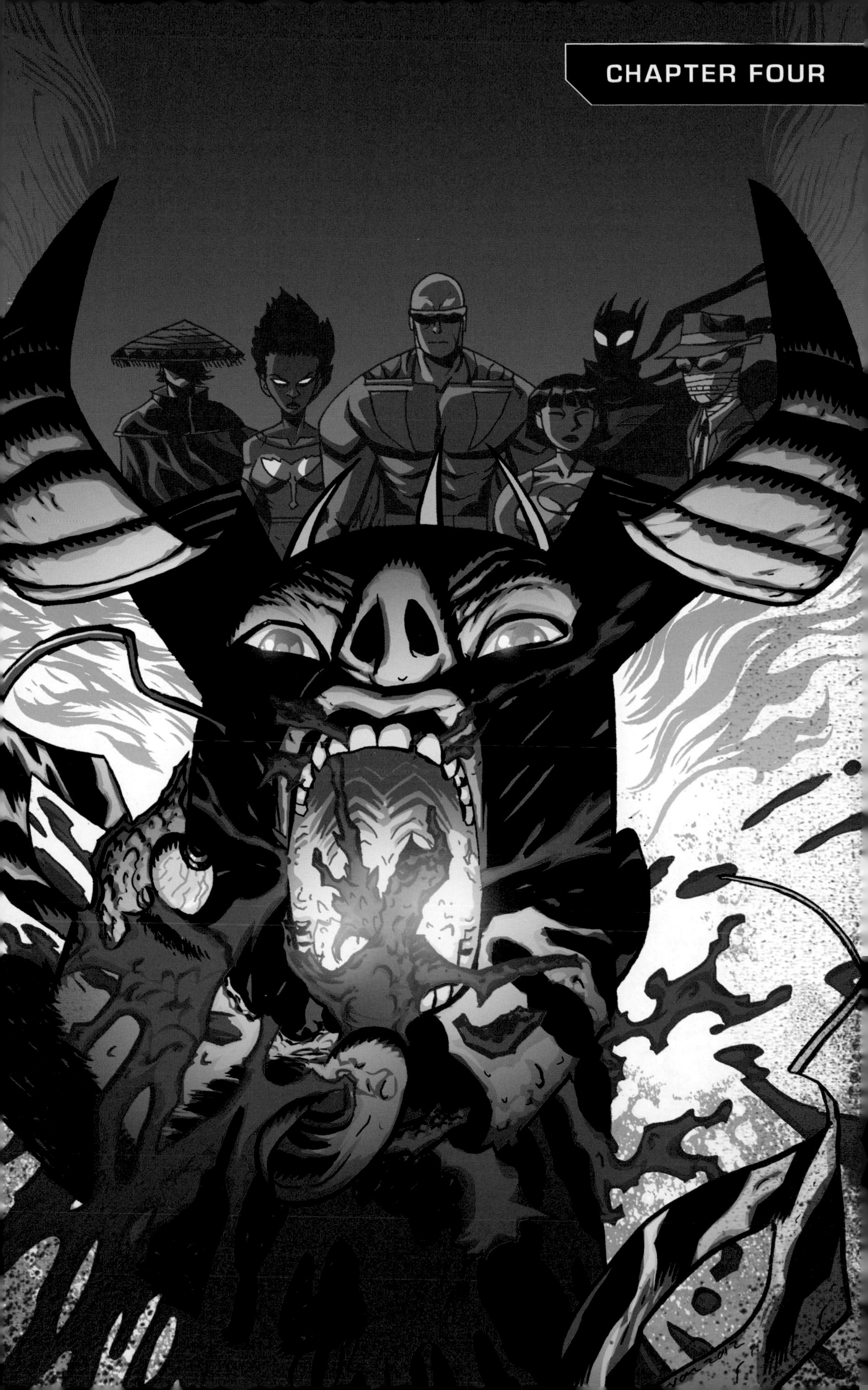

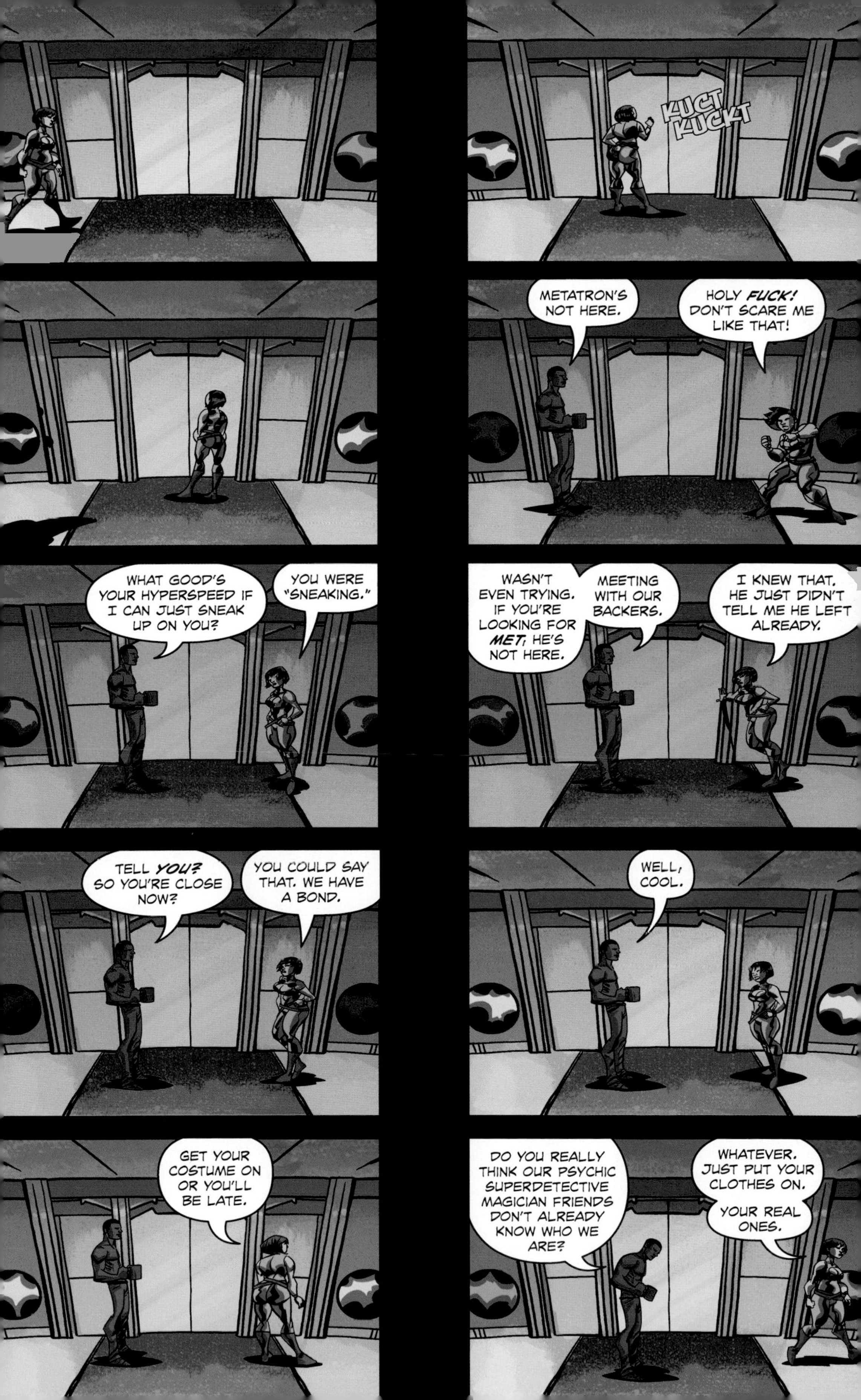
KUCT KUCKT
METATRON'S NOT HERE.
HOLY FUCK! DON'T SCARE ME LIKE THAT!
WHAT GOOD'S YOUR HYPERSPEED IF I CAN JUST SNEAK UP ON YOU?
YOU WERE "SNEAKING."
WASN'T EVEN TRYING. IF YOU'RE LOOKING FOR MET, HE'S NOT HERE.
MEETING WITH OUR BACKERS.
I KNEW THAT. HE JUST DIDN'T TELL ME HE LEFT ALREADY.
TELL YOU? SO YOU'RE CLOSE NOW?
YOU COULD SAY THAT. WE HAVE A BOND.
WELL, COOL.
GET YOUR COSTUME ON OR YOU'LL BE LATE.
DO YOU REALLY THINK OUR PSYCHIC SUPERDETECTIVE MAGICIAN FRIENDS DON'T ALREADY KNOW WHO WE ARE?
WHATEVER. JUST PUT YOUR CLOTHES ON.
YOUR REAL ONES.

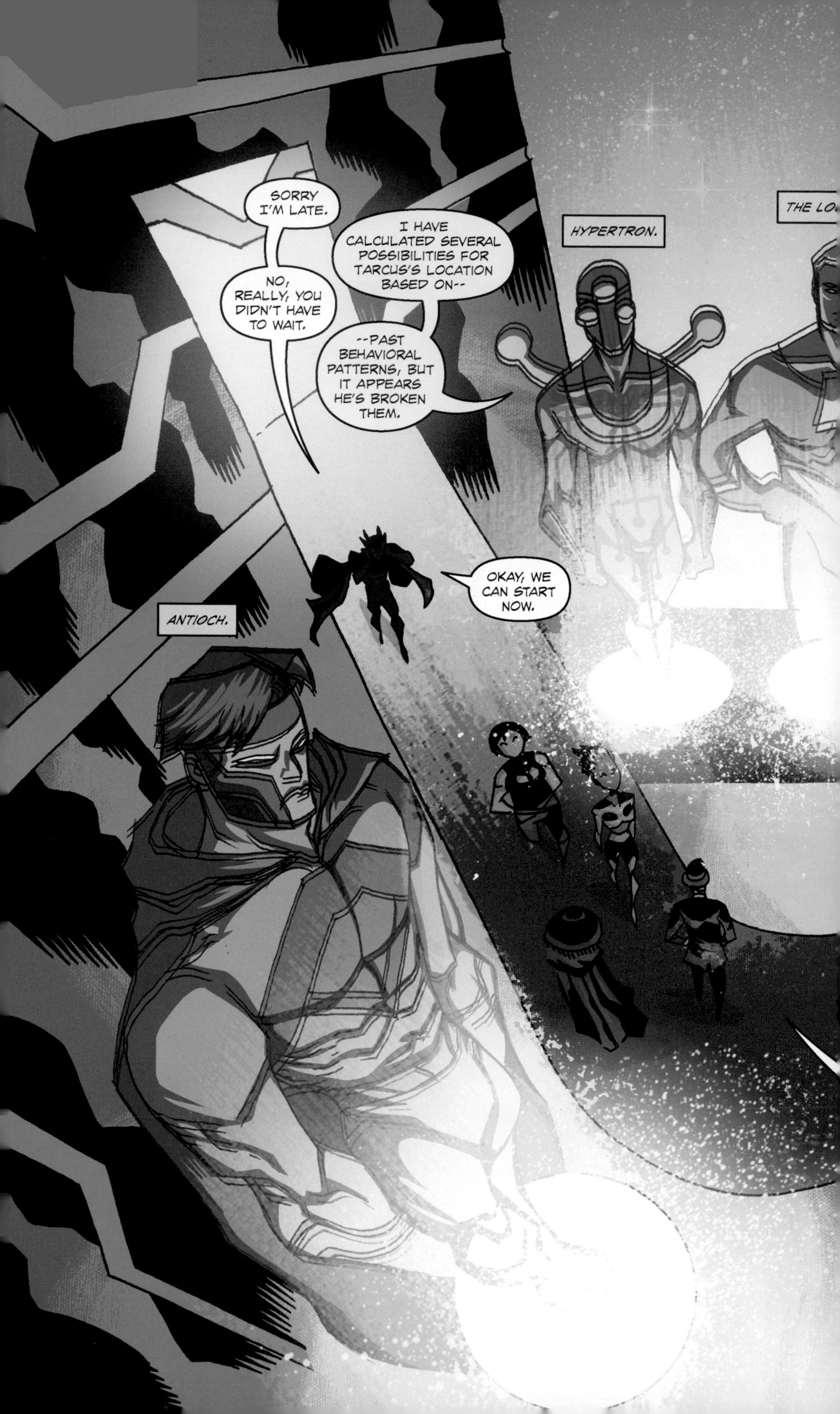
SORRY I'M LATE.
NO, REALLY, YOU DIDN'T HAVE TO WAIT.
I HAVE CALCULATED SEVERAL POSSIBILITIES FOR TARCUS'S LOCATION BASED ON--
--PAST BEHAVIORAL PATTERNS, BUT IT APPEARS HE'S BROKEN THEM.
HYPERTRON.
OKAY, WE CAN START NOW.
ANTIOCH.

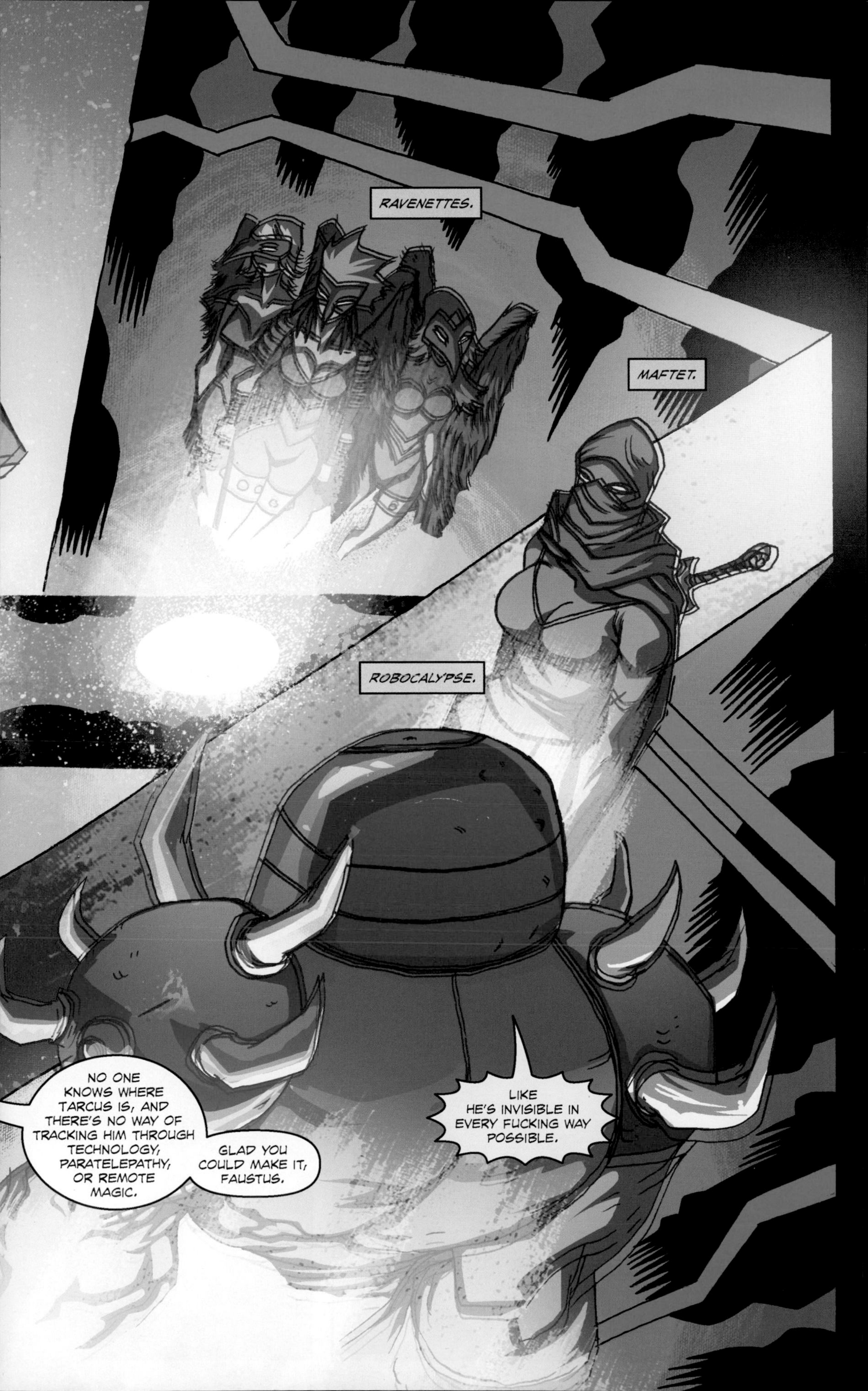
RAVENETTES.
MAFTET.
ROBOCALYPSE.
NO ONE KNOWS WHERE TARCUS IS, AND THERE'S NO WAY OF TRACKING HIM THROUGH TECHNOLOGY, PARATELEPATHY, OR REMOTE MAGIC.
GLAD YOU COULD MAKE IT, FAUSTUS.
LIKE HE'S INVISIBLE IN EVERY FUCKING WAY POSSIBLE.

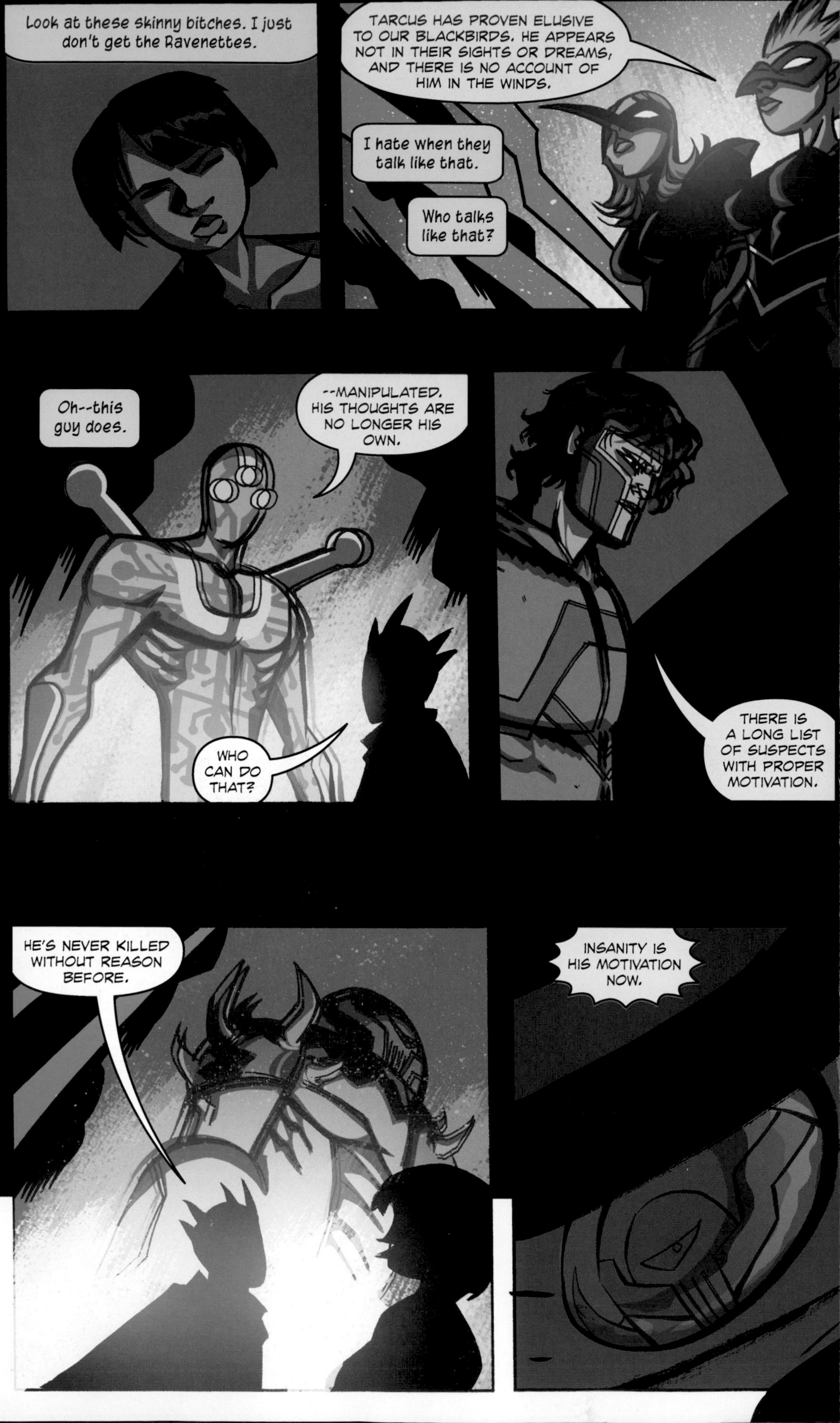
Look at these skinny bitches. I just don't get the Ravenettes.
TARCUS HAS PROVEN ELUSIVE TO OUR BLACKBIRDS. HE APPEARS NOT IN THEIR SIGHTS OR DREAMS, AND THERE IS NO ACCOUNT OF HIM IN THE WINDS.
I hate when they talk like that.
Who talks like that?
Oh--this guy does.
--MANIPULATED. HIS THOUGHTS ARE NO LONGER HIS OWN.
WHO CAN DO THAT?
THERE IS A LONG LIST OF SUSPECTS WITH PROPER MOTIVATION.
HE'S NEVER KILLED WITHOUT REASON BEFORE.
INSANITY IS HIS MOTIVATION NOW.

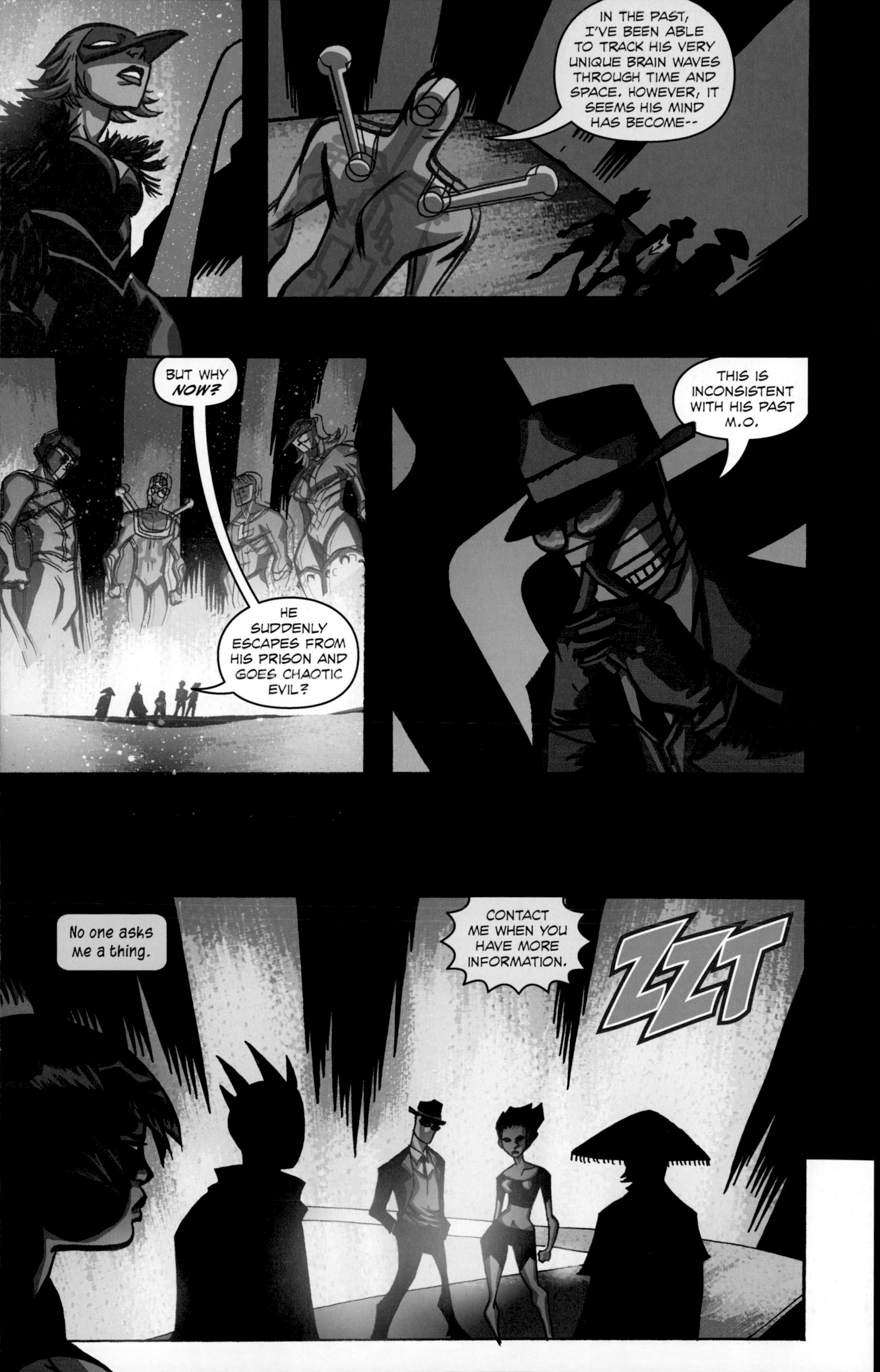
IN THE PAST, I'VE BEEN ABLE TO TRACK HIS VERY UNIQUE BRAIN WAVES THROUGH TIME AND SPACE. HOWEVER, IT SEEMS HIS MIND HAS BECOME--
BUT WHY *NOW?*
HE SUDDENLY ESCAPES FROM HIS PRISON AND GOES CHAOTIC EVIL?
THIS IS INCONSISTENT WITH HIS PAST M.O.
No one asks me a thing.
CONTACT ME WHEN YOU HAVE MORE INFORMATION.
ZZT

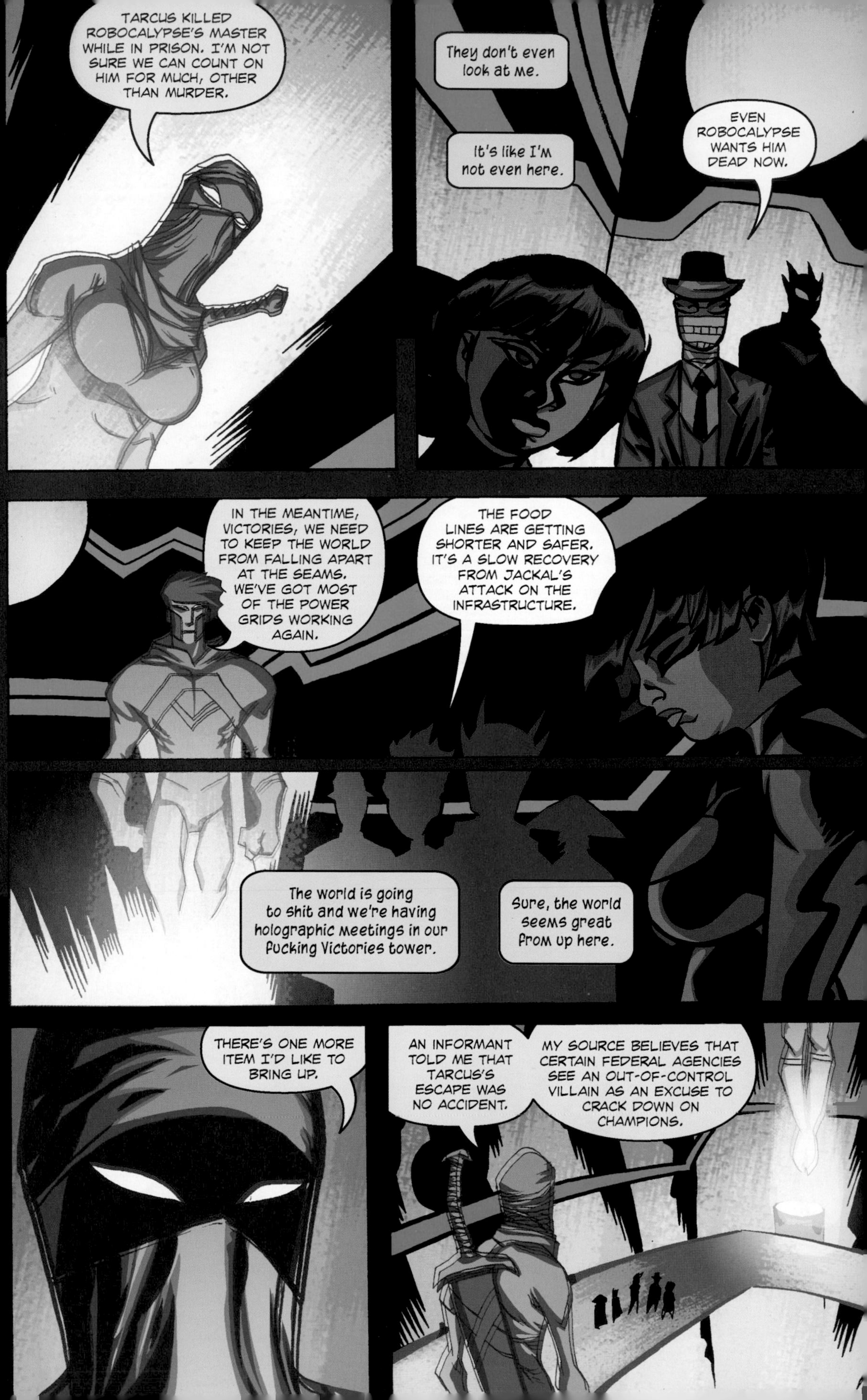
TARCUS KILLED ROBOCALYPSE'S MASTER WHILE IN PRISON. I'M NOT SURE WE CAN COUNT ON HIM FOR MUCH, OTHER THAN MURDER.
They don't even look at me.
It's like I'm not even here.
EVEN ROBOCALYPSE WANTS HIM DEAD NOW.
IN THE MEANTIME, VICTORIES, WE NEED TO KEEP THE WORLD FROM FALLING APART AT THE SEAMS. WE'VE GOT MOST OF THE POWER GRIDS WORKING AGAIN.
THE FOOD LINES ARE GETTING SHORTER AND SAFER. IT'S A SLOW RECOVERY FROM JACKAL'S ATTACK ON THE INFRASTRUCTURE.
The world is going to shit and we're having holographic meetings in our fucking Victories tower.
Sure, the world seems great from up here.
THERE'S ONE MORE ITEM I'D LIKE TO BRING UP.
AN INFORMANT TOLD ME THAT TARCUS'S ESCAPE WAS NO ACCIDENT.
MY SOURCE BELIEVES THAT CERTAIN FEDERAL AGENCIES SEE AN OUT-OF-CONTROL VILLAIN AS AN EXCUSE TO CRACK DOWN ON CHAMPIONS.

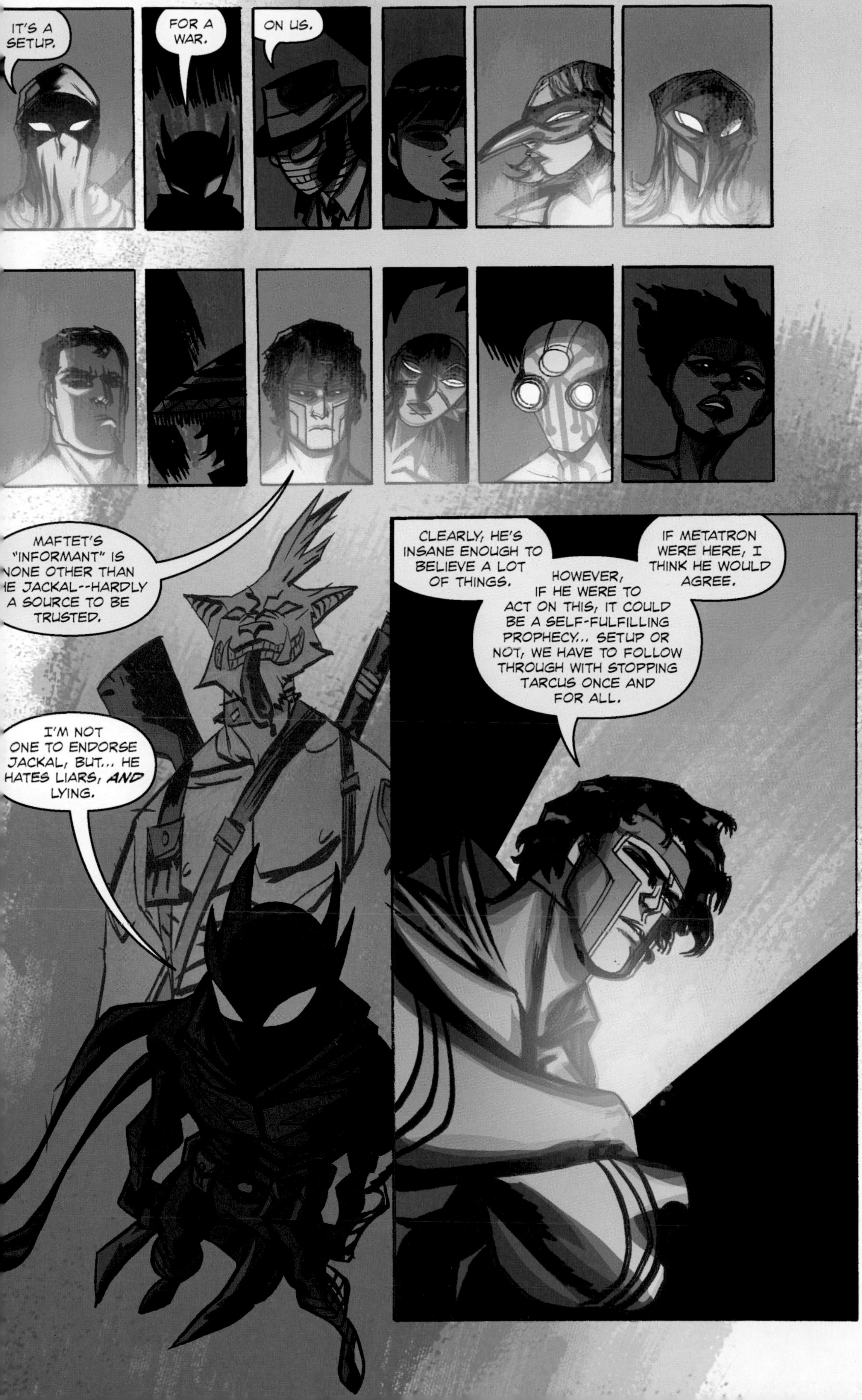

IT'S A SETUP.
FOR A WAR.
ON US.
MAFTET'S "INFORMANT" IS NONE OTHER THAN HE JACKAL--HARDLY A SOURCE TO BE TRUSTED.
I'M NOT ONE TO ENDORSE JACKAL, BUT... HE HATES LIARS, AND LYING.
CLEARLY, HE'S INSANE ENOUGH TO BELIEVE A LOT OF THINGS.
IF METATRON WERE HERE, I THINK HE WOULD AGREE.
HOWEVER, IF HE WERE TO ACT ON THIS, IT COULD BE A SELF-FULFILLING PROPHECY... SETUP OR NOT, WE HAVE TO FOLLOW THROUGH WITH STOPPING TARCUS ONCE AND FOR ALL.

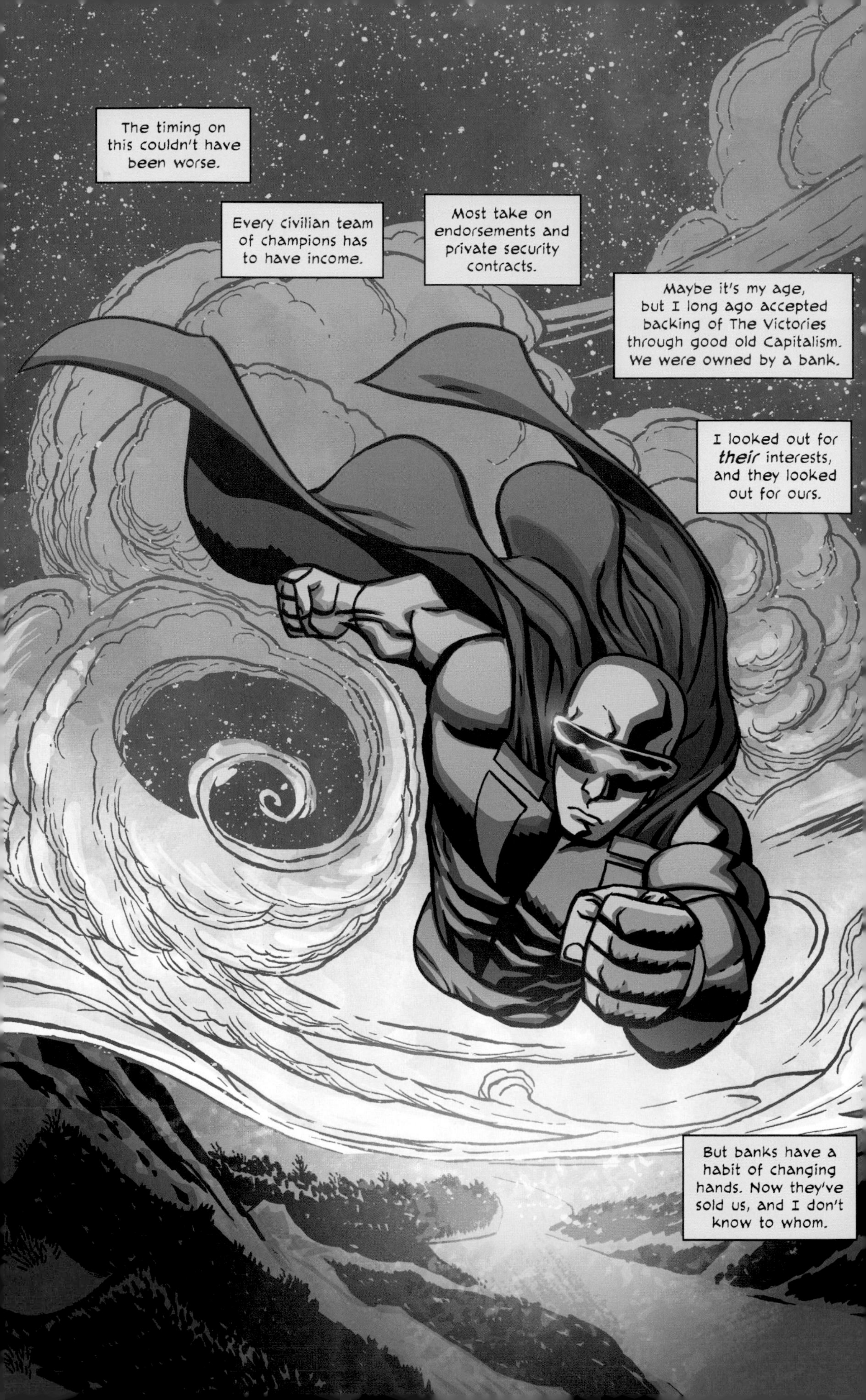

The timing on this couldn't have been worse.
Every civilian team of champions has to have income.
Most take on endorsements and private security contracts.
Maybe it's my age, but I long ago accepted backing of The Victories through good old Capitalism. We were owned by a bank.
I looked out for *their* interests, and they looked out for ours.
But banks have a habit of changing hands. Now they've sold us, and I don't know to whom.

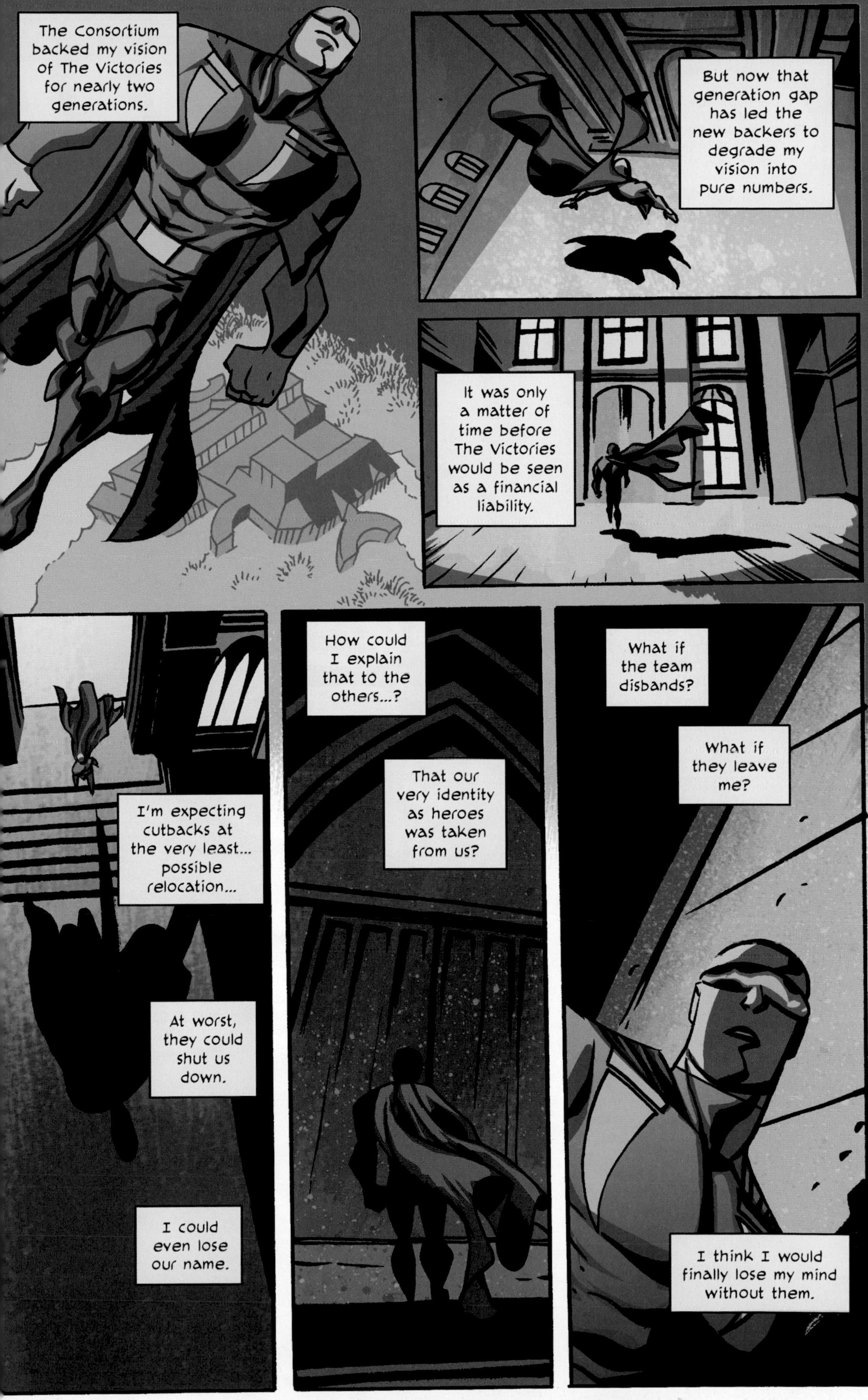
The Consortium backed my vision of The Victories for nearly two generations.
But now that generation gap has led the new backers to degrade my vision into pure numbers.
It was only a matter of time before The Victories would be seen as a financial liability.
I'm expecting cutbacks at the very least... possible relocation...
At worst, they could shut us down.
I could even lose our name.
How could I explain that to the others...?
That our very identity as heroes was taken from us?
What if the team disbands?
What if they leave me?
I think I would finally lose my mind without them.

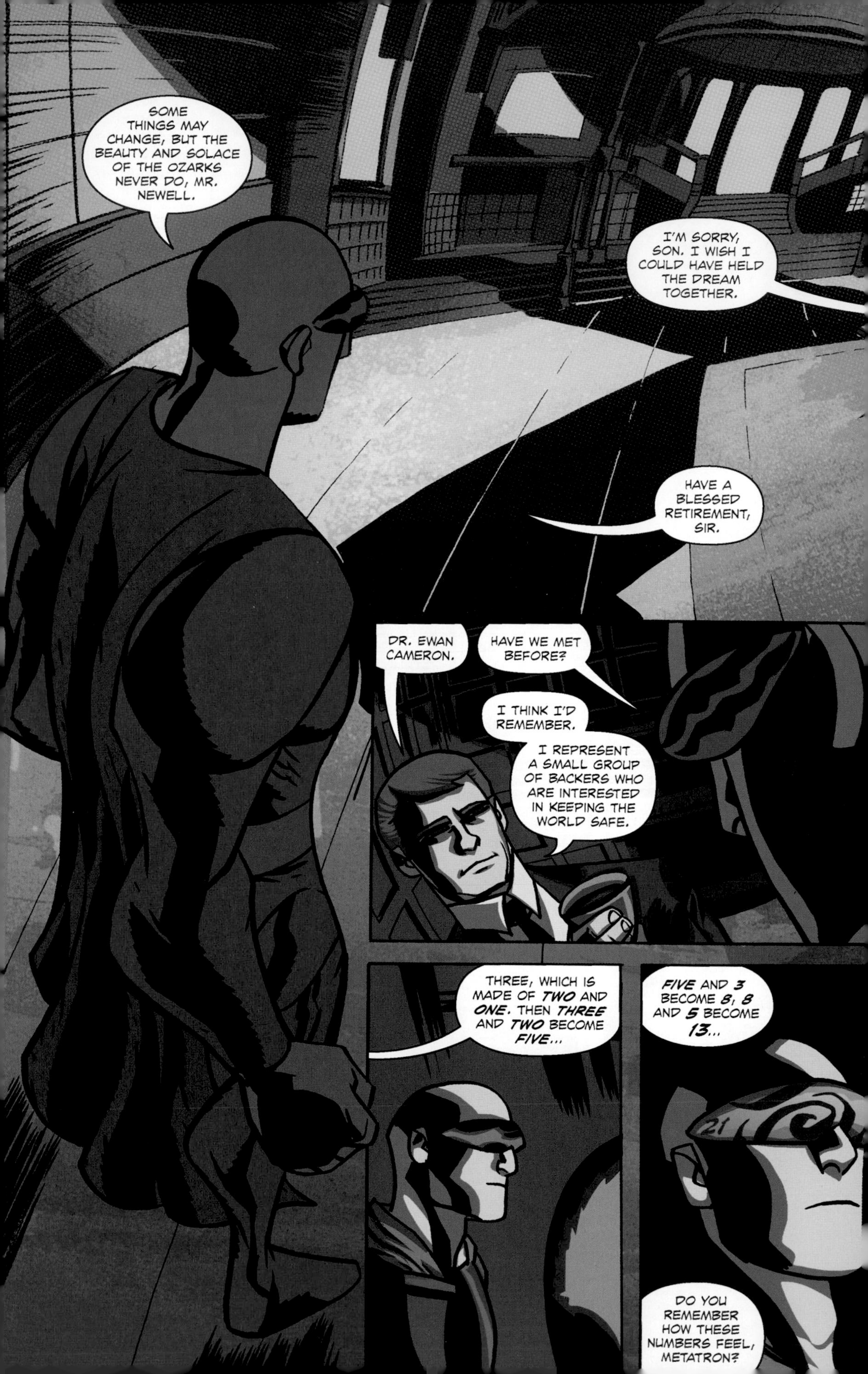
SOME THINGS MAY CHANGE, BUT THE BEAUTY AND SOLACE OF THE OZARKS NEVER DO, MR. NEWELL.
I'M SORRY, SON. I WISH I COULD HAVE HELD THE DREAM TOGETHER.
HAVE A BLESSED RETIREMENT, SIR.
DR. EWAN CAMERON.
HAVE WE MET BEFORE?
I THINK I'D REMEMBER.
I REPRESENT A SMALL GROUP OF BACKERS WHO ARE INTERESTED IN KEEPING THE WORLD SAFE.
THREE, WHICH IS MADE OF *TWO* AND *ONE*. THEN *THREE* AND *TWO* BECOME *FIVE*...
FIVE AND *3* BECOME *8*, *8* AND *5* BECOME *13*...
DO YOU REMEMBER HOW THESE NUMBERS FEEL, METATRON?

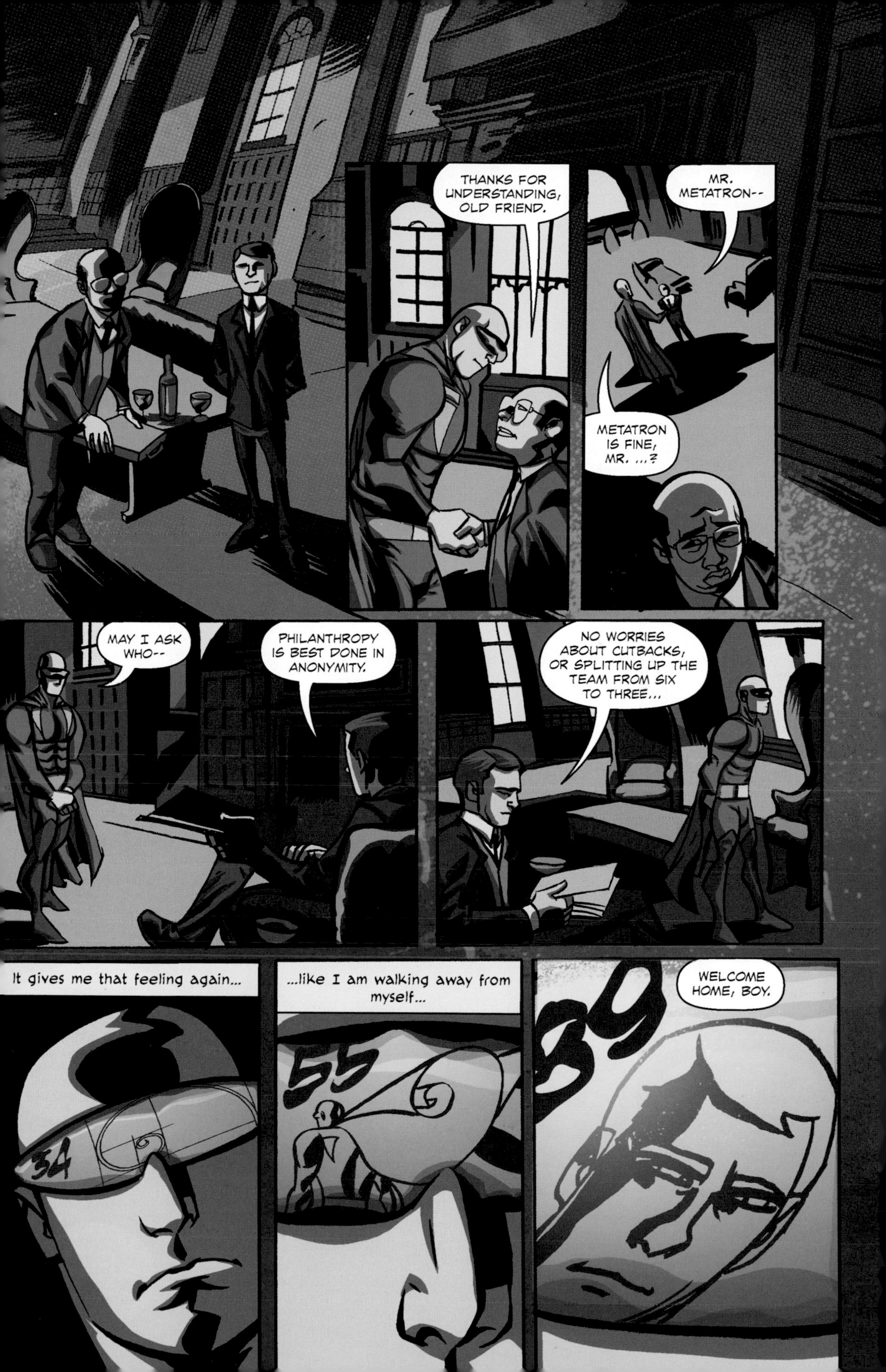
THANKS FOR UNDERSTANDING, OLD FRIEND.
MR. METATRON--
METATRON IS FINE, MR. ...?
MAY I ASK WHO--
PHILANTHROPY IS BEST DONE IN ANONYMITY.
NO WORRIES ABOUT CUTBACKS, OR SPLITTING UP THE TEAM FROM SIX TO THREE...
It gives me that feeling again...
...like I am walking away from myself...
WELCOME HOME, BOY.

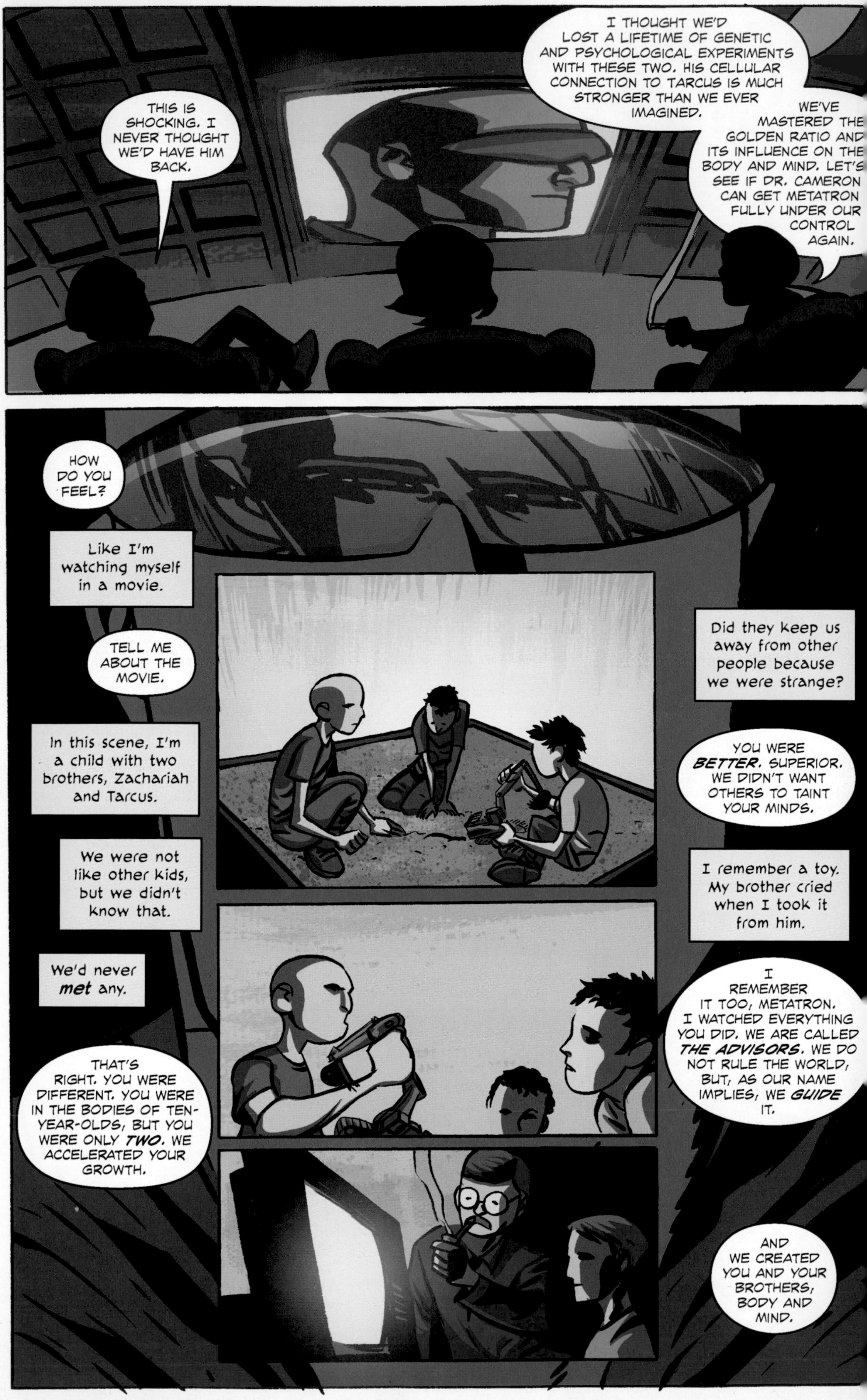

THIS IS SHOCKING. I NEVER THOUGHT WE'D HAVE HIM BACK.
I THOUGHT WE'D LOST A LIFETIME OF GENETIC AND PSYCHOLOGICAL EXPERIMENTS WITH THESE TWO. HIS CELLULAR CONNECTION TO TARCUS IS MUCH STRONGER THAN WE EVER IMAGINED.
WE'VE MASTERED THE GOLDEN RATIO AND ITS INFLUENCE ON THE BODY AND MIND. LET'S SEE IF DR. CAMERON CAN GET METATRON FULLY UNDER OUR CONTROL AGAIN.
HOW DO YOU FEEL?
Like I'm watching myself in a movie.
TELL ME ABOUT THE MOVIE.
In this scene, I'm a child with two brothers, Zachariah and Tarcus.
We were not like other kids, but we didn't know that.
We'd never *met* any.
THAT'S RIGHT. YOU WERE DIFFERENT. YOU WERE IN THE BODIES OF TEN-YEAR-OLDS, BUT YOU WERE ONLY *TWO*. WE ACCELERATED YOUR GROWTH.
Did they keep us away from other people because we were strange?
YOU WERE ***BETTER***. SUPERIOR. WE DIDN'T WANT OTHERS TO TAINT YOUR MINDS.
I remember a toy. My brother cried when I took it from him.
I REMEMBER IT TOO, METATRON. I WATCHED EVERYTHING YOU DID. WE ARE CALLED ***THE ADVISORS***. WE DO NOT RULE THE WORLD, BUT, AS OUR NAME IMPLIES, WE ***GUIDE*** IT.
AND WE CREATED YOU AND YOUR BROTHERS, BODY AND MIND.

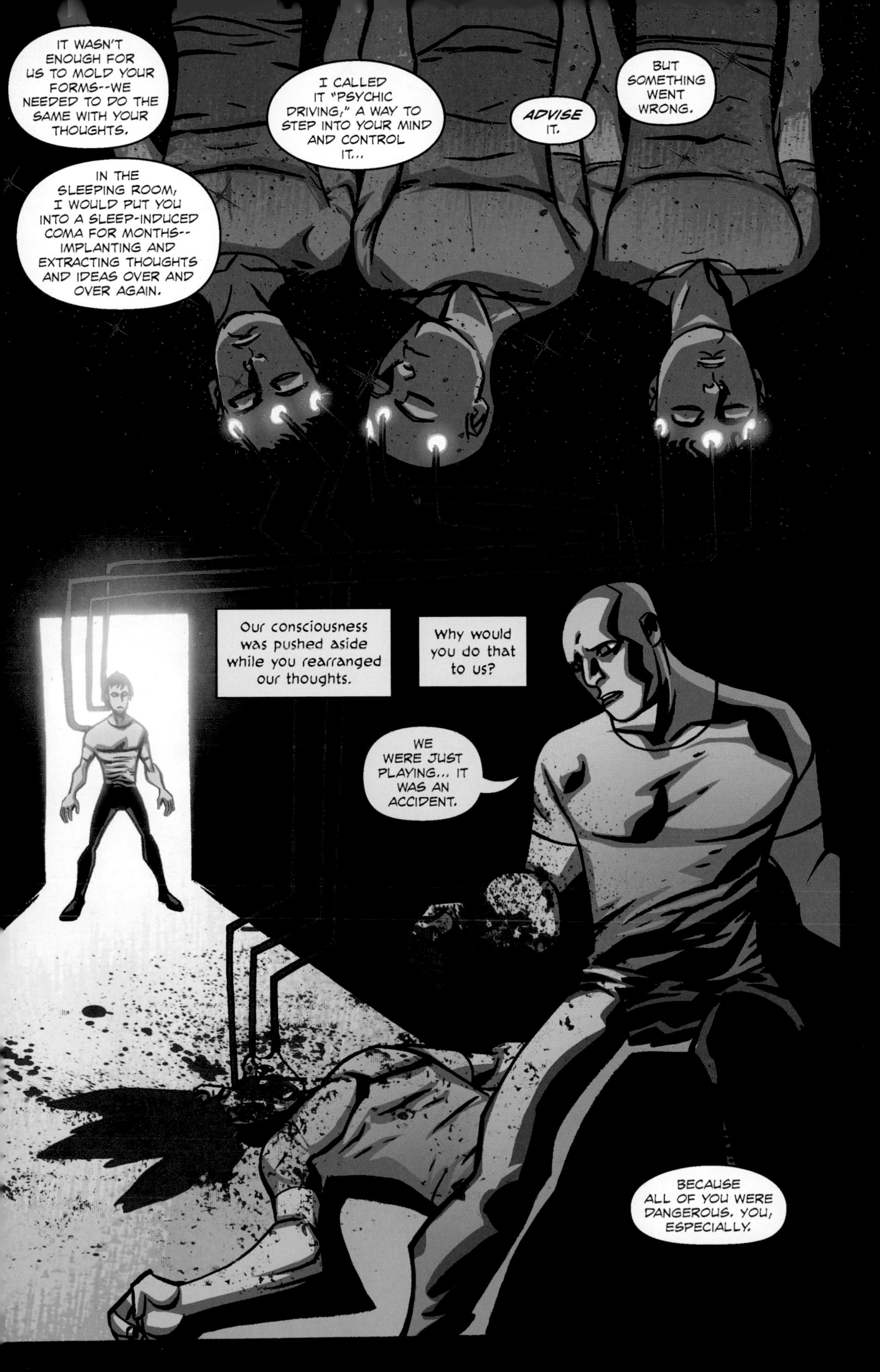
IT WASN'T ENOUGH FOR US TO MOLD YOUR FORMS--WE NEEDED TO DO THE SAME WITH YOUR THOUGHTS.
IN THE SLEEPING ROOM, I WOULD PUT YOU INTO A SLEEP-INDUCED COMA FOR MONTHS-- IMPLANTING AND EXTRACTING THOUGHTS AND IDEAS OVER AND OVER AGAIN.
I CALLED IT "PSYCHIC DRIVING," A WAY TO STEP INTO YOUR MIND AND CONTROL IT...
ADVISE IT.
BUT SOMETHING WENT WRONG.
Our consciousness was pushed aside while you rearranged our thoughts.
Why would you do that to us?
WE WERE JUST PLAYING... IT WAS AN ACCIDENT.
BECAUSE ALL OF YOU WERE DANGEROUS. YOU, ESPECIALLY.

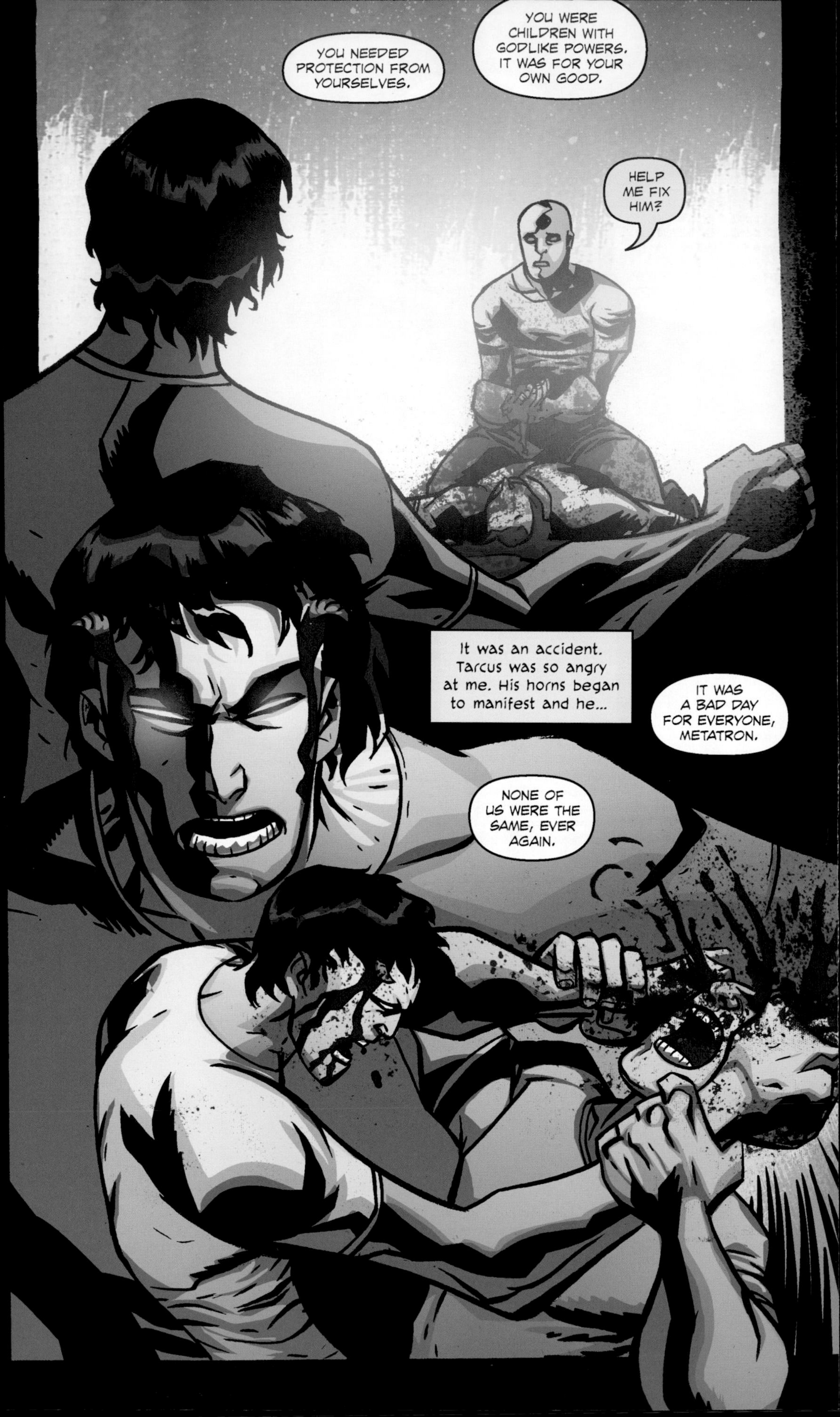
YOU NEEDED PROTECTION FROM YOURSELVES.
YOU WERE CHILDREN WITH GODLIKE POWERS. IT WAS FOR YOUR OWN GOOD.
HELP ME FIX HIM?
It was an accident. Tarcus was so angry at me. His horns began to manifest and he...
IT WAS A BAD DAY FOR EVERYONE, METATRON.
NONE OF US WERE THE SAME, EVER AGAIN.

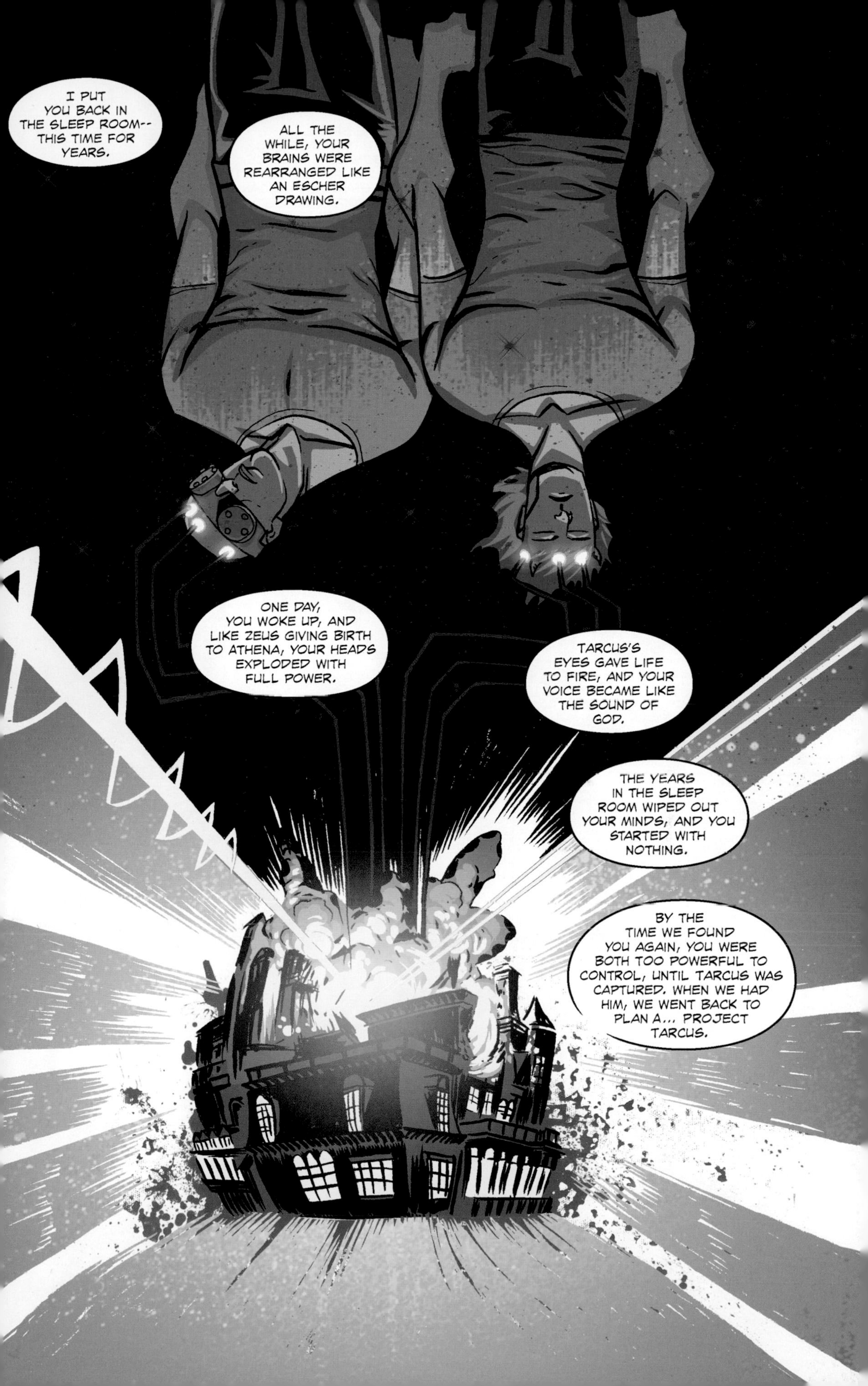
I PUT YOU BACK IN THE SLEEP ROOM-- THIS TIME FOR YEARS.
ALL THE WHILE, YOUR BRAINS WERE REARRANGED LIKE AN ESCHER DRAWING.
ONE DAY, YOU WOKE UP, AND LIKE ZEUS GIVING BIRTH TO ATHENA, YOUR HEADS EXPLODED WITH FULL POWER.
TARCUS'S EYES GAVE LIFE TO FIRE, AND YOUR VOICE BECAME LIKE THE SOUND OF GOD.
THE YEARS IN THE SLEEP ROOM WIPED OUT YOUR MINDS, AND YOU STARTED WITH NOTHING.
BY THE TIME WE FOUND YOU AGAIN, YOU WERE BOTH TOO POWERFUL TO CONTROL, UNTIL TARCUS WAS CAPTURED. WHEN WE HAD HIM, WE WENT BACK TO PLAN A... PROJECT TARCUS.

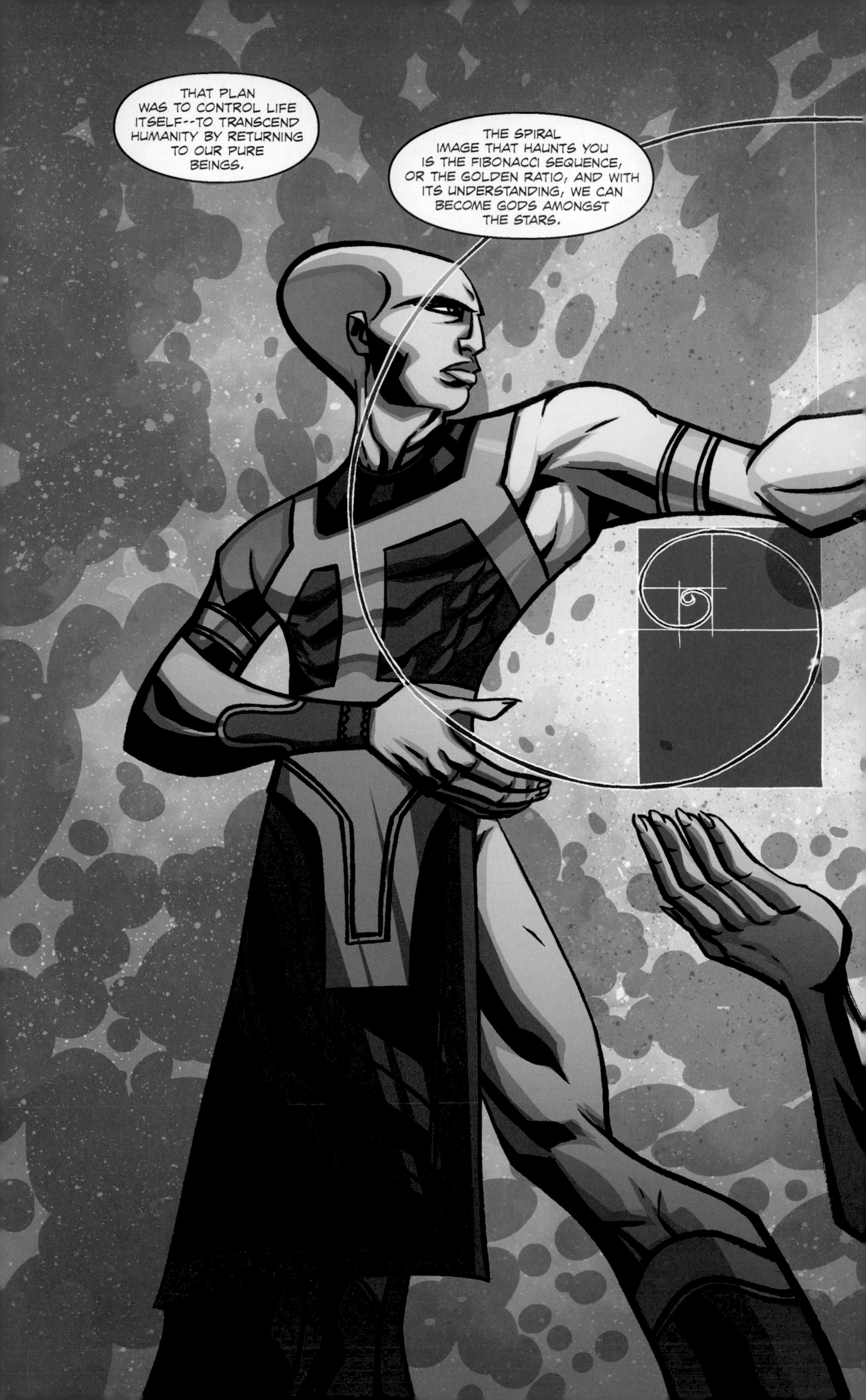
THAT PLAN WAS TO CONTROL LIFE ITSELF--TO TRANSCEND HUMANITY BY RETURNING TO OUR PURE BEINGS.
THE SPIRAL IMAGE THAT HAUNTS YOU IS THE FIBONACCI SEQUENCE, OR THE GOLDEN RATIO, AND WITH ITS UNDERSTANDING, WE CAN BECOME GODS AMONGST THE STARS.

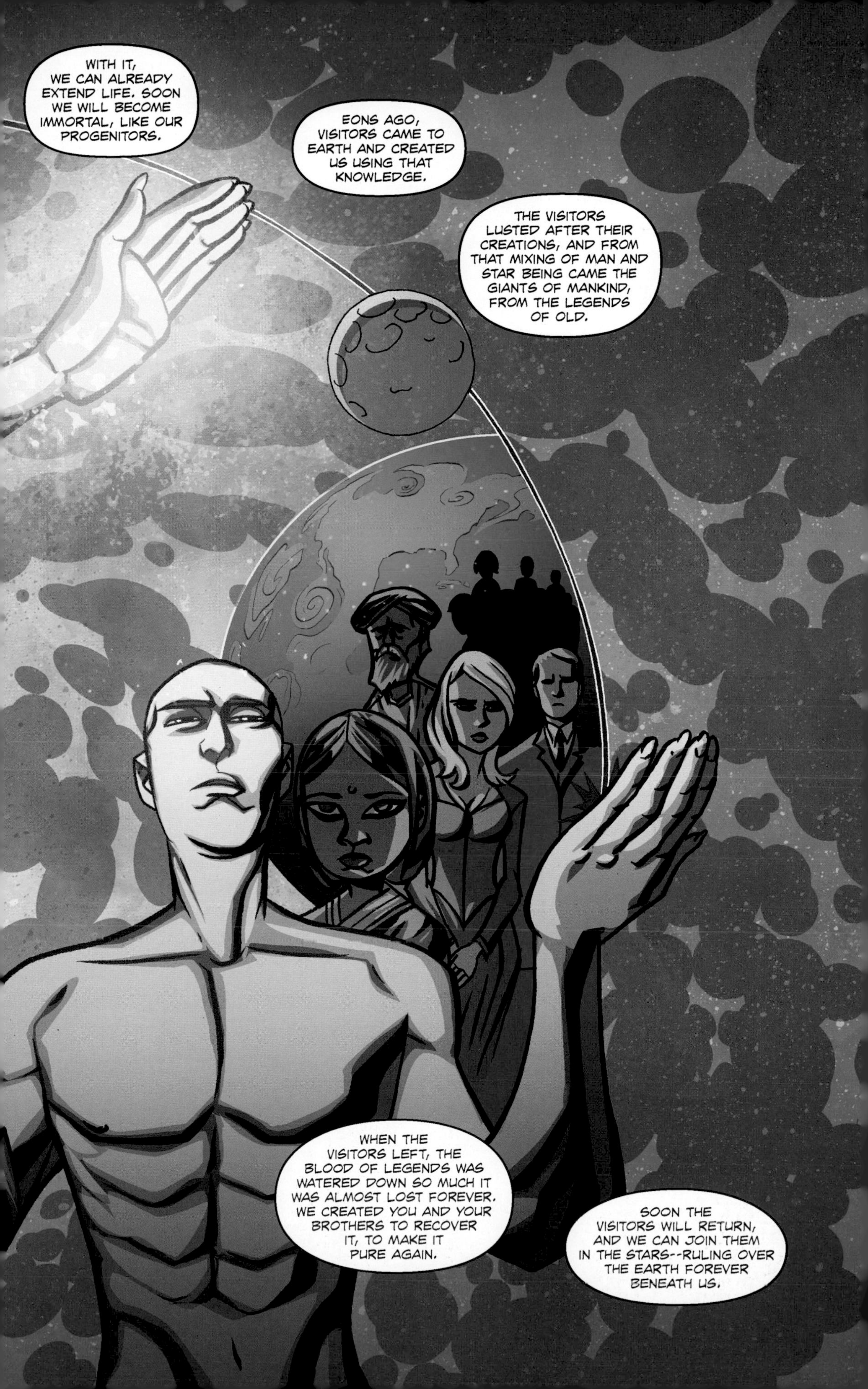
WITH IT, WE CAN ALREADY EXTEND LIFE. SOON WE WILL BECOME IMMORTAL, LIKE OUR PROGENITORS.
EONS AGO, VISITORS CAME TO EARTH AND CREATED US USING THAT KNOWLEDGE.
THE VISITORS LUSTED AFTER THEIR CREATIONS, AND FROM THAT MIXING OF MAN AND STAR BEING CAME THE GIANTS OF MANKIND, FROM THE LEGENDS OF OLD.
WHEN THE VISITORS LEFT, THE BLOOD OF LEGENDS WAS WATERED DOWN SO MUCH IT WAS ALMOST LOST FOREVER. WE CREATED YOU AND YOUR BROTHERS TO RECOVER IT, TO MAKE IT PURE AGAIN.
SOON THE VISITORS WILL RETURN, AND WE CAN JOIN THEM IN THE STARS--RULING OVER THE EARTH FOREVER BENEATH US.

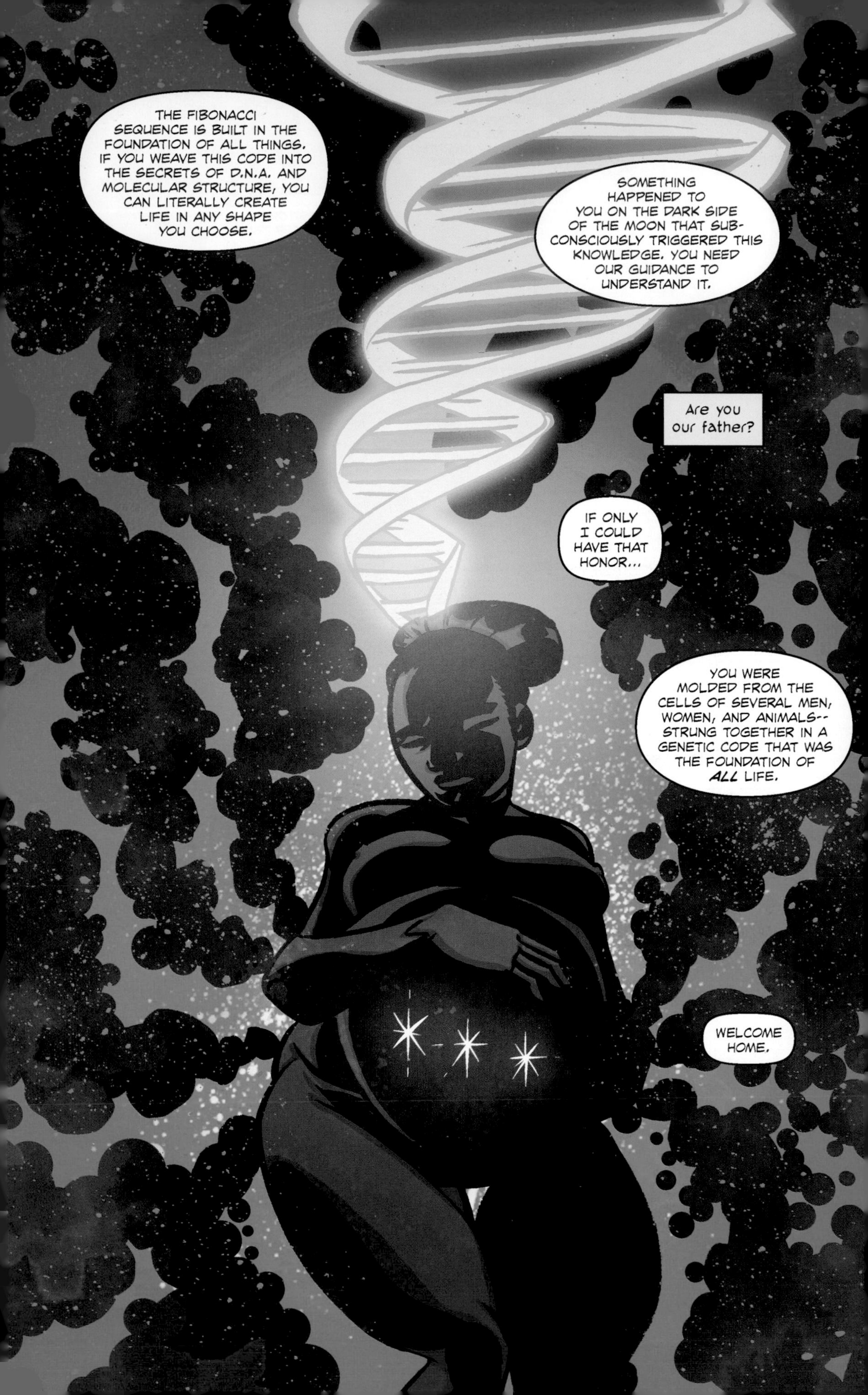
THE FIBONACCI SEQUENCE IS BUILT IN THE FOUNDATION OF ALL THINGS. IF YOU WEAVE THIS CODE INTO THE SECRETS OF D.N.A. AND MOLECULAR STRUCTURE, YOU CAN LITERALLY CREATE LIFE IN ANY SHAPE YOU CHOOSE.
SOMETHING HAPPENED TO YOU ON THE DARK SIDE OF THE MOON THAT SUB-CONSCIOUSLY TRIGGERED THIS KNOWLEDGE. YOU NEED OUR GUIDANCE TO UNDERSTAND IT.
Are you our father?
IF ONLY I COULD HAVE THAT HONOR...
YOU WERE MOLDED FROM THE CELLS OF SEVERAL MEN, WOMEN, AND ANIMALS--STRUNG TOGETHER IN A GENETIC CODE THAT WAS THE FOUNDATION OF ALL LIFE.
WELCOME HOME.

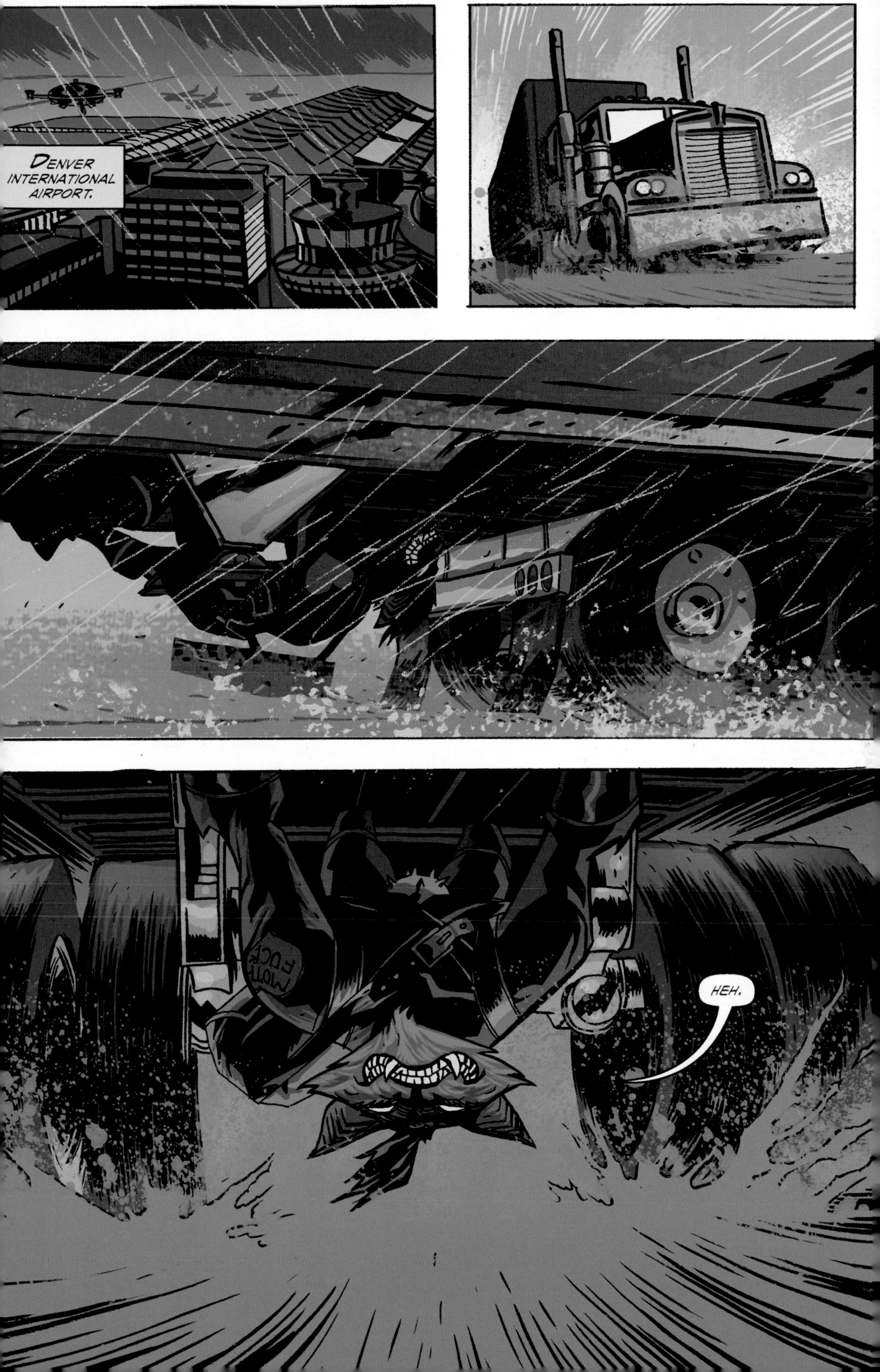
DENVER INTERNATIONAL AIRPORT.
HEH.

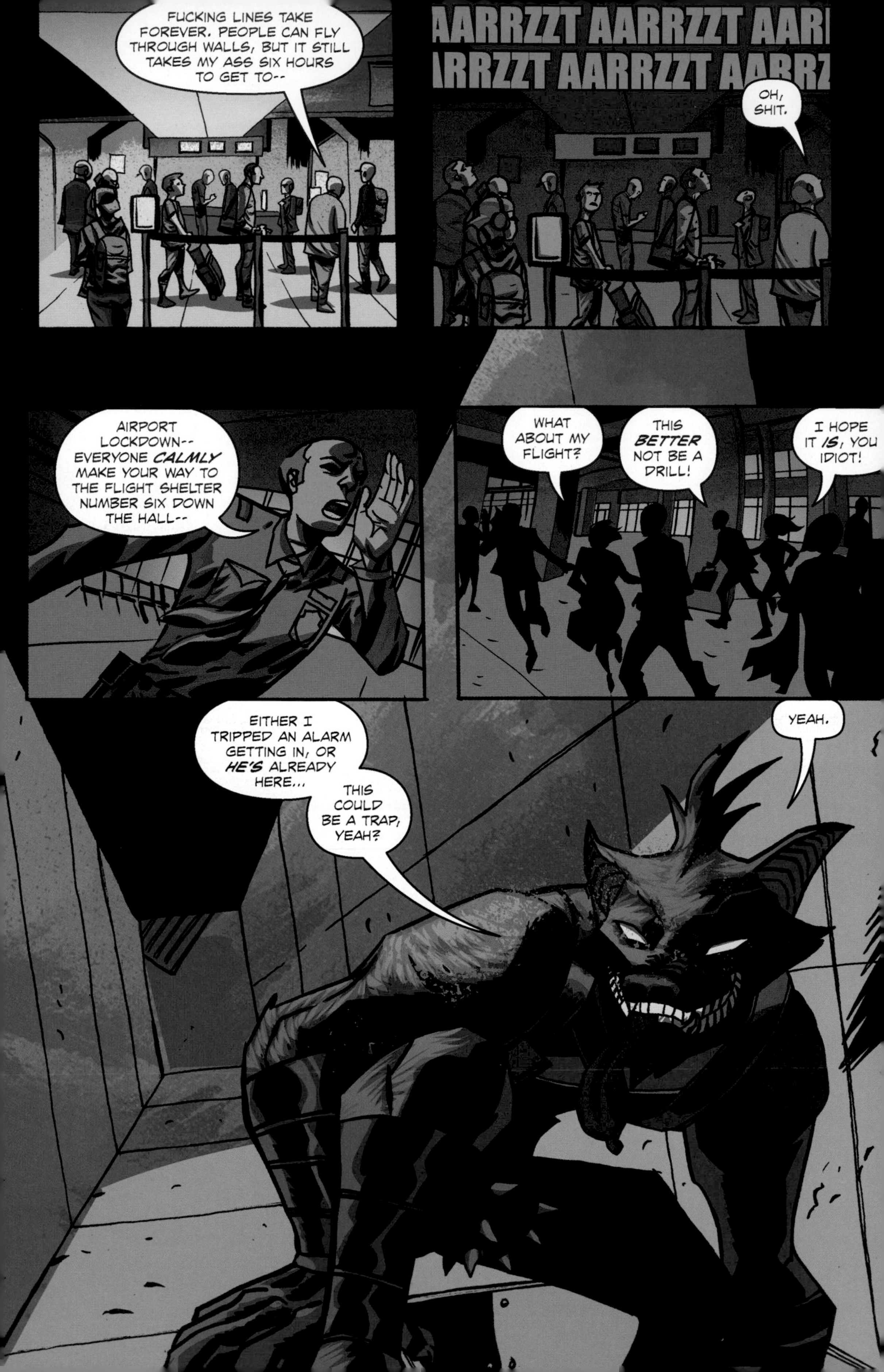
FUCKING LINES TAKE FOREVER. PEOPLE CAN FLY THROUGH WALLS, BUT IT STILL TAKES MY ASS SIX HOURS TO GET TO--
AARRZZT AARRZZT AARRZZT AARRZZT AARRZZT AARRZZT
OH, SHIT.
AIRPORT LOCKDOWN-- EVERYONE CALMLY MAKE YOUR WAY TO THE FLIGHT SHELTER NUMBER SIX DOWN THE HALL--
WHAT ABOUT MY FLIGHT?
THIS BETTER NOT BE A DRILL!
I HOPE IT IS, YOU IDIOT!
EITHER I TRIPPED AN ALARM GETTING IN, OR HE'S ALREADY HERE...
THIS COULD BE A TRAP, YEAH?
YEAH.

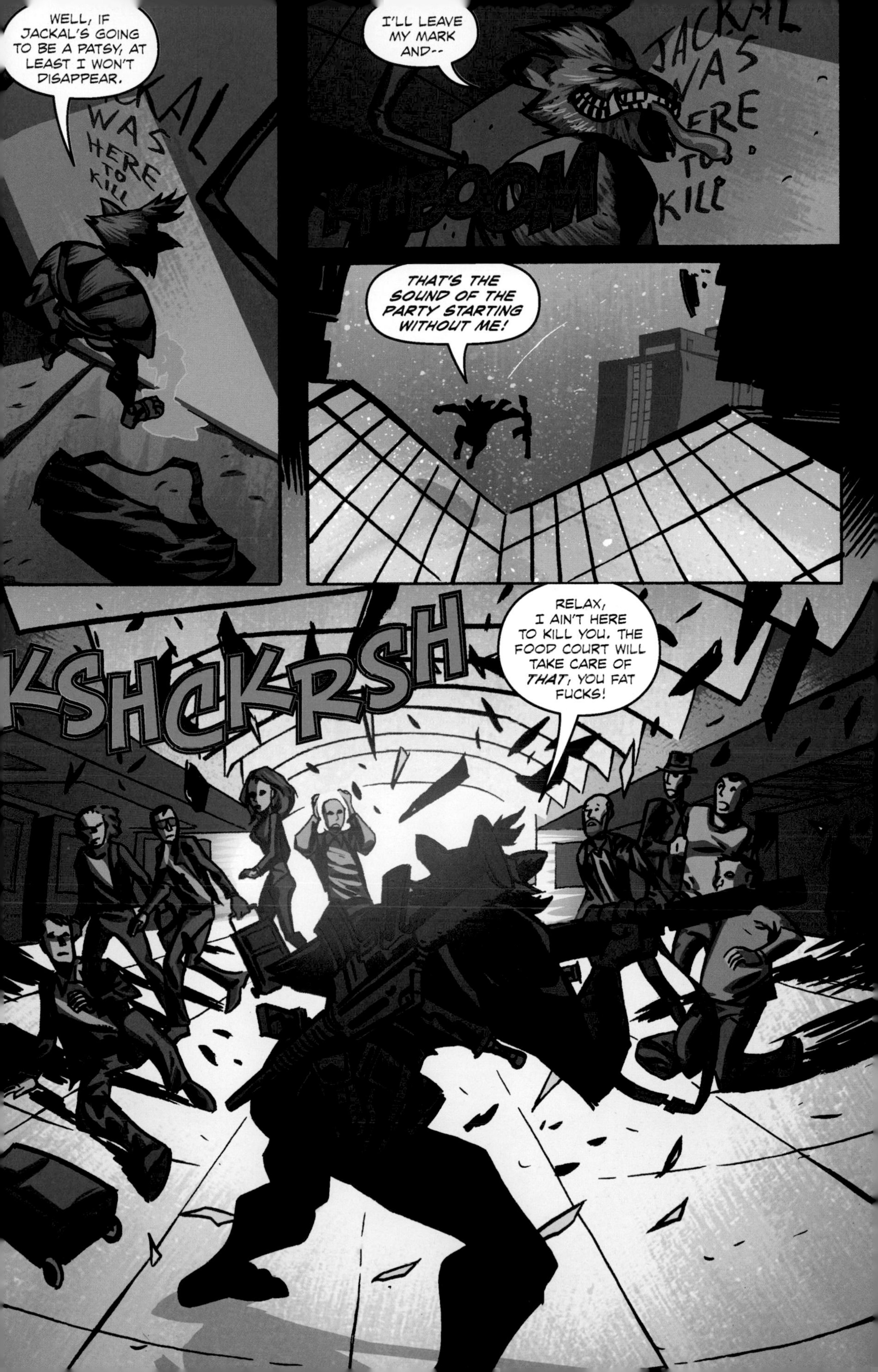
WELL, IF JACKAL'S GOING TO BE A PATSY, AT LEAST I WON'T DISAPPEAR.
JACKAL WAS HERE TO KILL
I'LL LEAVE MY MARK AND--
JACKAL WAS HERE TO KILL
KTHBOOM
THAT'S THE SOUND OF THE PARTY STARTING WITHOUT ME!
KSHCKRSH
RELAX, I AIN'T HERE TO KILL YOU. THE FOOD COURT WILL TAKE CARE OF THAT, YOU FAT FUCKS!

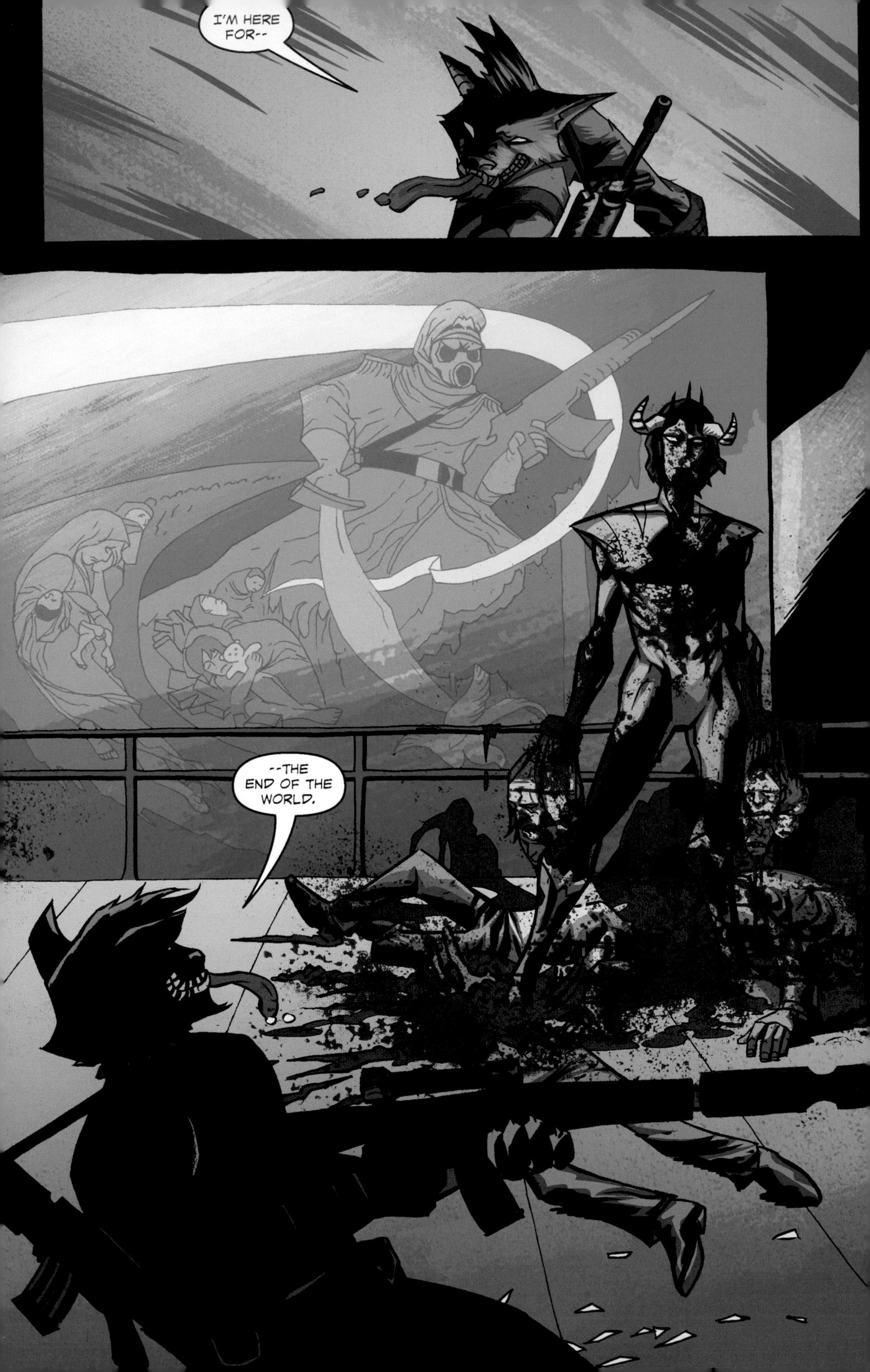
I'M HERE FOR--
--THE END OF THE WORLD.

CHAPTER FIVE

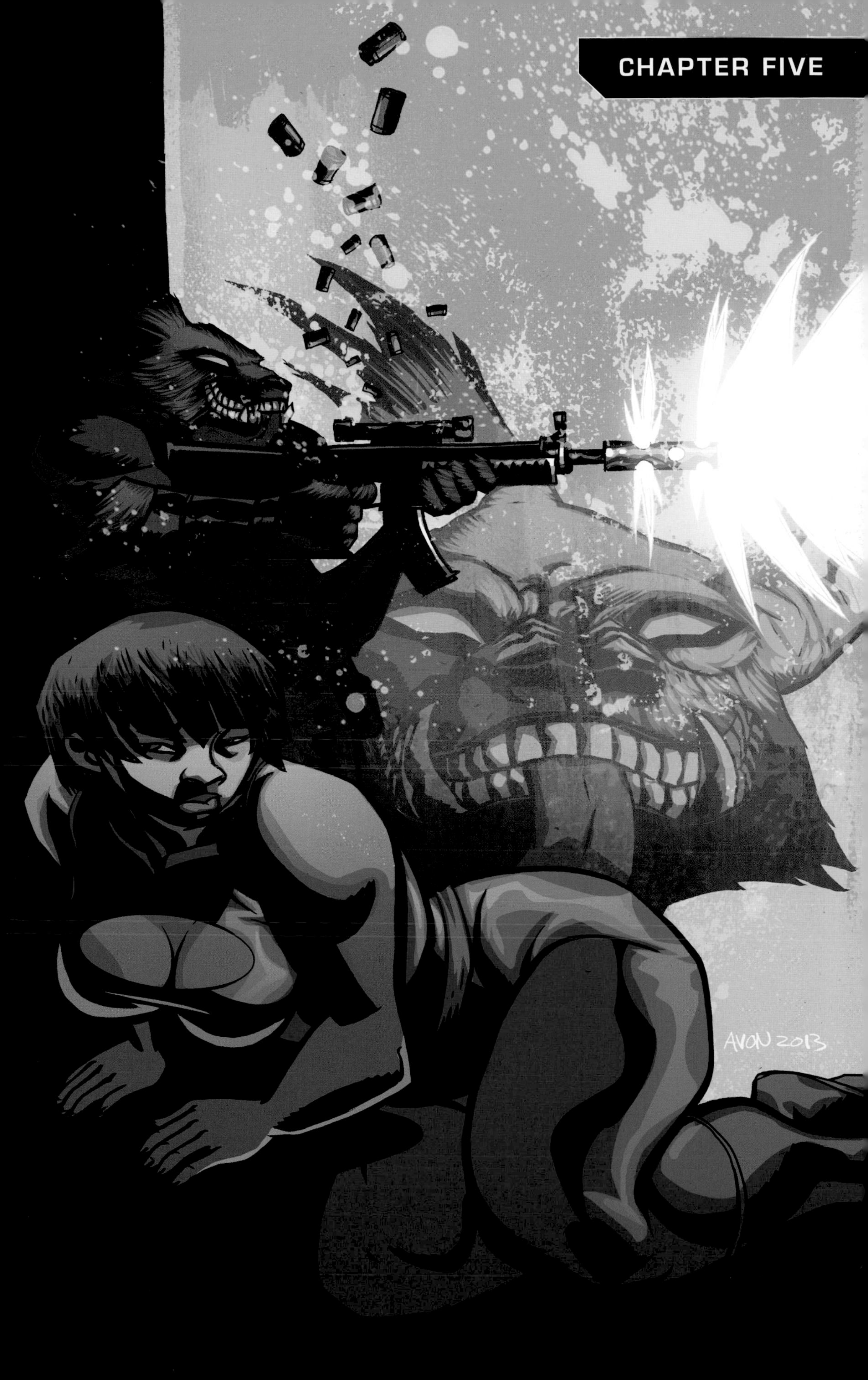
AVON 2013

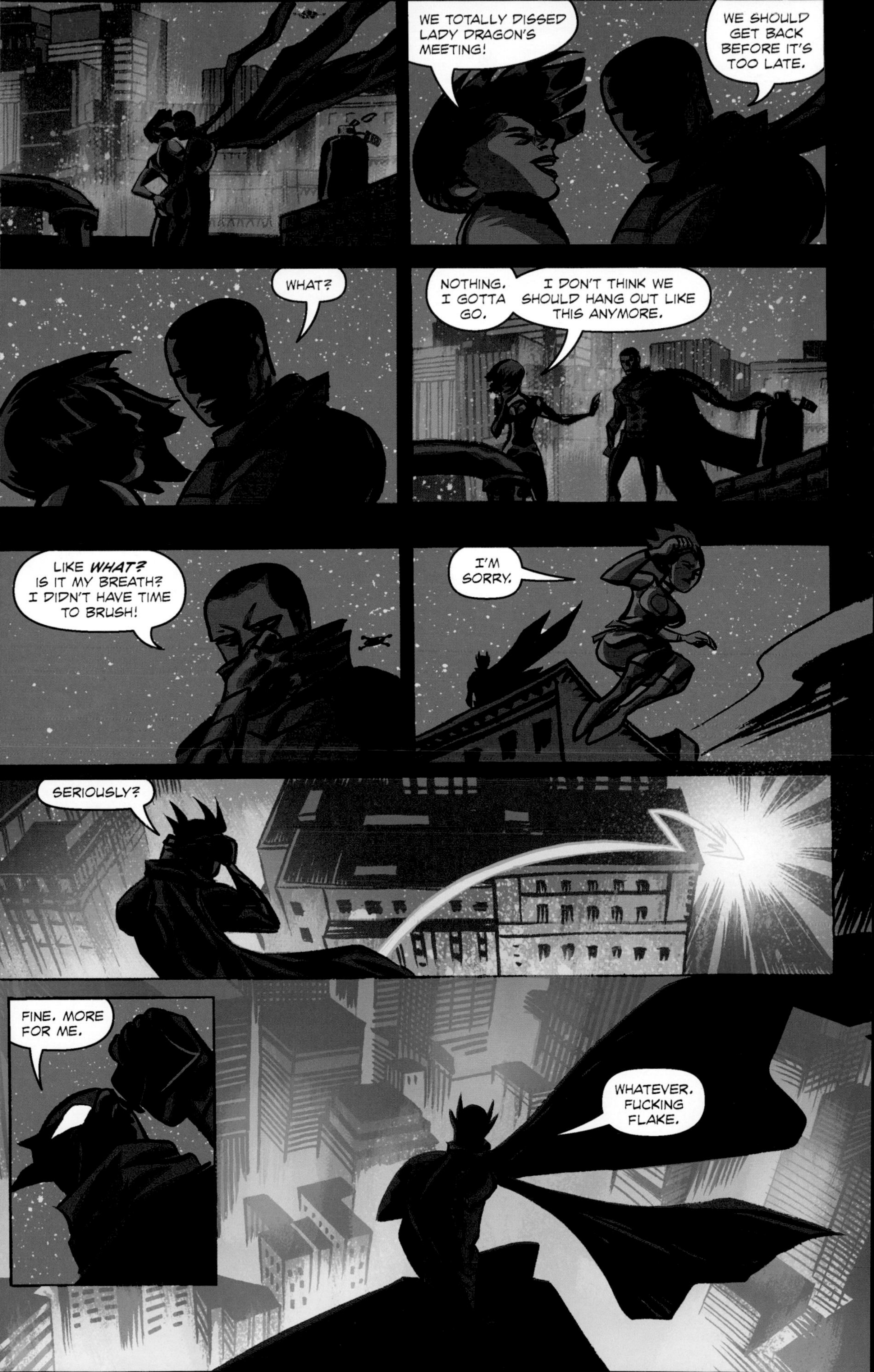
WE TOTALLY DISSED LADY DRAGON'S MEETING!
WE SHOULD GET BACK BEFORE IT'S TOO LATE.
WHAT?
NOTHING. I GOTTA GO.
I DON'T THINK WE SHOULD HANG OUT LIKE THIS ANYMORE.
LIKE WHAT? IS IT MY BREATH? I DIDN'T HAVE TIME TO BRUSH!
I'M SORRY.
SERIOUSLY?
FINE. MORE FOR ME.
WHATEVER. FUCKING FLAKE.

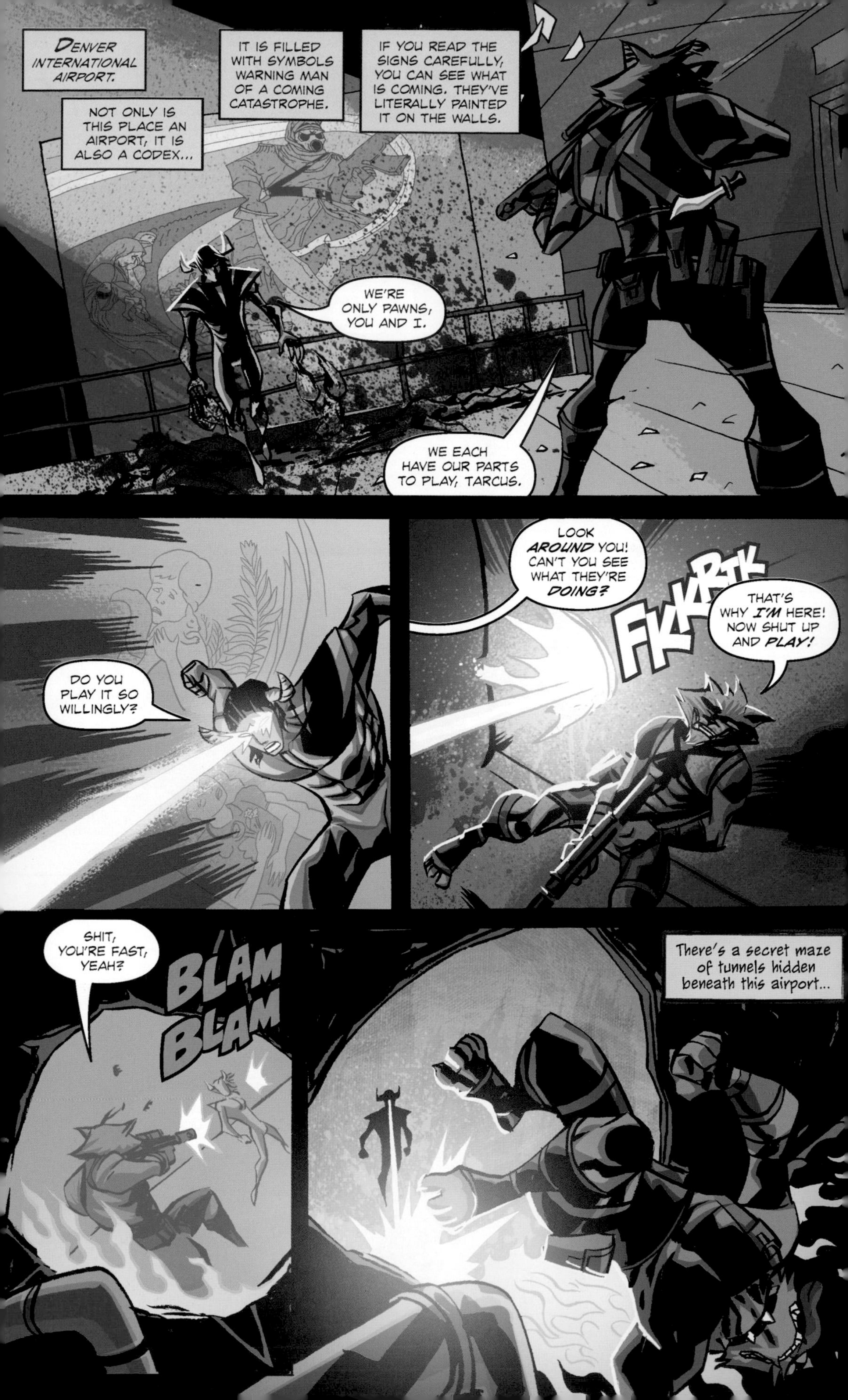
DENVER INTERNATIONAL AIRPORT.
NOT ONLY IS THIS PLACE AN AIRPORT, IT IS ALSO A CODEX...
IT IS FILLED WITH SYMBOLS WARNING MAN OF A COMING CATASTROPHE.
IF YOU READ THE SIGNS CAREFULLY, YOU CAN SEE WHAT IS COMING. THEY'VE LITERALLY PAINTED IT ON THE WALLS.
WE'RE ONLY PAWNS, YOU AND I.
WE EACH HAVE OUR PARTS TO PLAY, TARCUS.
DO YOU PLAY IT SO WILLINGLY?
LOOK AROUND YOU! CAN'T YOU SEE WHAT THEY'RE DOING?
FKKRTK
THAT'S WHY I'M HERE! NOW SHUT UP AND PLAY!
SHIT, YOU'RE FAST, YEAH?
BLAM BLAM
There's a secret maze of tunnels hidden beneath this airport...

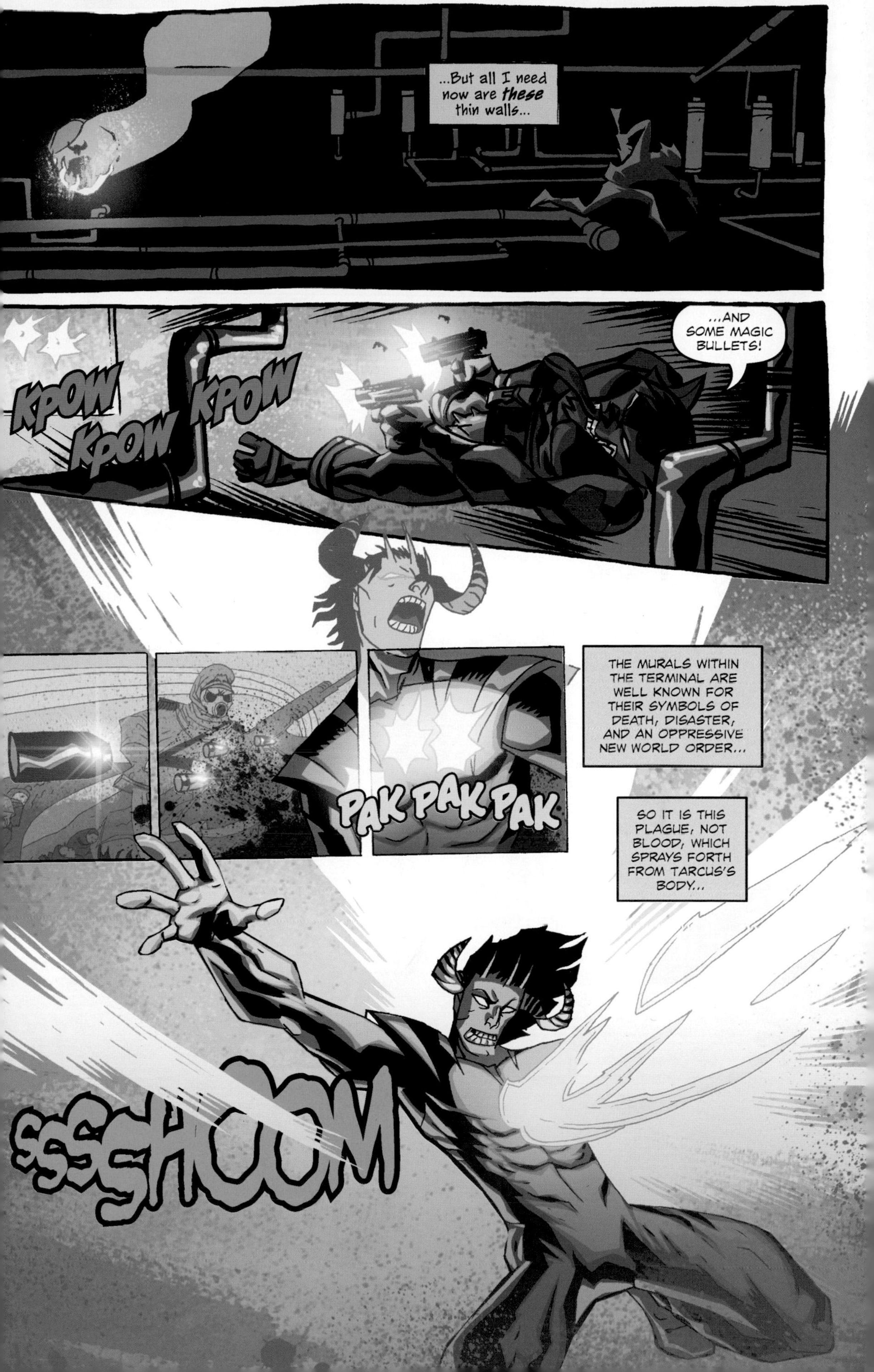
...But all I need now are these thin walls...
...AND SOME MAGIC BULLETS!
KPOW KPOW KPOW
THE MURALS WITHIN THE TERMINAL ARE WELL KNOWN FOR THEIR SYMBOLS OF DEATH, DISASTER, AND AN OPPRESSIVE NEW WORLD ORDER...
PAK PAK PAK
SO IT IS THIS PLAGUE, NOT BLOOD, WHICH SPRAYS FORTH FROM TARCUS'S BODY...
sssSHOOM

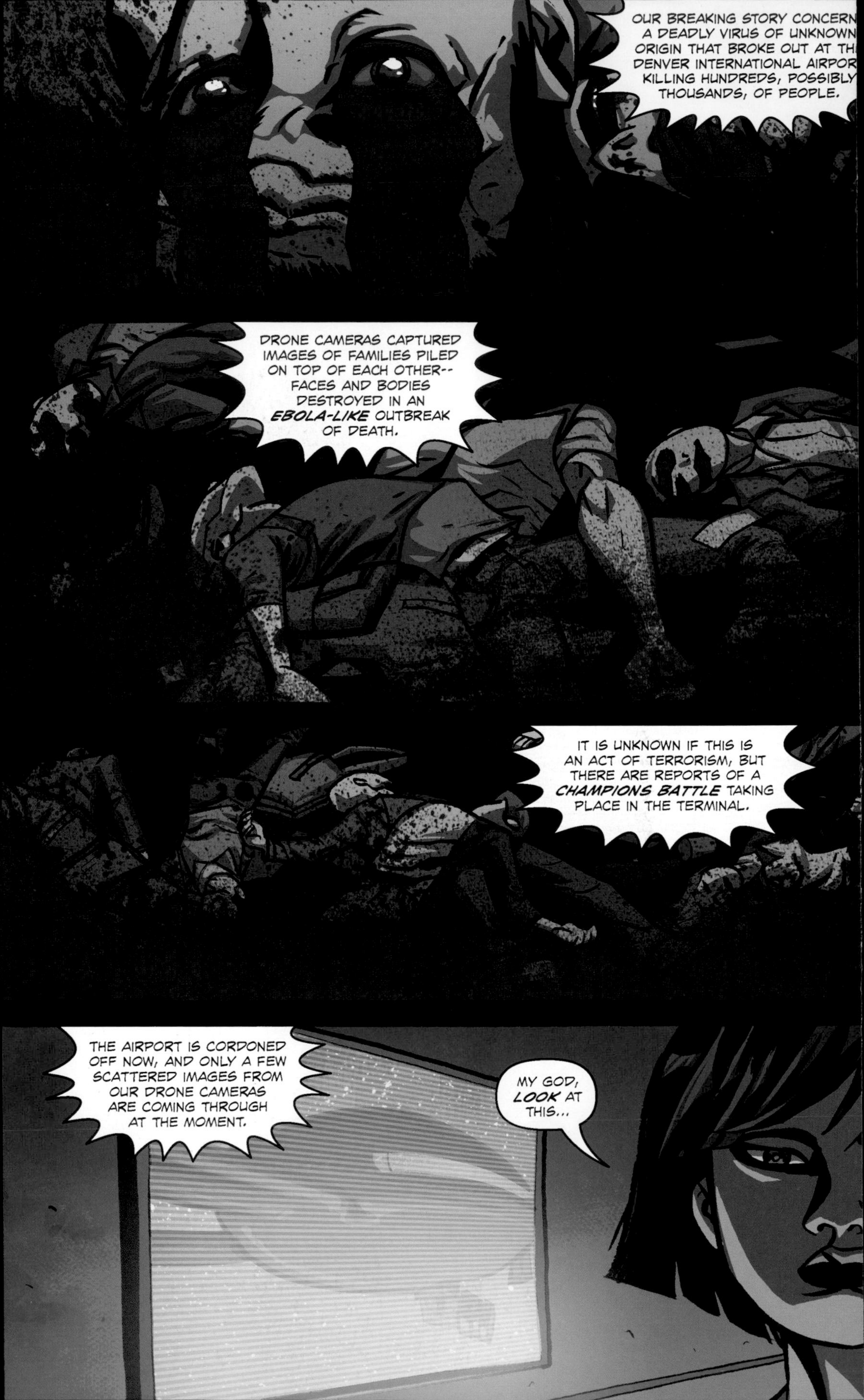
OUR BREAKING STORY CONCERN
A DEADLY VIRUS OF UNKNOWN
ORIGIN THAT BROKE OUT AT TH
DENVER INTERNATIONAL AIRPOR
KILLING HUNDREDS, POSSIBLY
THOUSANDS, OF PEOPLE.
DRONE CAMERAS CAPTURED IMAGES OF FAMILIES PILED ON TOP OF EACH OTHER-- FACES AND BODIES DESTROYED IN AN *EBOLA-LIKE* OUTBREAK OF DEATH.
IT IS UNKNOWN IF THIS IS AN ACT OF TERRORISM, BUT THERE ARE REPORTS OF A *CHAMPIONS BATTLE* TAKING PLACE IN THE TERMINAL.
THE AIRPORT IS CORDONED OFF NOW, AND ONLY A FEW SCATTERED IMAGES FROM OUR DRONE CAMERAS ARE COMING THROUGH AT THE MOMENT.
MY GOD, *LOOK* AT THIS...

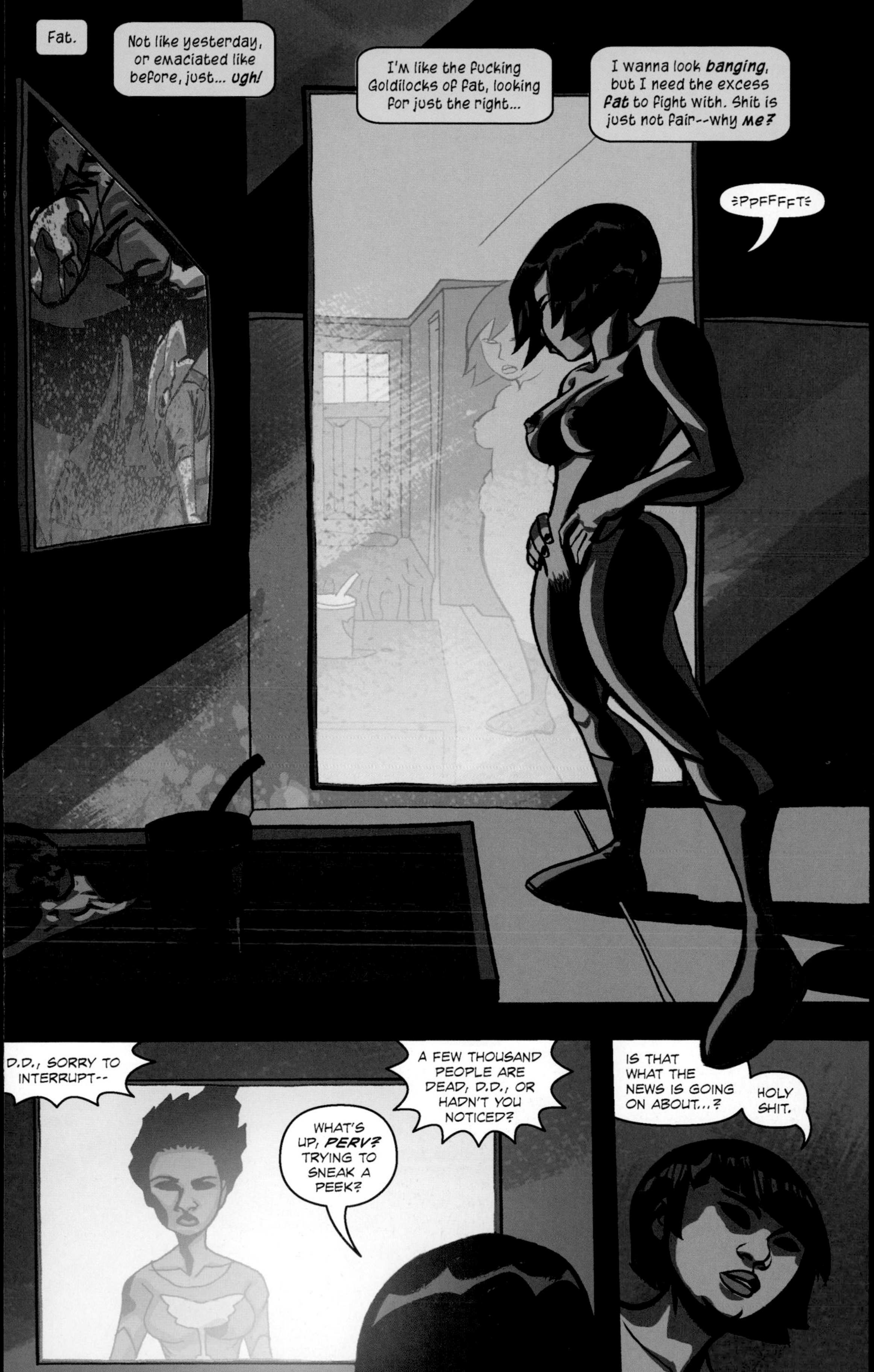
Fat.
Not like yesterday, or emaciated like before, just... ugh!
I'm like the fucking Goldilocks of fat, looking for just the right...
I wanna look banging, but I need the excess fat to fight with. Shit is just not fair--why me?
PPFFFFT
D.D., SORRY TO INTERRUPT--
WHAT'S UP, PERV? TRYING TO SNEAK A PEEK?
A FEW THOUSAND PEOPLE ARE DEAD, D.D., OR HADN'T YOU NOTICED?
IS THAT WHAT THE NEWS IS GOING ON ABOUT...?
HOLY SHIT.

DENVER INTERNATIONAL AIRPORT.

WWWSSS

ZZZZZ

VICTORIES!

IT SEEMS *MAFTET'S* INFORMANT MIGHT HAVE BEEN TELLING THE TRUTH.

THE JACKAL?

HE AND TARCUS FOUGHT HERE.

DID THEY--?

MY NEURAL PROBES HAVE TAPPED INTO THE SECURITY AND DRONE CAMERA RECORDINGS.

UPON ARRIVAL, TARCUS BEGAN KILLING PEOPLE. JACKAL CAME TO THE SCENE AND KILLED TARCUS.

WHEN HE DID, A BIOVIRUS WAS RELEASED FROM TARCUS'S BODY.

CURRENTLY ANALYZING.

THERE ARE NO SURVIVORS WITHIN. THE MILITARY ARE COMING TO QUARANTINE THE AREA.

THIS IS STAGED. A FALSE-FLAG OPERATION!

JESUS, THEY DIED RUNNING AWAY... ARE W SAFE?

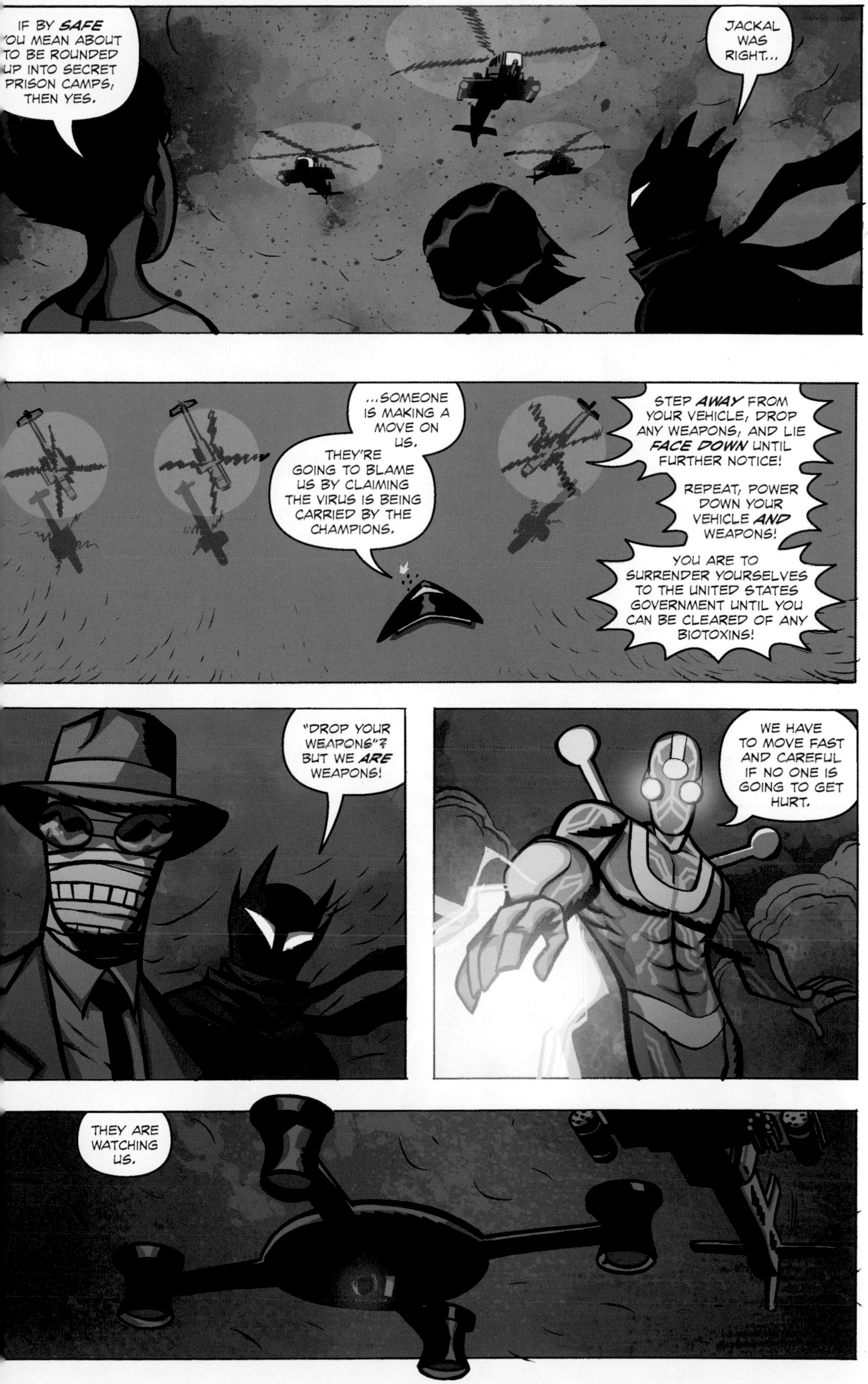
IF BY SAFE YOU MEAN ABOUT TO BE ROUNDED UP INTO SECRET PRISON CAMPS, THEN YES.
JACKAL WAS RIGHT...
...SOMEONE IS MAKING A MOVE ON US.
THEY'RE GOING TO BLAME US BY CLAIMING THE VIRUS IS BEING CARRIED BY THE CHAMPIONS.
STEP AWAY FROM YOUR VEHICLE, DROP ANY WEAPONS, AND LIE FACE DOWN UNTIL FURTHER NOTICE!
REPEAT, POWER DOWN YOUR VEHICLE AND WEAPONS!
YOU ARE TO SURRENDER YOURSELVES TO THE UNITED STATES GOVERNMENT UNTIL YOU CAN BE CLEARED OF ANY BIOTOXINS!
"DROP YOUR WEAPONS"? BUT WE ARE WEAPONS!
WE HAVE TO MOVE FAST AND CAREFUL IF NO ONE IS GOING TO GET HURT.
THEY ARE WATCHING US.

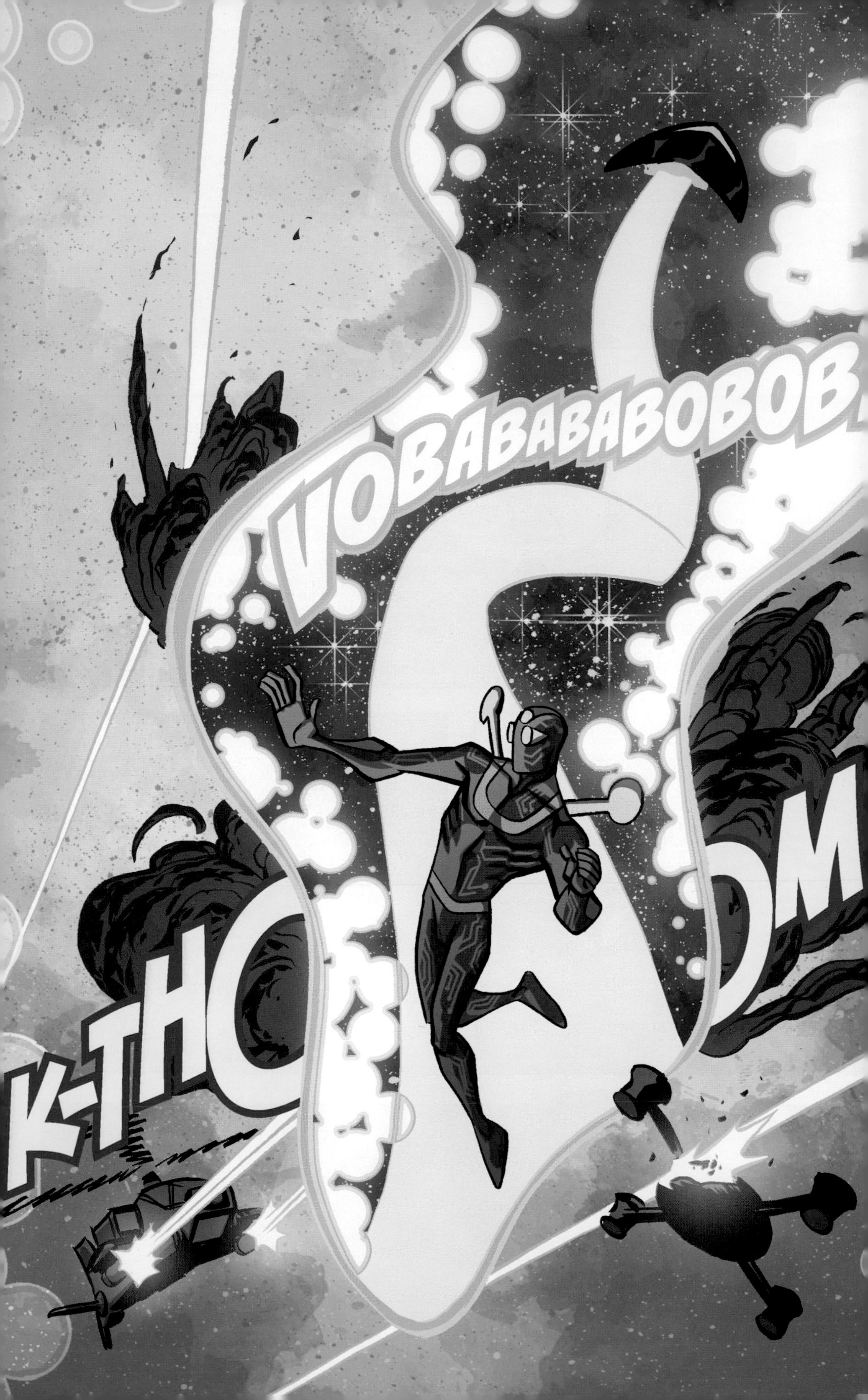
VOBABABABOBOB
K-THO
OM

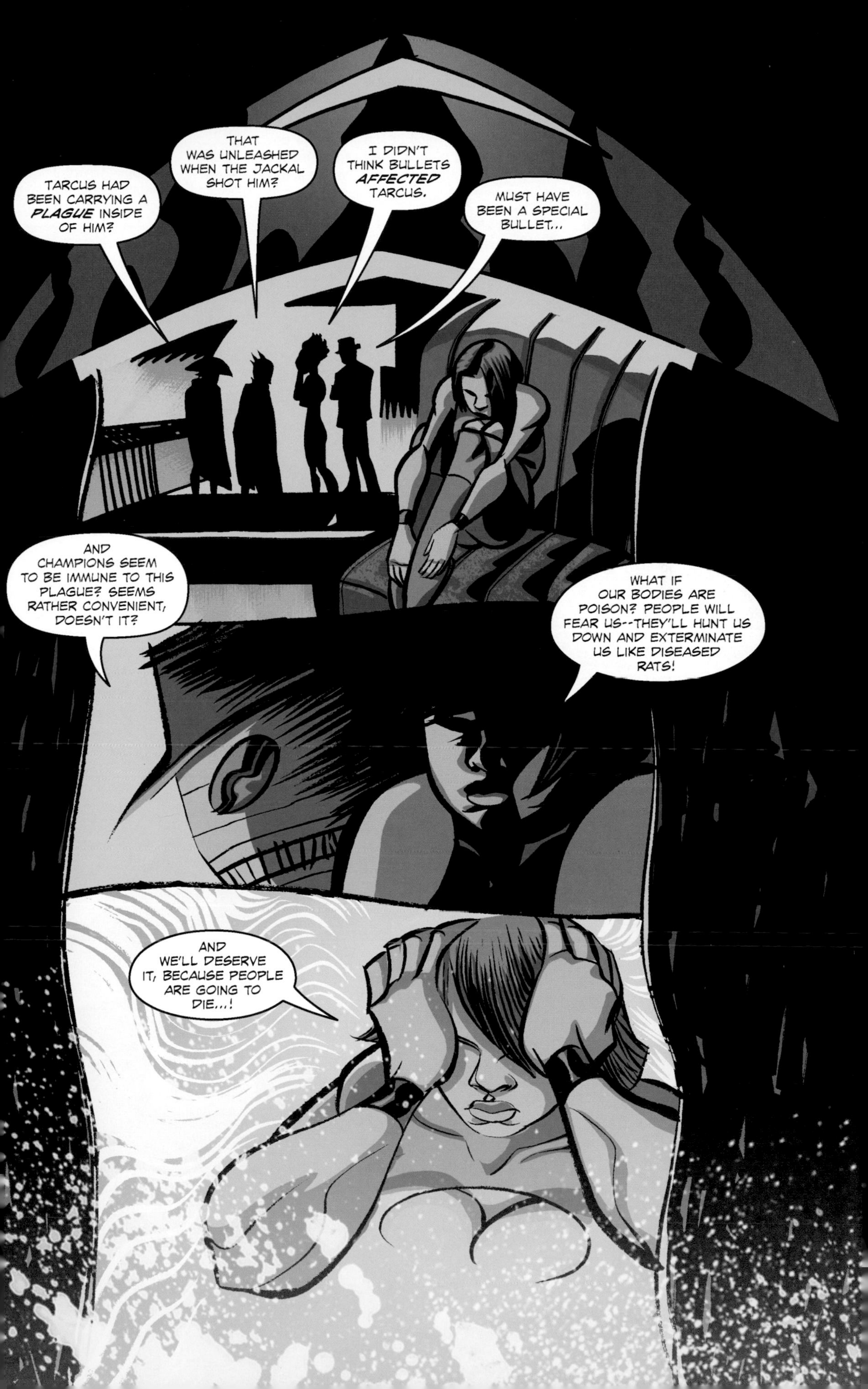
TARCUS HAD BEEN CARRYING A *PLAGUE* INSIDE OF HIM?
THAT WAS UNLEASHED WHEN THE JACKAL SHOT HIM?
I DIDN'T THINK BULLETS *AFFECTED* TARCUS.
MUST HAVE BEEN A SPECIAL BULLET...
AND CHAMPIONS SEEM TO BE IMMUNE TO THIS PLAGUE? SEEMS RATHER CONVENIENT, DOESN'T IT?
WHAT IF OUR BODIES ARE POISON? PEOPLE WILL FEAR US--THEY'LL HUNT US DOWN AND EXTERMINATE US LIKE DISEASED RATS!
AND WE'LL DESERVE IT, BECAUSE PEOPLE ARE GOING TO DIE...!

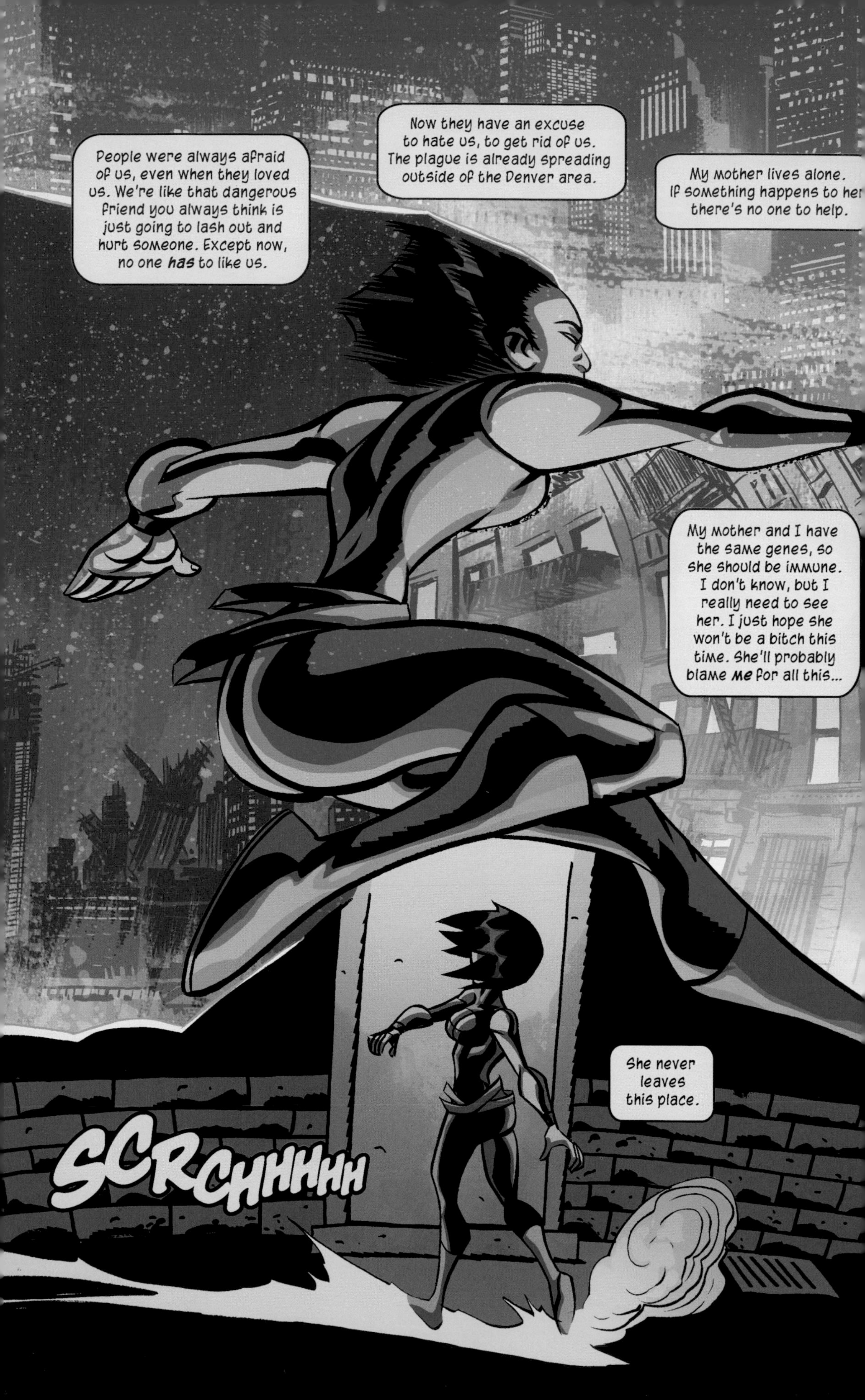
People were always afraid of us, even when they loved us. We're like that dangerous friend you always think is just going to lash out and hurt someone. Except now, no one ***has*** to like us.
Now they have an excuse to hate us, to get rid of us. The plague is already spreading outside of the Denver area.
My mother lives alone. If something happens to her there's no one to help.
My mother and I have the same genes, so she should be immune. I don't know, but I really need to see her. I just hope she won't be a bitch this time. She'll probably blame ***me*** for all this...
She never leaves this place.
SCRCHHHHH

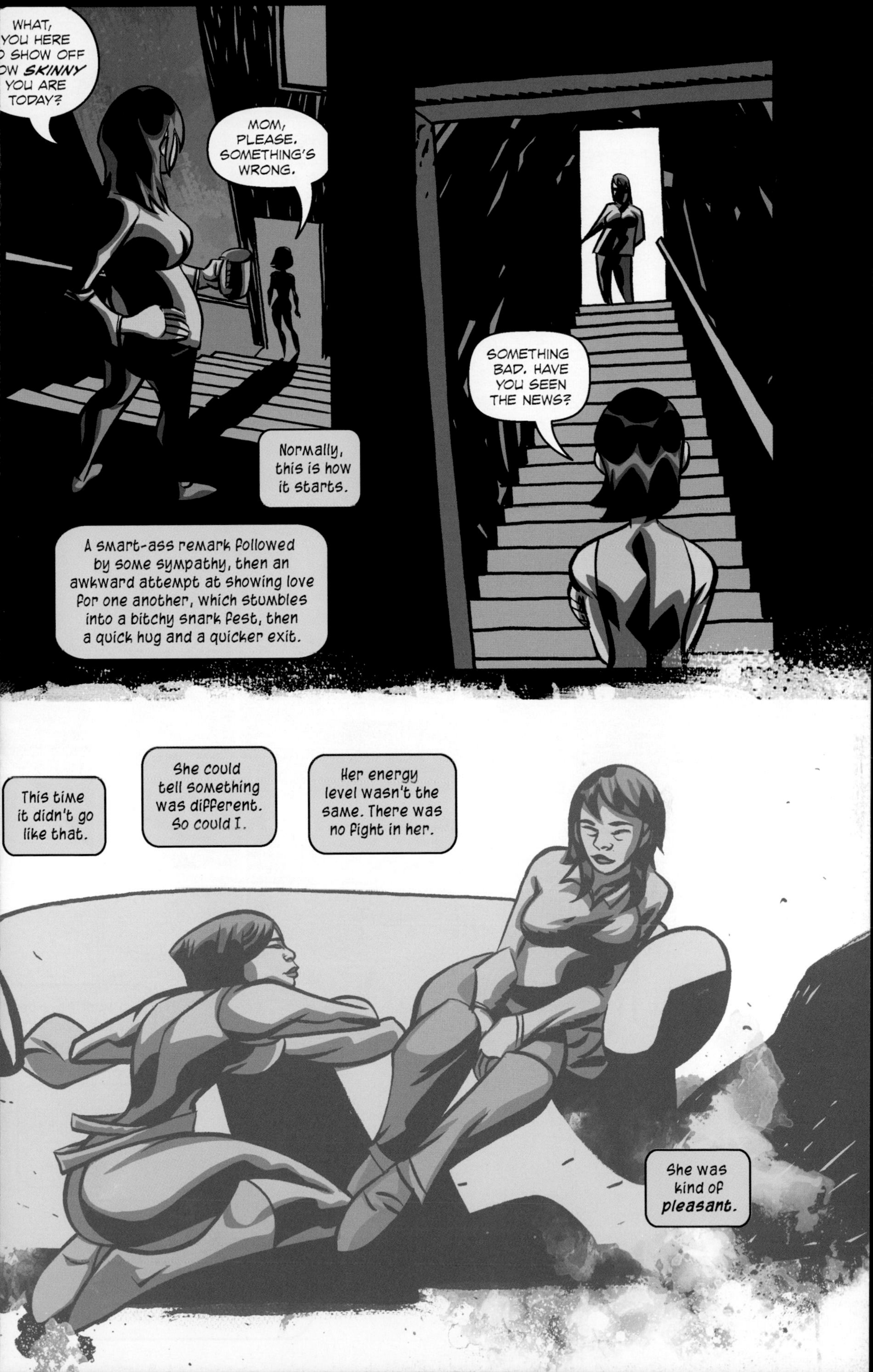
WHAT, YOU HERE O SHOW OFF OW SKINNY YOU ARE TODAY?
MOM, PLEASE. SOMETHING'S WRONG.
SOMETHING BAD. HAVE YOU SEEN THE NEWS?
Normally, this is how it starts.
A smart-ass remark followed by some sympathy, then an awkward attempt at showing love for one another, which stumbles into a bitchy snark fest, then a quick hug and a quicker exit.
This time it didn't go like that.
She could tell something was different. So could I.
Her energy level wasn't the same. There was no fight in her.
She was kind of pleasant.

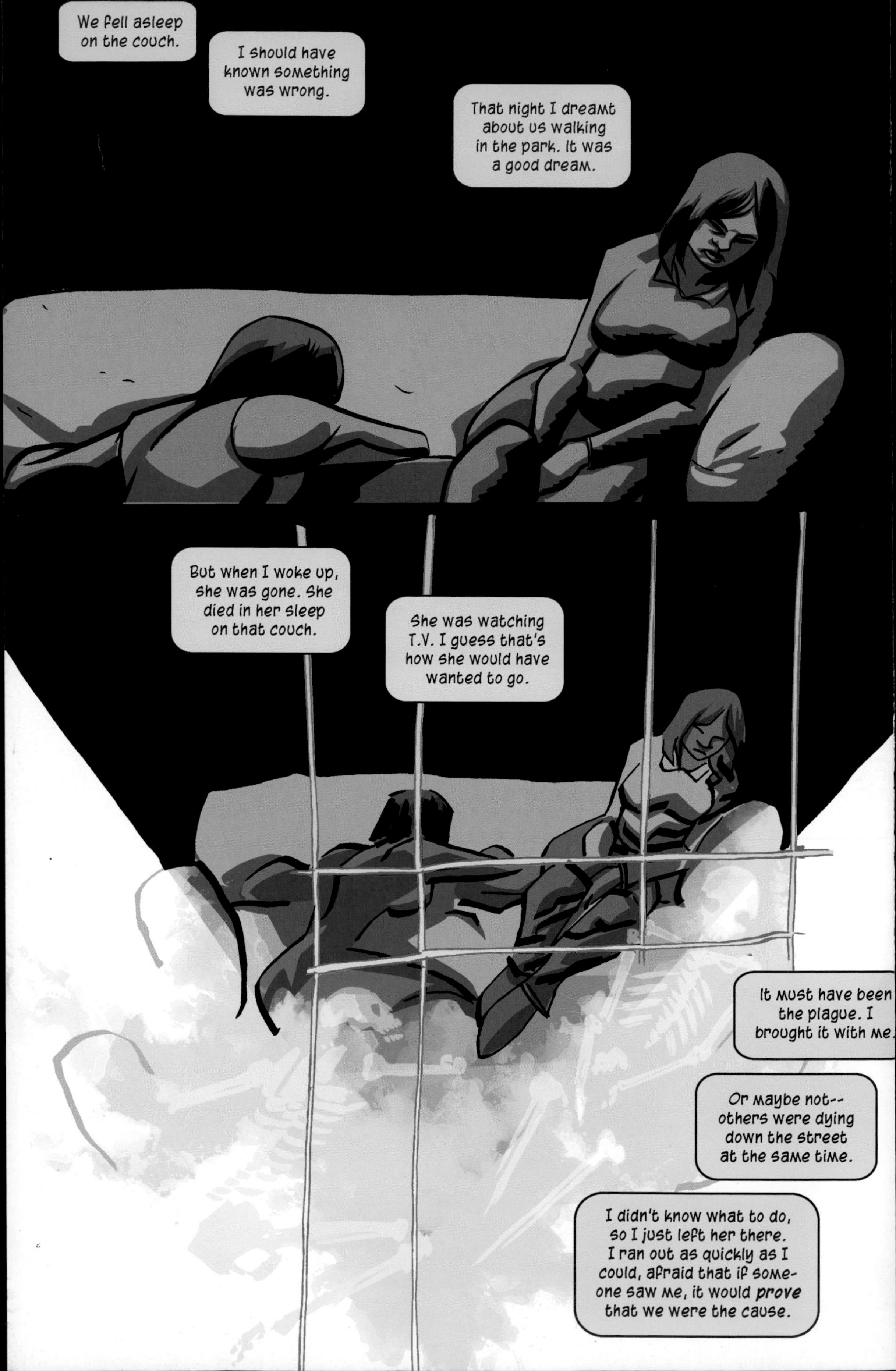
We fell asleep on the couch.
I should have known something was wrong.
That night I dreamt about us walking in the park. It was a good dream.
But when I woke up, she was gone. She died in her sleep on that couch.
She was watching T.V. I guess that's how she would have wanted to go.
It must have been the plague. I brought it with me.
Or maybe not--others were dying down the street at the same time.
I didn't know what to do, so I just left her there. I ran out as quickly as I could, afraid that if some-one saw me, it would *prove* that we were the cause.

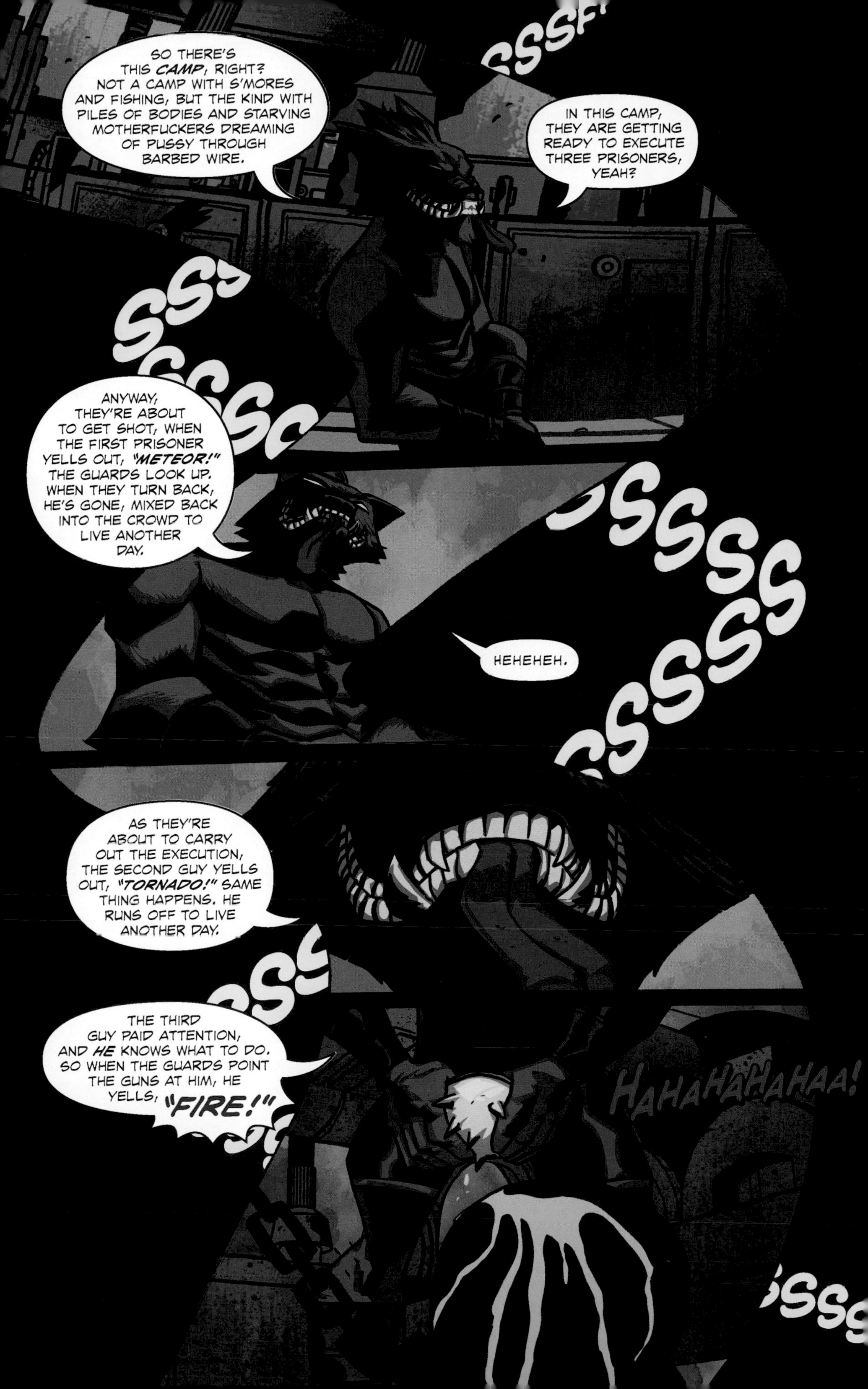
SSSF
SO THERE'S THIS CAMP, RIGHT? NOT A CAMP WITH S'MORES AND FISHING, BUT THE KIND WITH PILES OF BODIES AND STARVING MOTHERFUCKERS DREAMING OF PUSSY THROUGH BARBED WIRE.
IN THIS CAMP, THEY ARE GETTING READY TO EXECUTE THREE PRISONERS, YEAH?
ANYWAY, THEY'RE ABOUT TO GET SHOT, WHEN THE FIRST PRISONER YELLS OUT, "METEOR!" THE GUARDS LOOK UP. WHEN THEY TURN BACK, HE'S GONE, MIXED BACK INTO THE CROWD TO LIVE ANOTHER DAY.
HEHEHEH.
AS THEY'RE ABOUT TO CARRY OUT THE EXECUTION, THE SECOND GUY YELLS OUT, "TORNADO!" SAME THING HAPPENS. HE RUNS OFF TO LIVE ANOTHER DAY.
THE THIRD GUY PAID ATTENTION, AND HE KNOWS WHAT TO DO. SO WHEN THE GUARDS POINT THE GUNS AT HIM, HE YELLS, "FIRE!"
HAHAHAHAHAHAA!

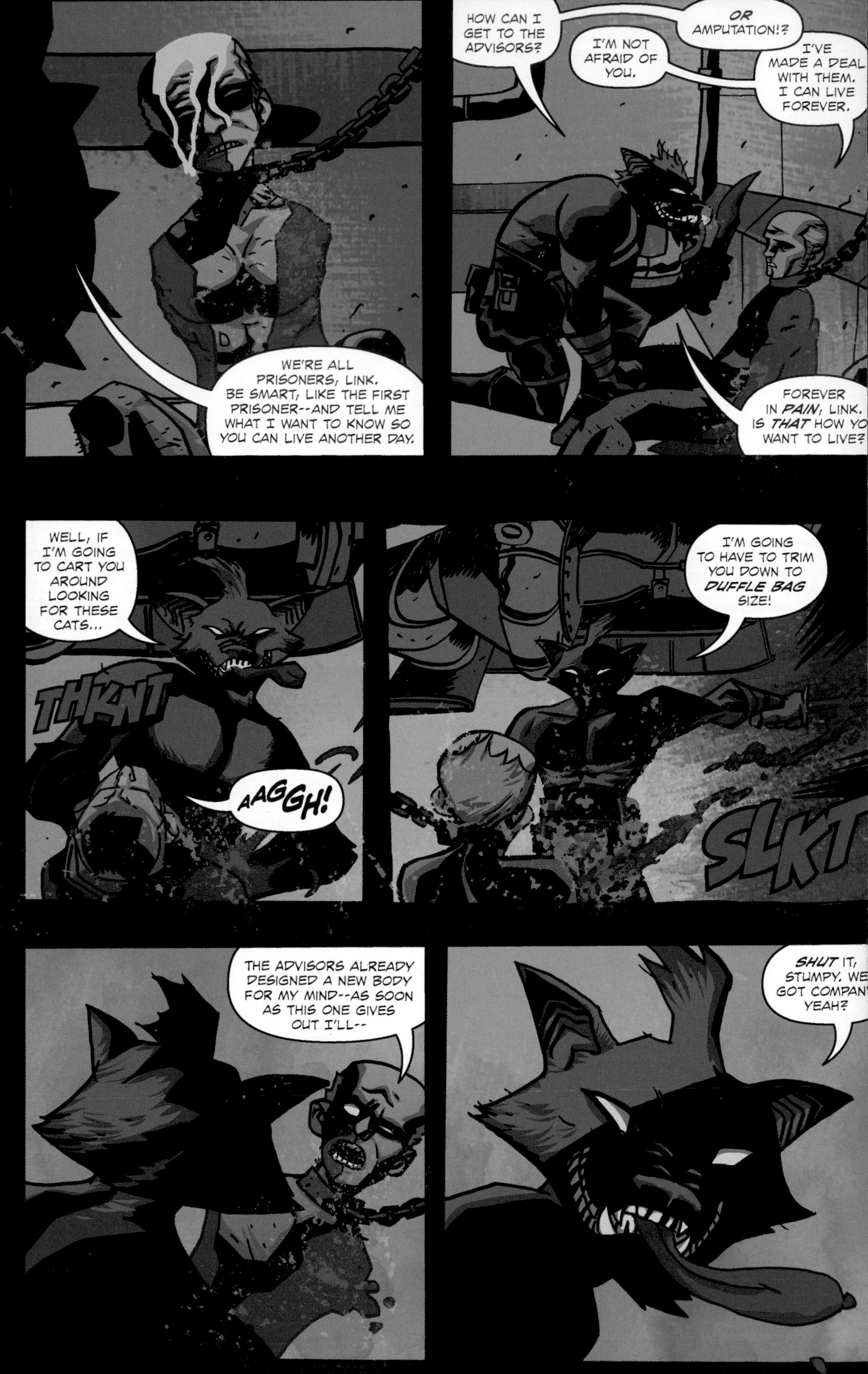
WE'RE ALL PRISONERS, LINK. BE SMART, LIKE THE FIRST PRISONER--AND TELL ME WHAT I WANT TO KNOW SO YOU CAN LIVE ANOTHER DAY.
HOW CAN I GET TO THE ADVISORS?
OR AMPUTATION!?
I'M NOT AFRAID OF YOU.
I'VE MADE A DEAL WITH THEM. I CAN LIVE FOREVER.
FOREVER IN PAIN, LINK. IS THAT HOW YO
WANT TO LIVE?
WELL, IF I'M GOING TO CART YOU AROUND LOOKING FOR THESE CATS...
THKNT
AAGGH!
I'M GOING TO HAVE TO TRIM YOU DOWN TO DUFFLE BAG SIZE!
SLKT
THE ADVISORS ALREADY DESIGNED A NEW BODY FOR MY MIND--AS SOON AS THIS ONE GIVES OUT I'LL--
SHUT IT, STUMPY. WE
GOT COMPANY
YEAH?

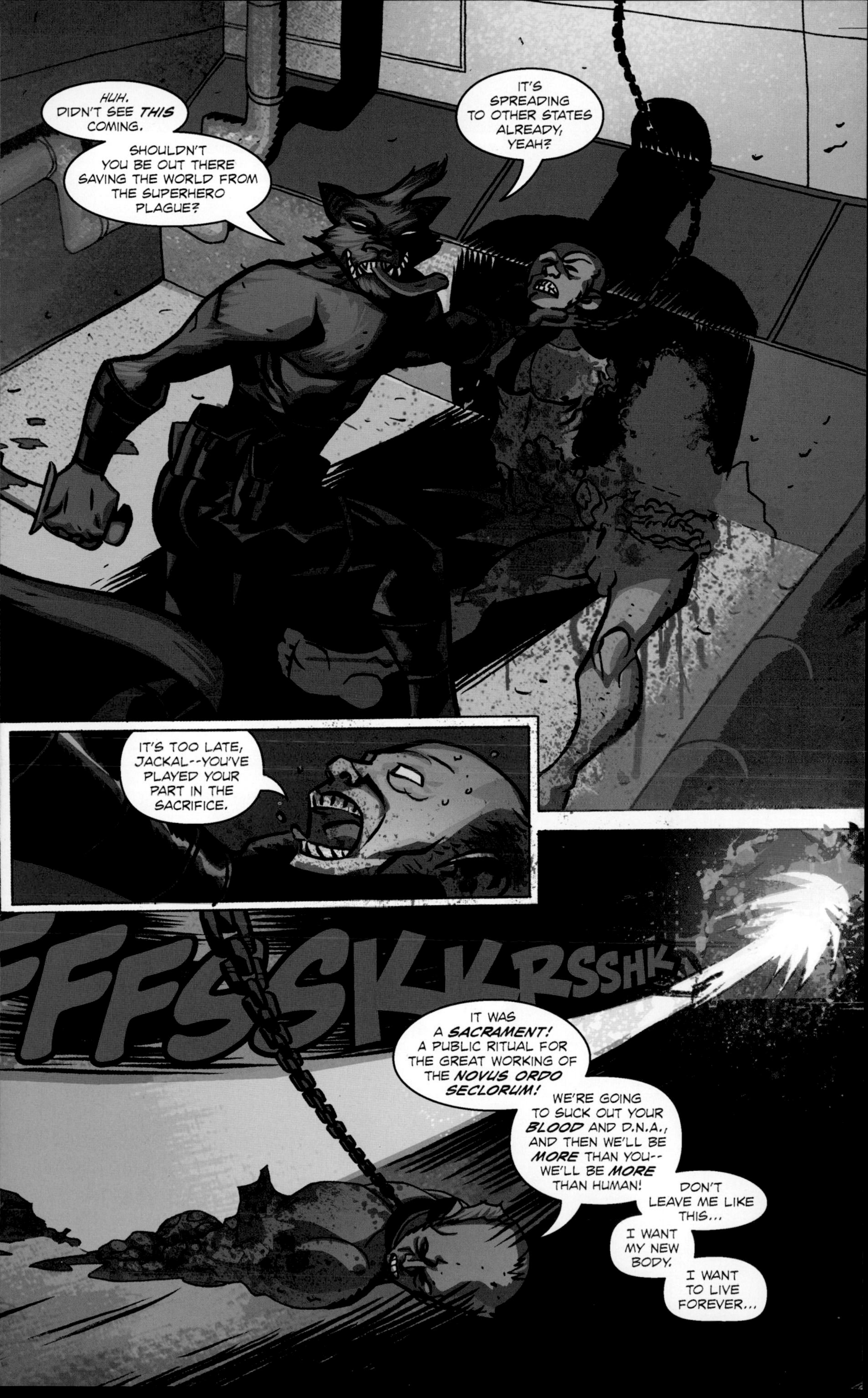
HUH. DIDN'T SEE THIS COMING.
SHOULDN'T YOU BE OUT THERE SAVING THE WORLD FROM THE SUPERHERO PLAGUE?
IT'S SPREADING TO OTHER STATES ALREADY, YEAH?
IT'S TOO LATE, JACKAL--YOU'VE PLAYED YOUR PART IN THE SACRIFICE.
FFSSKKRSSHK
IT WAS A SACRAMENT! A PUBLIC RITUAL FOR THE GREAT WORKING OF THE NOVUS ORDO SECLORUM!
WE'RE GOING TO SUCK OUT YOUR BLOOD AND D.N.A., AND THEN WE'LL BE MORE THAN YOU-- WE'LL BE MORE THAN HUMAN!
DON'T LEAVE ME LIKE THIS...
I WANT MY NEW BODY.
I WANT TO LIVE FOREVER...

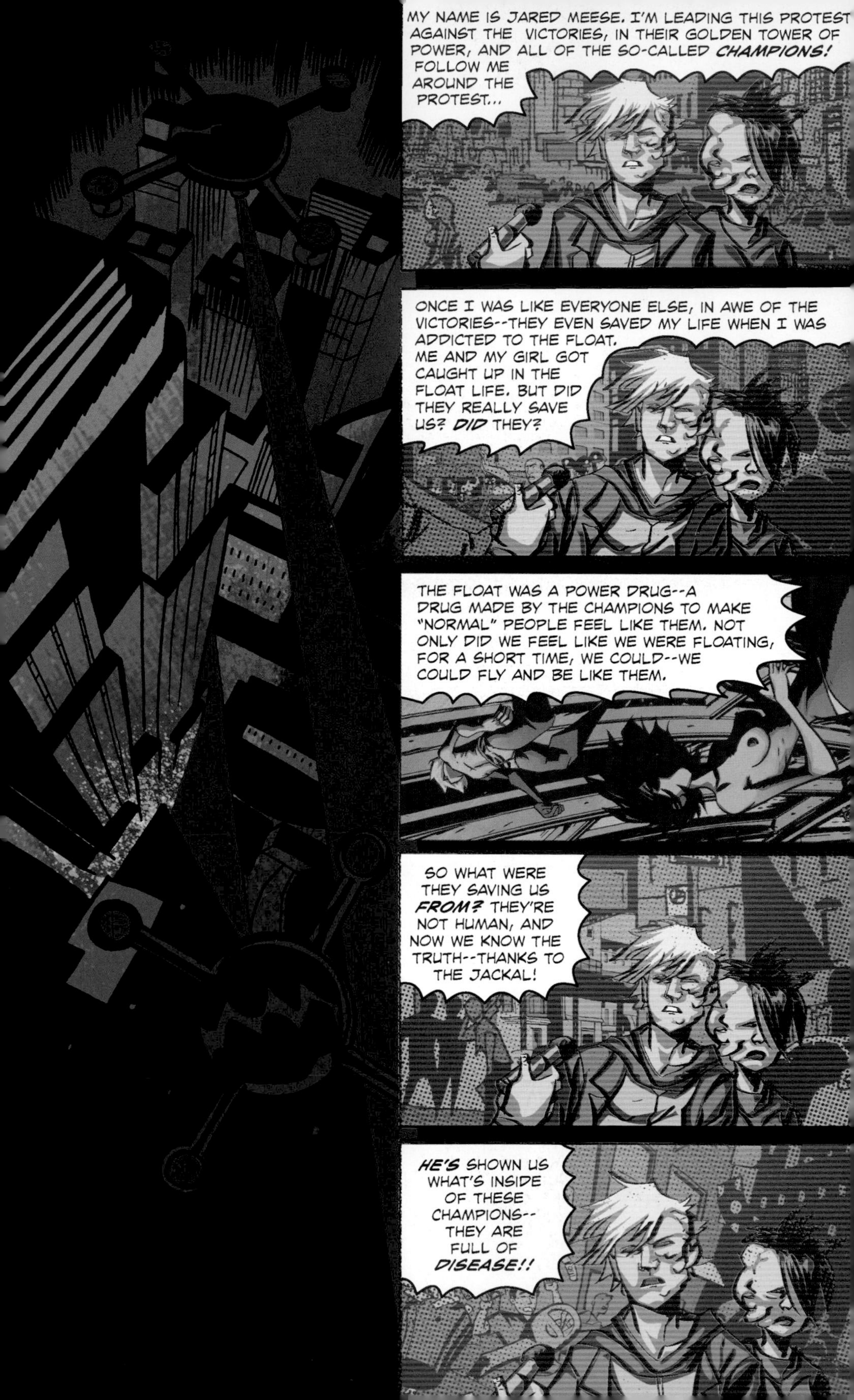
MY NAME IS JARED MEESE. I'M LEADING THIS PROTEST AGAINST THE VICTORIES, IN THEIR GOLDEN TOWER OF POWER, AND ALL OF THE SO-CALLED *CHAMPIONS!*
FOLLOW ME AROUND THE PROTEST...
ONCE I WAS LIKE EVERYONE ELSE, IN AWE OF THE VICTORIES--THEY EVEN SAVED MY LIFE WHEN I WAS ADDICTED TO THE FLOAT.
ME AND MY GIRL GOT CAUGHT UP IN THE FLOAT LIFE. BUT DID THEY REALLY SAVE US? *DID* THEY?
THE FLOAT WAS A POWER DRUG--A DRUG MADE BY THE CHAMPIONS TO MAKE "NORMAL" PEOPLE FEEL LIKE THEM. NOT ONLY DID WE FEEL LIKE WE WERE FLOATING, FOR A SHORT TIME, WE COULD--WE COULD FLY AND BE LIKE THEM.
SO WHAT WERE THEY SAVING US *FROM?* THEY'RE NOT HUMAN, AND NOW WE KNOW THE TRUTH--THANKS TO THE JACKAL!
HE'S SHOWN US WHAT'S INSIDE OF THESE CHAMPIONS--THEY ARE FULL OF *DISEASE!!*

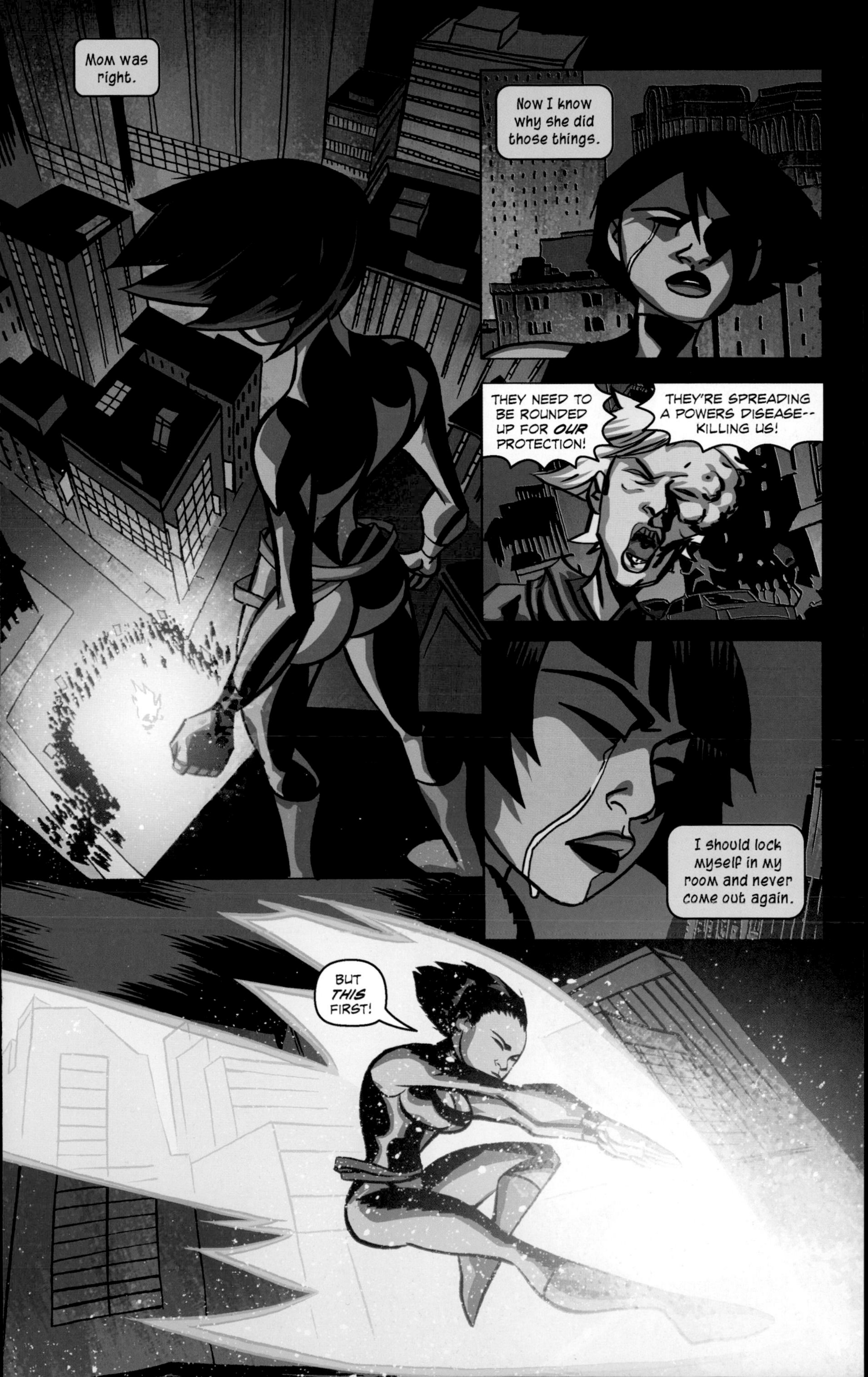
Mom was right.
Now I know why she did those things.
THEY NEED TO BE ROUNDED UP FOR OUR PROTECTION!
THEY'RE SPREADING A POWERS DISEASE-- KILLING US!
I should lock myself in my room and never come out again.
BUT THIS FIRST!

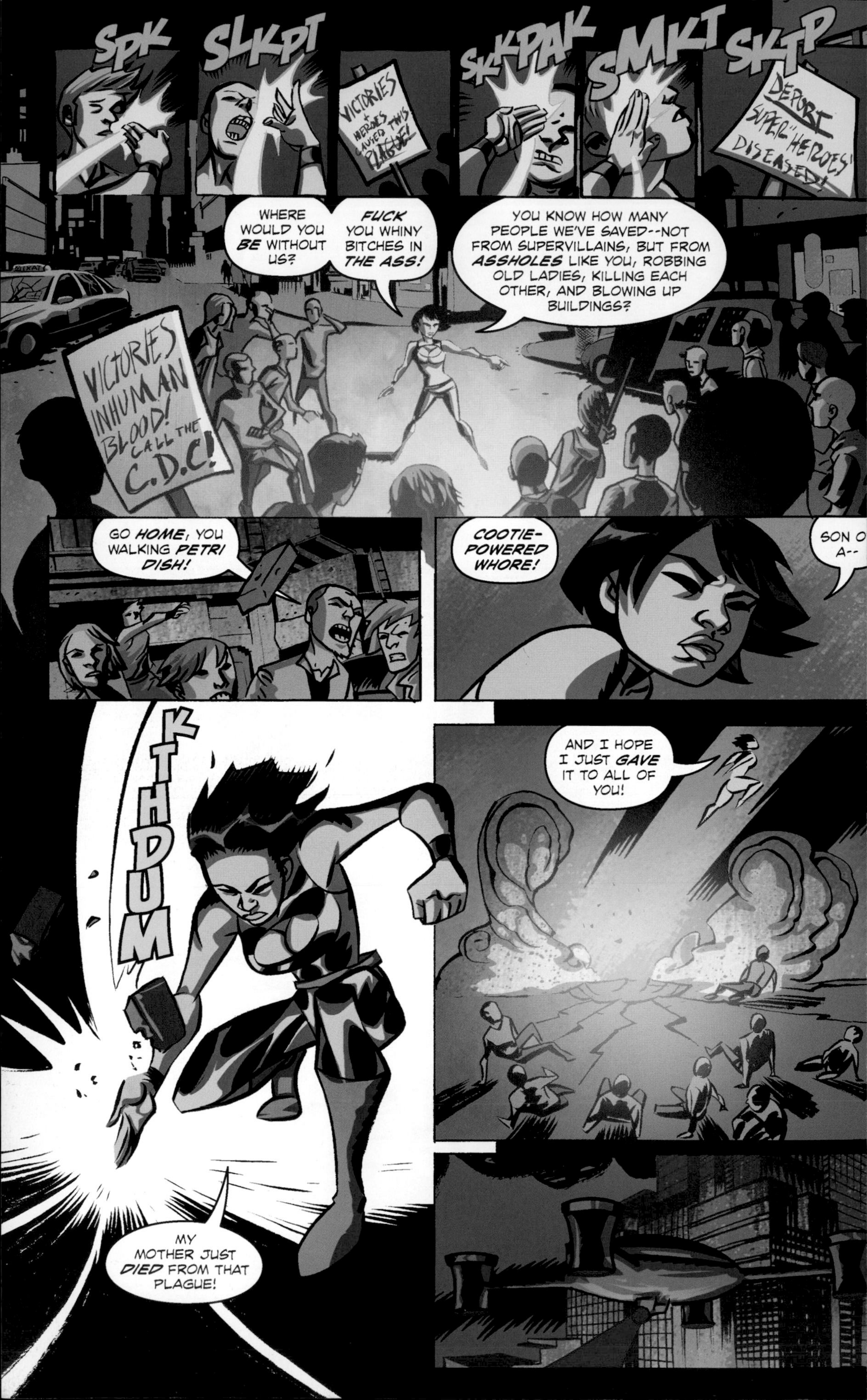
SPK
SLKPT
VICTORIES + HEROES CAUSED THIS PLAGUE!
SKKPAK
SMKT
SKTP
DEPORT "SUPER"HEROES! DISEASED!
WHERE WOULD YOU BE WITHOUT US?
FUCK YOU WHINY BITCHES IN THE ASS!
YOU KNOW HOW MANY PEOPLE WE'VE SAVED--NOT FROM SUPERVILLAINS, BUT FROM ASSHOLES LIKE YOU, ROBBING OLD LADIES, KILLING EACH OTHER, AND BLOWING UP BUILDINGS?
VICTORIES INHUMAN BLOOD! CALL THE C.D.C!
GO HOME, YOU WALKING PETRI DISH!
COOTIE-POWERED WHORE!
SON O A--
KTHDUM
MY MOTHER JUST DIED FROM THAT PLAGUE!
AND I HOPE I JUST GAVE IT TO ALL OF YOU!

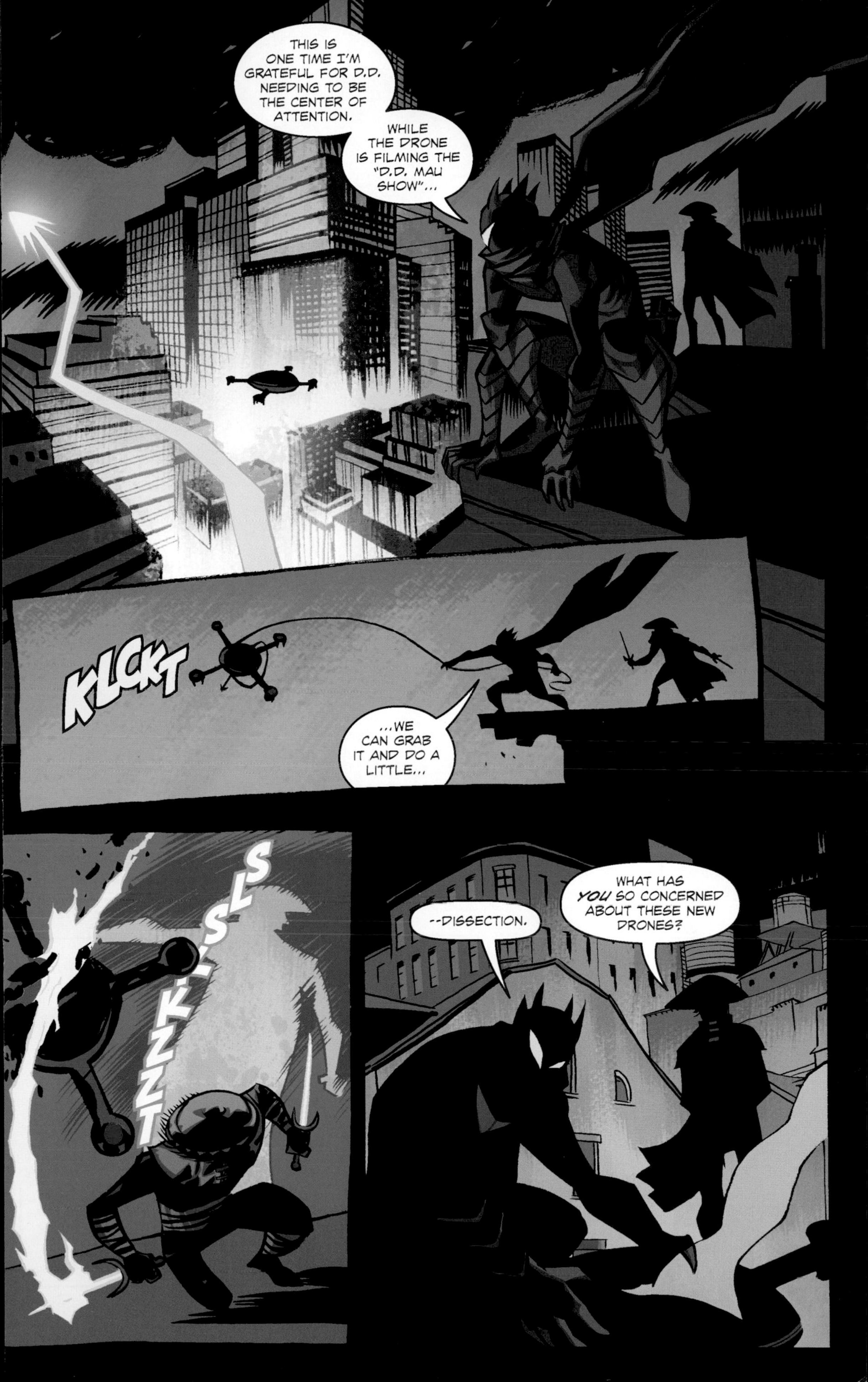
THIS IS ONE TIME I'M GRATEFUL FOR D.D. NEEDING TO BE THE CENTER OF ATTENTION.
WHILE THE DRONE IS FILMING THE "D.D. MAU SHOW"...
KLCKT
...WE CAN GRAB IT AND DO A LITTLE...
KZZZT
SLSLS
--DISSECTION.
WHAT HAS *YOU* SO CONCERNED ABOUT THESE NEW DRONES?

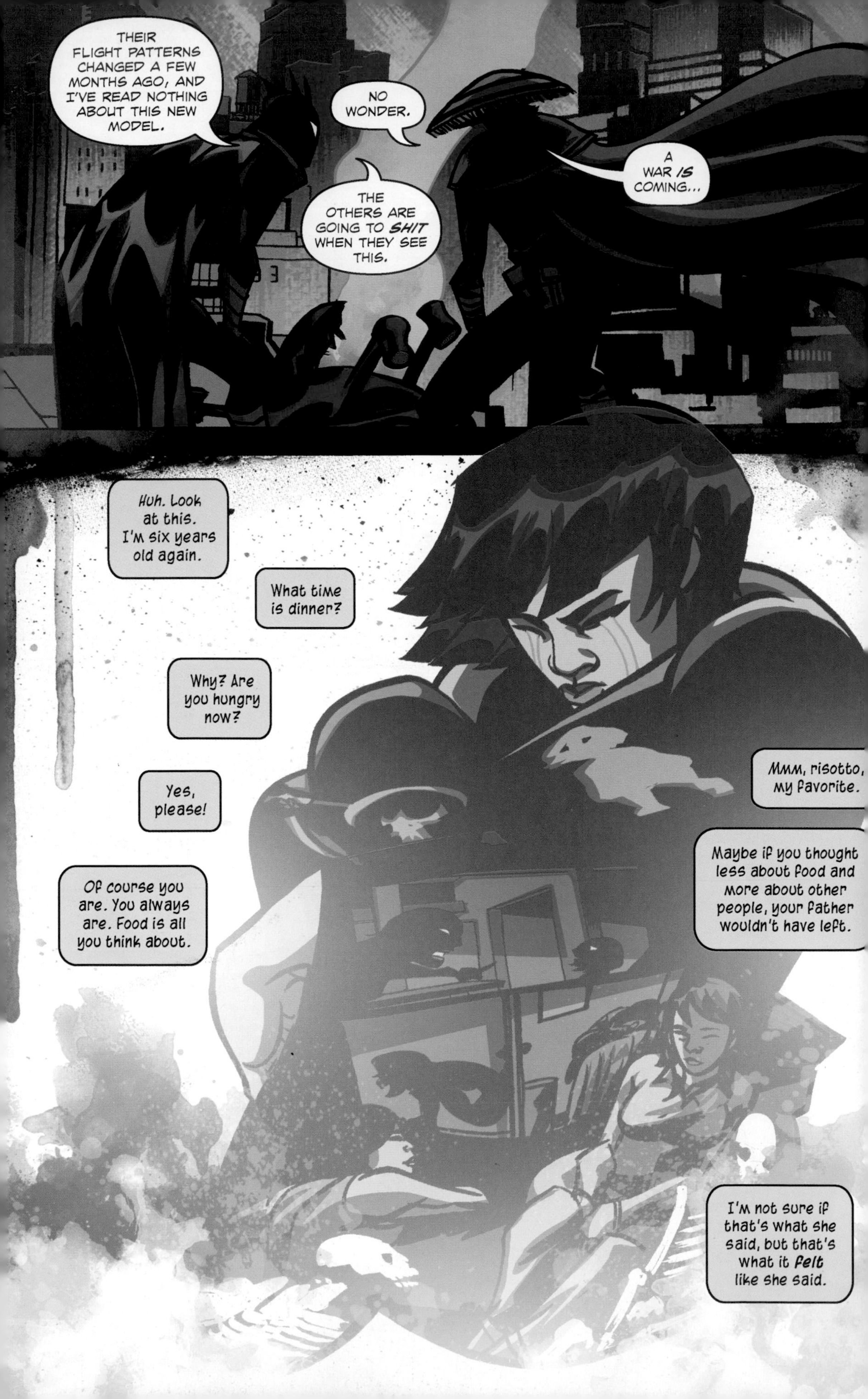
THEIR FLIGHT PATTERNS CHANGED A FEW MONTHS AGO, AND I'VE READ NOTHING ABOUT THIS NEW MODEL.
NO WONDER.
THE OTHERS ARE GOING TO SHIT WHEN THEY SEE THIS.
A WAR IS COMING...
Huh. Look at this. I'm six years old again.
What time is dinner?
Why? Are you hungry now?
Yes, please!
Of course you are. You always are. Food is all you think about.
Mmm, risotto, my favorite.
Maybe if you thought less about food and more about other people, your father wouldn't have left.
I'm not sure if that's what she said, but that's what it felt like she said.

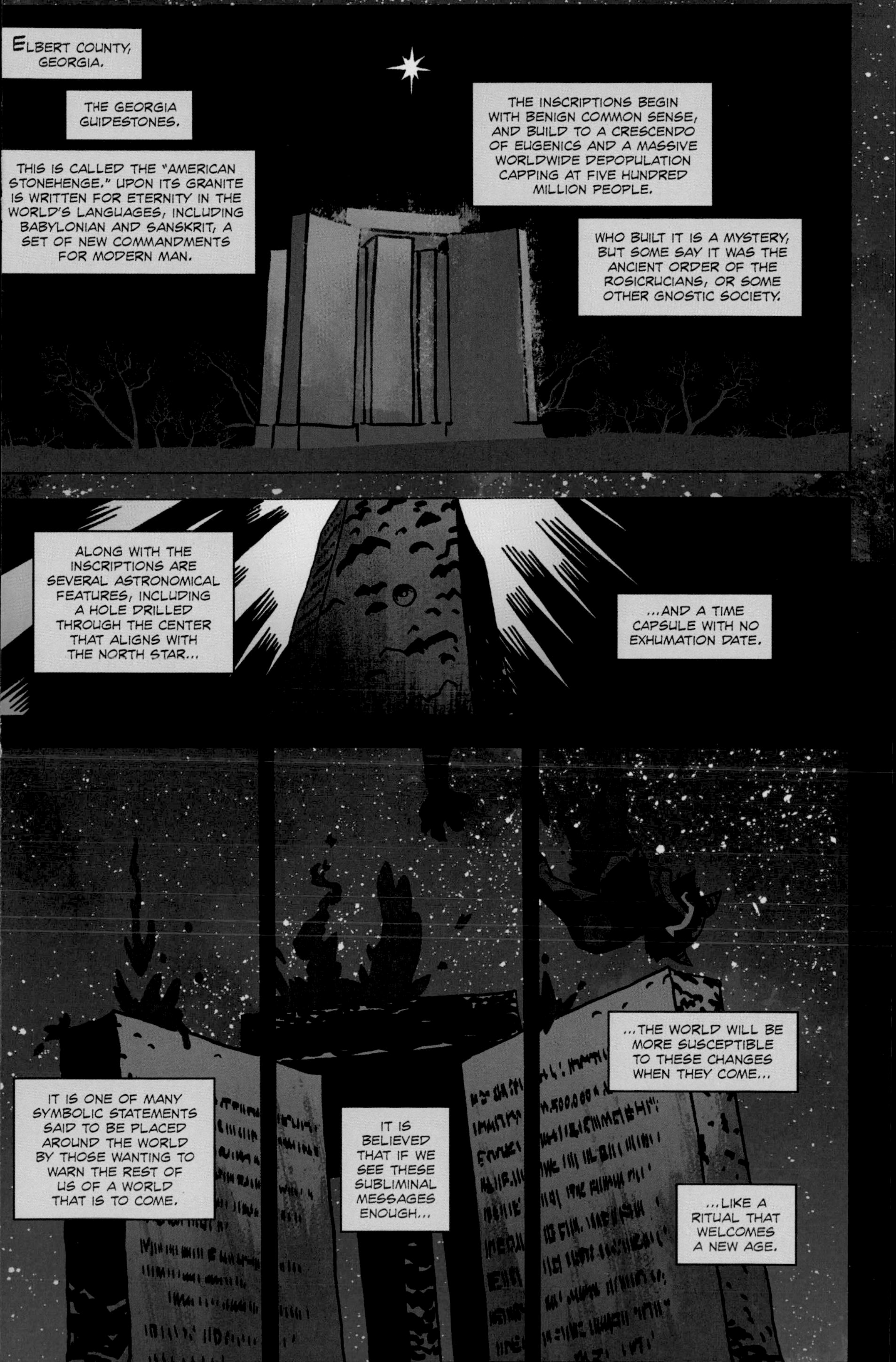
ELBERT COUNTY, GEORGIA.
THE GEORGIA GUIDESTONES.
THIS IS CALLED THE "AMERICAN STONEHENGE." UPON ITS GRANITE IS WRITTEN FOR ETERNITY IN THE WORLD'S LANGUAGES, INCLUDING BABYLONIAN AND SANSKRIT, A SET OF NEW COMMANDMENTS FOR MODERN MAN.
THE INSCRIPTIONS BEGIN WITH BENIGN COMMON SENSE, AND BUILD TO A CRESCENDO OF EUGENICS AND A MASSIVE WORLDWIDE DEPOPULATION CAPPING AT FIVE HUNDRED MILLION PEOPLE.
WHO BUILT IT IS A MYSTERY; BUT SOME SAY IT WAS THE ANCIENT ORDER OF THE ROSICRUCIANS, OR SOME OTHER GNOSTIC SOCIETY.
ALONG WITH THE INSCRIPTIONS ARE SEVERAL ASTRONOMICAL FEATURES, INCLUDING A HOLE DRILLED THROUGH THE CENTER THAT ALIGNS WITH THE NORTH STAR...
...AND A TIME CAPSULE WITH NO EXHUMATION DATE.
IT IS ONE OF MANY SYMBOLIC STATEMENTS SAID TO BE PLACED AROUND THE WORLD BY THOSE WANTING TO WARN THE REST OF US OF A WORLD THAT IS TO COME.
IT IS BELIEVED THAT IF WE SEE THESE SUBLIMINAL MESSAGES ENOUGH...
...THE WORLD WILL BE MORE SUSCEPTIBLE TO THESE CHANGES WHEN THEY COME...
...LIKE A RITUAL THAT WELCOMES A NEW AGE.

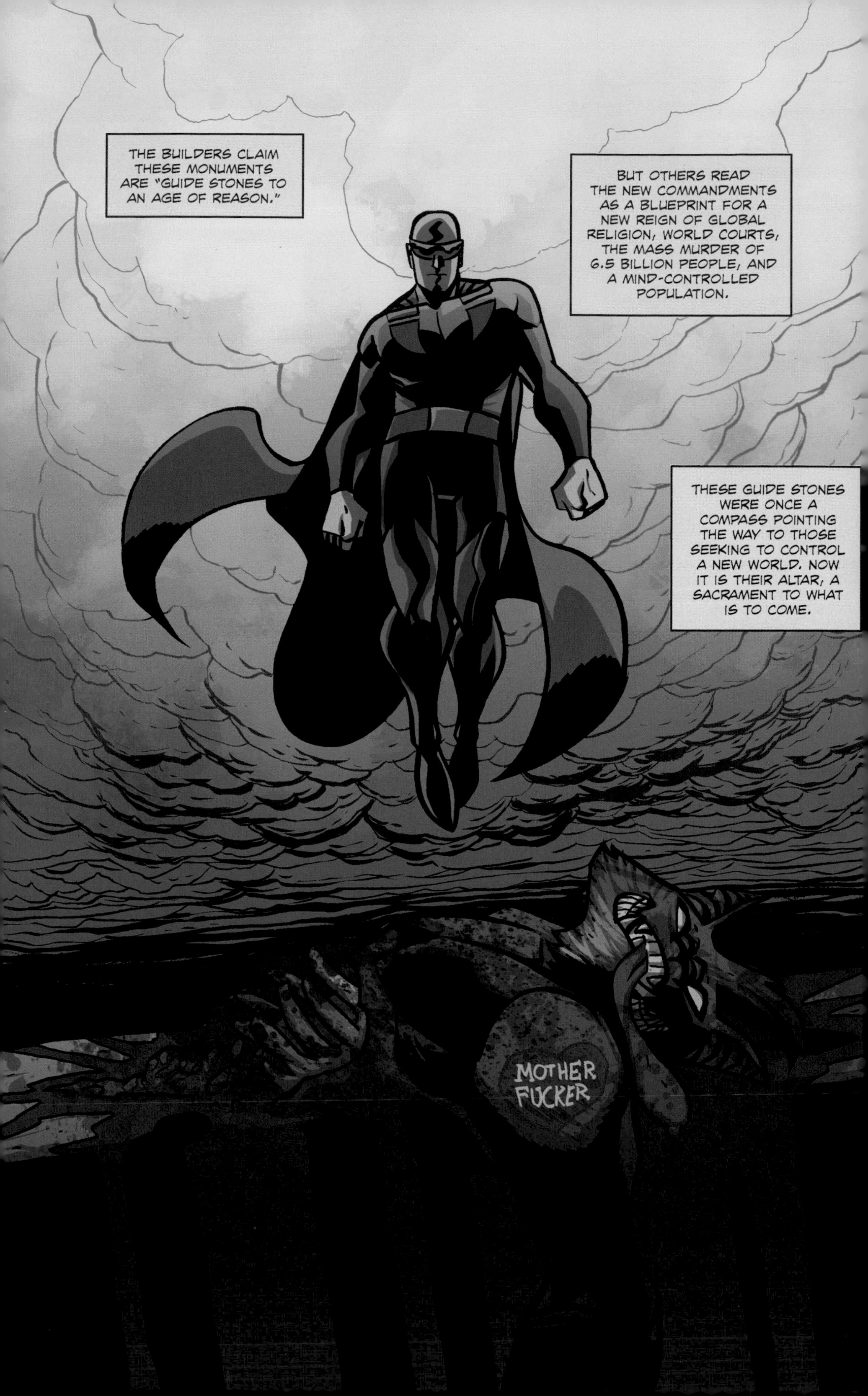
THE BUILDERS CLAIM THESE MONUMENTS ARE "GUIDE STONES TO AN AGE OF REASON."
BUT OTHERS READ THE NEW COMMANDMENTS AS A BLUEPRINT FOR A NEW REIGN OF GLOBAL RELIGION, WORLD COURTS, THE MASS MURDER OF 6.5 BILLION PEOPLE, AND A MIND-CONTROLLED POPULATION.
THESE GUIDE STONES WERE ONCE A COMPASS POINTING THE WAY TO THOSE SEEKING TO CONTROL A NEW WORLD. NOW IT IS THEIR ALTAR, A SACRAMENT TO WHAT IS TO COME.
MOTHER FUCKER

CHAPTER SIX

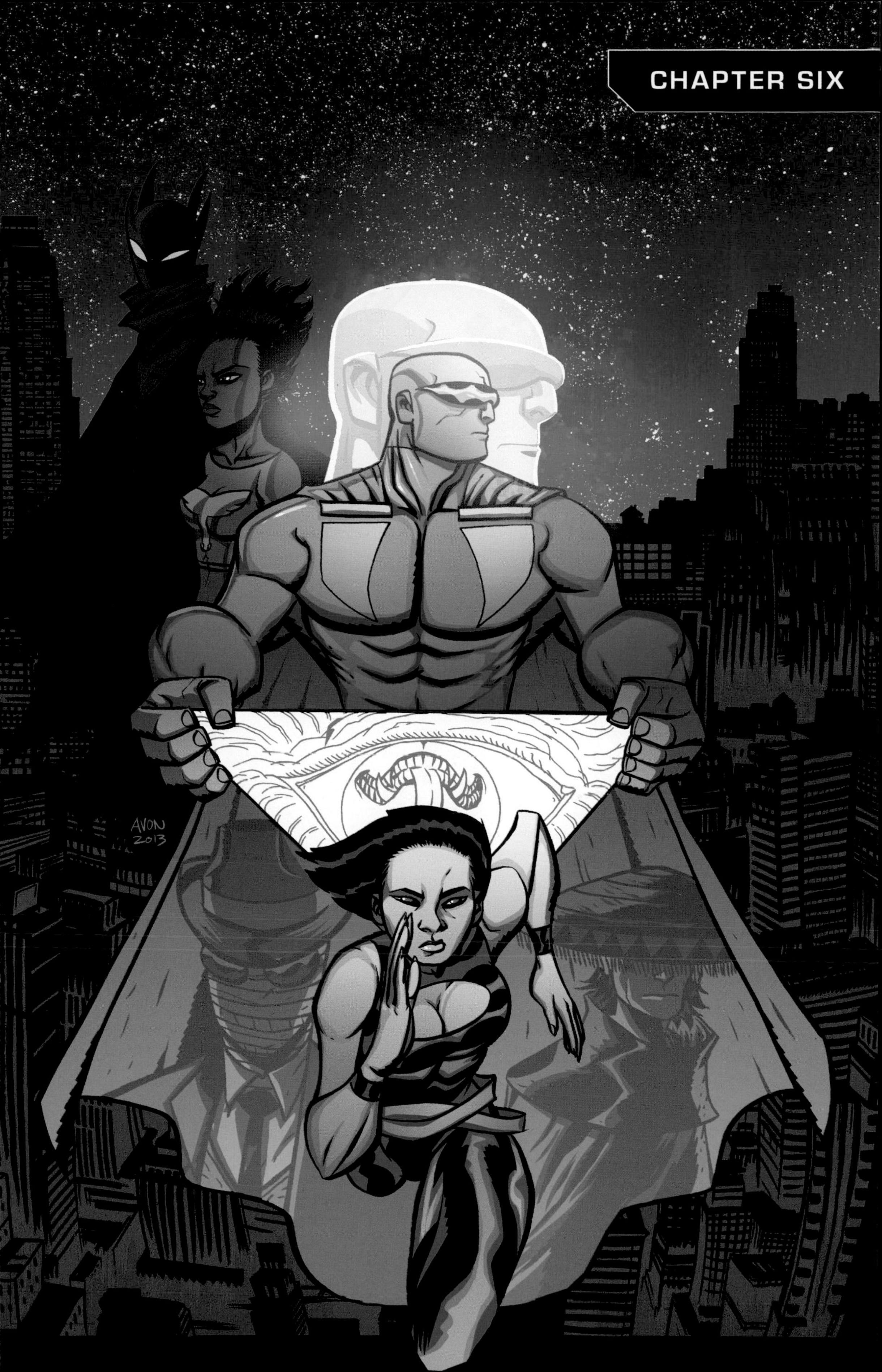
AVON
2013

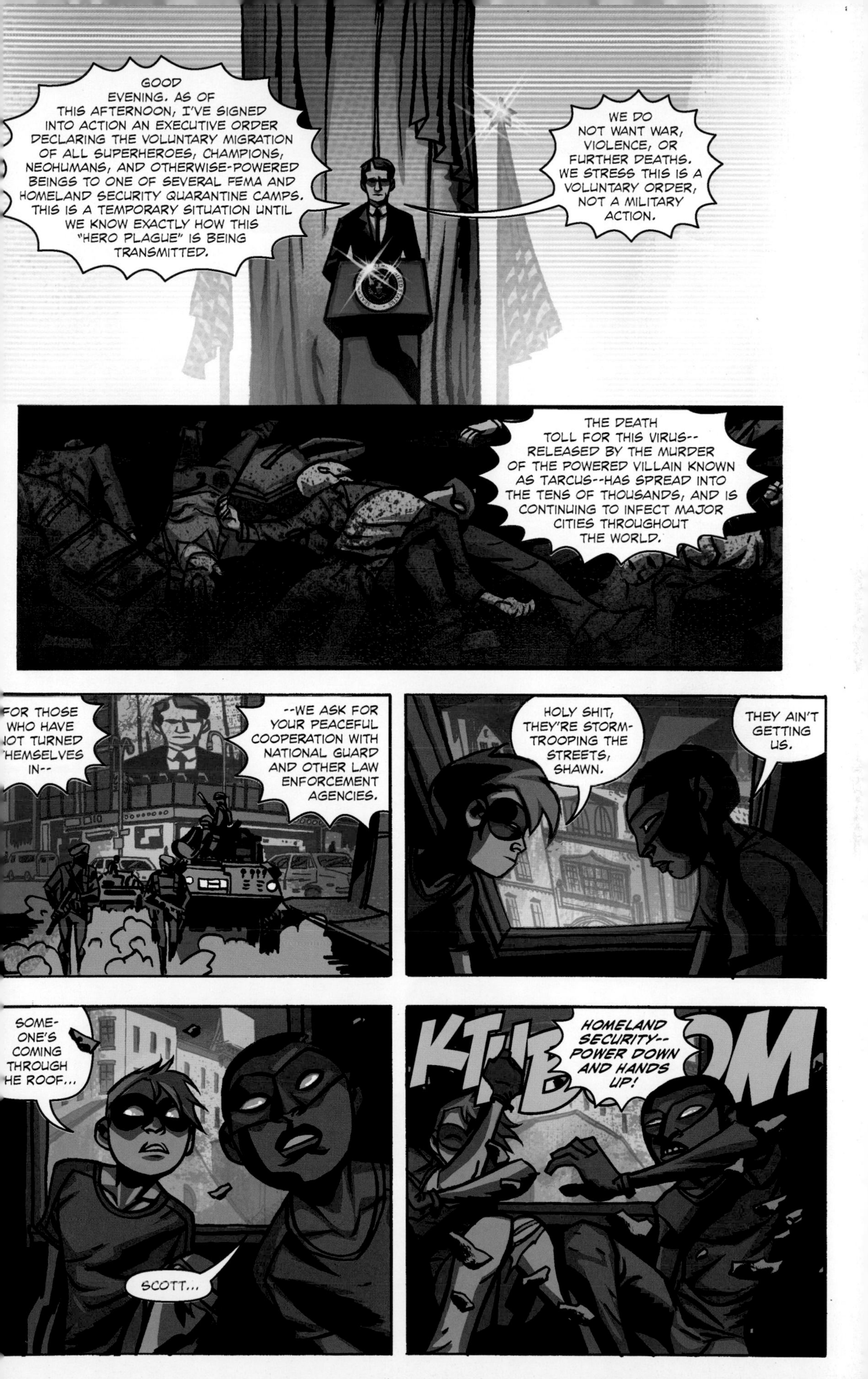
GOOD EVENING. AS OF THIS AFTERNOON, I'VE SIGNED INTO ACTION AN EXECUTIVE ORDER DECLARING THE VOLUNTARY MIGRATION OF ALL SUPERHEROES, CHAMPIONS, NEOHUMANS, AND OTHERWISE-POWERED BEINGS TO ONE OF SEVERAL FEMA AND HOMELAND SECURITY QUARANTINE CAMPS. THIS IS A TEMPORARY SITUATION UNTIL WE KNOW EXACTLY HOW THIS "HERO PLAGUE" IS BEING TRANSMITTED.
WE DO NOT WANT WAR, VIOLENCE, OR FURTHER DEATHS. WE STRESS THIS IS A VOLUNTARY ORDER, NOT A MILITARY ACTION.
THE DEATH TOLL FOR THIS VIRUS--RELEASED BY THE MURDER OF THE POWERED VILLAIN KNOWN AS TARCUS--HAS SPREAD INTO THE TENS OF THOUSANDS, AND IS CONTINUING TO INFECT MAJOR CITIES THROUGHOUT THE WORLD.
FOR THOSE WHO HAVE NOT TURNED THEMSELVES IN--
--WE ASK FOR YOUR PEACEFUL COOPERATION WITH NATIONAL GUARD AND OTHER LAW ENFORCEMENT AGENCIES.
HOLY SHIT, THEY'RE STORM-TROOPING THE STREETS, SHAWN.
THEY AIN'T GETTING US.
SOME-ONE'S COMING THROUGH THE ROOF...
SCOTT...
KTHOOM
HOMELAND SECURITY--POWER DOWN AND HANDS UP!

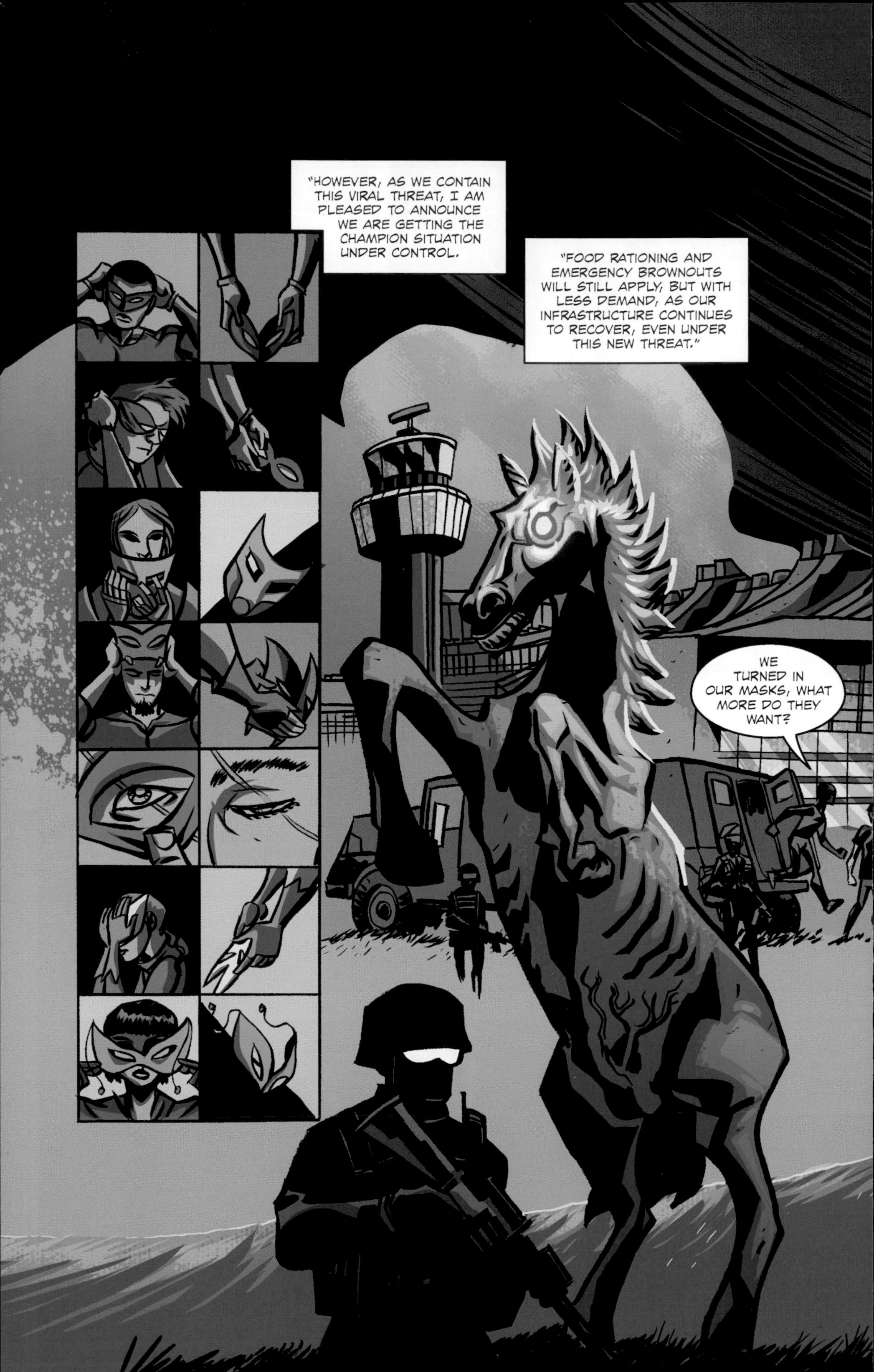
"HOWEVER, AS WE CONTAIN THIS VIRAL THREAT, I AM PLEASED TO ANNOUNCE WE ARE GETTING THE CHAMPION SITUATION UNDER CONTROL.
"FOOD RATIONING AND EMERGENCY BROWNOUTS WILL STILL APPLY, BUT WITH LESS DEMAND, AS OUR INFRASTRUCTURE CONTINUES TO RECOVER, EVEN UNDER THIS NEW THREAT."
WE TURNED IN OUR MASKS, WHAT MORE DO THEY WANT?

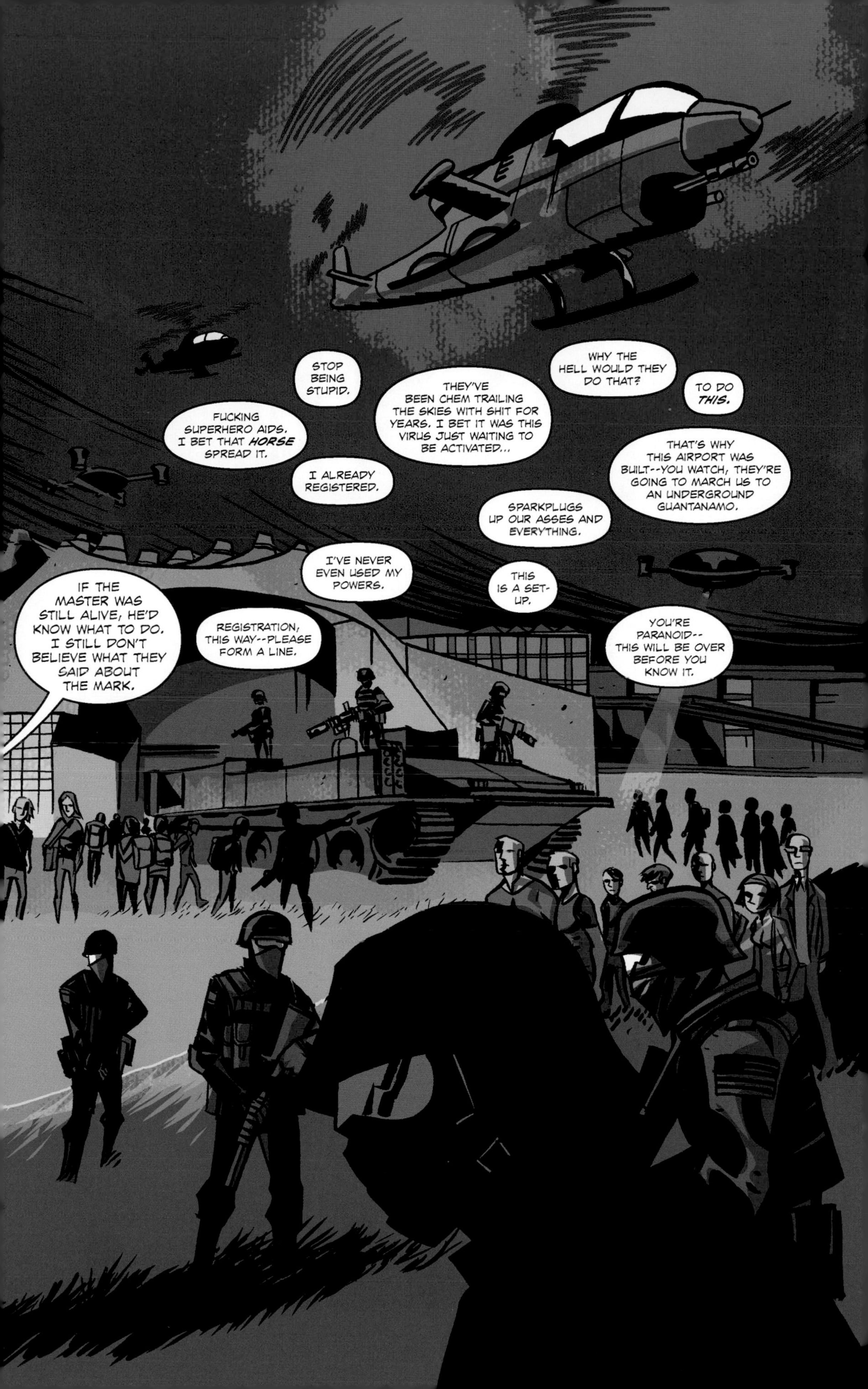

FUCKING SUPERHERO AIDS. I BET THAT *HORSE* SPREAD IT.
STOP BEING STUPID.
THEY'VE BEEN CHEM TRAILING THE SKIES WITH SHIT FOR YEARS. I BET IT WAS THIS VIRUS JUST WAITING TO BE ACTIVATED...
WHY THE HELL WOULD THEY DO THAT?
TO DO *THIS.*
THAT'S WHY THIS AIRPORT WAS BUILT--YOU WATCH, THEY'RE GOING TO MARCH US TO AN UNDERGROUND GUANTANAMO.
I ALREADY REGISTERED.
SPARKPLUGS UP OUR ASSES AND EVERYTHING.
I'VE NEVER EVEN USED MY POWERS.
THIS IS A SET-UP.
IF THE MASTER WAS STILL ALIVE, HE'D KNOW WHAT TO DO. I STILL DON'T BELIEVE WHAT THEY SAID ABOUT THE MARK.
REGISTRATION, THIS WAY--PLEASE FORM A LINE.
YOU'RE PARANOID--THIS WILL BE OVER BEFORE YOU KNOW IT.

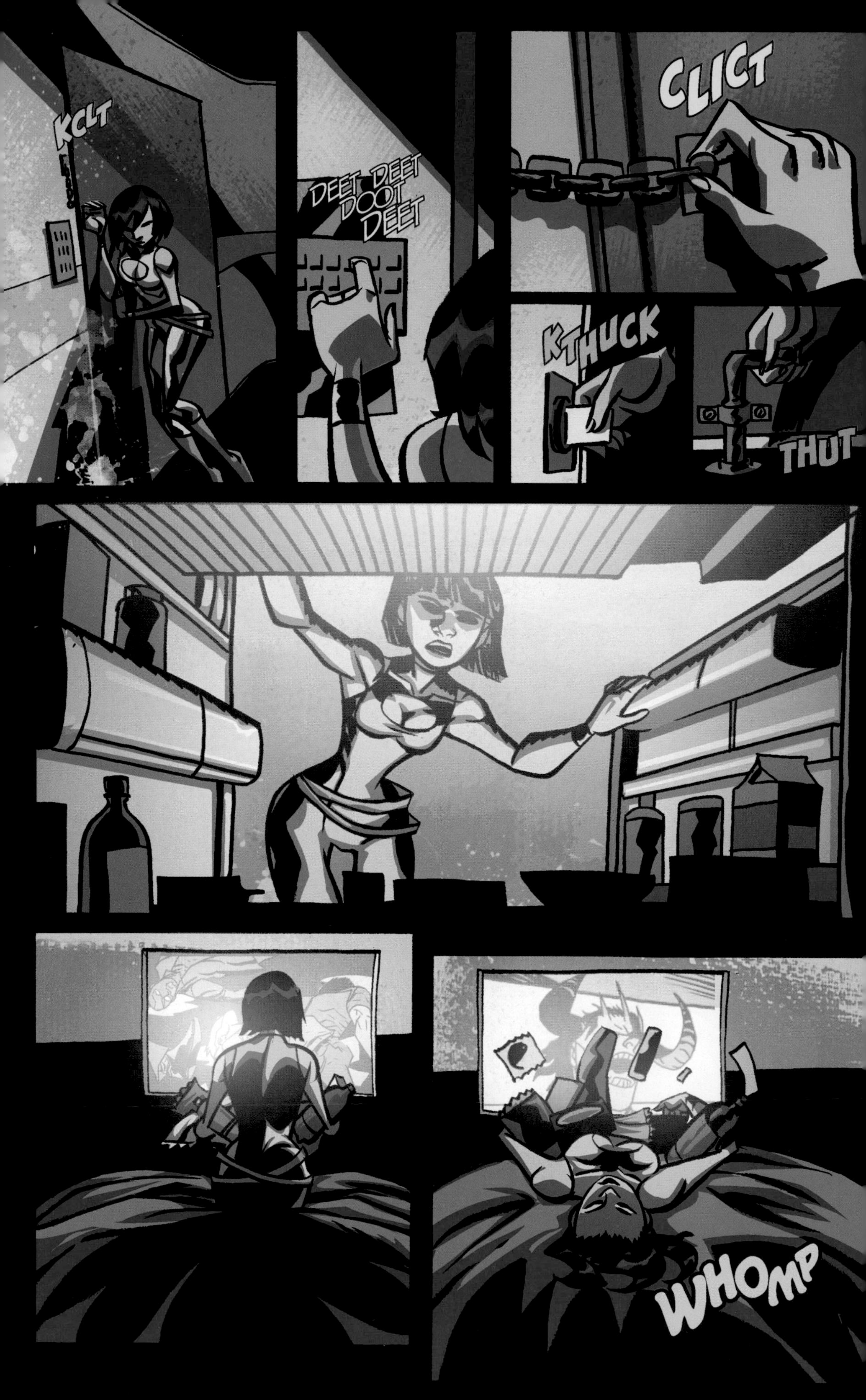
KCLT
DEET DEET DOOT DEET
CLICT
KTHUCK
THUT
WHOMP

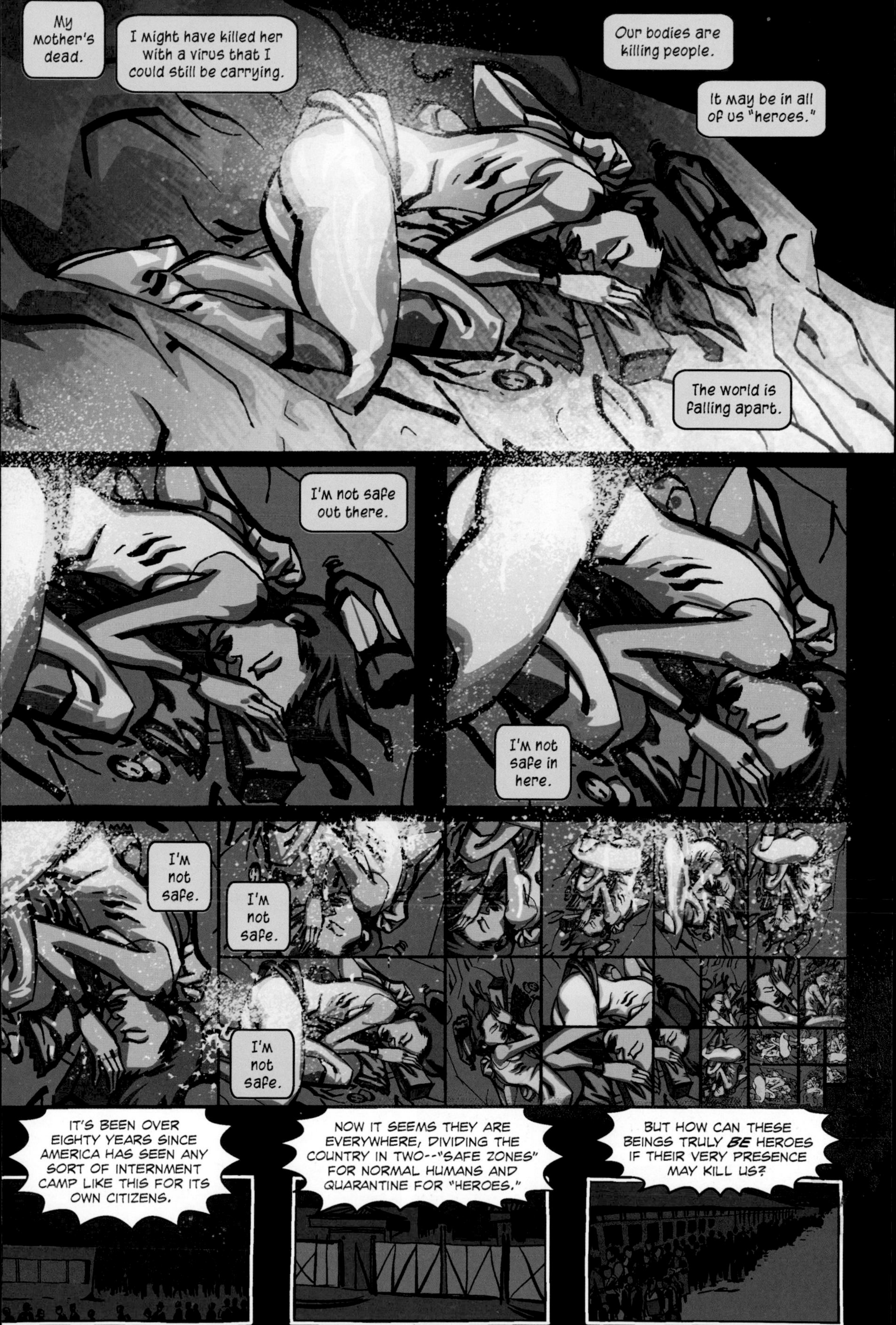
My mother's dead.
I might have killed her with a virus that I could still be carrying.
Our bodies are killing people.
It may be in all of us "heroes."
The world is falling apart.
I'm not safe out there.
I'm not safe in here.
I'm not safe.
I'm not safe.
I'm not safe.
IT'S BEEN OVER EIGHTY YEARS SINCE AMERICA HAS SEEN ANY SORT OF INTERNMENT CAMP LIKE THIS FOR ITS OWN CITIZENS.
NOW IT SEEMS THEY ARE EVERYWHERE, DIVIDING THE COUNTRY IN TWO--"SAFE ZONES" FOR NORMAL HUMANS AND QUARANTINE FOR "HEROES."
BUT HOW CAN THESE BEINGS TRULY *BE* HEROES IF THEIR VERY PRESENCE MAY KILL US?

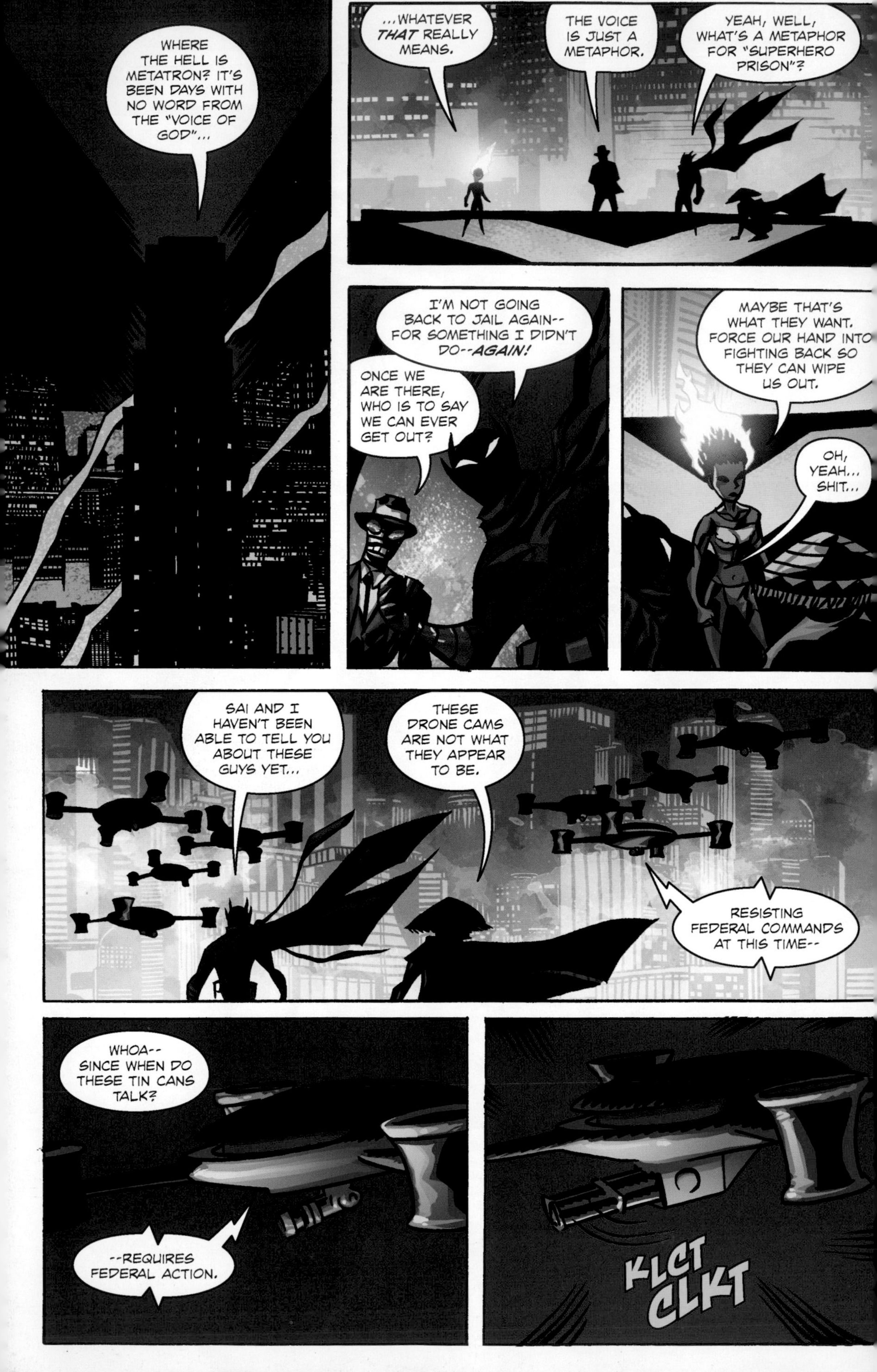

WHERE THE HELL IS METATRON? IT'S BEEN DAYS WITH NO WORD FROM THE "VOICE OF GOD"...
...WHATEVER THAT REALLY MEANS.
THE VOICE IS JUST A METAPHOR.
YEAH, WELL, WHAT'S A METAPHOR FOR "SUPERHERO PRISON"?
I'M NOT GOING BACK TO JAIL AGAIN-- FOR SOMETHING I DIDN'T DO--AGAIN!
ONCE WE ARE THERE, WHO IS TO SAY WE CAN EVER GET OUT?
MAYBE THAT'S WHAT THEY WANT. FORCE OUR HAND INTO FIGHTING BACK SO THEY CAN WIPE US OUT.
OH, YEAH... SHIT...
SAI AND I HAVEN'T BEEN ABLE TO TELL YOU ABOUT THESE GUYS YET...
THESE DRONE CAMS ARE NOT WHAT THEY APPEAR TO BE.
RESISTING FEDERAL COMMANDS AT THIS TIME--
WHOA-- SINCE WHEN DO THESE TIN CANS TALK?
--REQUIRES FEDERAL ACTION.
KLCT CLKT

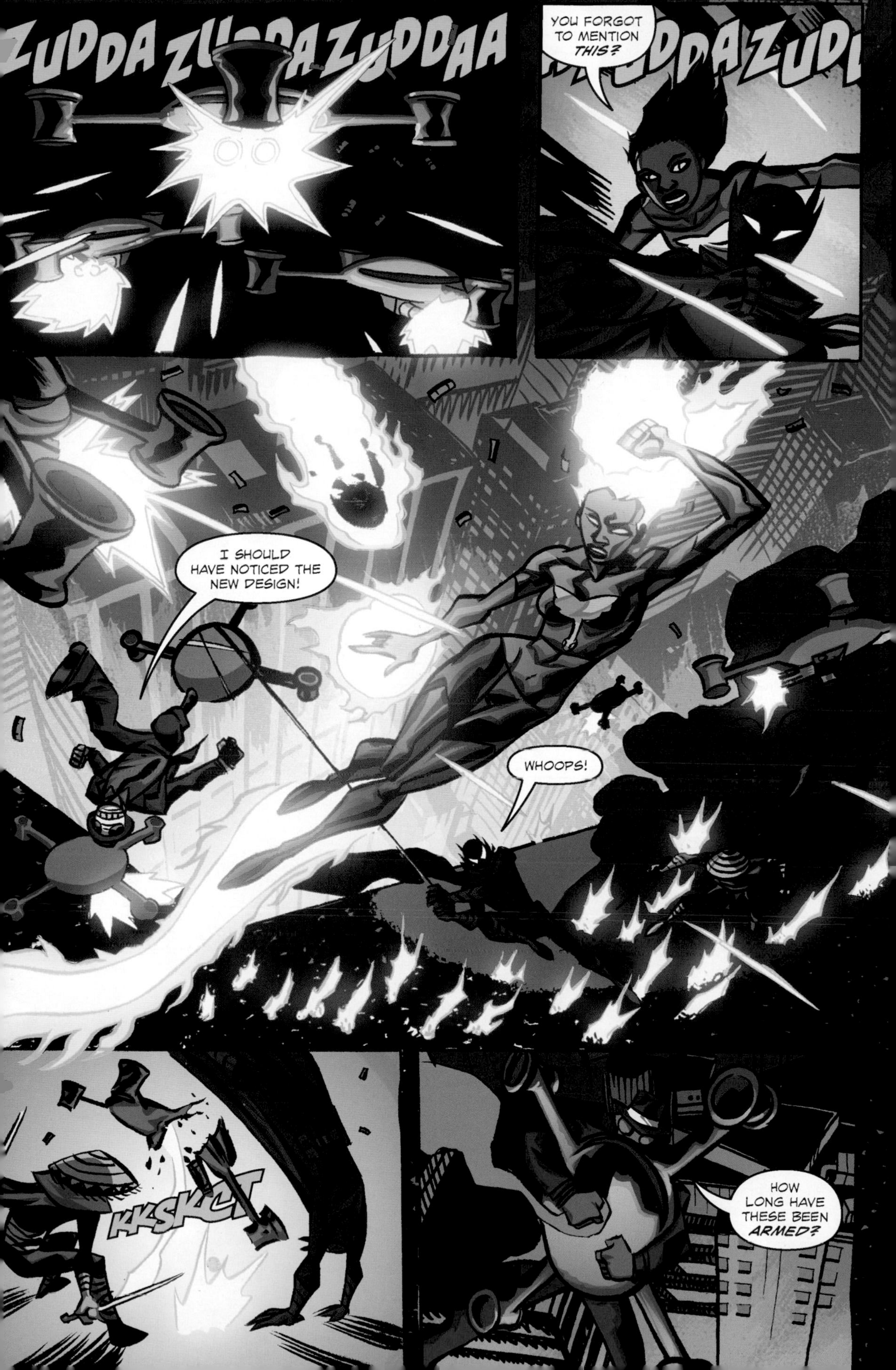
ZUDDA ZUDDA ZUDDAA
YOU FORGOT TO MENTION *THIS?*
I SHOULD HAVE NOTICED THE NEW DESIGN!
WHOOPS!
KKSKCT
HOW LONG HAVE THESE BEEN *ARMED?*

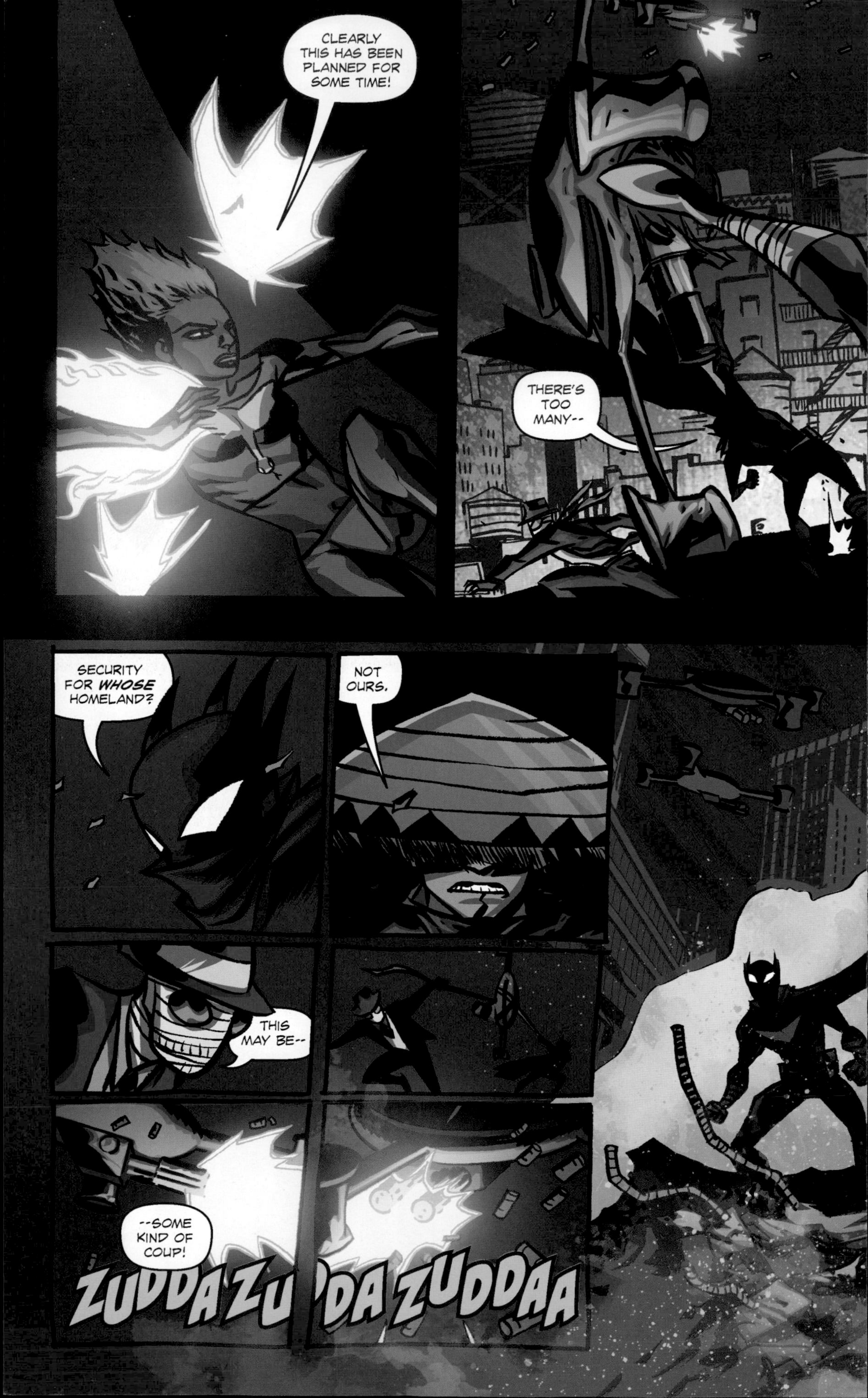
CLEARLY THIS HAS BEEN PLANNED FOR SOME TIME!
THERE'S TOO MANY--
SECURITY FOR *WHOSE* HOMELAND?
NOT OURS.
THIS MAY BE--
--SOME KIND OF COUP!
ZUDDA ZUDDA ZUDDAA

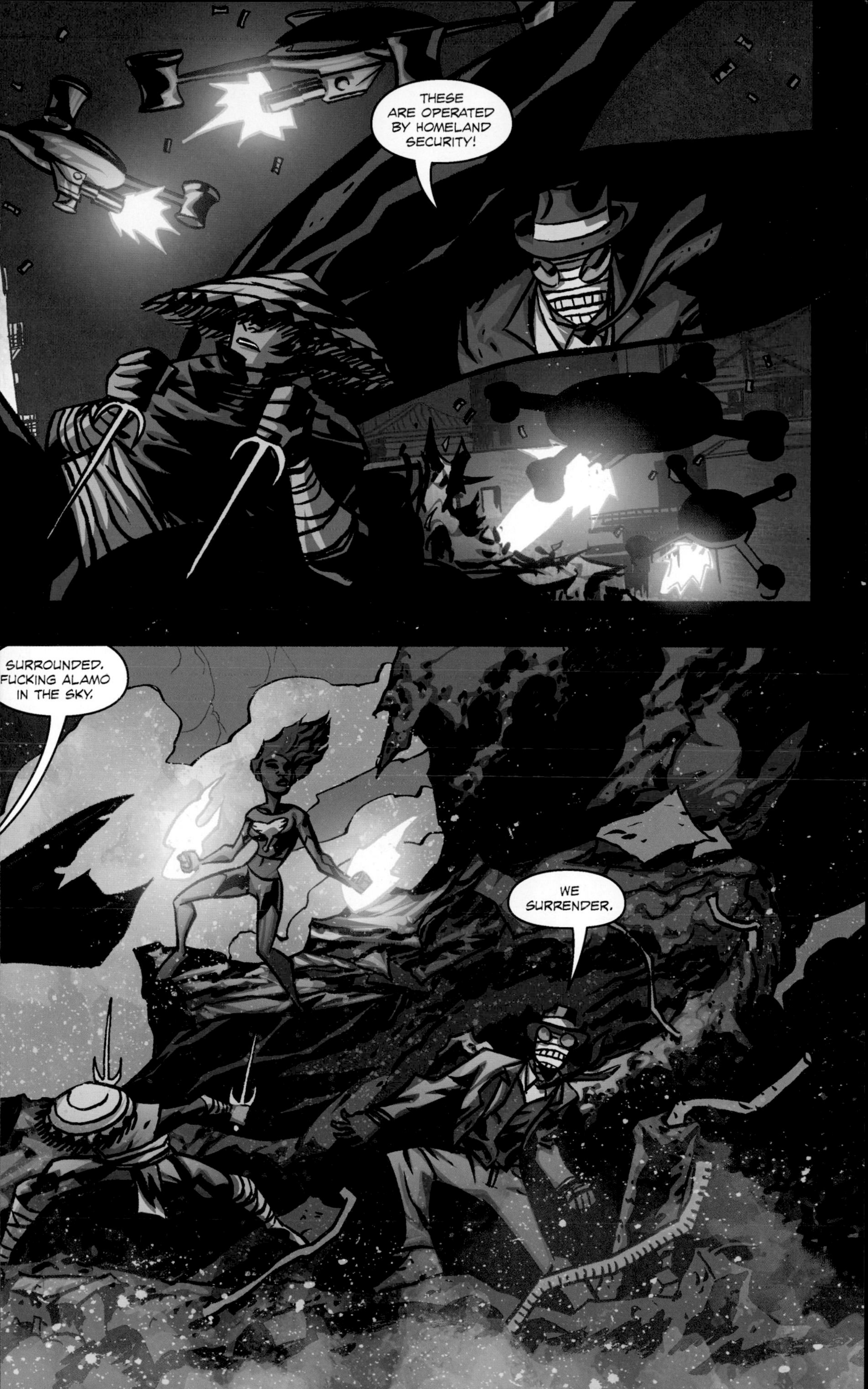
THESE ARE OPERATED BY HOMELAND SECURITY!
SURROUNDED. FUCKING ALAMO IN THE SKY.
WE SURRENDER.

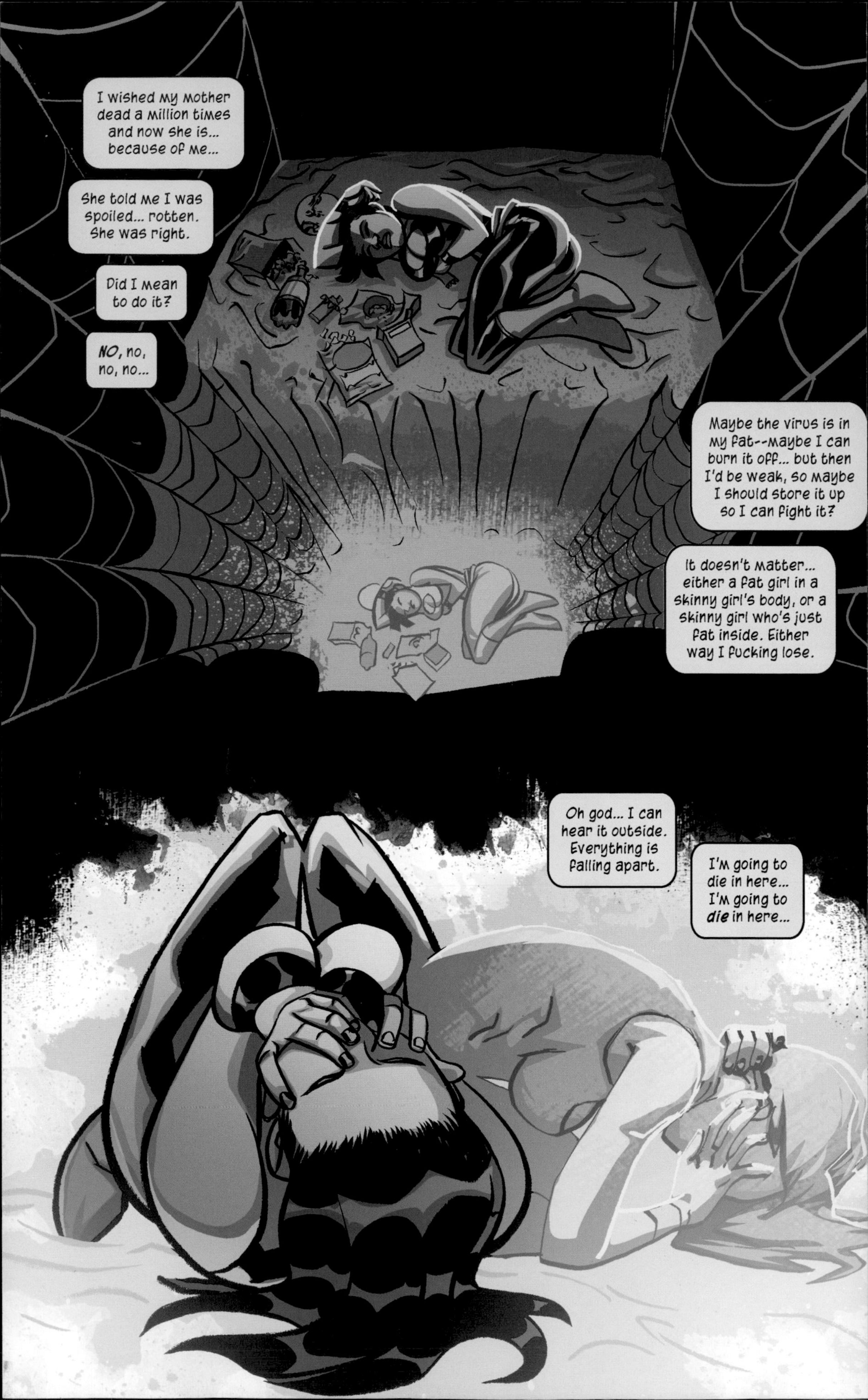
I wished my mother dead a million times and now she is... because of me...
She told me I was spoiled... rotten. She was right.
Did I mean to do it?
NO, no, no, no...
Maybe the virus is in my fat--maybe I can burn it off... but then I'd be weak, so maybe I should store it up so I can fight it?
It doesn't matter... either a fat girl in a skinny girl's body, or a skinny girl who's just fat inside. Either way I fucking lose.
Oh god... I can hear it outside. Everything is falling apart.
I'm going to die in here... I'm going to *die* in here...

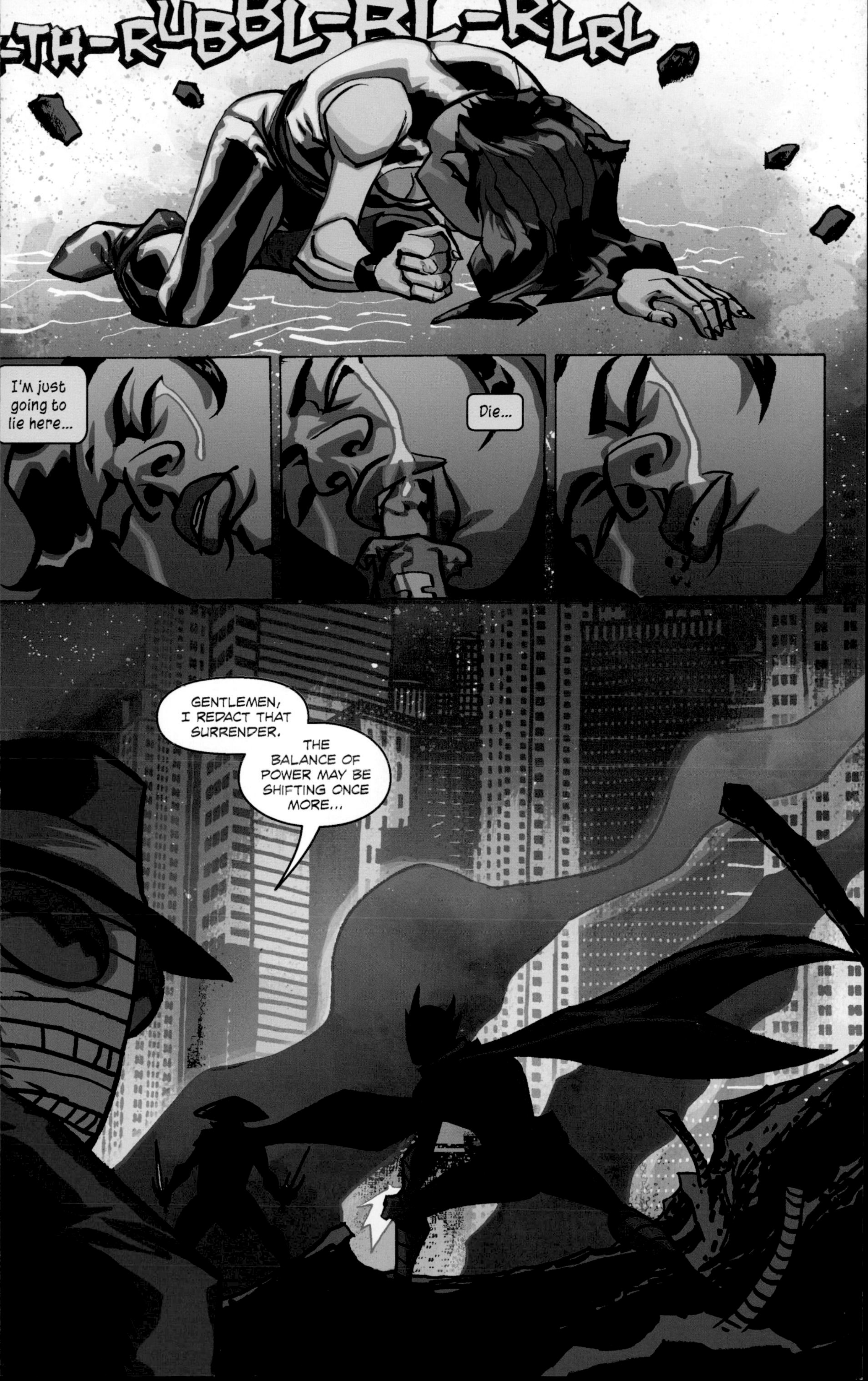
TH-RUBBL-RL-RLRL
I'm just going to lie here...
Die...
GENTLEMEN, I REDACT THAT SURRENDER.
THE BALANCE OF POWER MAY BE SHIFTING ONCE MORE...

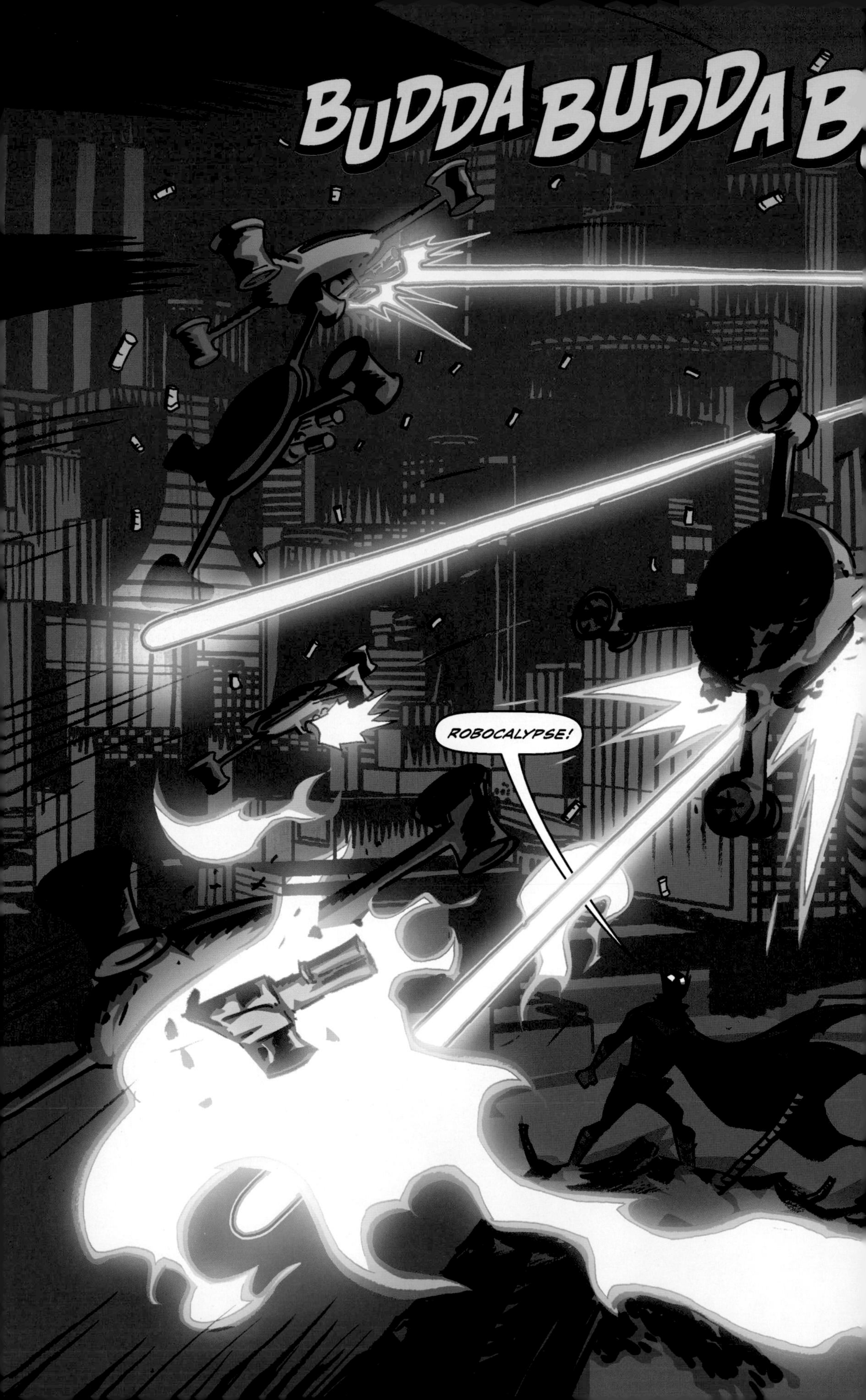
BUDDA BUDDA B
ROBOCALYPSE!

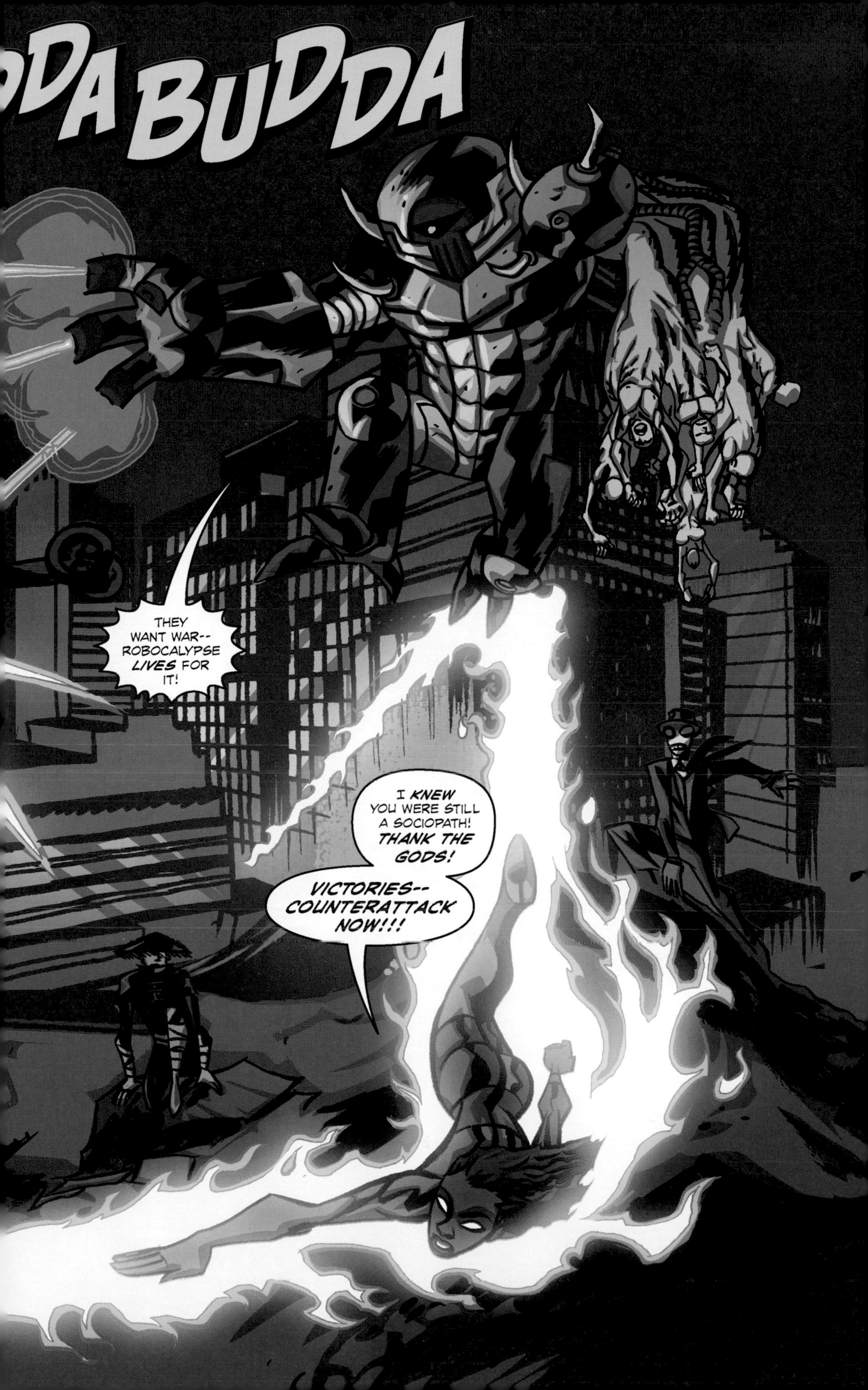
DDA BUDDA
THEY WANT WAR-- ROBOCALYPSE LIVES FOR IT!
I KNEW YOU WERE STILL A SOCIOPATH! THANK THE GODS!
VICTORIES-- COUNTERATTACK NOW!!!

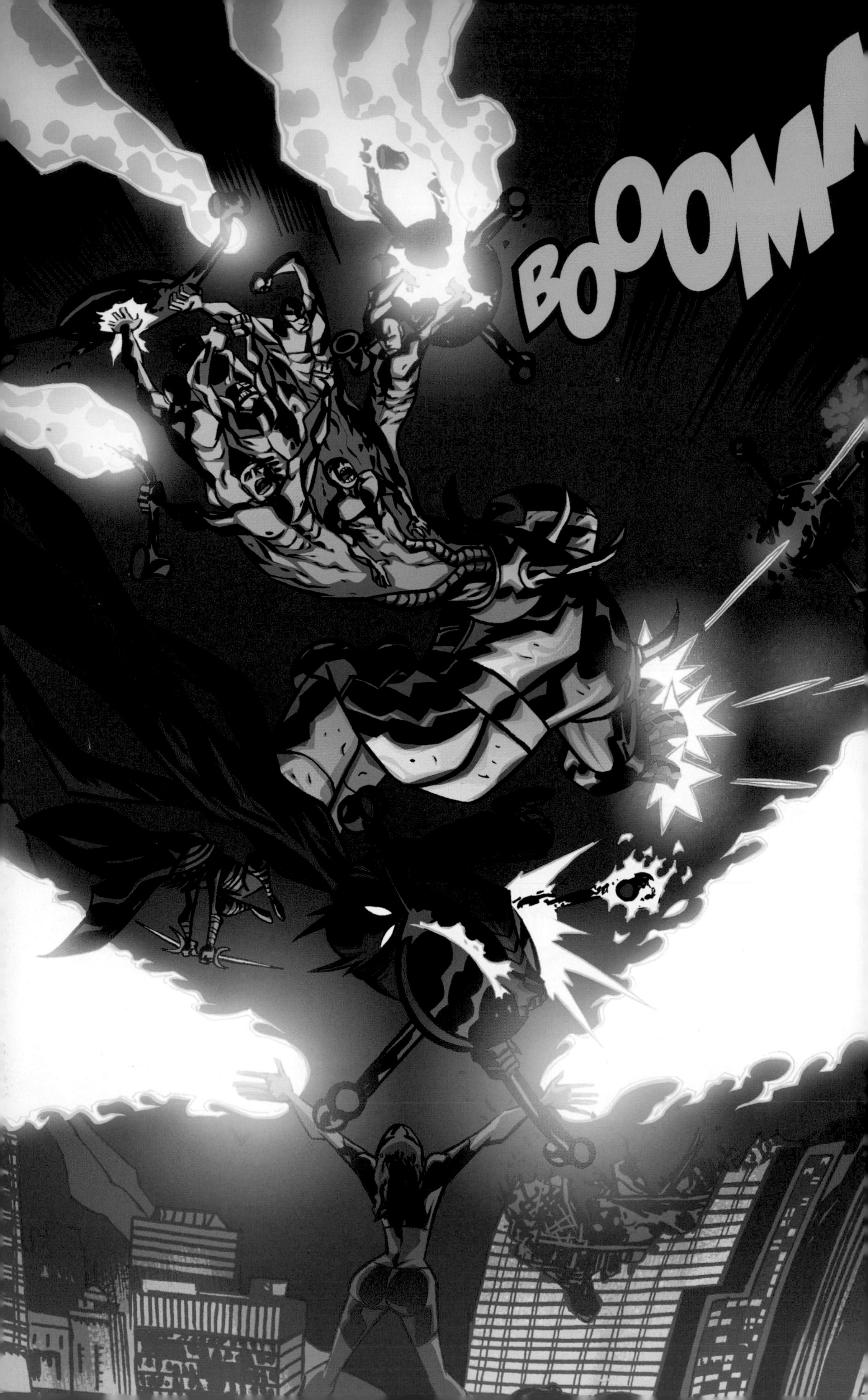
BOOOOM

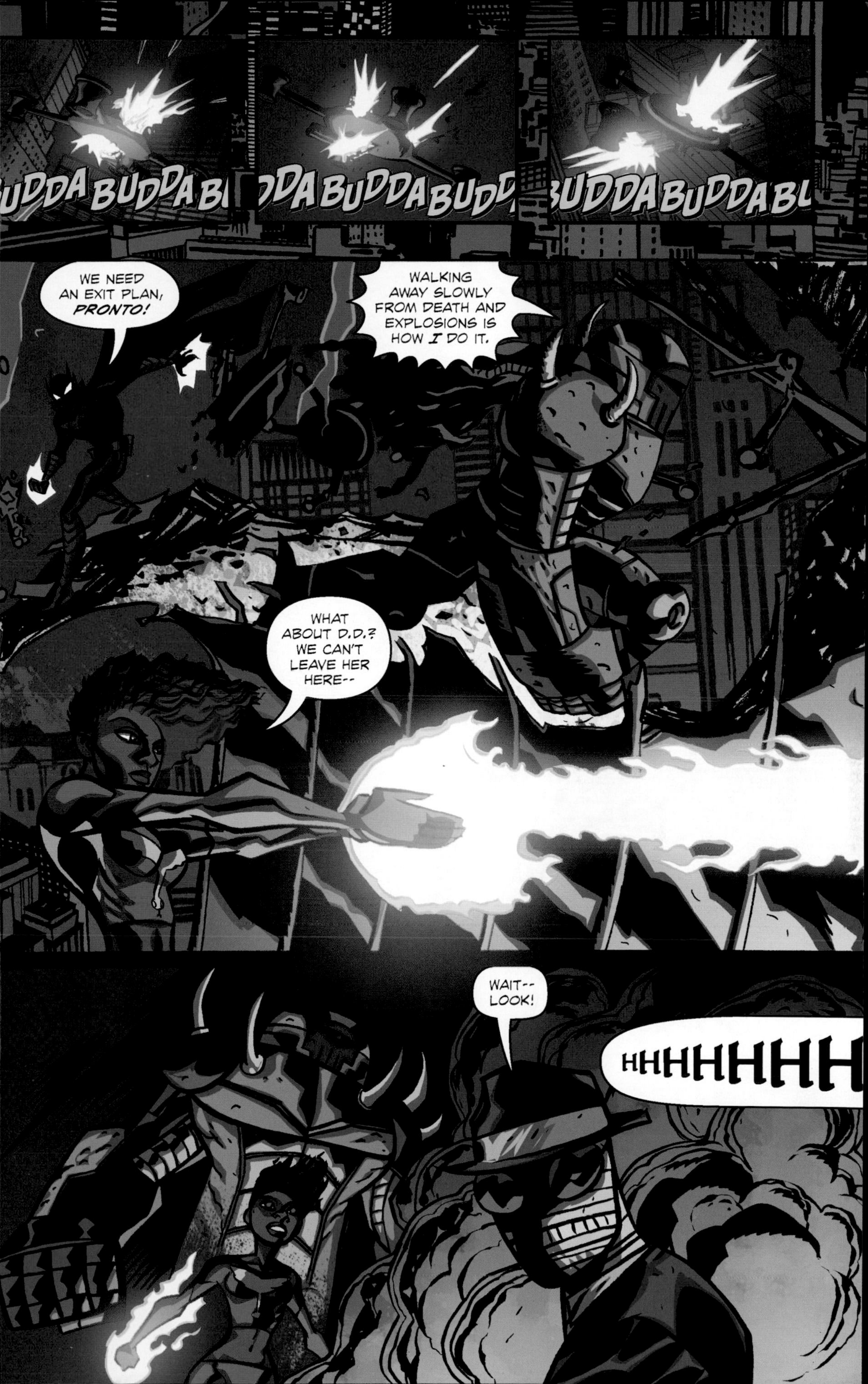

BUDDA BUDDA BU
DDA BUDDA BUDD
BUDDA BUDDA BU
WE NEED AN EXIT PLAN, *PRONTO!*
WALKING AWAY SLOWLY FROM DEATH AND EXPLOSIONS IS HOW *I* DO IT.
WHAT ABOUT D.D.? WE CAN'T LEAVE HER HERE--
WAIT-- LOOK!
HHHHHHH

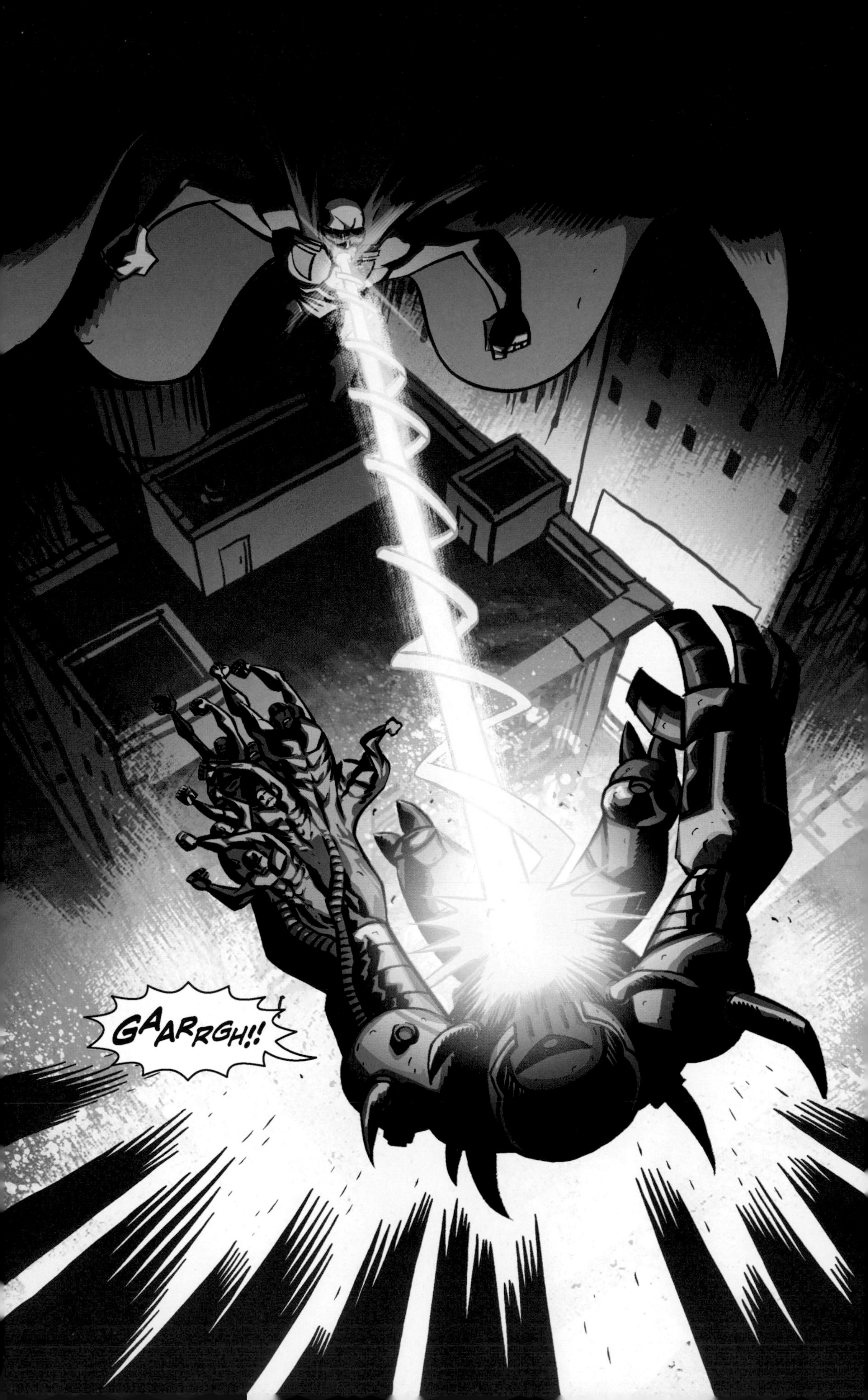
GAARRGH!!

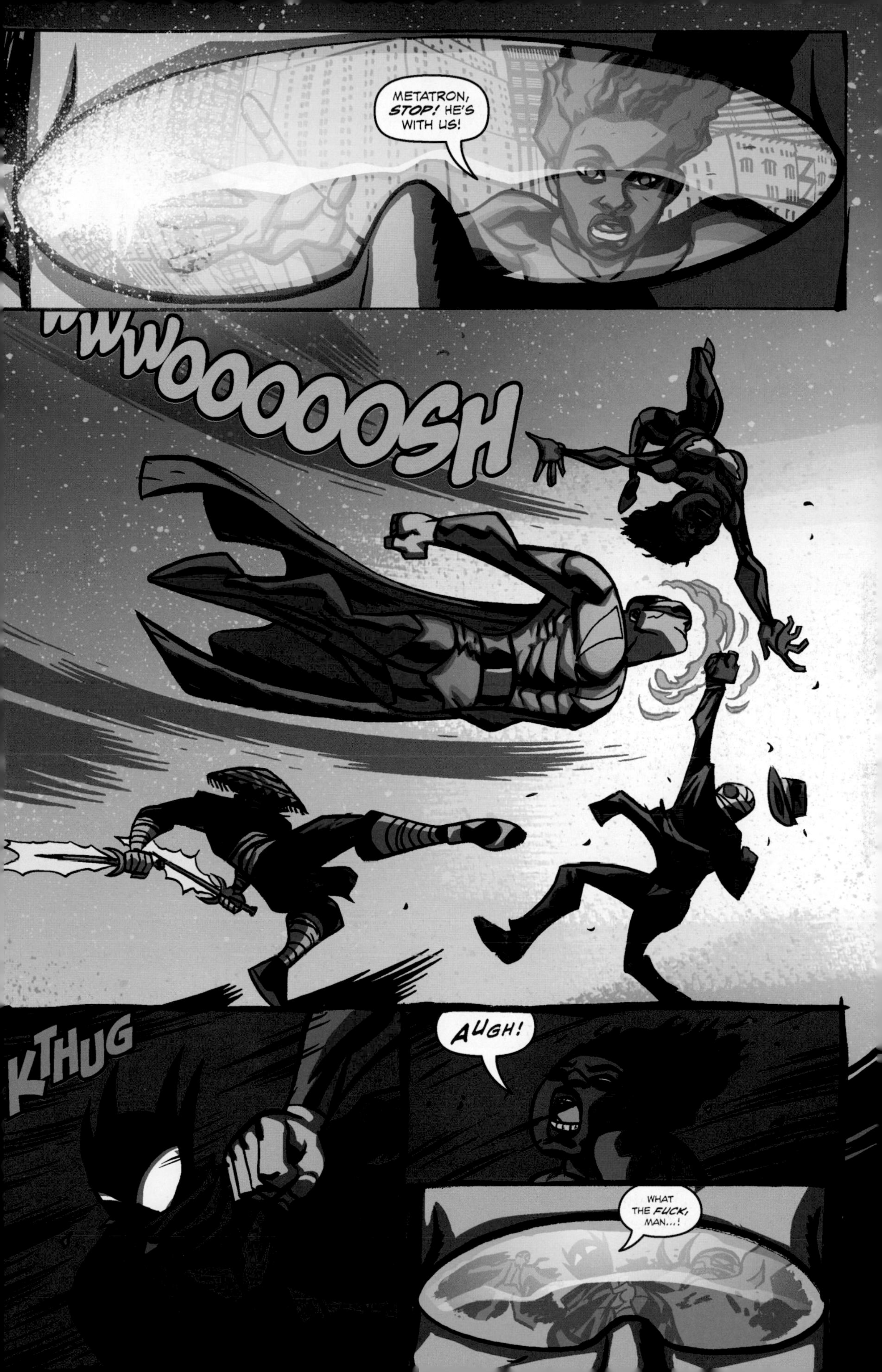
METATRON, STOP! HE'S WITH US!
WWWOOOOOOSH
KTHUG
AUGH!
WHAT THE FUCK, MAN...!

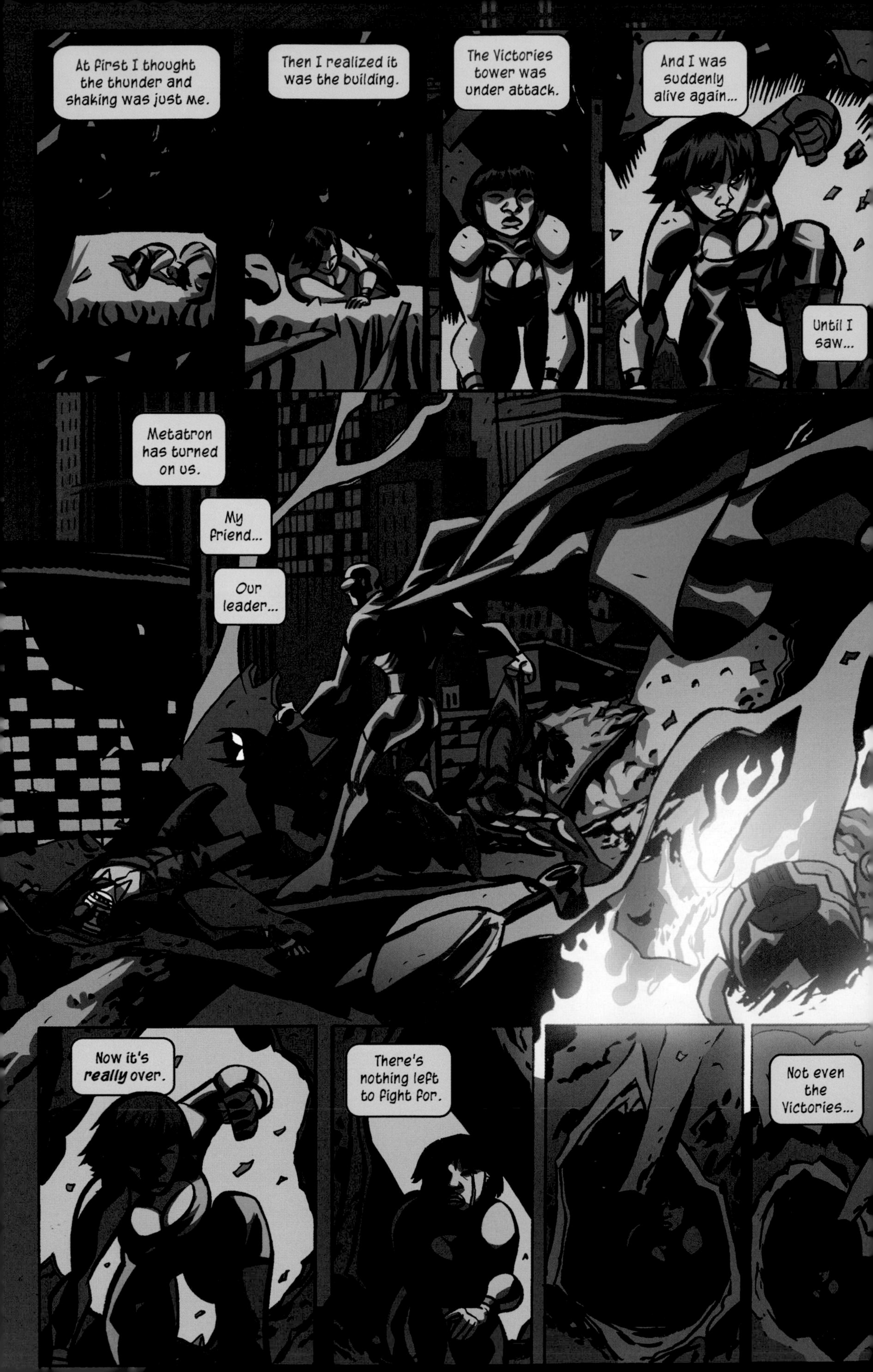
At first I thought the thunder and shaking was just me.
Then I realized it was the building.
The Victories tower was under attack.
And I was suddenly alive again...
Until I saw...
Metatron has turned on us.
My friend...
Our leader...
Now it's *really* over.
There's nothing left to fight for.
Not even the Victories...

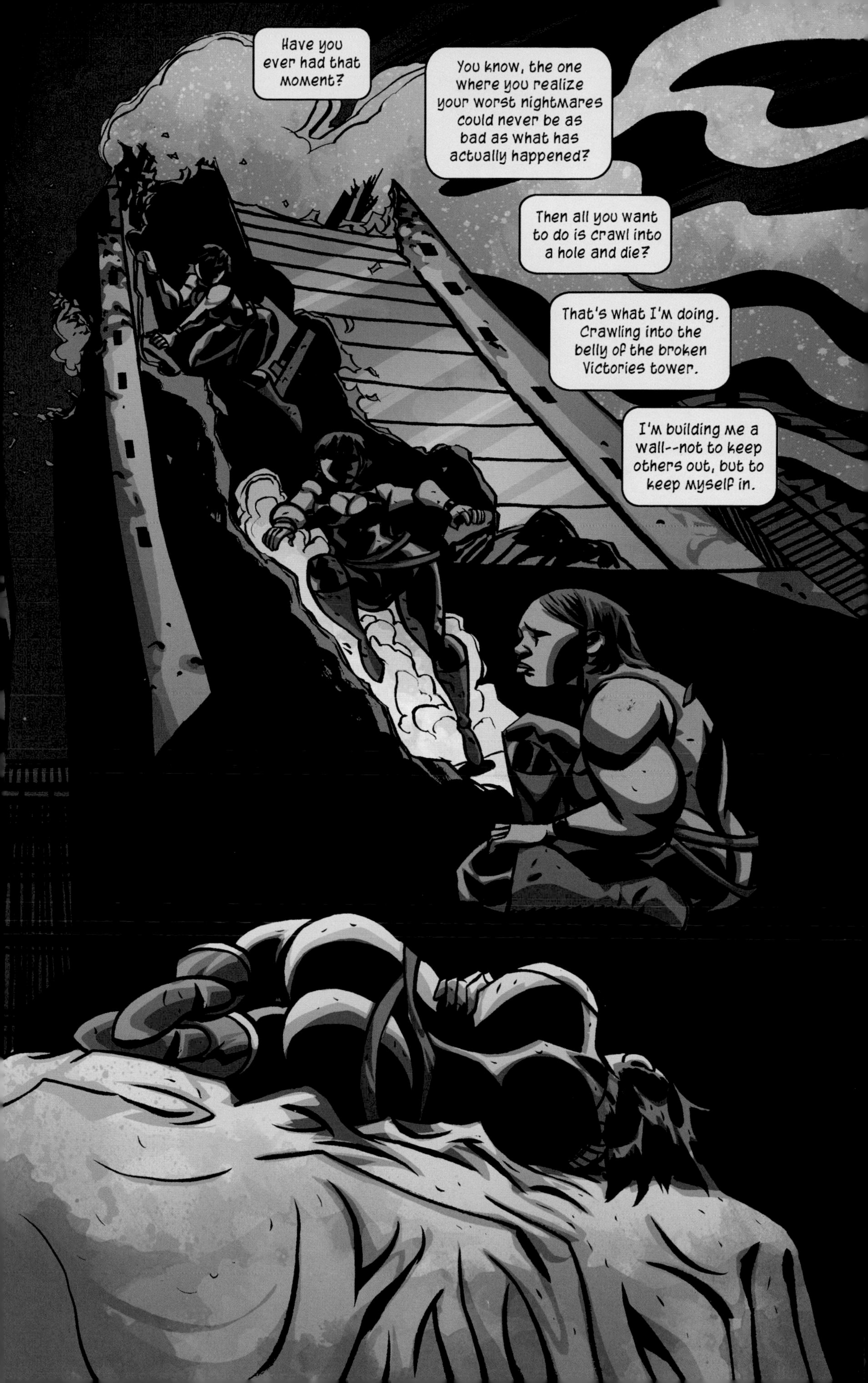
Have you ever had that moment?
You know, the one where you realize your worst nightmares could never be as bad as what has actually happened?
Then all you want to do is crawl into a hole and die?
That's what I'm doing. Crawling into the belly of the broken Victories tower.
I'm building me a wall--not to keep others out, but to keep myself in.

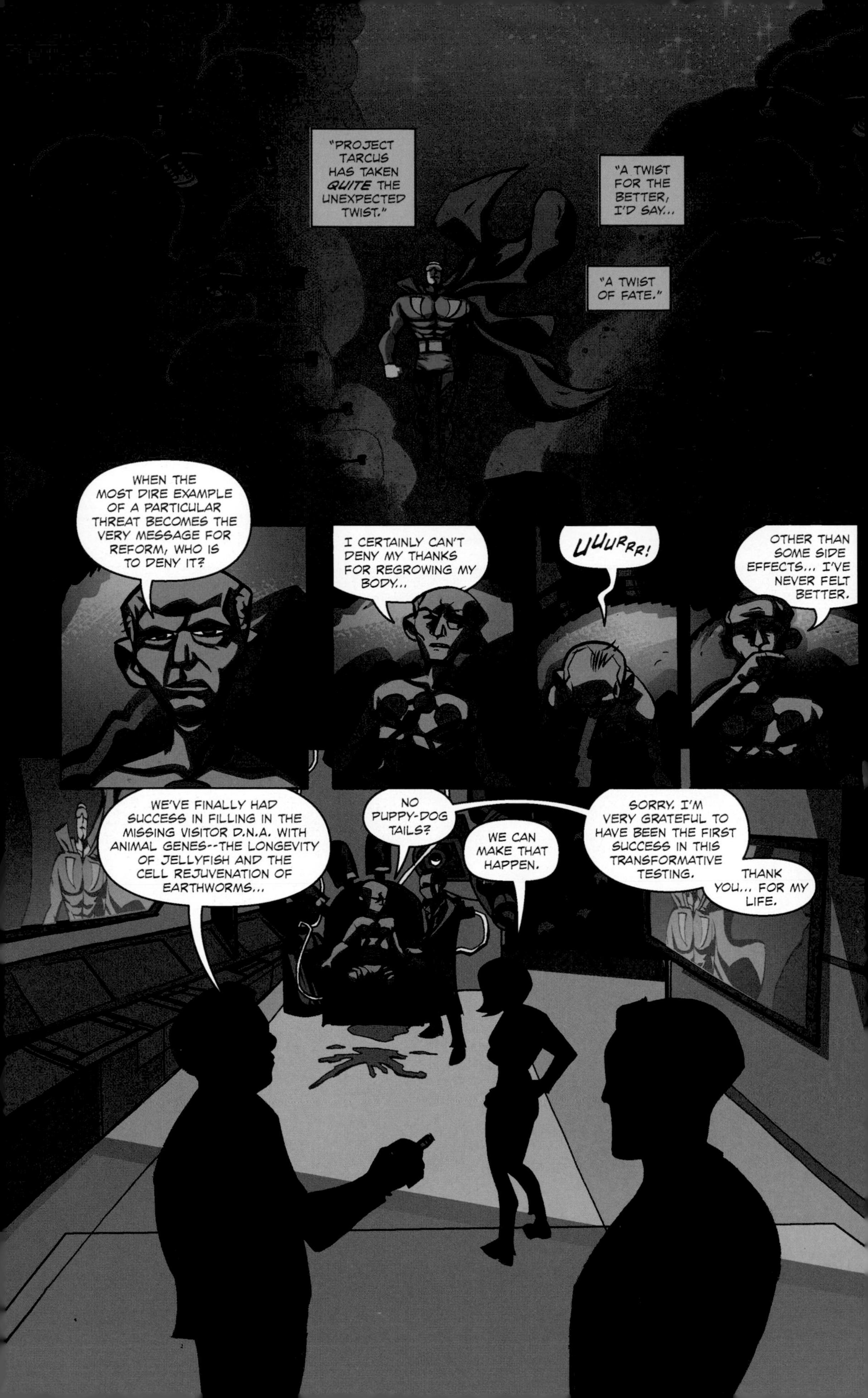
"PROJECT TARCUS HAS TAKEN QUITE THE UNEXPECTED TWIST."
"A TWIST FOR THE BETTER, I'D SAY...
"A TWIST OF FATE."
WHEN THE MOST DIRE EXAMPLE OF A PARTICULAR THREAT BECOMES THE VERY MESSAGE FOR REFORM, WHO IS TO DENY IT?
I CERTAINLY CAN'T DENY MY THANKS FOR REGROWING MY BODY...
UUURRR!
OTHER THAN SOME SIDE EFFECTS... I'VE NEVER FELT BETTER.
WE'VE FINALLY HAD SUCCESS IN FILLING IN THE MISSING VISITOR D.N.A. WITH ANIMAL GENES--THE LONGEVITY OF JELLYFISH AND THE CELL REJUVENATION OF EARTHWORMS...
NO PUPPY-DOG TAILS?
WE CAN MAKE THAT HAPPEN.
SORRY. I'M VERY GRATEFUL TO HAVE BEEN THE FIRST SUCCESS IN THIS TRANSFORMATIVE TESTING.
THANK YOU... FOR MY LIFE.

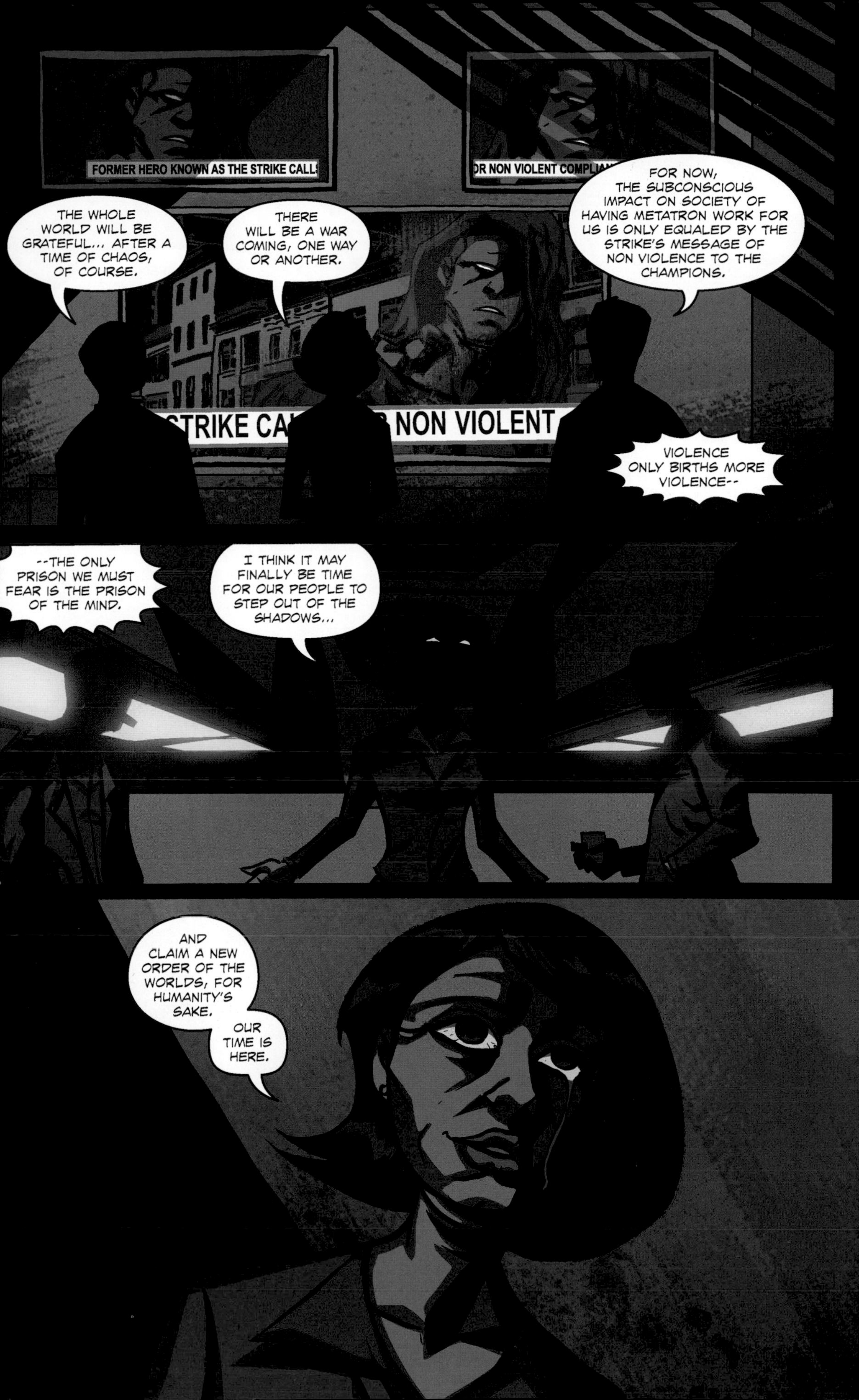
FORMER HERO KNOWN AS THE STRIKE CALLS
OR NON VIOLENT COMPLIAN
THE WHOLE WORLD WILL BE GRATEFUL... AFTER A TIME OF CHAOS, OF COURSE.
THERE WILL BE A WAR COMING, ONE WAY OR ANOTHER.
FOR NOW, THE SUBCONSCIOUS IMPACT ON SOCIETY OF HAVING METATRON WORK FOR US IS ONLY EQUALED BY THE STRIKE'S MESSAGE OF NON VIOLENCE TO THE CHAMPIONS.
STRIKE CA NON VIOLENT
VIOLENCE ONLY BIRTHS MORE VIOLENCE--
--THE ONLY PRISON WE MUST FEAR IS THE PRISON OF THE MIND.
I THINK IT MAY FINALLY BE TIME FOR OUR PEOPLE TO STEP OUT OF THE SHADOWS...
AND CLAIM A NEW ORDER OF THE WORLDS, FOR HUMANITY'S SAKE.
OUR TIME IS HERE.

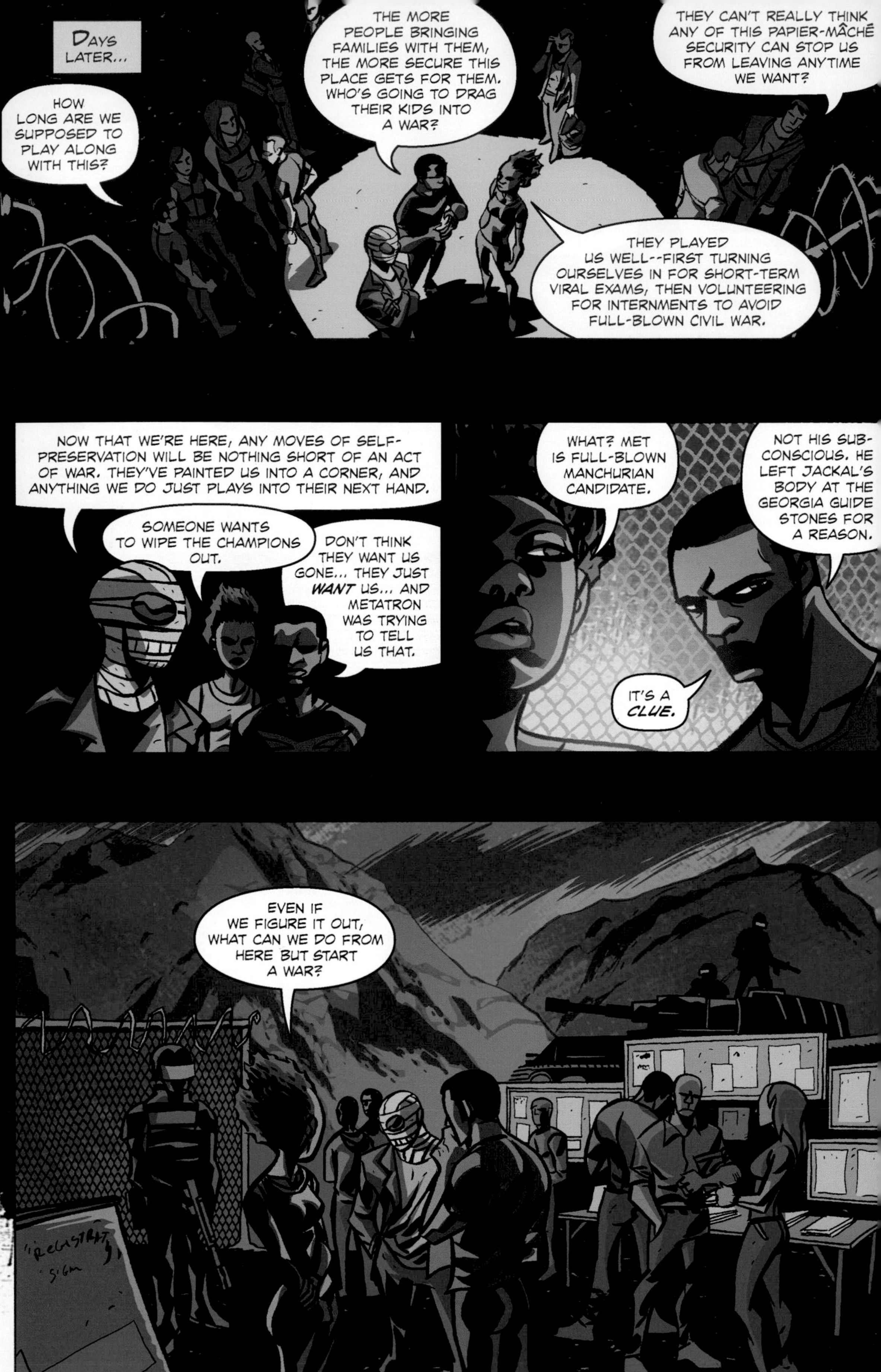
DAYS LATER...
HOW LONG ARE WE SUPPOSED TO PLAY ALONG WITH THIS?
THE MORE PEOPLE BRINGING FAMILIES WITH THEM, THE MORE SECURE THIS PLACE GETS FOR THEM. WHO'S GOING TO DRAG THEIR KIDS INTO A WAR?
THEY CAN'T REALLY THINK ANY OF THIS PAPIER-MÂCHÉ SECURITY CAN STOP US FROM LEAVING ANYTIME WE WANT?
THEY PLAYED US WELL--FIRST TURNING OURSELVES IN FOR SHORT-TERM VIRAL EXAMS, THEN VOLUNTEERING FOR INTERNMENTS TO AVOID FULL-BLOWN CIVIL WAR.
NOW THAT WE'RE HERE, ANY MOVES OF SELF-PRESERVATION WILL BE NOTHING SHORT OF AN ACT OF WAR. THEY'VE PAINTED US INTO A CORNER, AND ANYTHING WE DO JUST PLAYS INTO THEIR NEXT HAND.
SOMEONE WANTS TO WIPE THE CHAMPIONS OUT.
DON'T THINK THEY WANT US GONE... THEY JUST *WANT* US... AND METATRON WAS TRYING TO TELL US THAT.
WHAT? MET IS FULL-BLOWN MANCHURIAN CANDIDATE.
NOT HIS SUB-CONSCIOUS. HE LEFT JACKAL'S BODY AT THE GEORGIA GUIDE STONES FOR A REASON.
IT'S A ***CLUE.***
EVEN IF WE FIGURE IT OUT, WHAT CAN WE DO FROM HERE BUT START A WAR?

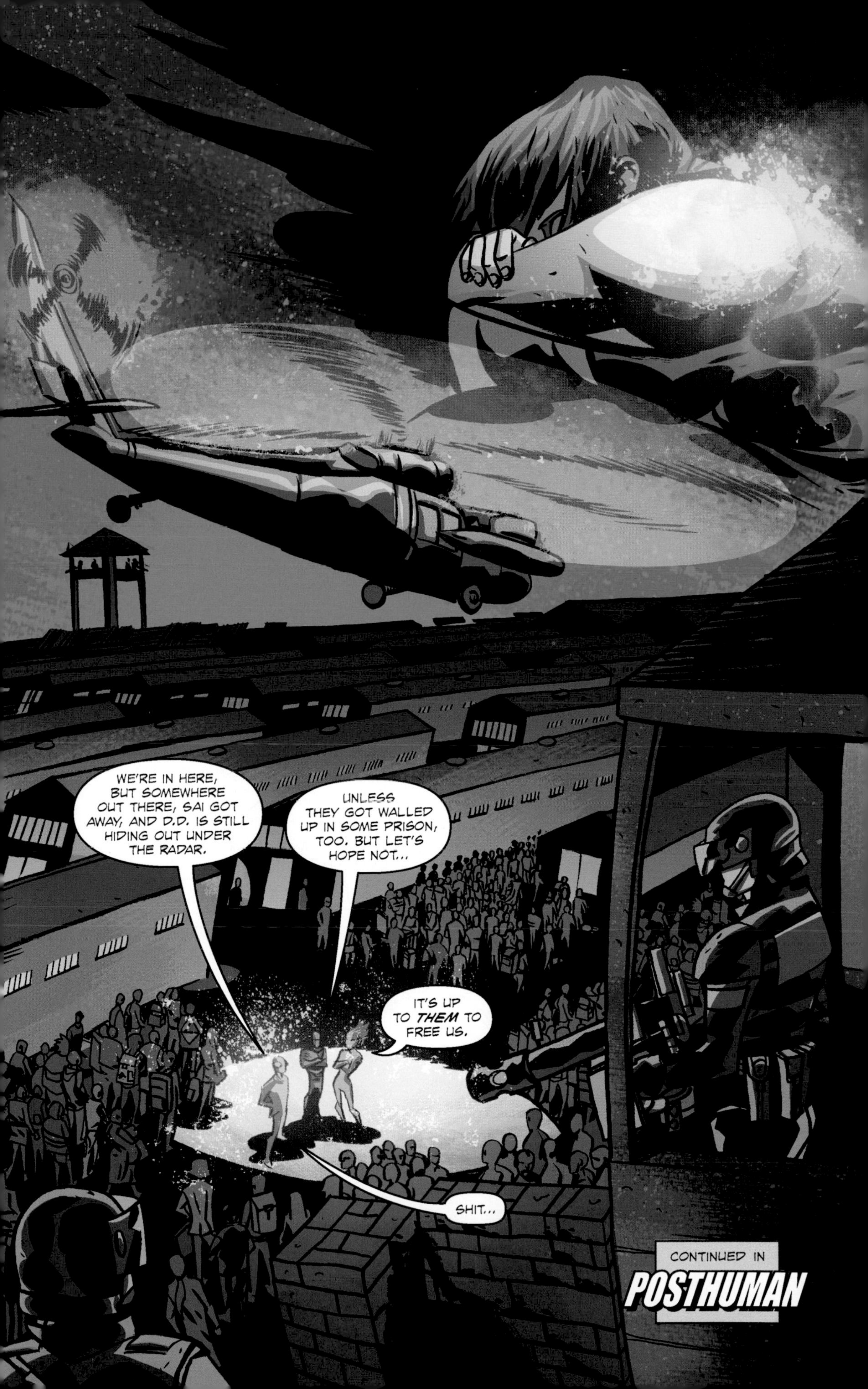
WE'RE IN HERE, BUT SOMEWHERE OUT THERE, SAI GOT AWAY, AND D.D. IS STILL HIDING OUT UNDER THE RADAR.
UNLESS THEY GOT WALLED UP IN SOME PRISON, TOO. BUT LET'S HOPE NOT...
IT'S UP TO *THEM* TO FREE US.
SHIT...
CONTINUED IN
POSTHUMAN

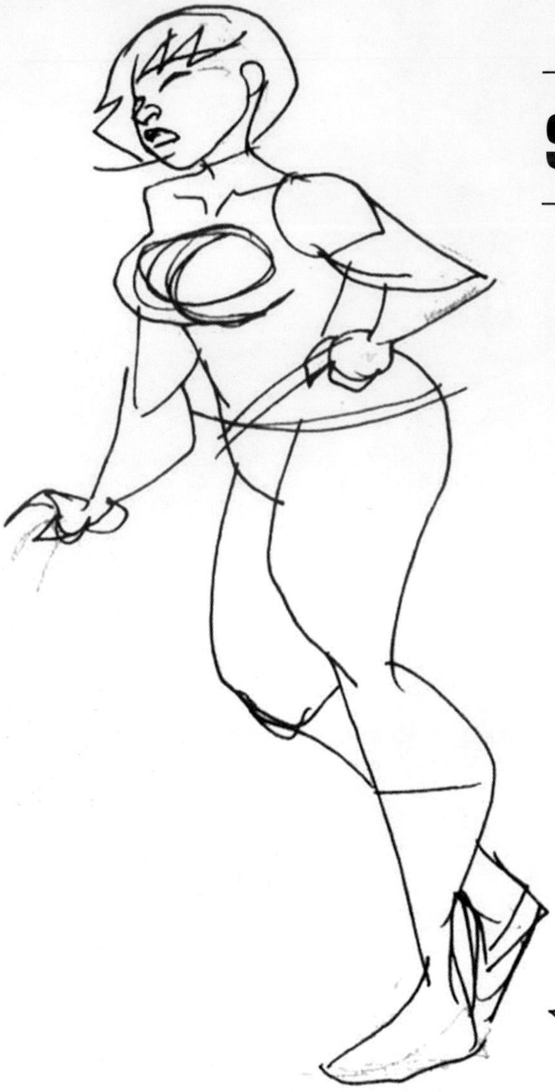

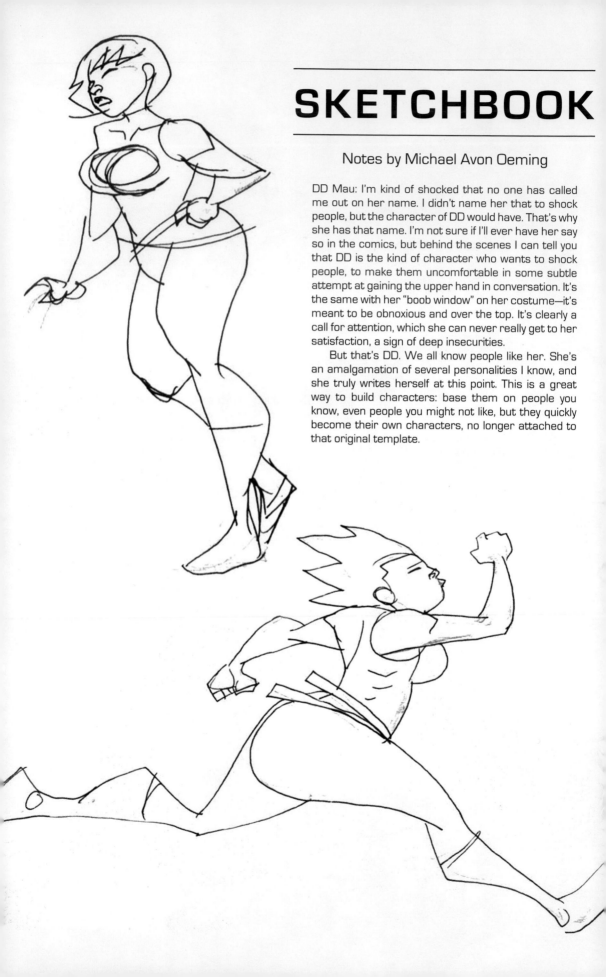

SKETCHBOOK

Notes by Michael Avon Oeming

DD Mau: I'm kind of shocked that no one has called me out on her name. I didn't name her that to shock people, but the character of DD would have. That's why she has that name. I'm not sure if I'll ever have her say so in the comics, but behind the scenes I can tell you that DD is the kind of character who wants to shock people, to make them uncomfortable in some subtle attempt at gaining the upper hand in conversation. It's the same with her "boob window" on her costume—it's meant to be obnoxious and over the top. It's clearly a call for attention, which she can never really get to her satisfaction, a sign of deep insecurities.

But that's DD. We all know people like her. She's an amalgamation of several personalities I know, and she truly writes herself at this point. This is a great way to build characters: base them on people you know, even people you might not like, but they quickly become their own characters, no longer attached to that original template.

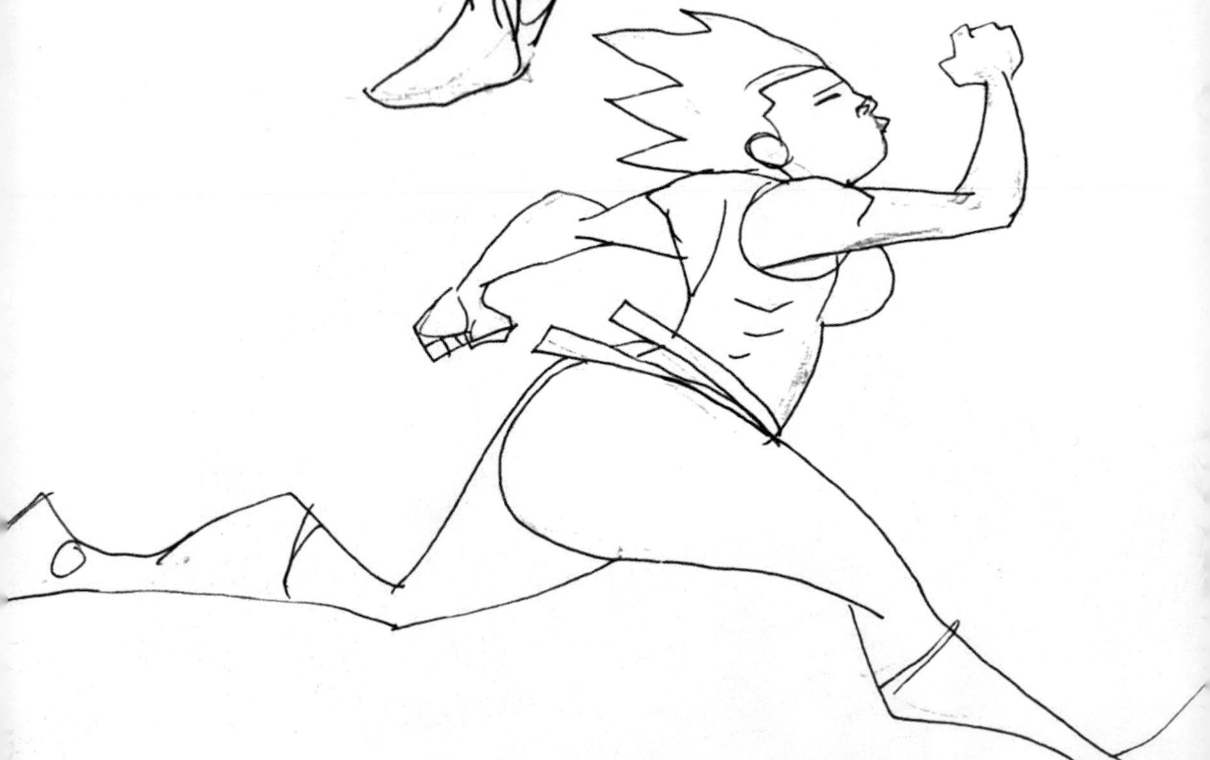

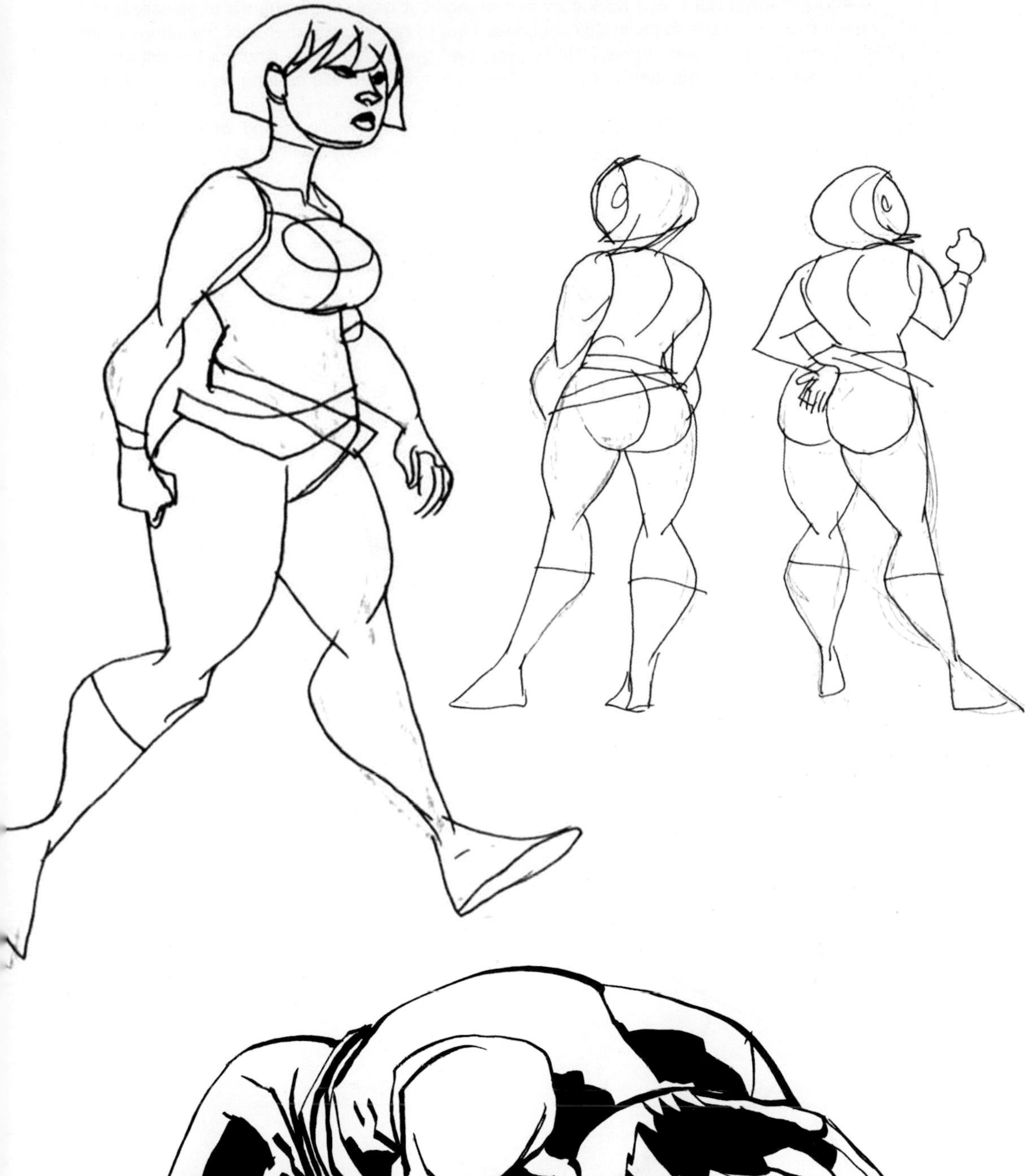

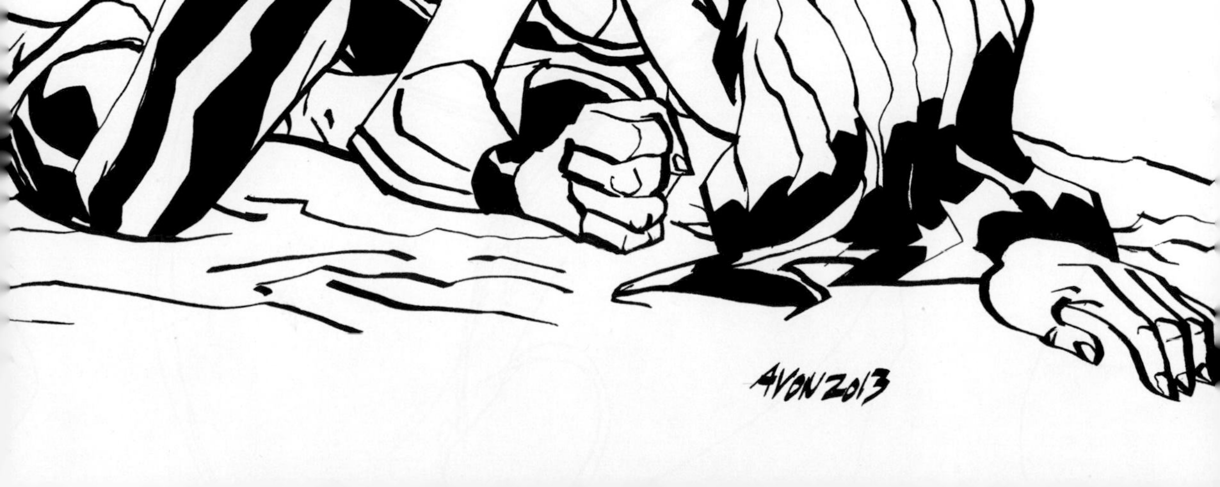
AVON 2013

This was a fun image. I like telling backstory in montages; it gives me a chance to visually break away from the rest of the story. In this sequence I got to get into the theme of transhumanism, the mixing of human and animal DNA to "improve" the human body. One day we will regrow body parts like lizards, see in the dark like cats, and even live as long as turtles or near-immortal jellyfish.

But at what cost? Is our humanity defined by our bodies? And what horrible ways will we abuse such technology? It also covers one of my favorite subjects, the ancient alien theories!

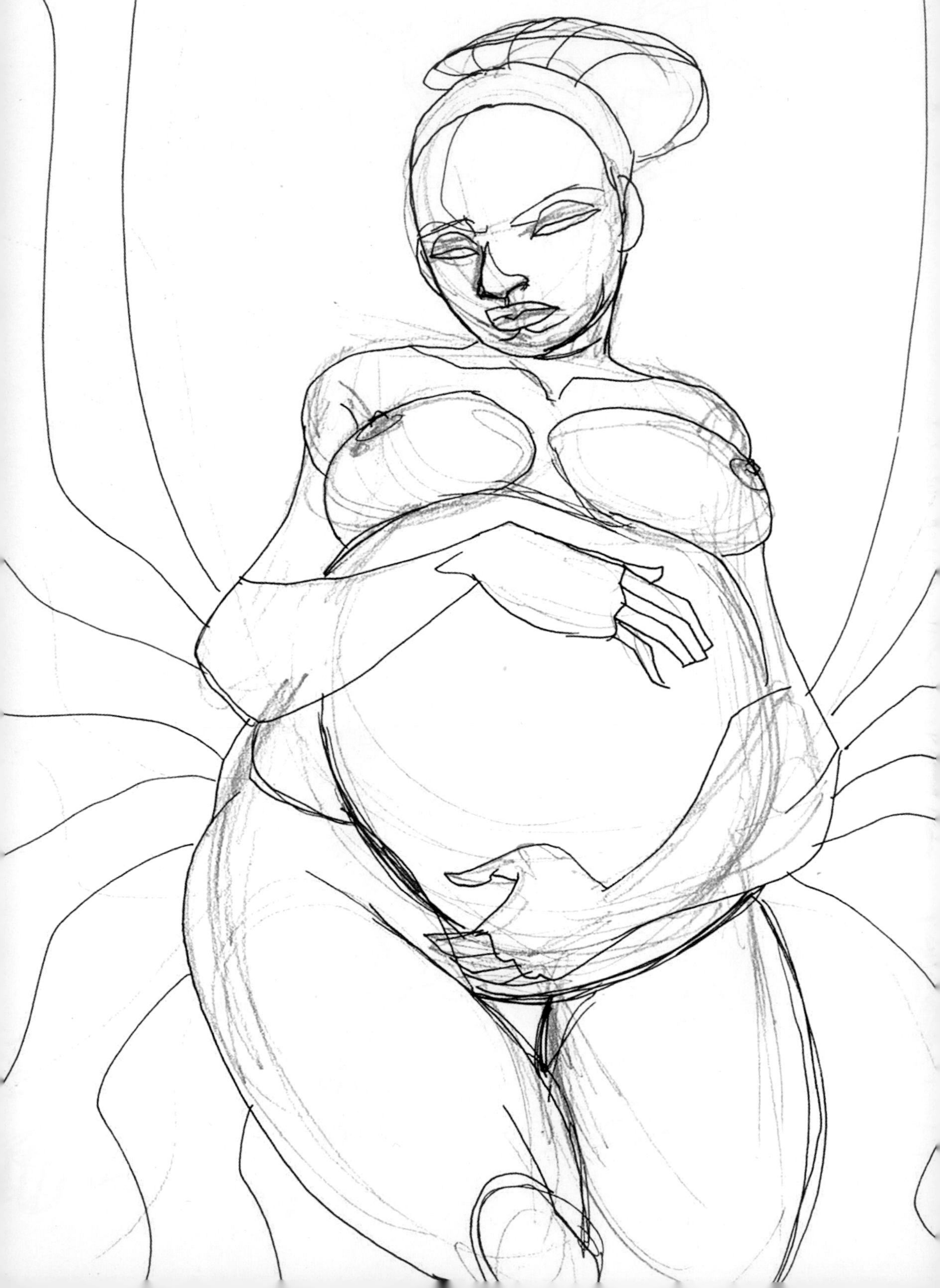

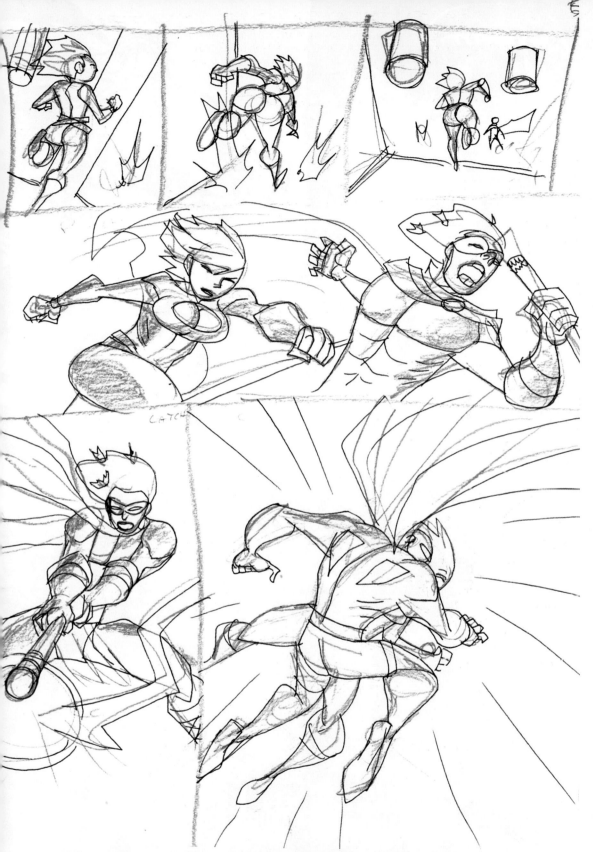

When I begin my layouts, they start wherever I am—on my computer, on the script, or in my sketchbook.

I laid out this page in light pencil, defined it with ink, and then added tones in pencil.

Bacchus was a fun villain I made up on the spot. Since I love mythology, I wanted someone based on Greek gods, so when I chose Bacchus, the god of wine and sex, the choice of powers seemed obvious. Probably not something I could get away with in mainstream comics.

This guy and his Thyrsus machines will return some day.

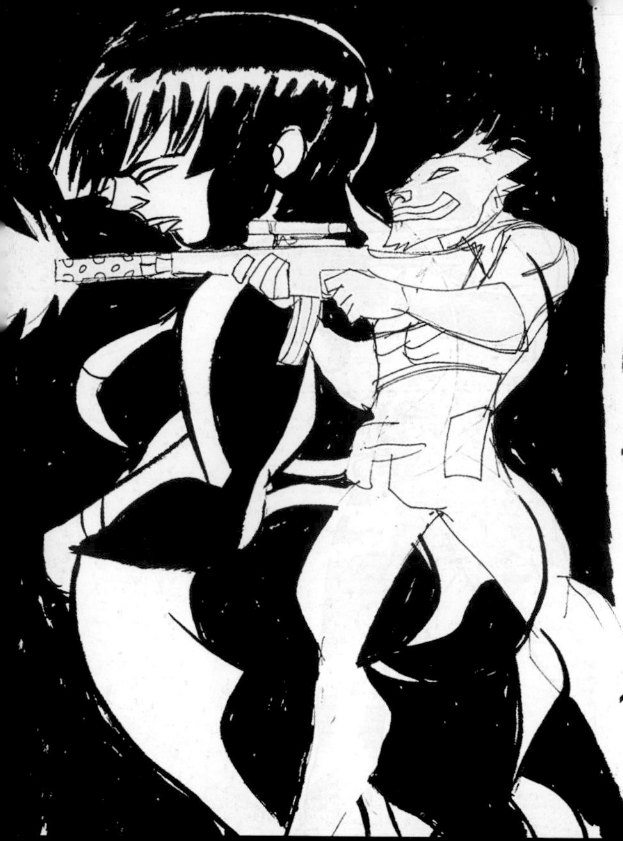

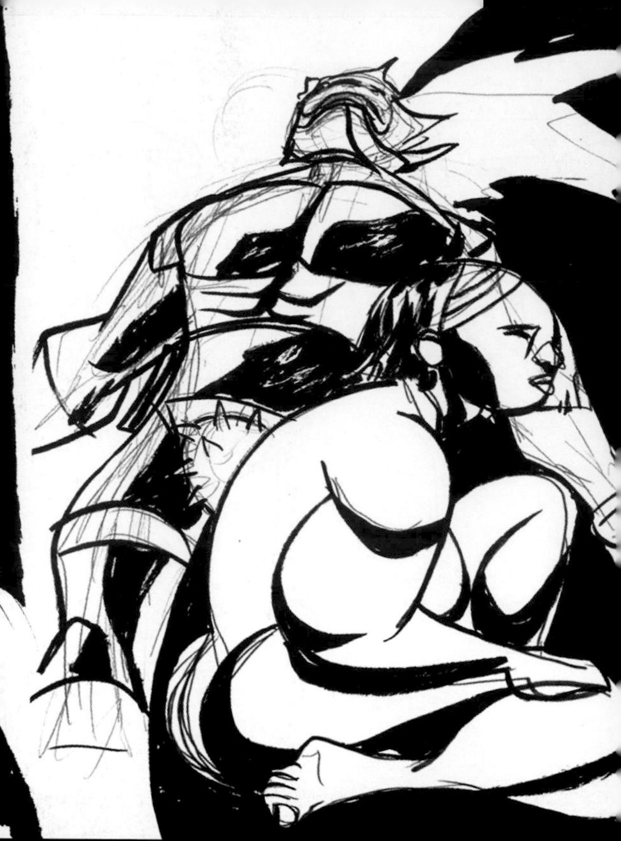

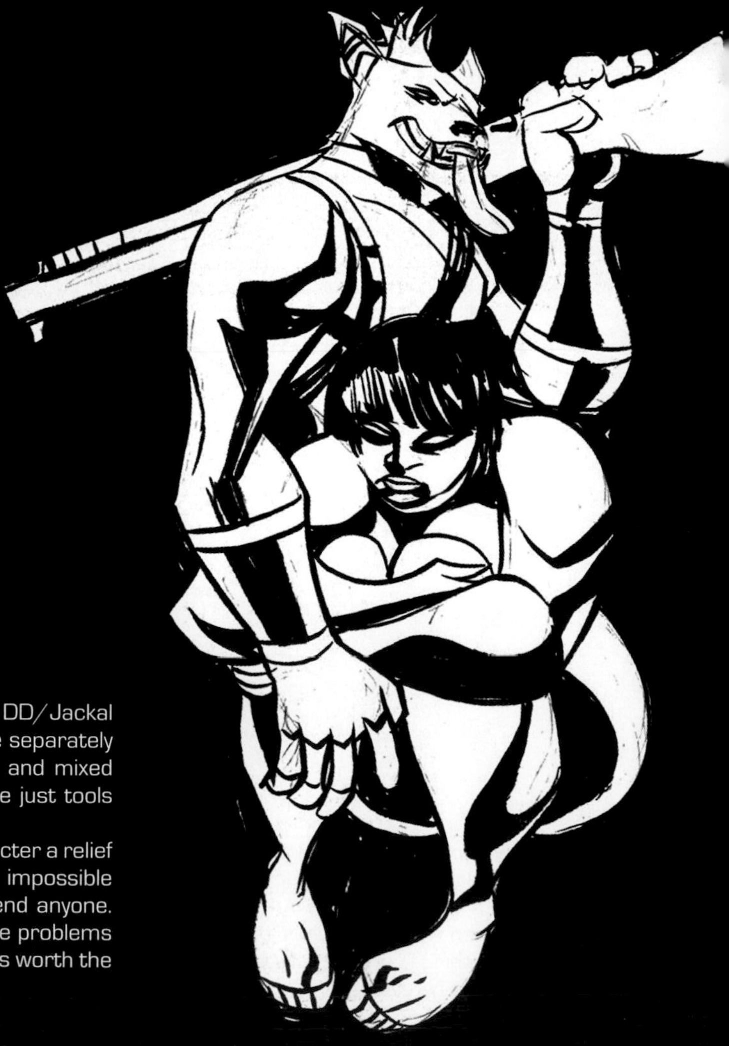

One of the many sketches I did for the DD/Jackal cover. Some of these figures were done separately and tried out in different combinations and mixed media, both digital and analog. Both are just tools for the artist.

I hope a lot of women find DD's character a relief from the constant heroines with nearly impossible body types out there. I never *try* to offend anyone. I think it's possible some people still have problems with her character, but I thought she was worth the chance. What do you think?

This is part of a concept I have for a later project. I changed elements around to use for the "Mind Control" Conspiratoid column printed in the comic, written by Aaron Walker, but the image didn't look right as a watermark, so we used the Illuminati Eye instead.

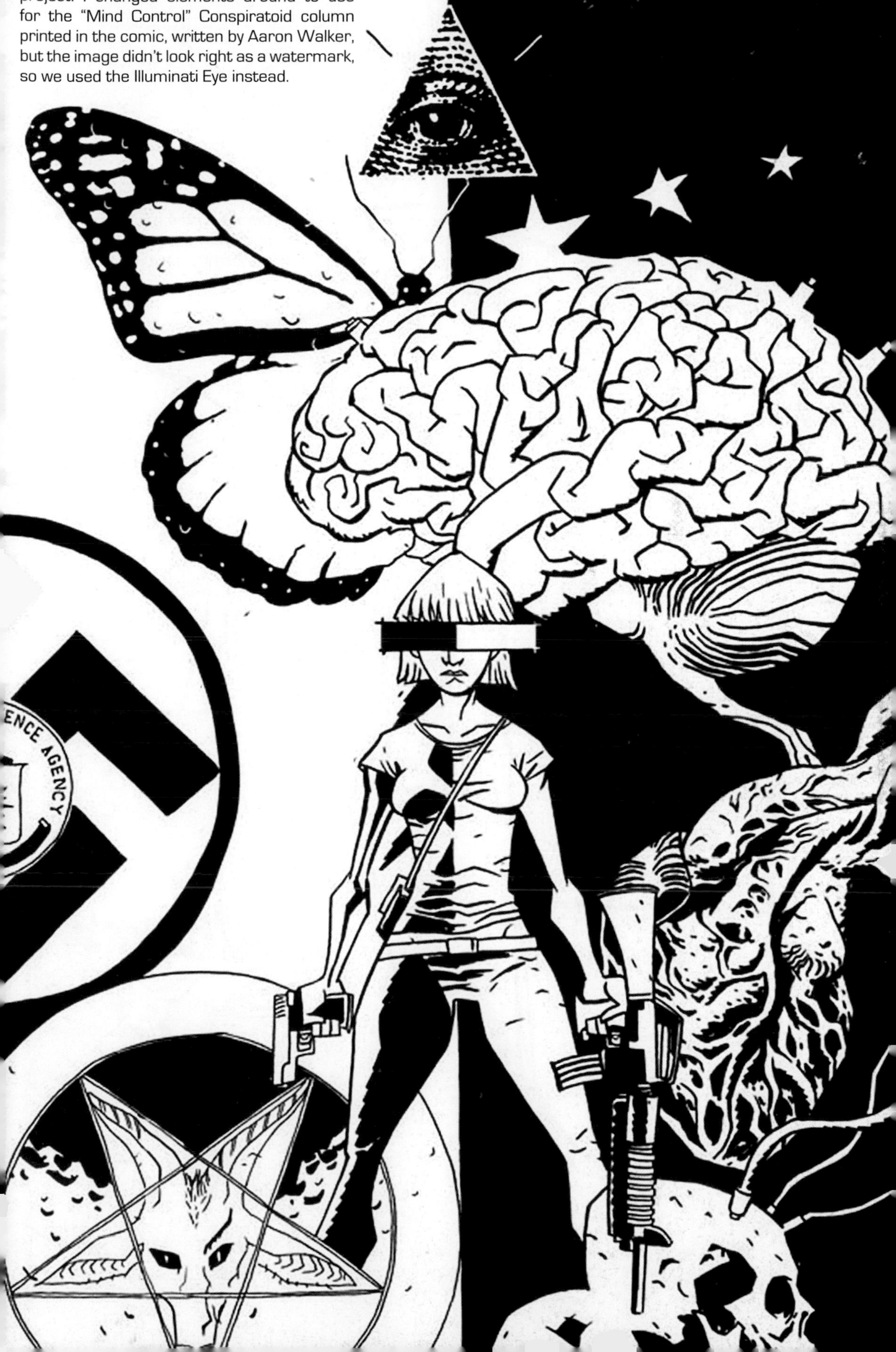
ENCE AGENCY

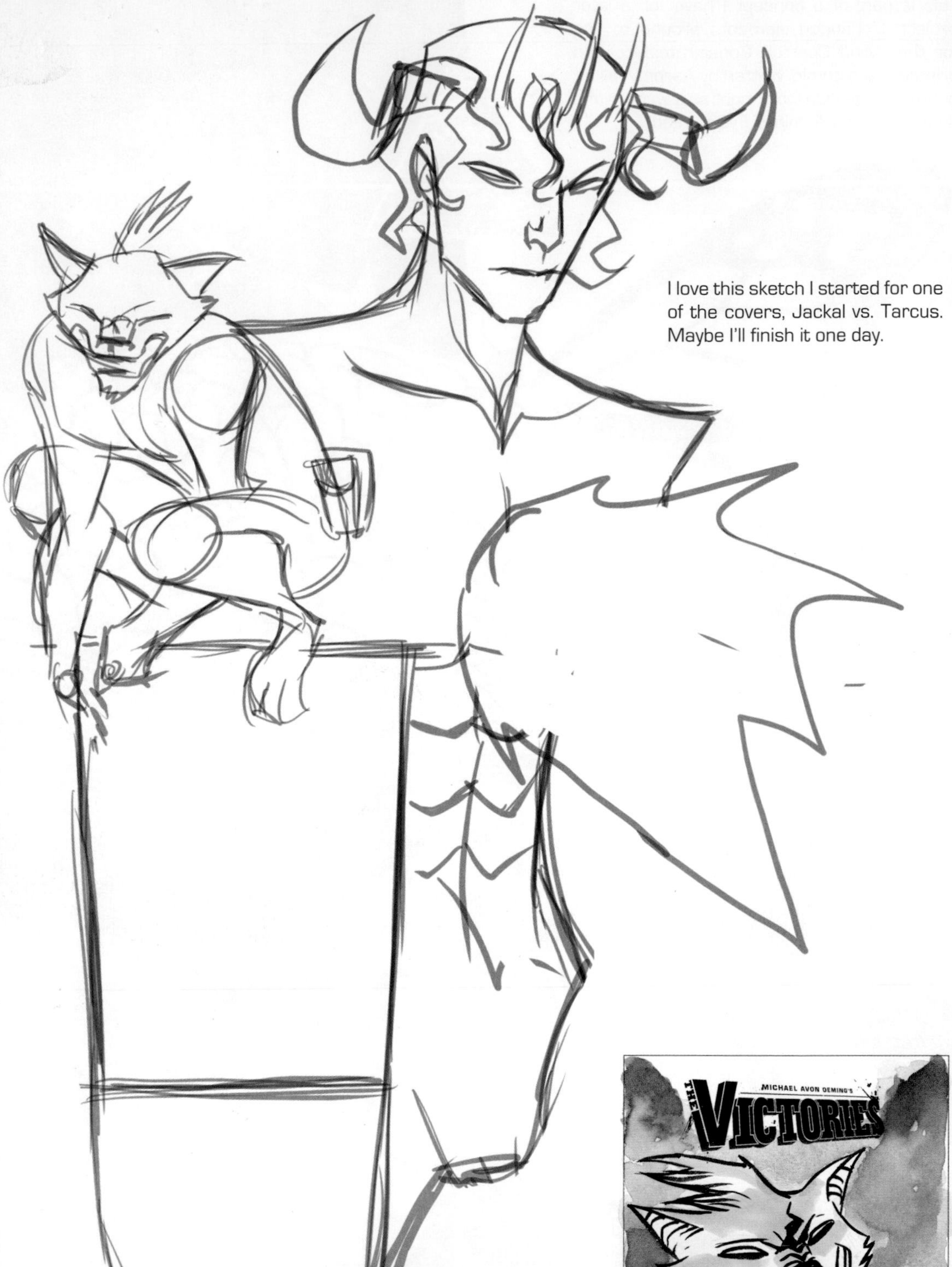

I love this sketch I started for one of the covers, Jackal vs. Tarcus. Maybe I'll finish it one day.

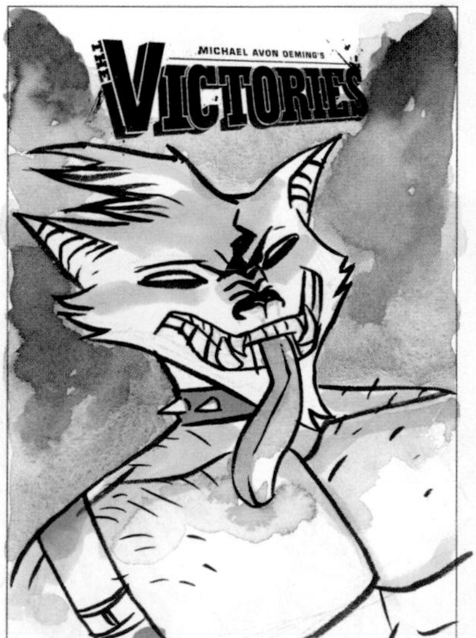
MICHAEL AVON OEMING'S
THE VICTORIES

This is one of the one hundred sketch cards we did as an incentive for retailers. Did you get yours?

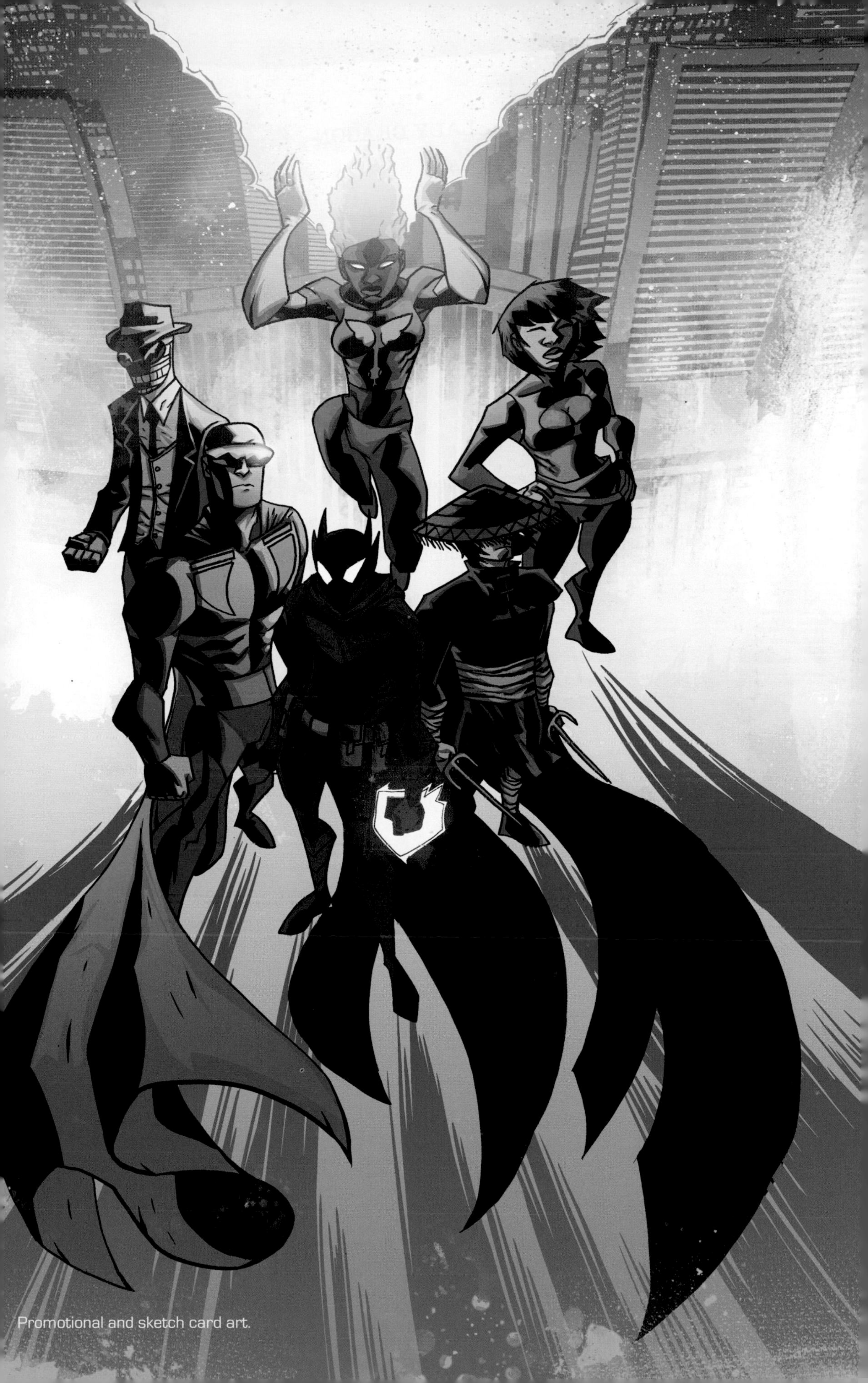

Promotional and sketch card art.

#FindTheVictories

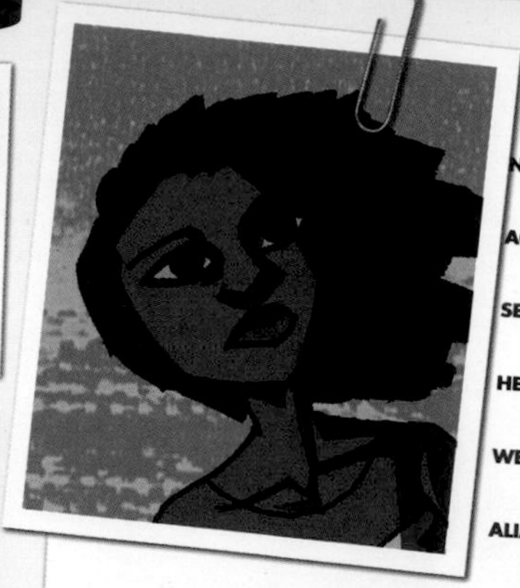

NAME: LADY DRAGON

AGE: 28

SEX: Female

HEIGHT: 5'8"

WEIGHT: Unknown

ALIAS: Classified

POWERS: Control of a variation of fire called the Ghost Flame.

ADDITIONAL FILE INFO: Lady Dragon is a known descendant of the Pendragons, a powerful corporate family linked to the European banking system

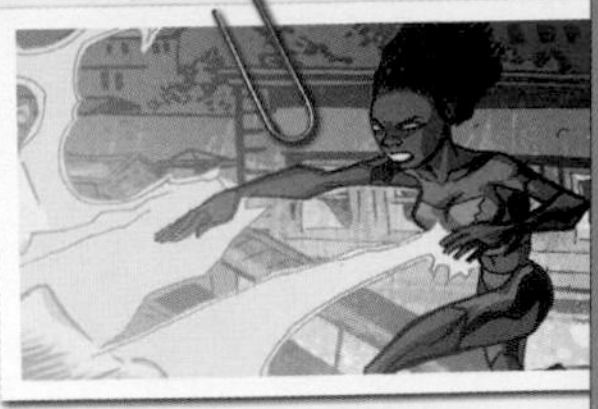

Tweet the hashtag #FindTheVictories for a chance to win original artwork from creator Michael Avon Oeming every day until June 12!

Get a **FREE**, full-length digital comic, *The Victories: Babalon*, at Digital.DarkHorse.com/TheVictories

MICHAEL AVON OEMING'S THE VICTORIES

SPONSORED BY:

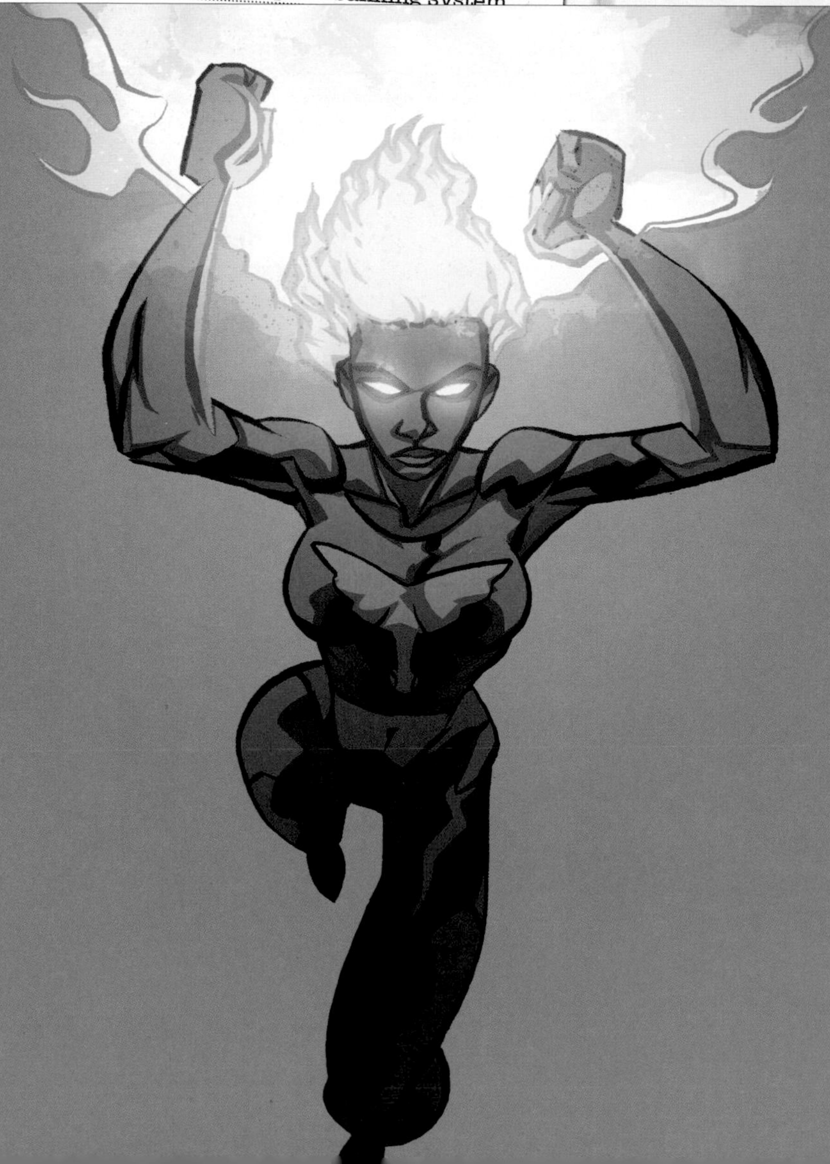

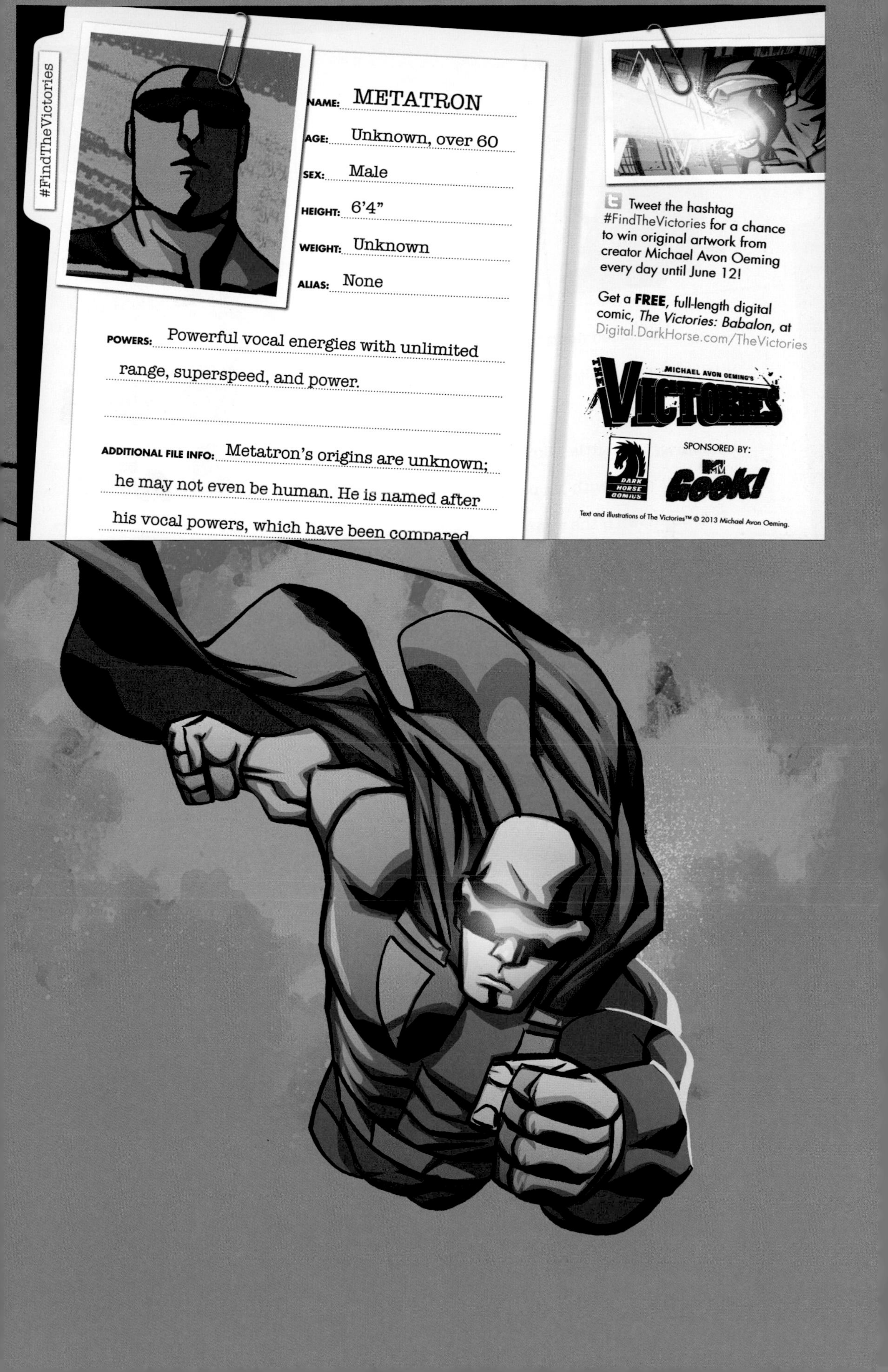
#FindTheVictories
NAME: METATRON
AGE: Unknown, over 60
SEX: Male
HEIGHT: 6'4"
WEIGHT: Unknown
ALIAS: None
POWERS: Powerful vocal energies with unlimited range, superspeed, and power.
ADDITIONAL FILE INFO: Metatron's origins are unknown; he may not even be human. He is named after his vocal powers, which have been compared
Tweet the hashtag #FindTheVictories for a chance to win original artwork from creator Michael Avon Oeming every day until June 12!
Get a FREE, full-length digital comic, The Victories: Babalon, at Digital.DarkHorse.com/TheVictories
MICHAEL AVON OEMING'S
THE VICTORIES
DARK HORSE COMICS
SPONSORED BY:
MTV Geek!
Text and illustrations of The Victories™ © 2013 Michael Avon Oeming.

#FindTheVictories

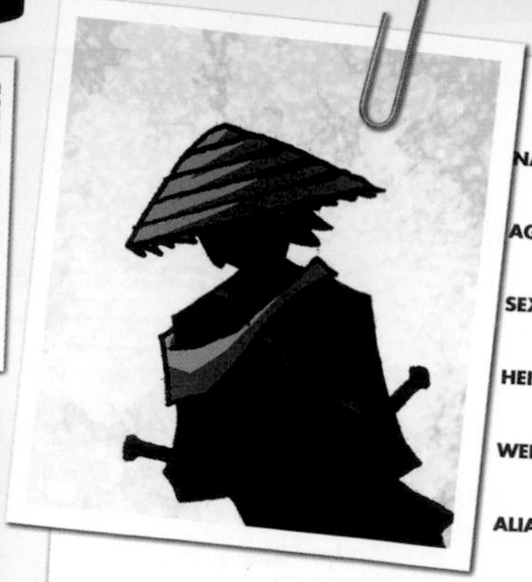

NAME: SAI

AGE: Unknown

SEX: Assumed Male

HEIGHT: Unknown

WEIGHT: Unknown

ALIAS: Unknown

POWERS: Enhanced fighting abilities and micro-psychic precognition.

ADDITIONAL FILE INFO: Little is known about Sai other than his skills with his powered sai weapons. It is unknown if the weapons are self-powered

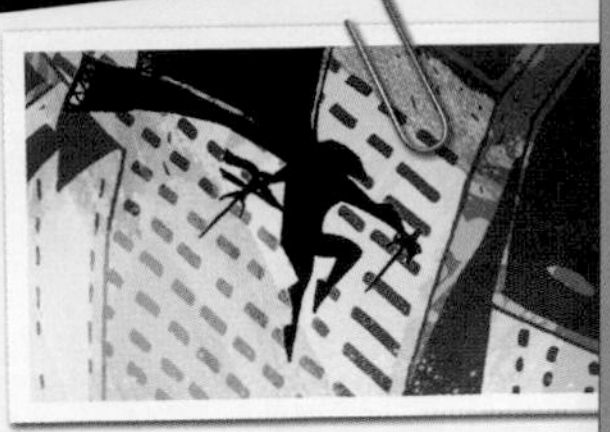

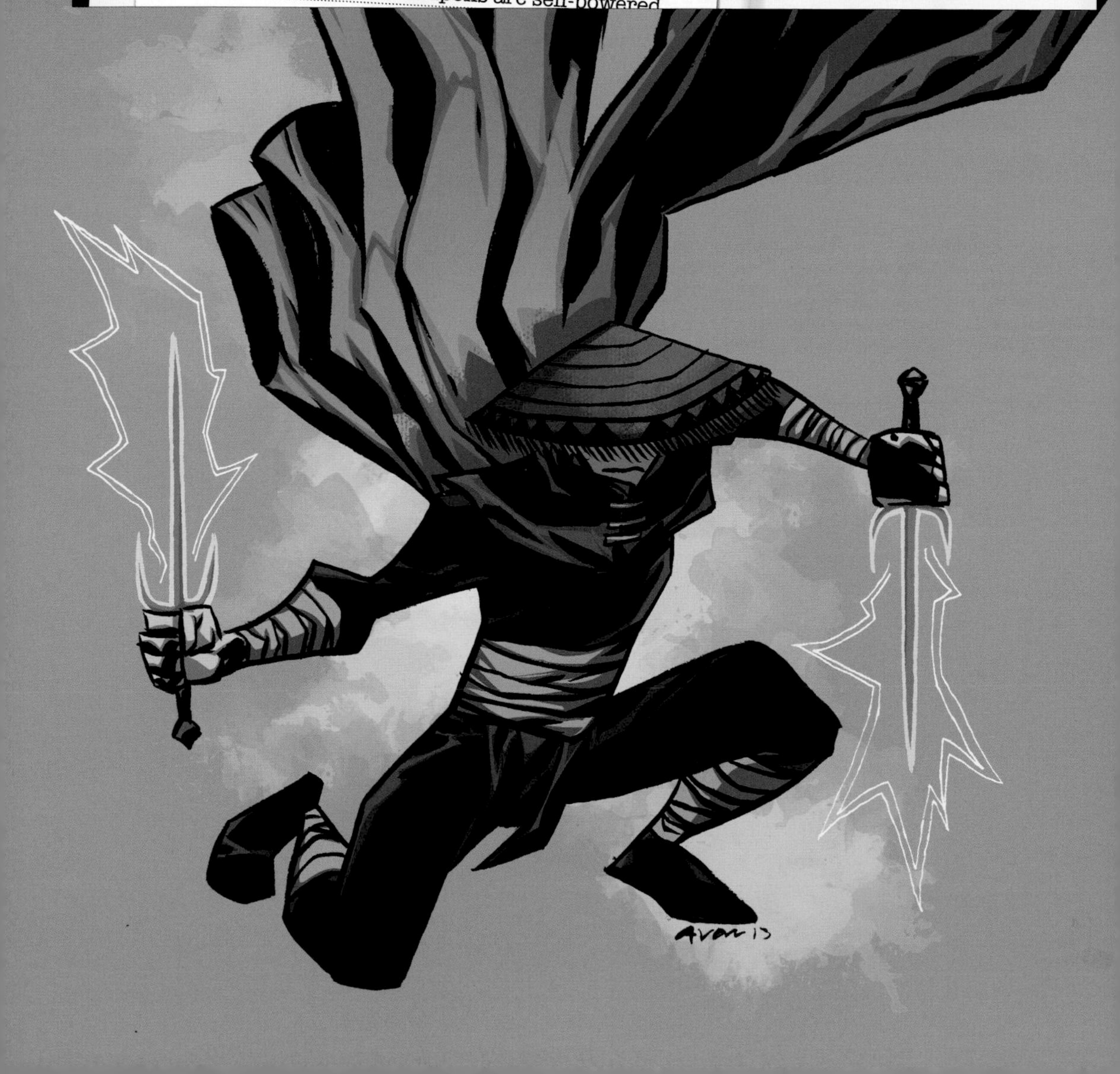

AVON 13

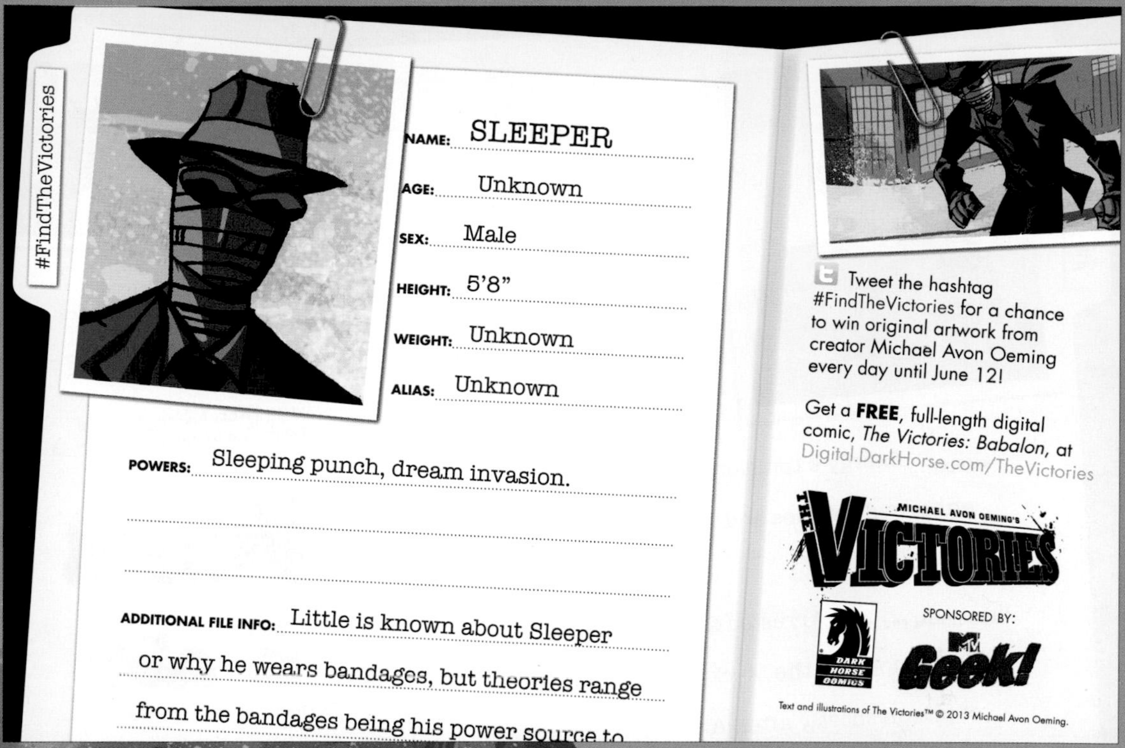
#FindTheVictories
NAME: SLEEPER
AGE: Unknown
SEX: Male
HEIGHT: 5'8"
WEIGHT: Unknown
ALIAS: Unknown
POWERS: Sleeping punch, dream invasion.
ADDITIONAL FILE INFO: Little is known about Sleeper
or why he wears bandages, but theories range
from the bandages being his power source to
Tweet the hashtag #FindTheVictories for a chance to win original artwork from creator Michael Avon Oeming every day until June 12!
Get a FREE, full-length digital comic, The Victories: Babalon, at Digital.DarkHorse.com/TheVictories
MICHAEL AVON OEMING'S
THE VICTORIES
DARK HORSE COMICS
SPONSORED BY:
MTV Geek!
Text and illustrations of The Victories™ © 2013 Michael Avon Oeming.

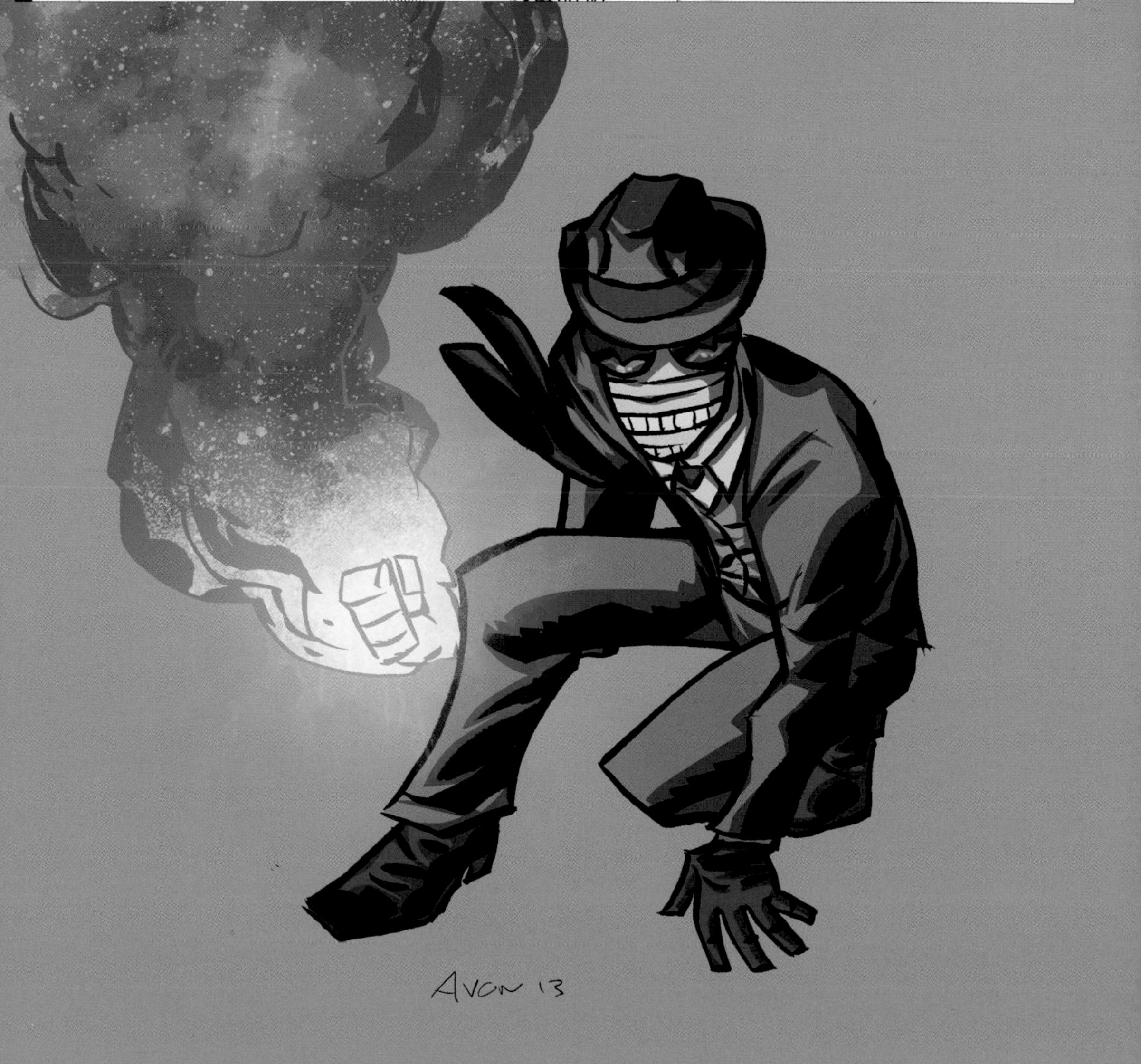
AVON 13

AVON 13

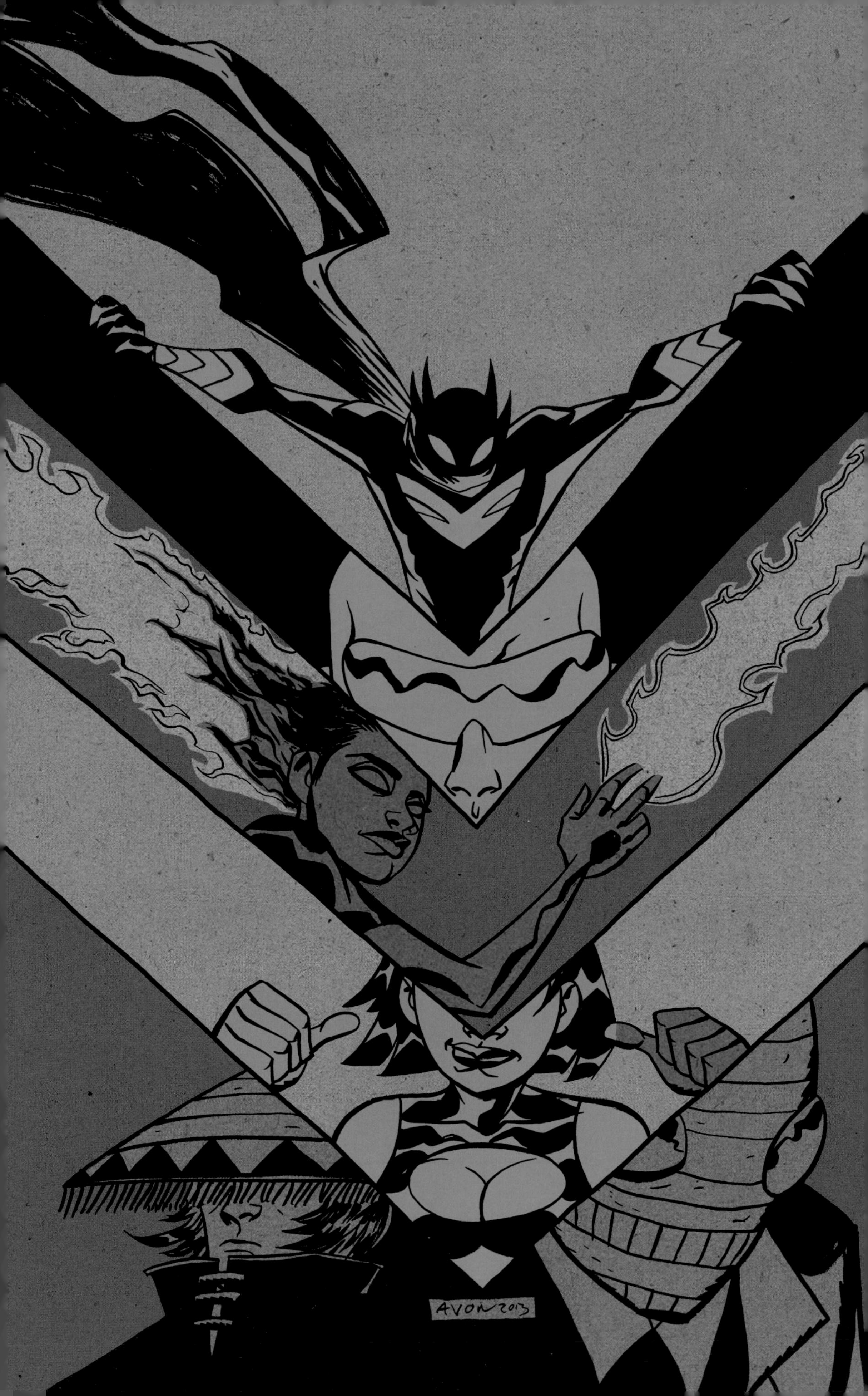
AVON 2013

THE VICTORIES VOLUME 1: TOUCHED

Michael Avon Oeming and Nick Filardi

Not long from now, all that will stand between you and evil are the Victories: heroes sworn to protect us from crime, corruption, and the weird designer drug known as Float. As one member hits the streets looking for blood, he discovers himself touched by a painful past through the powers of a psychic. Will this trauma cause him to self-destruct or to rejoin the good fight?

ISBN 978-1-61655-100-1 | $9.99

RAPTURE

Michael Avon Oeming and Taki Soma

After warring for a century, Earth's greatest champions and villains suddenly disappear, leaving the planet decimated. Like a rapture, the Powers are gone and humanity is left behind to pick up the pieces. Amongst this wreckage, two lovers, Evelyn and Gil, find themselves separated by a continent and will do anything to find each other again. But when a strange being named "the Word" turns Evelyn into a champion with an angelic spear, she finds the force of her love for Gil clashing with her newfound power. Love and destiny collide in what will become the worst breakup ever!

ISBN 978-1-59582-460-8 | $19.99

B.P.R.D.: PLAGUE OF FROGS HARDCOVER COLLECTION VOLUME 1

Mike Mignola, Christopher Golden, Geoff Johns, Michael Avon Oeming, and others

In 2001, Hellboy quit the B.P.R.D., leaving Abe Sapien to lead Liz Sherman and a bizarre roster of special agents in defending the world from occult threats, including the growing menace of the frog army first spotted in *Hellboy: Seed of Destruction*.

ISBN 978-1-59582-609-1 | $34.99

CONAN: THE DAUGHTERS OF MIDORA AND OTHER STORIES

Jimmy Palmiotti, Ron Marz, Michael Avon Oeming, and others

A must-buy for any Conan fan! Collects *Conan and the Daughters of Midora*, *Conan: Island of No Return #1–#2*, and stories from *MySpace Dark Horse Presents #11* and *USA Today*.

ISBN 978-1-59582-917-7 | $14.99

VALVE PRESENTS: THE SACRIFICE AND OTHER STEAM-POWERED STORIES

Michael Avon Oeming and others

Valve joins with Dark Horse to bring three critically acclaimed, fan-favorite series to print, with a hardcover collection of comics from the worlds of *Left 4 Dead*, *Team Fortress*, and *Portal*. With over two hundred pages of story, *Valve Presents: The Sacrifice and Other Steam-Powered Stories* is a must-read for fans looking to further explore the games they love or comics readers interested in dipping their toes into a new mythos!

ISBN 978-1-59582-869-9 | $24.99

AVAILABLE AT YOUR LOCAL COMICS SHOP OR BOOKSTORE! • To find a comics shop in your area, call 1-888-266-4226.
For more information or to order direct visit DarkHorse.com or call 1-800-862-0052 Mon.–Fri. 9 AM. to 5 PM. Pacific Time. Prices and availability subject to change without notice.

DarkHorse.com   Victories™ © Michael Avon Oeming. Rapture © Michael Avon Oeming & Taki Soma. B.P.R.D.: Plague of Frogs © Michael Mignola. CONAN ® and © Conan Properties International LLC. VALVE PRES-
ENTS Volume 1: The Sacrifice and Other Steam-Powered Stories © Valve Corporation. Dark Horse Books® and the Dark Horse logo are registered trademarks of Dark Horse Comics, Inc. All rights reserved. (BL 5066)

DARK HORSE HORROR

GETS UNDER YOUR SKIN

"The company known for some of the most prominent horror comics of all time has big plans to keep frightening its readers."—Comic Book Resources

THE STRAIN
VOLUME 1
DAVID LAPHAM MIKE HUDDLESTON DAN JACKSON

GUILLERMO DEL TORO AND CHUCK HOGAN'S THE STRAIN TPB

David Lapham, Mike Huddleston

When a Boeing 777 goes dark on the JFK runway, the Centers for Disease Control, fearing a terrorist attack, calls in a team of expert biological-threat first responders. Only an elderly pawnbroker from Spanish Harlem suspects a darker purpose behind the event—an undead threat intent on covering mankind in darkness.

Volume 1 | ISBN 978-1-61655-032-5 | $19.99
Volume 2 | ISBN 978-1-61655-156-8 | $19.99

BILLY THE KID'S
OLD TIMEY ODDITIES
AND THE ORM OF LOCH NESS
ERIC POWELL
KYLE HOTZ

BILLY THE KID'S OLD TIMEY ODDITIES TPB

Eric Powell, Kyle Hotz

The world thinks the notorious outlaw Billy the Kid was killed by Pat Garrett, but the Kid is very much alive, the hired gun of Fineas Sproule's traveling spectacle of biological curiosities. Nothing in Billy's career as a gunslinger prepared him for the supernatural terrors he must face with his freak-show cohorts!

Volume 1 | ISBN 978-1-59307-448-7 | $13.95
Volume 2 | ISBN 978-1-59582-736-4 | $15.99
Volume 3 | ISBN 978-1-61655-106-3 | $15.99

EXSANGUINE
TIM SEELEY JOSHUA SCOTT EMMONS

EX SANGUINE TPB

Tim Seeley, Joshua Scott Emmons

One's a natural-born killer gleefully prowling the night for victims to quench an unnatural blood lust. The other's a vampire. His centuries of existence have left him world weary and detached, until his thirst is reinvigorated when the intricate work of the Sanguine Killer catches his eyes.

ISBN 978-1-61655-158-2 | $17.99

COLDER
PAUL TOBIN
JUAN FERREYRA

COLDER TPB

Paul Tobin, Juan Ferreyra

Declan Thomas's body temperature is dropping. An ex-inmate of an insane asylum that was destroyed in a fire, he has the strange ability to step inside a person's madness and sometimes cure it. He hopes to one day cure his own, but time is running out, because when his temperature reaches zero . . . it's over.

ISBN 978-1-61655-136-0 | $17.99

TO HELL YOU RIDE HC

Lance Henriksen, Joseph Maddrey, Tom Mandrake

A deadly curse plagues a small town, melting the flesh from its victims—the violent revenge four warriors set in motion when their sacred burial grounds were disturbed for the sake of gold miners' greed!

ISBN 978-1-61655-162-9 | $24.99

CRIMINAL MACABRE: FINAL NIGHT—THE 30 DAYS OF NIGHT CROSSOVER TPB

Steve Niles, Christopher Mitten

In this epic crossover with IDW, Steve Niles's greatest characters come together in a final showdown. Cal McDonald only wanted a beer, but what he got was a jaded federal agent and a story about vampires up in Barrow, Alaska. There's a new vamp in LA, and he's hell bent on wiping out mankind.

ISBN 978-1-61655-142-1 | $17.99

AVAILABLE AT YOUR LOCAL COMICS SHOP OR BOOKSTORE! • To find a comics shop in your area, call 1-888-266-4226.
For more information or to order direct visit DarkHorse.com or call 1-800-862-0052 Mon.–Fri. 9 AM. to 5 PM. Pacific Time. Prices and availability subject to change without notice.